INTERNATIONAL PAVILIONS AT THE 1964/1965 WORLD'S FAIR

VENEZUELA

UNITED STATES

VATICAN

UNITED ARAB REPUBLIC

THAILAND

SWITZERLAND

SWEDEN

REPUBLIC OF KOREA

SUDAN

LEBANON

MEXICO

PHILIPPINES

SIERRA LEONE

MOROCCO

MALAYSIA

POLYNESIA

PAKISTAN

SPAIN

Cover Photo:

Unisphere® presented by (USS) United States Steel

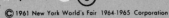

© 1961 New York World's Fair 1964-1965 Corporation

THE BOOK OF
KNOWLEDGE
ANNUAL 1965

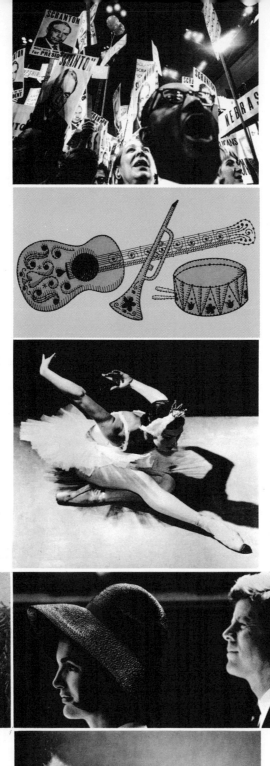

THE BOOK OF KNOWLEDGE ANNUAL 1965

Grolier
INCORPORATED
New York

Grolier Society
of Canada Limited
Toronto

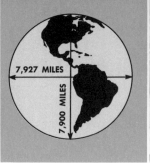

Editorial Director   LOWELL A. MARTIN
Graphics Coordinator   FRANK SAYLES

Editor in Chief   WILLIAM E. SHAPIRO
Art Director   RUSSELL J. SULLY
Assistant Editor   NANCY ABOLIN HARDIN

EDITORIAL STAFF

Production Editor   HELEN RIEHL HITCHCOCK
Production Assistant   CHARLES PAUL MAY
Copy Editor   HELEN HYNSON MERRICK
Style Editors   J. M. A. RAIKES
MARION LEE JOHNSON
Researchers   FERN MAMBERG
J. BEN TORMA
SERGIO BARZANTI
Indexer   KATHLEEN LEERBURGER
Staff Assistants   ELEANOR C. WOOD
TOR MALLON

ILLUSTRATION STAFF

Art Assistants   RHONY SANCHEZ
WALTER SCHWARZ
Picture Editor   JOYCE DEYO
Production Editor   ISABEL VESA
Production Assistant   CARMEN ASTEINZA

CONTENTS

CONTRIBUTORS

AUTHORS

LORRAINE ABELSON *Ludwig Erhard* page 112
Research Coordinator for FLAIR REPORTS, American Broadcasting Company.

NORMAN D. ANDERSON *Experiments in Astronomy* page 398
Assistant Professor of Science Education, North Carolina State of the University of North Carolina.

JIM BECKER *Winter Olympics* page 204
Sportswriter, Associated Press; contributor to sports magazines and to BEST SPORTS STORIES ANNUAL.

CHARLES F. BERLITZ *English—A World Language?* page 281
Vice-President, Berlitz School of Languages and Berlitz Publications; author, BERLITZ METHOD BOOKS in 23 languages, LANGUAGE SERIES FOR CHILDREN, and others.

WILLIAM BERNS *New York World's Fair 1964-1965* page 37
Vice-President of Communications and Public Relations for the World's Fair Corp.

MARGARET BOURKE-WHITE *A Career in Photography* page 378
Staff photographer, LIFE; author, PORTRAIT OF MYSELF, HALFWAY TO FREEDOM, DEAR FATHERLAND, REST QUIETLY, PURPLE HEART VALLEY, YOU HAVE SEEN THEIR FACES.

ROBERT I. BOWMAN *The Galapagos International Scientific Project*
page 357
Associate Professor of Biology, San Francisco State College; Co-director of the 1964 Galapagos International Scientific Project and secretary for the Americas of the Charles Darwin Foundation for the Galapagos Islands.

K. L. BOYNTON *Animal Camouflage and Disguise* page 360
President, Boynton Associates; author, NATURE'S WAYS IN THE ANIMAL WORLD; contributor, HIGHLIGHTS FOR CHILDREN, WOMAN'S DAY, INSTITUTIONS, TWELVE TO FIFTEEN.

ARNOLD C. BRACKMAN *Asia* page 415
Writer and consultant on Asian affairs; author, INDONESIAN COMMUNISM: A HISTORY.

WALTER BRIGGS *Japan's Twin Revolutions* page 192
International-relations consultant; formerly, Far East correspondent, NEW YORK HERALD TRIBUNE; consultant, Republic of Korea Government.

ERWIN J. BULBAN *Aviation Highlights* page 308
Southwest Editor, AVIATION WEEK & SPACE TECHNOLOGY, McGraw-Hill, Inc.; contributor to the AMERICAN AVIATION HISTORICAL SOCIETY JOURNAL.

BRYAN BUNCH *Sets* page 272
Science Review page 327
Chief Mathematics Editor, Harcourt, Brace & World, Inc.

JOHN CABOT *A Career in the Foreign Service* page 368
Ambassador of the United States of America to the Polish People's Republic; author, THE RACIAL CONFLICT IN TRANSYLVANIA, TOWARD OUR COMMON AMERICAN DESTINY.

OLEG CASSINI *A Career in Fashion Designing* page 371
Head of the House of Cassini; official designer for Mrs. Jacqueline Kennedy, 1960-63; official representative of U. S. fashion at the 1964-65 New York World's Fair.

WALTER CRONKITE *Top of the News* page 50
CBS News correspondent.

EDWARD R. DYER, JR.   *International Years of the Quiet Sun*   *page 301*
Executive Secretary, U. S. National Committee for the IQSY; since 1959 a member of the staff of the National Academy of Sciences' Space Science Board.

HAROLD FABER   *Political Conventions*   *page 97*
Assistant National News Editor, THE NEW YORK TIMES.

SAL FODERARO   *United States Review of the Year*   *page 78*
Associate Editor, THE AMERICANA ANNUAL.

THOMAS M. FRANCK   *Africa*   *page 140*
Legal advisor, Government of Tanzania; Visiting Professor of Law, Stanford Law School, University of East Africa; Professor of Law, New York University.

BLAIR FRASER   *Quebec Separatism*   *page 189*
Ottawa Editor, MACLEAN's magazine, 1943-60 and currently; Editor in Chief, MACLEAN's magazine, 1960-62; political commentator, Canadian Broadcasting Corp.

HARVEY GINSBERG   *Summer Olympics*   *page 200*
                              Sports in 1964   *page 210*
Sportswriter; Senior editor, G. P. Putnam's Sons.

GEOFFREY L. GRIFFITH   *Australia*   *page 150*
Associate Editor and feature writer, THE AUSTRALIAN, Sydney, New South Wales; author, GUIDE TO LAW COURT REPORTING.

DORA JANE HAMBLIN   *Fads*   *page 388*
Staff writer, LIFE; contributor, SPORTS ILLUSTRATED, NEW SOCIETY (London).

ROBERT HAWK   *Motion Pictures*   *page 247*
Contributing writer and reviewer, NEW YORK HERALD TRIBUNE Lively Arts magazine.

JOHN HAYDEN   *Protecting Our Wildlife*   *page 349*
Free-lance writer.

JOHN L. HOCHMANN   *Latin America*   *page 154*
Editor, Time, Inc.

JAMES WONG HOWE   *Cinematography*   *page 269*
Director of Photography on such films as THE OUTRAGE, HUD, SONG WITHOUT END, PICNIC, THE ROSE TATTOO, SWEET SMELL OF SUCCESS, BODY AND SOUL, AIR FORCE, KING'S ROW, TRANSATLANTIC; winner of two Academy Awards (1956, 1964).

ROBERT W. HOWE   *Ecology Projects and Experiments*   *page 404*
Assistant Professor of Science Education, Ohio State University.

CHARLES J. JONES   *Lyndon Baines Johnson*   *page 126*
Free-lance writer; formerly, Dean, Manhattan Tutoring School.

KATHARINE JONES   *Fairs and Expositions*   *page 44*
Staff editor, THE AMERICAN PEOPLES ENCYCLOPEDIA.

CLAUDIA LEWIS   *Young People's Books*   *page 229*
Specialist in children's literature, Bank Street College of Education; author, WRITING FOR YOUNG CHILDREN, WHEN I GO TO THE MOON.

LOUIS E. LOMAX   *History of Negro Protest*   *page 105*
Writer, television personality and lecturer; author, THE RELUCTANT AFRICAN, THE NEGRO REVOLT, WHEN THE WORD IS GIVEN: contributor, LIFE, LOOK, THE SATURDAY EVENING POST, THE NATION, THE NEW LEADER, HARPER'S.

JAMES LORD   *Alberto Giacometti*   *page 116*
Novelist, playwright, free-lance writer on art subjects; contributor, HORIZON, BOTTEGHE OSCURE, LA REVUE DE PARIS; long-time friend of Giacometti's.

ROBERT LOSADA, JR.   *Latin-American Poetry*   *page 238*
Translator; assistant editor, ODYSSEY REVIEW.

DAVID O. SELZNICK   *Producing*   *page 268*
Producer of GONE WITH THE WIND, REBECCA, DAVID COPPERFIELD, SPELLBOUND, DUEL IN THE SUN, THE PARADINE CASE, ANNA KARENINA (Garbo version), among many others.

LOU SHAINMARK   *New York City: Commerce*   *page 32*
Managing editor, NEW YORK CITY COMMERCE NEWS; Public Relations Advisor to the New York City Department of Commerce and Industrial Development.

PHILLIP BENNETT SHEPPARD   *Nursery Rhymes*   *page 244*
Free-lance writer and editor.

JOHN W. SHRUM   *The Amateur Fossil Hunter*   *page 392*
Assistant Professor of Science Education and Geology, Ohio State University.

R. D. HILTON SMITH   *Canada*   *page 152*
Advisory Editor, ENCYCLOPEDIA CANADIANA.

ROBERT L. SMITH   *New York City Architecture: 1664-1964*   *page 25*
Teacher, Benjamin Franklin High School, New York City.

EDWARD DURELL STONE   *A Career in Architecture*   *page 374*
Architect of such buildings as the Museum of Modern Art, N.Y.; the Foods Building, New York World's Fair; U.S. Embassy, New Delhi, India; Stanford Medical Center, Calif.; the John F. Kennedy Center for the Performing Arts in Washington, D.C.

LUTHER L. TERRY   *Smoking and Health*   *page 321*
Surgeon General, Public Health Service, U.S. Department of Health, Education and Welfare.

MARIE TORRE   *Television during the Year*   *page 254*
TV Newscaster, Westinghouse Broadcasting Company; former TV-Radio columnist of NEW YORK HERALD TRIBUNE; contributor, LOOK, MCCALL'S, REDBOOK, COSMOPOLITAN.

ELI WALLACH   *Acting*   *page 266*
A well-known actor who has appeared in films such as BABY DOLL, THE MISFITS, THE MAGNIFICENT SEVEN, HOW THE WEST WAS WON, THE VICTORS and on Broadway in MR. ROBERTS, THE ROSE TATTOO, TEAHOUSE OF THE AUGUST MOON, and LUV.

SANFORD R. WHITE   *Television and Radio Ratings*   *page 257*
Free-lance writer; contributor, THE READER'S DIGEST, THE EVERGREEN REVIEW, ARGOSY.

ARTISTS

GEORGE BAKACS
BILL CASTIMORE
LEONARD COLE
FRANK GIUSTO
GRAPHIC ARTS INTERNATIONAL

JEPPESEN & COMPANY
STEVEN RODGERS PECK
STONEHILL STUDIO
FRANCES A. WAINWRIGHT
BLAISE ZITO

SPECIAL CREDITS

Pages 2, 3: A. W. Ambler, National Audubon Society; Gene Daniels, Black Star; Wayne Shilkret, Hurok Inc; Max Scheler, Black Star; Edgerton, Germeshausen & Grier; Alexander Marshack, PIX; 1964 Scholastic Photography Awards; Bettman Archives.
Pages 4, 5: Annan Photos; Marc Riboud, Magnum; Photo Researchers; Friedman-Abeles; Ringling Museum of Art.
Pages 6, 7: Joe Covello, Black Star; The Metropolitan Museum of Art, gift of Annette Young, 1956, in memory of her brother Innis Young; Robert Capa, Magnum; Tom King, Black Star; Warner Bros.
Pages 8, 9: The Solomon R. Guggenheim Museum; Australian News & Information Bureau.
Pages 10, 11: Union Pacific Railroad; Black Star.
Page 165: Rykov, Underwood & Underwood; all others, Sovfoto.
Pages 235–36: "Collected Poems" published by Cassell; "New Poems" and "5 Pens in Hand" published by Doubleday; portrait drawn from photo by Larry Colwell.
Page 239: "Una Hoja No Más" by Carlos Castro Saavedra published by Editorial Antonio Nariño, Manizales, Colombia, 1962, in "Obra Selecta."
Page 240: "Oda de Invierno al Río Mapocho" by Pablo Neruda published by Editorial Losada, Buenos Aires, Argentina, 1955, in "Canto General," Tomo II.
Page 242: "Masa" by César Vallejo published by Editorial Losada, Buenos Aires, Argentina, 1961, in "Poemas Humanos; España, aparta de mi este cáliz." "Pureza" by Efraín Barquero published by Editorial Nascimento, Santiago, Chile, 1960, © 1960 by Efraín Barquero, in "El Pan del Hombre."
Page 330: Adapted from "The Worm Runner's Digest."
Pages 366–67: From "The Picture Book of Symbols," by Ernst Lehner, Tudor Publ. Co.

A TRIBUTE

TO JOHN F. KENNEDY

On November 22, 1964, the first anniversary of the assassination of President John F. Kennedy was observed. The release of the Warren Commission Report and the unveiling of plans for President Kennedy's tomb at Arlington National Cemetery both thrust the image of this vital man back into our awareness. Clearly, since his death the memory of him, rather than diminishing, has grown stronger.

PRESIDENT

Fred Ward, Black Star

Owen, Black Star

FATHER

WIT AND ORATOR

Artist's model of the John F. Kennedy
Tomb at Arlington National Cemetery.

President Kennedy remembered: in the United States and in
many other countries place-names have been changed.

HUSBAND

To the presidency John Kennedy brought youth,
vitality, style, wit. Though his concrete accom-
plishments were many, it is for these qualities that
most remember him. During his tenure, these qualities were evidenced in the many roles he filled—
father to Caroline and John, Jr.; husband to
Jacqueline; patron of the arts, who opened the
doors of the White House to writers, poets, musicians and artists; witty orator and verbal duelist.
Here, John Kennedy is shown in some of these
roles, which he filled so well.

13

CITIES: From Nineveh to New York

A CITY starts in a certain place because the founders of that city had a good reason to settle there. The earliest cities were often established at places that could be easily defended, such as a hill or a peninsula. Rome, for example, was founded where it is because its seven hills were surrounded by marshes. However, a city could not prosper just by being located at an easily defended site.

For a city to survive and flourish, its artisans and merchants had to trade their goods for food and raw materials. Since land transportation was so difficult, traveling by boat was the only practical way to trade. Cities were therefore likely to be established at the crossings of trade routes— where land and water or ocean and river transportation met. In such places merchants gathered to exchange goods and news. It was no accident that in the ancient eastern world the first large cities, such as Nineveh, Thebes and Babylon, were located on large rivers. Similarly, in the New World, Montreal was founded on an island near where the St. Lawrence and Ottawa rivers meet.

Ancient cities were very different from modern cities. Many of them were enclosed by protective walls. Inside these walls conditions were often chaotic. The layout of most cities was almost completely unplanned.

After the fall of the Roman Empire and the barbarian invasions in the fourth century, cities all but disappeared from western Europe. Trade routes were broken and commerce gradually came to a halt. The people who lived in the cities fled to the country. There they lived in the protective shadow of the fortified houses of the Romans or barbarians. Society became rural. Few people traveled away from the self-sufficient feudal manors. Constantinople, with its 100,000 people, was the only large city in Europe during this period.

But in the Middle Ages, around the tenth century, peace was slowly established. Commerce started up once more. The Crusades of the next two centuries stimulated trade. Cities such as Venice, Florence, Hamburg, Ghent and Bruges flourished. With their growth the feudal system died out. By 1500, six European cities each had populations of 100,000 or more. Around this time America was discovered. New trade routes to the East were opened. Powerful national states, such as Spain, France and England, came into being. Trade became worldwide instead of local. Coastal towns prospered and grew. But because robbers made roads unsafe, inland towns still did not thrive.

The walled medieval city offered a welcome refuge to tradesmen, artisans and merchants. Like ancient cities, medieval cities were unplanned, and grew haphazardly, the streets winding aimlessly in all directions. At the center of each city was a cathedral, a guild hall, a castle and a market square. Private homes bordered most of the streets. Because these walled cities could not easily expand beyond the walls, they often became overpopulated. Because of this and the fact that there were no sewer systems, epidemics started easily and spread rapidly.

Cities as we know them today came into being in the 1700's, during the industrial revolution. Before then, 90 per cent of the world's people lived on farms. During the industrial revolution new ways of transporting supplies and goods were invented and developed. A city no longer needed to be near water to flourish. Railroads, paved roads, and canals were built. Steamships carried goods from all over the world.

At the same time, better farming methods and equipment enabled a much smaller percentage of a country's population to raise an adequate amount of food. People who were no longer needed for farming went to work in mills and factories. For convenience, they settled near these industrial areas, which became the centers for new cities. Cities also grew up near sources of raw materials and fuel. In the United States, especially, cities sprang up along newly built railroad lines.

By 1964, there were more than fifty cities in the world each with populations of 1,000,000 or more. New York City, which celebrated its 300th anniversary in 1964, is one of these. This metropolis has a population of more than 8,000,000. It is the third-largest city in the world, and the center of the world's largest metropolitan area.

1664 NEW YORK CITY 1964

IN 1964, New York City celebrated the 300th anniversary of its founding. For it was in 1664 that the British captured New Amsterdam from the Dutch and renamed it New York. Then New York was just a small settlement at the southern tip of Manhattan Island: only about 1,500 people lived there. In the three centuries that followed, the city grew at an enormous rate. In 1764, more than 12,000 people lived there; in 1864 almost 1,000,000 people called New York home; and in 1964 the city boasted more than 8,000,000 inhabitants. The small community in the area south of Wall Street had grown into the 300-square-mile metropolis we know today.

New York owes its rapid growth to the influx of immigrants. First of course there were the Dutch and the English. Before the Civil War many Germans came; then the Irish; later the Italians; and, in the latter half of the nineteenth century, Jews from eastern and southern Europe. Most of these immigrants went on to settle in other parts of the country but many stayed in the city. After 1924, when the immigration laws were made more restrictive, the flow of people from other countries slowed down. But then the city received streams of Spanish-speaking United States citizens from Puerto Rico and southern Negroes moving north. The result is that New York City today has more foreign-born people and more ethnic groups than any other city in the world.

Almost as diverse as the city's people is the city's architecture, for this too is a product of three hundred years of change. In New York, outstanding public buildings, commercial structures and historic houses show a wide variety of style. In fact, one disadvantage of the city's thriving and ever-expanding commercial activity is that all too often irreplaceable examples of New York's architectural heritage are torn down to make way for business projects.

In the articles that follow we examine these two aspects —the people and the architecture—of New York City, and how they have changed in the last three hundred years. Other articles examine the historic growth of New York's commerce and transportation.

In its three hundred years of growth New York City has become a tourist's mecca. Coincidental with the city's tercentenary was the opening of the 1964–1965 World's Fair, which millions of visitors from all over the world came to see. The highlights of this fair are also presented to you in this special section on New York City and the Fair.

The Bettmann Archive

. . . it has taken New York just 300 years to transform itself from a rural settlement into a huge city

New Amsterdam scene in 1660.

Times Square, the heart of New York City, today.

Dick Hanley, Photo Researchers

In this print showing a typical New York Harbor scene in 1667, the water is already crowded with a variety of vessels.

Three centuries later, the same view across the East River has been transformed by huge skyscrapers, modern ships and new trucks.

18

Martin Helfer, DPI

NEW YORK TODAY:
A CITY OF CONTRASTS

A hot-dog vendor peddles his wares against a backdrop of glittering luxury—a modern skyscraper.

Fritz Henle, Photo Researchers

Fruit and vegetable pushcarts line a street of rundown buildings in a less-fashionable setting in lower Manhattan.

Tom Hollyman, Photo Researchers

Immigrants landing at Ellis Island in New York Bay at the turn of the century.

The People of New York

By RICHARD J. MARGOLIS

NEW YORK CITY is home to more than 8,000,000 people, and most of them belong to some kind of minority group. In most other parts of the United States minority groups are the exception. In New York City they are the rule. The world's many nationalities, religions and races are all represented there. And to a surprising extent they have all kept their distinctions intact.

New York is a crowded, bustling and confusing place. No one can possibly stay in step with all its rhythms. To the slum dweller in Harlem, New York is noisy, dirty and full of troubles, To the homeowner in Queens, where there are trees and grass, New York is something like the suburbs—quiet and orderly. And to the young artist just come to the city from his hometown, New York is full of bright lights and promise.

If New York is all things to all people, it is because sooner or later all kinds of people find their way there. The 370,000 suburbanites who commute to the city each weekday see New York through the distorting glass of their train and office windows. As a rule, they see it through a glass hurriedly, because it is rush hour and they must get to work on time. The city's famous frenzied pace—of which visitors often complain—is the pace of the commuter, not of the New Yorker.

To the millions of tourists who visit the city each year, New York is a collection of towering skyscrapers (the city has 50,000

21

Some of New York City's newspapers that serve minority groups. From top, clockwise: Polish, Irish, Hungarian, German, Italian and Spanish.

elevators!), noisy hotel lobbies, fancy restaurants and expensive shops. The visitor tends to see the typical New Yorker as a person with his hand always outstretched —waiting to be paid.

New York is all of these things and more. But the average New Yorker, when he thinks of his city, thinks of his neighborhood. For New York is a city of small, closely knit neighborhoods. Each has its main street, its main traditions and its special atmosphere. In a large and crowded city, the small neighborhood preserves some of the niceties of village life. In your own neighborhood you know the names of many of the people you pass on the street—and they know yours. The shopkeepers recognize their customers.

Even the policeman is a familiar figure.

"I have an idea," E. B. White has observed in *Here Is New York,* "that people from villages and small towns, people accustomed to the convenience and the friendliness of neighborhood over-the-fence living, are unaware that life in New York follows the neighborhood pattern. The city is literally a composite of tens of thousands of tiny neighborhood units." If you ask a man from Flatbush, Brooklyn, how to get to a place in Jackson Heights, Queens, he is likely to answer, "How should I know? I've never been there."

Many of New York's neighborhoods are populated by members of a single national, racial or religious group. There are, for example, Irish neighborhoods, Jewish neighborhoods, Italian neighborhoods, Polish neighborhoods, Greek neighborhoods, German neighborhoods, Chinese neighborhoods, Negro neighborhoods and Puerto Rican neighborhoods. There is even an Arab neighborhood in Brooklyn.

Such communities are remarkably self-sufficient. They have their own churches, their own social centers and often their own newspapers. Of the city's 232 newspapers, 87 are neighborhood weeklies. And many of the others, while not confined to a single neighborhood, do serve a single minority group. A few of the names will give you an idea of how varied an audience they serve: the *Atlantis Greek Daily, El Diario-La Prensa* (Spanish), *Al-Islaah* (Arabic), the *Jewish Daily Forward*, the *Irish World,* the *Amsterdam News* (Negro), the *Hungarian Daily Nepszava* and the *Staats-Zeitung und Herold* (German).

The city, as Mayor Robert F. Wagner has remarked, is not so much a melting pot as it is "a pressure cooker with separate compartments." Individuals from the various groups work together, cheer the Mets or Yankees together, and ride the subways together. But each returns to his own little community, his separate compartment.

New York is a place of many opinions—and all of them get loudly expressed. The street-corner speaker is a less frequent but still important figure in the city. Newspapers are filled with "letters to the editor" on topics ranging from crime in the streets to leaks in bathroom showers. New Yorkers are constantly circulating petitions to abolish this and establish that. And new organizations seem to spring up overnight. Typical are groups like the Society for the Prevention of World War III, the Committee to Aid Heidelberg Students, the Committee of French-American Wives, the Society of Colonial Wars and the Committee to Preserve Penn Station.

It is often said that if you have ten New Yorkers you may end up with ten com-

Burt Glinn, Magnum

Young residents of New York during a celebration in Chinatown on Manhattan's Lower East Side.

mittees. You may also have ten languages, ten nationalities and ten religions. By and large New York has thrived on people's differences. In 1660, when the city belonged to the Dutch, the colony's governor noted that 18 different languages were spoken at or near Fort Amsterdam in lower Manhattan. It is still true today, though some of the languages have no doubt changed. Today's languages would include Italian, Spanish, Yiddish, Chinese, Japanese and Russian.

For three centuries, then, New York has gotten much of its strength and vitality from newcomers. They have shaped the city, just as the city has shaped them.

"Give me your tired, your poor, your huddled masses yearning to breathe free," wrote the poet Emma Lazarus. Her poem is inscribed on the Statue of Liberty. Millions of tired, poor immigrants have seen it as their ship glided into the city's harbor. Some have come seeking freedom; others have sought fortune. Each has added his special talent and outlook to the city's crazy-quilt pattern.

According to the 1960 census, nearly half the city's people were born in a foreign country or have parents who were born in a foreign country. Of these, 859,-000 were from Italy; 564,000 were from Russia; 389,000 were from Poland; 312,-000 were from Ireland; 175,000 were from Great Britain; and 56,000 were from Greece. There is hardly a nation, in fact, that does not have a sizable representation in New York City.

And what is true of nationalities is also true of religions. New York has some 3,000 churches and synagogues, serving a remarkable variety of beliefs. About one fourth of the city's population is Jewish; about one fifth is Roman Catholic. All the Protestant denominations have representation in the city. And there are more than one hundred other religions and sects. These range from Buddhism and Islam to Ethical Culture and the Church of Latter-Day Saints. In New York City, as a local minister has observed, "every church has a belief and every belief has a church."

As a rule, the immigrants brought their religions with them. Thus many of the churches have a strong national flavor. These include Dutch Reformed, Greek Orthodox, German Methodist and the Japanese United Church of Christ.

The most recent newcomers to the city are Puerto Ricans and Negroes. They are not immigrants, of course, but migrants. That is, they have not come from foreign countries. The Puerto Ricans have migrated some 3,000 miles—from their Caribbean island (a commonwealth associated with the United States). Most of the Negroes have come to New York from states in the South.

Fifty years ago the city had only 7,000 Puerto Rican residents and 61,000 Negro residents. Today the Puerto Rican population has grown to 623,000. And Negroes in New York now number more than 1,000,000.

Both these groups have come up against many problems in the city. Many had been accustomed to farm life, not city life. The adjustment has not been easy. Of course, this is an old story in New York. All newcomers have had a bad time of it at first. It has been the business of the city to help each successive group of newcomers to learn the ropes—to send the children to school, to help the fathers get jobs, to give the families a useful place in the community.

But the city's "pressure cooker" magic has not worked so well with today's newcomers. This is partly because unskilled jobs are not so plentiful as they once were. Also white prejudice often bars Negroes (and some Puerto Ricans) from normal advancement. Thus the newcomers, unlike those who came before them (the Irish, the Jews, the Italians), have been unable to join the mainstream of city life. They are forced to live in the slums which other groups abandoned years ago. Helping Negroes and Puerto Ricans to win acceptance has become the city's major challenge.

The challenge is part of a broader problem now confronting all big cities: the problem of holding its residents. The suburbs have attracted hundreds of thousands of New Yorkers. The city is in danger of becoming a playground for the rich and a prison for the poor. The great middle-income group (the children and grandchildren of immigrants) is fleeing to little towns in Westchester, in New Jersey and on Long Island. And the old vital neighborhoods, which only yesterday made life in New York worth living, are in danger of becoming tomorrow's slums.

New York City Architecture: 1664-1964

By ROBERT L. SMITH

THE City of New York changes almost daily. The little, out-of-the-way restaurant or shop you found on your last trip to the city may not be there today. New Yorkers who do not visit a favorite street or neighborhood for a few months may not recognize it the next time they see it.

New York City is now in the midst of one of its greatest building booms. This frenzy of construction has caused some beautiful old buildings and sections to be leveled. Too often they have been replaced by luxury apartments or office buildings that look like brick barracks or glass rabbit warrens. However, some of the new buildings are attractive. They look like shining towers that seem to reach up to the sky.

Famed as it is now for its towering skyscrapers and magnificent skyline, New York was once nothing more than a tiny rural community. In those days it was called New Amsterdam. Three hundred years ago, in 1664, the British took New Amsterdam from the Dutch. They renamed it New York. Then the entire city was concentrated south of Wall Street. The buildings, of course, were of Dutch design. Almost all of these buildings have long since been gobbled up by the steam shovels of progress. A few Dutch farmhouses are left, but only one—the Dyckman House—is in Manhattan.

Up until the American Revolution, architecture in New York showed a strong

The bronze and glass Seagram Building, designed by Mies van der Rohe and Philip Johnson.
Louis Goldman, Rapho-Guillumette

A. Devaney, Inc.

Dyckman House, built by the Dutch founders of New York City more than three hundred years ago, is at Broadway and 204th Street in Manhattan.

The New York Convention & Visitors Bureau

City Hall, completed in 1811, is a beautiful example of postcolonial architecture. The mayor, the City Council and the Board of Estimate have offices here.

British influence. So strong was this influence that buildings dating from this period are called Georgian. This name refers to the three Georges (I, II, III) who ruled, one after another, in England then. Georgian architecture, especially in churches, was quite elaborate, with towers, pillars and large windows. One example that still stands today is St. Paul's Chapel, where George Washington worshiped. Another is the Jumel Mansion. At one time this building was Washington's headquarters. It was from here that he sent Nathan Hale on his last mission. Still another Georgian building is Fraunces Tavern. This structure was built in 1719 and is one of the city's oldest houses. Here Revolutionary leaders met and plotted. And here Washington bade his men farewell in 1783. Today Fraunces Tavern is a restaurant and a museum.

After the American colonies won their independence, a great reaction came against all things British. The Americans wanted an architecture of their own. So from 1789 to about 1825, the elegant and simple Federal style came into being. As you might expect, it was quite different from the Georgian style. Little decoration was used. Windows and doors were plain. Pillars were done in the simplest and oldest style of the Greeks, the Doric. The beauti-

ful City Hall building, where New York's mayor and his staff work, is an example of this postcolonial style. The mayor also lives in a Federal-style building—Gracie Mansion. The Commandant's House in the Brooklyn Navy Yard, the Hamilton Grange and the James Watson House are other examples of this style of architecture.

Following the Federal period, architects tried very hard to copy architectural styles found in other countries. So during most of the nineteenth century, one so-called revival followed another. The most important were the Greek, the Gothic, the Italianate, the French and the Romanesque revivals.

The Greek Revival was inspired by the Greek struggle to gain independence from Turkey between 1821 and 1832. Buildings of this period were massive. They had broad flat surfaces and huge porticos and colonnades. Greek ornaments, such as may be seen on ancient temples, were often used. The Classic craze reached such heights that some ridiculous effects were produced. For example, American leaders were portrayed in paintings and sculptures wearing togas. And elaborate colonnades were tacked onto simple farmhouses. Many Greek Revival buildings are

French Gothic in design, Saint Patrick's Cathedral on Fifth Avenue took about twenty years to build.

The controversial Guggenheim Museum at Fifth Avenue and 89th Street was designed by Frank Lloyd Wright. It is made of cast concrete. Paintings are exhibited along a continuous spiraling ramp.

quite beautiful though. Among them are the Federal Hall National Memorial, the main offices of the First National City Bank, Brooklyn's Borough Hall and the houses along the north side of Washington Square.

After the Greek Revival came the Gothic and Italianate revivals. The picturesque and romantic Gothic style was used mostly for churches, academic buildings and grand, Victorian-type town houses. It featured many towers, balconies and loggias (porches with arches). Gothic architecture was inspired in part by the novels of Sir Walter Scott and the glamorous age of chivalry. Some examples are Trinity Church, St. Patrick's Cathedral and Grace Church.

The Italianate Revival came to the United States via travelers to Italy. They described the Roman country villas which they saw on their trips. Soon American architects were using low-pitched roofs, balconies and loggias in their own buildings. The most famous remnants of this style are the brownstones. These once covered block after block of New York City above 14th Street. Now they are disappearing. New housing projects are taking their place. Examples of individual buildings in the Italianate style are the Sun Building,

Plymouth Church of the Pilgrims, the Friends Meeting House and the Litchfield Mansion.

In 1848 the first cast-iron building in New York City went up on the northwest corner of Washington and Murray streets. Now a warehouse, it is the ancestor of the steel-skeleton buildings which later completely changed architecture. Less than ten years later, the first practical elevator was installed by Elisha Graves Otis in a department store at Broadway and Broome streets. Without this invention, the later development of skyscrapers would not have been possible.

From 1864 to 1873 there was a great interest in the French Second Empire and the glamorous court of Napoleon III and Eugénie. Structures were built with coupled columns, round or segmented arched windows and mansard roofs (two slopes on each side). The best New York City example is the Manhattan Club.

The Romanesque Revival is often called the Richardson Revival. This is because the great American architect Henry Richardson helped establish it in this country. There were two phases of this revival. The first, 1845 to 1860, took place before Richardson became well known. Buildings in this phase were usually brick. They had round arched openings and extra pilasters (dummy pillars). This style was used mostly for commercial buildings, churches, armories, private stables, and the like. Examples are the Marble Collegiate Church and the Church of the Pilgrims.

Richardson studied medieval architecture. He favored the dark colors, arches and towers of the Middle Ages. Richardson's own work is not found in New York City, but he had many followers. They built the south wing of the American Museum of Natural History, the De Vinne Press Building and the Hotel Margaret in Brooklyn Heights.

The Romanesque Revival came to an end in 1893. This year also brought the beginning of a new era in American architecture. Both the end of the old and the beginning of the new appeared at the World's Columbian Exposition in Chicago in 1893. Along the shores of Lake Michigan a White City was built. It consisted of 150 buildings in Romanesque, Greek and Renaissance styles. These buildings were made of imitation marble.

The exposition introduced the idea of town planning and landscaping. It was also the beginning of eclecticism, as the choosing from many different styles of architecture is called. Eclecticism differed from the previous revivals. A Romanesque Revival building would be in Romanesque *style*. A Romanesque eclectic building would be an exact *reproduction*. The Bowery Savings Bank on East 42d Street is Romanesque eclectic.

Eclecticism lasted until the late 1920's. Many praised it, saying that now architects had a rich field of possibilities to choose from. Others ridiculed it. They felt that it was uncreative and had stopped the development of a native American architecture.

There were many types of eclecticism. Some notable New York City examples are the American Telephone & Telegraph Building and almost every bank put up between 1893 and 1920 (Roman eclectic); U. S. Government Customs House and New York Public Library (*beaux-arts* eclectic); Duke Mansion (French Classic eclectic); West End Collegiate Church (Flemish Renaissance eclectic); Dakota Apartments (German Renaissance eclectic); Woolworth Building, St. Thomas' Church and the older buildings of City College (Gothic eclectic).

By 1930, borrowing from classic styles had ended. Advances in steel fabrication, alloys and glass encouraged architects to use their imaginations. Improved, high-speed elevators made skyscrapers possible. The Flatiron Building and the Woolworth Building showed landowners that sky-high buildings could produce sky-high profits from office rentals. As a result the skyline of the city rose upward. The Chrysler Building was followed by the Empire State Building, Rockefeller Center, and very recently the Pan Am Building. Rockefeller Center, one of the world's greatest tourist attractions, is New York City's only coordinated set of skyscrapers. Gardens, promenades, open-air restaurants and buildings were planned and built as one unit.

A striking feature of modern New York City is the growing use of sheet glass for entire walls. This was begun in New York City in 1948 with the construction of the United Nations Building. Other notable examples followed, including Lever House in 1952, the Seagram Building in 1958, and the Kips Bay apartments in 1963.

Another striking feature of the city today is the reappearance of cast concrete. This is a technique that was known to the Romans. With cast concrete a building may be given a variety of shapes. Two examples are the TWA Building at Kennedy International Airport and Frank Lloyd Wright's Guggenheim Museum.

For better or worse, New York City has changed beyond recognition in three hundred years. It will keep on changing, and volumes will be written about the changes. How will the city look in 2264? We cannot even guess.

Metropolitan Transportation

Traffic congestion in New York City has become a serious problem. In fact the old joke to the effect that it takes longer to make your way across town today than it did a century ago is no longer a laughing matter. Despite the city's 4,000 buses, 8,500 subway trains and 12,000 taxis, New York's losing struggle to keep its 8,000,000 inhabitants moving leads to daily tie-ups, confusion, delays, lost tempers and nostalgia for the days of horse-drawn trollies, hansom cabs and stagecoaches.

Traffic comes in all shapes and sizes on New York City's Second Avenue.

Larry Fried, PIX

One of the few ferries still in operation, the Staten Island Ferry offers commuters an unsurpassed view of lower Manhattan's skyline and the Statue of Liberty, all for only a nickel.

Early (circa 1915) versions of the double-decker Fifth Avenue buses (themselves replaced in the 1950's).

Brand-new subway cars on their way to start carrying the 4,600,000 passengers who ride New York's fifty-year-old subway system each weekday.

On April 29, 1878, crowds gathered and horses reared in excitement as the first train on the Gilbert Elevated Railroad passed through Sixth Avenue near the Jefferson Market Court House, which is still standing.

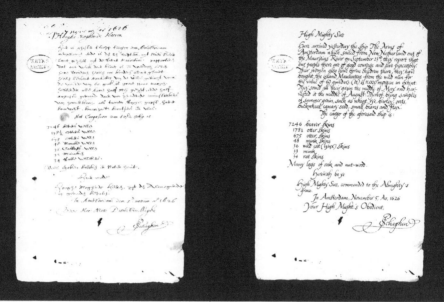

Letter of 1626 (with translation), recording purchase of Manhattan from the Indians.

New York City: Commerce

By LOU SHAINMARK

NEW YORK was founded as a commercial city. The Dutch traders who came to Manhattan Island in the early 1600's were attracted by its harbor. They promptly began doing business with the Indians. For food and furs, the traders gave the Indians colored beads known as wampum. They sent pelts and timber to Amsterdam in exchange for guilders. In 1621 they organized the Dutch West India Company as a trading monopoly. The city's rise to fame and fortune was under way.

In 1624 the Dutch arranged a business bargain that made history. They bought Manhattan Island from the Indians for 60 guilders worth of trinkets—equal to $24. It was named Nieuw Amsterdam. Today the real estate of Manhattan Island is worth over $12,000,000,000. New York is now the greatest commercial city in the world and in history. It is first in finance, manufacturing, wholesale and retail trade, transportation and services.

Soon after settling Nieuw Amsterdam, the colonists began to build ships for trade. They erected windmills and breweries and bakeries. They put up housing and they built schools and churches. They set up annual agricultural fairs and weekly meat markets. Besides fur and lumber, they traded in meat, shellfish, fruit and tobacco. As early as 1629, their exports totalled 130,000 guilders. Imports were valued at 113,000 guilders.

The English seized Nieuw Amsterdam from the Dutch in 1664 and changed its name to New York. But this hardly ruffled the city's economy. In fact business thrived. In 1678, an official act gave New York a monopoly in bolting cloth and packing flour for export. Neighboring settlements were jealous and the act was repealed in 1694. Meantime the value of yearly exports tripled, going from £2,000 to £6,000. Ships berthing at the harbor multiplied many times over. Shipping expanded to the southern colonies and the West Indies. In addition, the printing industry had its start in New York City late in the century when William Bradford moved his presses from Philadelphia.

In the early days of the eighteenth century, many craftsmen settled in the city. Specialization of trades began. Silversmiths and blacksmiths gathered at the tip of Manhattan alongside shippers and traders. Tanners and shoemakers moved "uptown" to Maiden Lane. Bradford began publishing New York's first newspaper, the *New York Gazette,* in 1725. The colonists imported molasses from the West Indies and began the sugar-refining and rum-making industries. In 1752 they set up the first Merchant's Exchange. By the middle of the century, New York had become the leading commercial city in the New World, outstripping Philadelphia and Boston.

During the Revolutionary War, the city's trade came to a standstill. But with peace, the economy revived. New York became the financial center of the new United States of America. The first bank, the Bank of New York, came into existence in 1784. The first insurance concern, the Mutual Fire Insurance Company, opened its doors in 1787. About 1784, John Jacob Astor came to the city. He set up a string of fur-trading posts in the North American interior. For these pelts, which he shipped to China, he traded sandalwood, tea and silks. New York's exports reached $20,-000,000 annually, and the city now counted 60,000 inhabitants.

An important event in financial history took place in 1792. A group of traders gathered under a buttonwood tree at what is now 68 Wall Street. There they organized the first money and securities mart. This was to become officially the New York Stock Exchange in 1817. In the course of its existence, the exchange has saved nations from economic collapse. It has financed wars and built railroads. It has also given financial backing to corporations, big and small, in oil, steel, utili-

Cal Bernstein, Black Star

Delivery trucks and carts packed with clothing and fabrics jam New York's garment center.

Cioffero, Fundamental Photographs

Macy's—one of the department stores that make New York the shopping center of the world.

the middle of the century, the Cunard Line was established. It was soon followed by other great ocean lines.

Other aspects of the economy grew just as quickly. The city's first horse-drawn railroad, the New York and Harlem, made its appearance in 1831. It was a forerunner of the great transcontinental carriers. In 1853 New York City achieved world status by putting on the first World's Fair in the New World. And the census taken a few years earlier counted 500,000 inhabitants in the city.

Industry and commerce became more varied. Before the beginning of the eighteenth century, the Schieffelin family had led in the founding of the drug industry in New York. Early in the 1800's, Thomas Kensett and Ezra Daggett introduced the canning of seafood. Abram Hewitt, who later served as mayor, began to manufacture iron ware. Robert Colgate opened a soap factory. The Steinway family came to the city in the 1850's to build pianos. Charles Pratt began refining oil.

Merchant princes rose during that era. They laid the foundations that have made New York the shopping center of the world. Arnold Constable, A. T. Stewart, the Gimbel family, John Wanamaker, John H. Browning, Benjamin Altman, the Bloomingdale brothers, and Isidor and Nathan Straus established magnificent department stores. Many of these men came to New York as immigrants.

The strength of New York's economy was proved after the panic of 1857. Whole industries were paralyzed and nearly 1,000 companies went bankrupt with debts of $12,000,000. But only two years later the city boasted 70 banks, 106 insurance companies, 11 markets, 18 steamboat companies, several thousand factories, jobbing houses and retail establishments. Then came the war between the states, economic disaster—and, again, quick recovery. Because business was so good, labor organized and demanded a share of the profits. In the mid-1870's New York City saw its first

ties and many other fields. In its early days, it sold United States securities, thus strengthening the financial structure of the young republic. In recent years it helped develop aviation, electronics, missiles and nuclear energy.

New York City made the great economic leap forward in the nineteenth century. Prosperity came in like a floodtide. Businessmen with daring and vision came to the city from all parts of the world. They made fortunes and history.

The shipping industry raced forward. In 1801 the Federal Government established the New York Naval Shipyard in Brooklyn. The first steam vessel, Robert Fulton's *Clermont,* chugged up the Hudson River in 1807. Ten years later the Black Ball Packet Line began to send ships regularly between New York, Liverpool and London. In 1825, the Erie Canal opened a water trade route to the interior of the United States. In

1850   THE NEW YORK STOCK EXCHANGE   1964

N. Y. Stock Exchange

great strike—one put on by house painters and allied trades. The rise of unionism, with union benefits for many workers (especially in the garment trades), followed.

The latter half of the nineteenth century was marked by great financial exploits. A handful of men changed the face of the country. J. P. Morgan had moved his activity from Boston to New York in 1835. The Rothschilds sent August Belmont from Germany to help finance the growing industries. Wall Street became a battleground of financial wizards, some of them not given to the highest principles. Such men as Daniel Drew, Jim Fisk, Jay Cooke, E. H. Harriman and Jay Gould fought and cornered markets. At the end of the century, the survivors were organizing giant monopolies.

During this period the population of New York City grew enormously. Irish and German immigrants flocked to the city in the mid-1800's. Jewish migrations began to swell in the 1870's. In the 1890's Italians came in throngs. The immigrants brought with them the physical, mental and cultural resources of their origins. Hardworking, ambitious and imaginative, they came with an overpowering faith in the golden opportunities that America offered them. They increased the great variety of the city's industry and commerce. They spread from Manhattan into neighboring areas of Brooklyn, the Bronx, Queens and Richmond. Then in 1898 the five counties united as Greater New York. The population in 1900 totalled 3,350,000.

The economy of New York—interrupted only briefly by a panic in 1907—continued to grow at a fantastic pace in the twentieth century. Skyscrapers began to dot the skyline. The 26-story Pulitzer Building rose in 1890. The Flatiron Building, scaling 20 stories, was erected in 1902. Eleven years later these buildings were dwarfed by the 60-story Woolworth Building. It in turn was topped by the 77-story Chrysler Building in 1929.

A few years later the Empire State Building pierced the clouds with 102 stories.

World War I pressed New York into a war economy. It came out as the world's creditor. Soon after the war ended in 1918, New York was electrified by the birth of a new industry—radio. Economic growth continued until nearly the end of 1929. Then the stock market collapsed. The crash plunged the entire world into a great depression. Thousands of businesses went bankrupt and hundreds of thousands of workers were thrown out of jobs. New York City was just shaking off the depression when World War II began. The city again got onto a war footing. But as before, the city was quickly transferred to a peace economy at the close of the war in 1945. New industries—television, air conditioning, plastics, synthetics, aviation, nuclear energy and, more recently, automation and computers—brought new excitement and growth to New York City's business life.

In the mid-1960's, New York City's population totalled 8,000,000. Of these, 4,000,000 have daily jobs. The city contains 35,000 factories, which employ more than 900,000 persons. The clothing trades make up the largest industrial complex. More than 250,000 people are employed here. Printing is second with 125,000 jobs. The city's retail stores record $12,000,000,000 in sales yearly. Deposits in New York's commercial and savings banks total nearly $70,000,000,000. The city has become the corporation headquarters of the world. Trade from every corner of the globe is carried to the city by 170 steamship lines, 16 railroads, 39 airlines and 10,000 motor trucks.

New York City is also the greatest consumer in the world. New Yorkers spend close to $25,000,000,000 a year on food, clothing, housing, services, education and entertainment. Automobiles are owned by 1,440,000 residents. Every year the city plays host to 14,000,000 visitors. New York has become the greatest tourist attraction in history.

New York World's Fair 1964-1965

By WILLIAM BERNS

Swiss Sky Ride. During this thrilling five-minute ride 112 feet above the ground, airborne passengers can view the entire fairgrounds.

HAVE you ever eaten in an African tree-house? Heard a Chinese opera? Weighed yourself on an atomic scale? Taken a make-believe journey to the moon? Watched the nation's top athletes competing in Olympic trials? Or seen Michelangelo's beautiful sculpture, the *Pietà?*

This is just a small sampling of the delights and wonders at New York's World's Fair. More than 70,000,000 visitors are expected to visit the 646-acre fair in 1964 and 1965. At the fair, governments and industries have presented their arts, skills and discoveries. They have created a huge showcase of man's achievements.

"Peace through Understanding" is the theme of the fair. The fair was planned with the idea that a free exchange of ideas will encourage respect and understanding among people. The fair's symbol, the Unisphere, emphasizes this theme. It expresses the idea of a shrinking planet (in the sense that nations are becoming less and less independent of other nations) within an expanding universe.

(Continued on page 41)

37

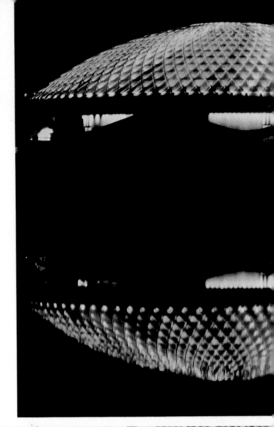

"Pietà." Michelangelo's famed and beautiful sculpture is in the Vatican Pavilion.

Performers at the Mexican Pavilion, which also features Mexican paintings and sculpture.

A colorful view of the fair at night, reflected in the waters of the Pool of Industry. Left, General Electric Pavilion; center-right, the Tower of Light.

Native dancers and singers at the African Pavilion. Nearby, built around a huge tree trunk, is a tree-house restaurant with genuine African food.

William E. Shapiro

GENERAL MOTORS FUTURAMA

General Motors presents to fairgoers a glimpse into the future on the moon and here on earth.

All photos, General Motors

In the future, men will work and live in the frozen wastelands of the Antarctic.

A "lunar crawler" creeps across the craggy, cratered contour of the moon.

The city of the future will feature superskyscrapers and moving sidewalks.

On the whole, the fair's exhibits were planned to appeal to as many people as possible. However, about 25 per cent of the people in the United States are of school or college age. Thus, many of the fair's exhibits have been planned to interest and instruct young people. Because a fair is a carnival as well as a classroom, an effort has been made to make learning fun.

In contrast, the fair's Lake Amusement Area has a holiday feeling. It is full of laughter and lighthearted entertainment. There are fancy stage shows and a circus. There are also puppets, performing porpoises, and ducks. And there is a wax museum and a replica of the *Santa Maria*. Hula dancers, dancing columns of water, and thrilling rides in the air and on water add to the fun.

A few of the fair's exhibits have been planned especially for younger children. In the children's room of the United States Pavilion's library exhibit, youngsters have storytelling hours and film showings. Youngsters can meet some of New York's small animals—live otters, beavers, raccoons and bear cubs—in that state's pavilion. There is a mazelike Nonsense Machine in the Johnson's Wax Pavilion. It is full of interesting surprises. For little girls, especially, there is a Land of Enchantment in the Simmons Pavilion. It is peopled with little pixies that move and fairy princesses.

A boat ride takes visitors around the world in the Pepsi-Cola Pavilion. There lifelike, moving figures of children in national costume sing and dance. In the Long Island Railroad exhibit, a tiny train carries youngsters through a landscaped acre of Long Island countryside.

Denmark's outstanding sculptors and artists have created a playground for the Danish Pavilion. It is modeled after the playground in Copenhagen's famous Tivoli Gardens. It features carved animals, a dipsy-doodle slide and a glass-mosaic labyrinth.

Teachers from all over the United States are at the Child's World Center in the Better Living Center. Here children can play with all sorts of experimental toys. They can watch chicks hatching and see what goes on in a beehive and ant colony. They can even churn butter and make their own ice cream.

To attract visitors, industrial pavilions have hired talented people from Broadway and Hollywood. They have added a theatrical touch to many of the industrial pavilions. In the Ford Pavilion, Walt Disney has created a fantasy journey. This journey takes visitors from the prehistoric past into the world of the future. Here you will see moving reproductions of life-size cavemen and huge monsters. *The Brightest Show on Earth* in the Tower of Light Pavilion also has lifelike figures that move. In the Better Living Center, there is a short musical comedy starring Borden's Elsie the Cow.

Puppets made by the famous puppeteer Bil Baird perform in a musical comedy at the Chrysler Pavilion. This pavilion also features a "zoo" made of car parts. Life-size dinosaurs, some of them moving, attract young and old to Sinclair's Dinoland.

Fairgoers can take a walking tour of the world in the Coca-Cola Pavilion. Here they visit strange ports, complete with sounds and smells. Or they can watch world-famous performers make the bells ring out on the world's largest electric carillon.

The 2,500,000,000-year story of life on our planet is reviewed pictorially in the Travelers Insurance Pavilion. Life-size figures and special sound effects are used in this exhibit. In the Continental Insurance Pavilion, events in American history are presented in a series of unusual slide cartoons. The Du Pont Pavilion features the *Wonderful World of Chemistry*. This original musical revue cleverly combines live performers, who sing, dance and talk, with figures on the screen. Animated gas appliances pop out of the ceilings and walls in the Gas Pavilion's Fun House of the Future. Bodies float about in General Cigar's Hall of Magic. And an Enchanted Forest comes alive in the Scott Paper Pavilion.

Those who enjoy movies can spend days seeing free film showings. Or they can see a camera obscura, the granddaddy of today's film projectors, in the Dynamic Maturity Pavilion. Television fans can watch a TV show being put together at the RCA Pavilion. They can also see themselves on monitor sets.

Countless international friendships will be started via Parker Pen's pen-pal project. For Scouts, the Wonderful World of Scouting is a home away from home.

The fair reflects what is going on around us in the world. Thus research efforts in atomic physics, computer mathematics and space exploration are emphasized in many educational exhibits. These exhibits try to show how industry uses scientific theories to change our daily lives. For example, in the General Electric Pavilion, a Disney-created show demonstrates how man has harnessed nature's energy sources. The story takes the viewer from primitive man's discovery of fire to modern uses of atomic energy. It ends by showing controlled nuclear fusion for the first time in public.

In the Bell System Pavilion the story of human communications—from smoke signals to the Telstar satellite—is shown in an original theatrical production. Puppets, films and drawings explain such subjects as miniaturization and the probability theory at the IBM Pavilion. A "machine game room" in the National Cash Register Pavilion lets visitors match wits with computers. They can also join in games that teach them the basic rules of computer arithmetic.

General Motor's Futurama ride suggests a world some fifty years in the future. In this world, man will have learned to use areas of the world where no one can live now. Whole towns will be built in today's jungles, Antarctic wastelands and beneath the seas.

In the Transportation and Travel Pavilion, visitors are taken on a make-believe trip to the moon. There they can see a lunar-exploration team at work. In the Hall of Science, there is a demonstration of a rendezvous in space. Two real orbital space vehicles are used.

The scientific exhibits are the most spectacular. But man himself is the center of all activity. Thus, many exhibits are about

The Republic of China pavilion at the New York World's Fair.

man's problems and his culture. The United States Federal and state pavilions and the international pavilions all present fascinating pictures of people and countries. These exhibits add new meaning to social-studies, geography and history textbooks.

At the fair are art masterpieces and archeological treasures never before shown in the United States. American "Pop" art can also be seen. Performers introduce visitors to the literature, music and dance of many parts of the world. Exhibits of handicraft and manufacture show the economic development of these nations.

Within the International Area, the fair visitor can take a tour covering more than 65 nations. In the United States Federal and States Area, various states display their contributions to American history.

The treasures at the fair are countless. Interested in art? There are original Goyas, El Grecos, Picassos and Miros in the Spanish Pavilion. Diego Rivera and Orozco murals may be seen in the Mexican Pavilion. Pre-Columbian art decorates the Florida Pavilion. There is also primitive African sculpture. And contemporary American artwork is shown. Antiquities? There is a King Tutankhamen collection in the U.A.R. Pavilion. The Dead Sea Scrolls may be seen at the Jordan Pavilion. Forty centuries of Oriental art are housed in the Republic of China Pavilion. Fifth-century Indian sculpture is also on exhibit.

The performing arts are well represented. You can watch folk dancers from the Philippines, African Watusi dancers, dancing drummer girls from Korea, flamenco dancers and Guinea's ballet troupe. There are also dancers from Indonesia, Venezuela, Hawaii, Polynesia and the Caribbean. The voices of Irish actors read from the works of Shaw, Joyce and other Irish-born writers. Arabic songs are sung in Morocco's Pavilion. Greek musicians perform on guitars and *bouzouki*. There are Caribbean calypso singers and Mexi-

can mariachi bands. American music is represented by a symphony orchestra from Oklahoma, a New Orleans jazz group and the Mormon Tabernacle Choir.

For a further look into interesting worlds, you can visit an Alaskan Eskimo village, an ancient Hawaiian village and a Belgian village. Tea ceremony and the art of flower arranging are taught in Japan's Pavilion. You can take a make-believe helicopter ride around a huge scale model of New York City. You can take lessons in fly casting, trout fishing and archery from Wisconsin's experts. You can also enter a West Virginia coal mine, see how tin is mined in Malaysia and watch shipbuilders at work on real boats in the New Jersey Pavilion. At the fair you can also see craftsmen tooling leather, hammering brass, carving in wood and ivory and making beautiful glass objects.

At fair President Robert Moses' request, major religions have their own pavilions for the first time in any World's Fair. Stirring art treasures add to these exhibits. The historic, gem-covered Holy Icon of the Virgin of Kazan can be seen in the Pavilion of the Russian Orthodox Greek-Catholic Church of America. There are sculptures and murals at the Mormon Pavilion. The Protestant and Orthodox Center has beautiful stained-glass windows. The Vatican Pavilion has the fair's most famous attraction—Michelangelo's *Pietà*. Never before has this statue been moved from its location in St. Peter's Cathedral in Rome.

The fair itself sponsors many free events. For music lovers there are band concerts, jazz concerts, choral groups and barbershop quartets. Folk dancing and baton twirling may also be seen. The fair's athletic program includes National AAU events.

A fountain show with taped music and fireworks accompanying brilliant water patterns climaxes the day's events.

At the 1964-65 New York World's Fair there is something for everyone.

An engraving by William Hogarth of the Southwark Fair in 1733.

Fairs and Expositions

By KATHARINE JONES

WHEN you want to buy something today, all you have to do is go to a store. It may be but a few minutes or half an hour away. You can even place your order by mail or telephone and have things sent to you.

It was not always so. In ancient, medieval and even more recent times, most people lived in the country. To buy the goods they needed they had to go to the towns and cities where there were bazaars or marketplaces. They couldn't go often because they had to work long hours in their fields and pastures.

But there were occasions when all the countrypeople flocked to the towns for religious festivals. In Egypt, in ancient times just as today, the Nile River overflowed its banks once each year and watered the farmlands. At that time the farmers would gather in their temple cities to give thanks to their gods for this heaven-sent blessing.

Similar religious events were common in Greece and all the other lands around the Mediterranean Sea. Mecca was a gathering place for Arab worshipers long before the time of Mohammed. So, too, did temples draw people to the cities of ancient India and China, and in the lands of the Inca, the Maya and the Aztec in far-off America.

Each great gathering of people provided a good opportunity for merchants to display their goods. Some merchants would even come from distant lands with perfumes, spices, colorful bird feathers and other exotic things to sell. They might set up tents or stalls in the marketplace or simply display their wares in the streets for visitors to see and buy. People thronged into the marketplace. Farmers bartered their products for the goods the merchants offered. Livestock and sometimes slaves were traded.

So what started out as a religious holiday became a *fair*—an assembly of people for the purpose of trade. In fact our word "fair" comes from an old Latin word that means "holiday" or "festival." But the fairgoers were interested not only in worship and trade. They also wanted to be amused. So there were magicians, jugglers, clowns, trained animals and many other entertainers on hand to please the crowds for the reward of a few coins.

It might seem that fairs would be out of place in our day of big department stores, shopping centers and neighborhood shops. With home television hardly anyone has to travel far for entertainment. But fairs are still popular all over the world.

Many are just local fairs where farm crops and livestock are the centers of interest. Then there are flower fairs, trade fairs and book fairs and other special kinds of fairs.

The biggest fairs of all are the international expositions or world's fairs. At these, many countries build pavilions, places where they tell about their land, their people, their way of life, their products and their achievements in the arts and other fields. Business concerns display new inventions and demonstrate

new products and services. Colorful shows, fireworks, thrilling rides and many other kinds of entertainment help attract millions of visitors.

Some great fairs of the Middle Ages

During the Middle Ages the most important fairs took place in the French province of Champagne. Merchants came there from all corners of Europe to trade their wares—such things as cloth, furs, leather, livestock, spices and even slaves. Puppet shows, plays, singers and masquerades offered a wide range of entertainment.

During fair time no warfare was allowed in the province. Merchants coming from enemy lands on their way to and from the fair were assured of a safe journey. A special police force in Champagne helped to keep trading honest.

The Stourbridge Fair, first chartered in 1211 by King John, was perhaps the most popular in England. Daniel Defoe, who wrote *Robinson Crusoe,* wrote of his visit to the Stourbridge Fair in 1723. According to his account, the shops were placed in rows, and many things, including silver, china, pewter, glass, food, clothing and toys, were offered for sale. Defoe also wrote that little ferryboats carried people to the fair along the River Cam, which flowed near the fairground. Defoe described such amusements as puppet shows, tightrope walkers and horse races.

At some of the early English fairs was a special court called piepowder court. It dealt with people who committed crimes at the fair. The name of the court came from the French words *pied poudreux,* meaning "dusty foot." It probably referred to merchants who had become dusty from their travels to the fair.

Similar to the Stourbridge Fair was the great fair in Russia, which began in the 13th century. It was held at a town named Nizhni Novgorod (now the city of Gorki) at the meeting point of two rivers. Goods from distant Asian and European countries were brought by boat and caravan to Nizhni Novgorod in midsummer of each year.

Great quantities of tea, sugar, iron, cotton, linen, silks, dried fruits, furs and timber were bought and sold. Some of these products came from so far away that it took many months for them to reach the fair. Tea was brought overland across Asia from China. Rugs began their journey to the fair from Persia (Iran) and Turkestan. The chief form of entertainment was a theater that featured an excellent ballet.

The fair at Nizhni Novgorod lasted after many fairs in other parts of the world had stopped. The Soviet Government finally closed it in 1930.

The trade in books
and furs at Leipzig Fair

More than four hundred years ago a small commercial fair began at Leipzig, Germany. In the course of time this fair became famous throughout the world for its sale of furs and books. Leipzig was a closely built medieval city with little extra room for all its visitors at fair time. Visiting retail merchants were housed in wooden booths that were owned by the city. These booths were built right in the streets the night before the fair opened. Wholesalers at the fair usually rented stores, while the owners of the stores lived in cellars and garrets. Sometimes space was so valuable that even windows were removed so that goods could be packed high on the sills.

All the publishers of Germany were represented at the Leipzig Fairs. Their books were shown in a special building belonging to them. There, in the 1800's, business was done in cash, the only money allowed being gold coin. Accounts were settled in one large room with galleries at each end.

The fur trade at the Leipzig Fair was for many years thought to be the greatest in the world. Valuable furs were brought from North America, central Europe, Russia and Asia. The traders appeared in native dress. There was a noisy scene when persons of many different nationalties bargained in perhaps a dozen different languages.

Agricultural fairs
and livestock shows

The fairgoing of farmers in times past was by no means limited to those fairs that were most famous. Local fairs devoted largely to farmers' interests have been held in Great Britain and other lands for several hundred years. There were agricultural fairs in colonial America too. These were forerunners of the county, state and provincial fairs that became such an important part of life in the 19th century.

The first county fair in the United States was organized by Elkanah Watson and held at Pittsfield, Massachusetts, in 1810. It was then called the Berkshire Cattle Show.

Agricultural fairs are still a regular feature of North American life. Most of them are held in late summer. On the fairgrounds may be some permanent exhibition buildings and very often a horse-racing track with grandstand. Additional tents and booths are set up at fair time for exhibitors of tools and other products related to agriculture.

Farmers show their finest cattle, hogs and other livestock. Housewives enter homemade pies and cakes, preserves and fancy needlework. Young people, such as members of 4-H Clubs, exhibit the results of their farm projects. All the work is carefully judged by experts, and prize ribbons are awarded for the best. The farm people also come to the fair to see demonstrations of new agricultural machinery and up-to-date methods. Many of them take advantage of the opportunity to enjoy such amusements as races, merry-go-rounds and carnival-type shows. Rodeos are a feature of western livestock shows.

The 1893 World's Columbian Exposition in Chicago, Illinois.

Some agricultural fairs are national in scope. For instance, Canada's prize livestock, poultry and other farm products are exhibited at the Royal Agricultural Winter Fair at Toronto. The International Livestock Exposition is an annual event in Chicago.

In the United Kingdom the royal agricultural societies of England, Scotland, Wales and Ulster (Northern Ireland) sponsor annual fairs or shows. The London Dairy Show and the Smithfield Show for beef cattle are also major events. Important agricultural fairs are held in each of the states of Australia as well as in New Zealand. The Palermo Show in Argentina is one of the world's most important livestock exhibitions.

Industrial as well as farm products are shown at the Canadian National Exhibition. This famous fair, which began in 1846, is held every summer in Toronto. Its permanent grounds and buildings are on the shores of Lake Ontario.

Trade fairs and
other specialized exhibitions

The industrial revolution that began in the 18th century brought an important change in the nature of fairs. With new machines, goods could be made so much alike that people did not have to inspect each item they bought. New, rapid means of transportation made trade easier too. Buyers could choose things they wanted from samples and have the merchandise shipped to them. So the fair became less of an occasion for direct trade and more a means for promoting trade through displays and demonstrations.

International trade fairs play as important a part in commerce today as the old Leipzig trade fair did in the past. Several such fairs are held every year in various parts of the world.

Some trade fairs are concerned with only one industry or line of products. Automobile shows, where manufacturers exhibit their latest models to the public,

47

have become very popular. Business machines, communication methods and devices, motorboats and fashions in clothing are only a few of many other subjects of trade exhibits.

The special interests of large numbers of people are also recognized by garden shows, bookfairs, art exhibitions, science fairs and hobby shows.

The modern growth of
international expositions

Most of the fairs and expositions mentioned so far have been regular annual events. But for at least two hundred years there have been special expositions on particular occasions. Some, like the Lewis and Clark Exposition in Portland, Oregon, in 1905 and the Texas Centennial in Dallas in 1936, marked anniversaries. Others were strictly national in scope. The Festival of Britain in London in 1951 is an example of this type. The Chicago Railroad Fair of 1948-49 was devoted to a single industry.

The first truly international exposition was the Great Exhibition in London in 1851. Prince Albert, the husband of Queen Victoria, brought it about. There were displays of goods from all over the British Empire and from many other countries as well. From the United States were sent such things as McCormick's reaper, vulcanized rubber and false teeth.

One of the highlights of the exhibition was the huge building in which it was held. It was built in Hyde Park and was named the Crystal Palace. This was a very large structure of iron and glass, so large that full-grown trees grew under the roof. In 1854 the Crystal Palace was moved to the outskirts of London. The building was destroyed by fire in 1936 and its remains torn down in 1941.

The exposition was a success from the beginning, and the idea of the international exposition became popular.

Expositions, also called exhibitions and world's fairs, have been held often since

A. Devaney, Inc.

The eye-catching Perisphere and Trylon became familiar to the whole world as the symbol of the 1939-40 New York World's Fair.

1851, particularly in France, Britain and the United States. Many of them have left some permanent structures by which they are remembered. And most have contributed in some way to scientific or artistic progress.

The first exposition in the United States was held in New York in 1853. Like the 1851 London exposition, it was held in a building named the Crystal Palace. In 1876 the second great fair in the United States took place in Philadelphia. This fair celebrated the 100th anniversary of the Declaration of Independence. Here visitors viewed the very newest inventions —the typewriter, an automatic telegraph and a "machine that talked"—the telephone.

The 400th anniversary of Columbus' discovery of America was celebrated a year late—in 1893—by the World's Columbian Exposition at Chicago. It was the biggest and finest exposition ever held up to that time. Electric lighting was available by then. Many countries and states had pavilions of their own in which to exhibit their products. The buildings of the "White City," noted for their beauty, had a strong influence upon architecture at the time.

Other notable international expositions in the United States included the Pan-American Exposition in Buffalo in 1901; the Louisiana Purchase Exposition in St. Louis in 1904; the 1915 Panama-Pacific Exposition in San Francisco, marking the opening of the Panama Canal; and the Philadelphia Sesquicentennial Exposition of 1926. A second Chicago World's Fair, called A Century of Progress, was held in 1933 and 1934.

Some buildings erected for the Brussels, Belgium, exposition of 1935 have since been used for an annual trade fair. Paris was the site of a 1937 international exposition. Its theme was international progress in arts, crafts and sciences.

The New York World's Fair in 1939 and 1940 had as its theme "Building the World of Tomorrow." A 1,200-acre plot near Flushing, Long Island, was changed from an ugly dump heap into a beautiful park for the fair. A time capsule was buried during the fair. Inside were objects familiar to people of the 20th century, such as knives and forks, alarm clocks and baseballs. There were also films of books and newspapers. The capsule is marked to be opened in the year 6939 to give the people of that age an idea of life in our times.

Held at the same time as the New York World's Fair, the Golden Gate International Exposition marked the completion of the two great bridges that span San Francisco Bay. The fair was held on a man-made island called Treasure Island in the bay between San Francisco and Oakland. The fair glorified the Pacific lands—the Orient, Latin America, the American West and the Pacific islands. One of the most interesting buildings was the Tower of the Sun, representing the religious rites of ancient peoples.

Brussels in 1958 held a fair in honor of the atomic age. From the center of the grounds soared an enormous structure called an Atomium, a model of a molecule enlarged many million times.

The theme of the Seattle World's Fair of 1962 was "Man in the Space Age." Exhibitions featured life in the next century. The 600-foot-high Space Needle, with a restaurant in its slowly rotating top, was the most popular attraction. A monorail, an elevated train on one track, carried visitors to the fair from the center of Seattle.

The New York World's Fair of 1964-65 was built on the site of the 1939-40 fair on Long Island. The theme was "Peace through Understanding." A giant-sized globe of the world, called the Unisphere, was erected near the heart of the fair-grounds. In addition to the many industrial exhibits and the pavilions of other nations, much space was devoted to science, religion and the arts. Among many fine works of art on display was Michelangelo's famous sculpture of the Madonna and the dead Christ, *Pietà,* on loan from the Vatican.

An international organization called the International Bureau of Exhibitions was set up in 1928 to control and limit the number of world's fairs. Because the New York World's Fair was the second one to be held in the United States in the 1960's and was scheduled to last more than six months, it was not recognized by the bureau. Therefore, member countries like the United Kingdom, France, West Germany and Canada were not permitted to erect official government pavilions at the New York fair.

Even as New York was holding its fair, preparations were under way for another international exposition at Montreal in 1967. Two islands in the St. Lawrence River were selected as the site. This fair was planned to mark the hundredth anniversary of the year in which Canada became a self-governing nation. "Man and His World" was chosen as the theme.

JANUARY

PANAMA CANAL CRISIS. On January 9 violence broke out between Panamanians and United States soldiers and civilians who live and work in the Canal Zone. When it was over, 21 Panamanians and 4 U.S. soldiers were dead and about 350 people were injured.

The crisis had its roots in sixty years of history. In 1903, Panama, which was then a province of Colombia, revolted and declared its independence. It was aided by the United States, which was anxious to build a canal across Panama. For its aid the United States was granted from Panama a 10-mile-wide, 50-mile-long strip of land on which to build a canal. There the U.S.–Panama treaty gave the United States the right to act as "if it were sovereign."

The Panama Canal was opened to ships in 1914. Since that year it has become a source of irritation to Panama. There are 1,000,000 Panamanians, most of whom live in poverty. In the Canal Zone there are 36,000 United States soldiers and civilians. They live in relative prosperity. In addition, Panamanians say that they are paid less than Americans for the same jobs in the Canal Zone. And they feel that they should have more say in and benefit more from the operation of the canal. But perhaps the most important issue in the crisis is nationalism. Resentment against "Yankee imperialism" has grown over the years. The fact that the Panamanians wanted their flag to be flown in the Canal Zone led to riots in 1959. Finally, in 1963 the United States agreed to fly both flags together.

But many American students in the zone resented this. They refused to fly the Panamanian flag in front of their schools. As a result, it was decreed that no flags—U. S. or Panamanian—would be flown in front of schools. However, on January 9, American students raised the U. S. flag in front of their high school at Balboa. Panamanians marched on the school to plant their own flag. It was taken down by the students, who also drove out the Panamanians. Hundreds of irate Panamanians stormed the zone. Snipers fired at Americans, and U. S. soldiers fired back. When the violence ended, Panama had broken diplomatic relations with the United States and was demanding a revision of the 1903 treaty. At month's end, the United States and Panama were trying to iron out their differences to avoid further crises and bloodshed.

Wide World

Riots resulted when American students flew U. S. flag by itself.

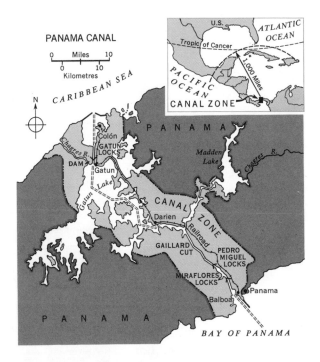

PANAMA CANAL

Miles 0 10

Kilometres 0 10

ATLANTIC OCEAN

U.S.

Tropic of Cancer

PACIFIC OCEAN

CANAL ZONE

1,000 Miles

N

CARIBBEAN SEA

Colón
GATUN LOCKS
Chagres R.
DAM
Gatun
Gatun Lake

PANAMA

Madden Lake

Chagres R.

CANAL ZONE

Darien

Railroad

GAILLARD CUT

PEDRO MIGUEL LOCKS

MIRAFLORES LOCKS

Panama

Balboa

PANAMA

BAY OF PANAMA

Panamanians gather under an anti-American banner to demonstrate in memory of the students who were killed during the January rioting.

UPI

KEES GO HOME
IANS OUT

NEWS FLASHES

JANUARY 1964

			1	2	3	4
5	6	7	8	9	10	11
12	13	14	15	16	17	18
19	20	21	22	23	24	25
26	27	28	29	30	31	

4. Pope Paul VI began a three-day trip to Jordan and Israel.

7. Britain sold 450 buses to Cuba, ignoring the U.S. economic blockade.

8. In his first State of the Union Message, President Johnson called for a $500,000,000 reduction in Federal spending, a "war against poverty" in the United States, and a 25 per cent cutback in uranium production for nuclear weapons.

12. Zanzibar's predominantly Arab Government was overthrown by armed African rebels.

15. Jack Teagarden, jazz trombonist and singer, died at 58.

22. Composer Marc Blitzstein, 58, was fatally beaten by three sailors in Martinique.

23. The anti-poll-tax 24th Amendment to the U. S. Constitution was ratified when South Dakota became the 38th state to approve it.

25. At the request of the governments of Tanganyika, Kenya and Uganda, British troops were rushed to those three newly independent African states where they put down mutinies in the armed forces.

27. The French Government announced its establishment of diplomatic relations with Communist China.

29. Movie actor Alan Ladd, 50, died in Palm Springs.

30. South Vietnam's ruling military junta was overthrown by dissident military officers under Major General Nguyen Khanh.

FEBRUARY

GUANTANAMO WATER CUT OFF BY CASTRO. On February 6 Cuban Premier Fidel Castro ordered the water supply to the United States Naval Base at Guantanamo Bay cut off, except for one hour daily. According to Castro, this action was taken in retaliation for the seizure of 38 Cuban fishermen and their boats in Florida waters four days earlier. Castro warned that the water would stay off until the men and boats were released.

President Johnson hurriedly began plans to make Guantanamo independent of Cuba for its water supply. He ordered water tankers to the base and initiated a project to desalt seawater. On February 17 the commander of Guantanamo cut the water pipeline, refusing to use even the small flow of water allowed by the Cubans.

Guantanamo, which is in southeast Cuba, is considered vital to United States defenses in the Caribbean. For one thing, it guards the approaches to the Panama Canal. Since coming to power in 1960, Castro has repeatedly demanded that the United States get out of Guantanamo. The United States has refused, for it has had treaty rights to the base since 1903. In 1898, as a result of the Spanish-American War, Cuba was freed from Spanish control by the United States. United States troops then occupied the island until 1902, when Cuba became independent. However, the United States insisted upon the right to buy or lease naval bases from Cuba. Reluctantly, the Cubans agreed to this. A treaty was then signed in 1903, and the United States leased Guantanamo. In 1934 a new treaty was signed. In effect, it gave the United States permanent possession of the base. This treaty cannot be nullified without the consent of both the United States and Cuba.

Thus, legally Castro cannot end the treaty rights of the United States. Nor can he take the base by force, for the United States has superior military strength. Thus it seemed to many observers that Castro used the seizure of the fishermen as an excuse to focus world attention on the fact that the United States has bases on foreign soil. This would perhaps increase anti-American sentiment in Latin America, particularly after the January riots in Panama. Nevertheless, by month's end, Guantanamo was getting by without Cuban water, the Cuban fishermen had been fined and released, and the Guantanamo incident seemed to be just that—an incident and not a portent of a more belligerent Cuban attitude.

A U.S. marine stands guard at Guantanamo Naval Base.

Wide World

A water tanker delivers water to Guantanamo after the base water supply was ordered cut off by Cuban Premier Fidel Castro on February 6.

Rear Admiral John Bulkeley, Guantanamo commander, supervises removal of a section of water pipe after Cuba accused U. S. of stealing water.

NEWS FLASHES

FEBRUARY 1964

						1
2	3	4	5	6	7	8
9	10	11	12	13	14	15
16	17	18	19	20	21	22
23	24	25	26	27	28	29

10. The National Chinese Government announced that it had broken diplomatic relations with France because of French recognition of Communist China.

16. Former Premier George Papandreou's Center Union Party was victorious in the Greek national elections; Papandreou became premier again.

17. The Supreme Court ruled in a 6-3 decision that the Constitution requires that Congressional districts within each state be approximately equal in population.

18. The United States curtailed aid to Britain, France, Yugoslavia, Spain and Morocco because of their refusal to halt trade with Cuba.

19. French troops put down a revolt against the Gabon Government and restored President Léon M'ba to power.

25. Grace Metalious, controversial novelist (*Peyton Place*), died at the age of 39. . . . Cassius Clay won the world heavyweight championship by a TKO when Sonny Liston was unable to answer the bell for the seventh round.

26. President Johnson signed the tax-cut-and-reform bill after it was passed by Congress. It provides for the biggest tax reduction in United States history: $11,500,000,000 per year.

29. President Johnson revealed that the United States had developed in secrecy a jet airplane, the A-11, capable of flying at more than 2,000 miles per hour at altitudes of over 70,000 feet.

MARCH

ALASKAN EARTHQUAKE. On the evening of March 27, one of the most powerful of earthquakes in modern times struck southern Alaska. Hardest hit was Anchorage, the state's largest city. There, buildings collapsed and great fissures opened up in the streets. The downtown section of the city was almost entirely destroyed. Also hard hit were Seward, Valdez, Cordova, Kodiak and Kenai. About 65 people were killed. Property damage was estimated at $500,000,000.

UN TROOPS IN CYPRUS. For the fourth time in its history, the United Nations sent troops to a troubled area of the world. First it was the Gaza Strip in the Middle East, then New Guinea, then the Congo. In March 1964 it was the island-nation of Cyprus.

There are about 500,000 Greek Cypriots and 100,000 Turkish Cypriots. When Cyprus won its independence from Great Britain in 1960, its new constitution gave the Turkish minority a veto over the actions of the Greek majority. The Turks feel that this veto is necessary to protect their rights. The Greeks, led by Cypriot President Archbishop Makarios, say that the veto makes majority government unworkable. Thus when Makarios tried to change the constitution in December 1963, fighting broke out between the two communities.

Under the 1960 constitution, Britain has the right to "protect peace and freedom" on Cyprus. So British troops stepped in between the warring Greeks and Turks. They prevented a full-scale war from breaking out. But they did not prevent the Greeks from making significant advances against the outnumbered Turks. As a result, Turkey threatened to intervene to protect the Turkish Cypriots. Greece, in turn, warned that if Turkey sent troops to Cyprus it would also.

The situation became more and more ominous as the two NATO allies seemed to be heading toward war. Then, on March 4, the UN Security Council voted to send a peace-keeping force to the island. The first contingent, French-Canadian troops of the Royal 22d Canadian Regiment, landed on March 22. On the 27th, the UN formally took over from the British. Finnish ambassador to Sweden, Sakari S. Tuomioja, was named UN mediator. However, even with UN troops on the island, fighting continued and the threat of war between Greece and Turkey remained.

After playing the bugle in a ceremoni parade at the United Nations base on th island of Cyprus, a line of troopers marche from the grounds.

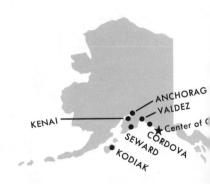

Map indicates the area hit by Alaska earthquake, which left widespread scene of destruction similar to this one of street in Anchorage's business distric

UPI
Pictorial Parade

NEWS FLASHES

MARCH 1964

1	2	3	4	5	6	7
8	9	10	11	12	13	14
15	16	17	18	19	20	21
22	23	24	25	26	27	28
29	30	31				

6. Sixty-two-year-old King Paul of Greece died; his son, Crown Prince Constantine, was proclaimed king.

10. Queen Elizabeth II of England gave birth to her fourth child in London. It was her third son.

14. Jack L. Ruby was convicted and sentenced to death in Dallas, Texas, for the murder of Lee Harvey Oswald, accused assassin of President John F. Kennedy. Ruby's lawyers, led by Melvin Belli, said they would appeal the verdict.

18. Dr. Norbert Wiener, American mathematician and scientist considered to be the father of automation, died at 69 in Stockholm.

20. Brendan Behan, Irish playwright (*The Quare Fellow, The Hostage*), died at 41 in Dublin.

23. Peter Lorre, 59, noted Hungarian-born screen villain, died in Hollywood.

24. United States Ambassador to Japan Edwin O. Reischauer was stabbed in the thigh by a youthful Japanese fanatic. His condition was not considered serious. . . . French President de Gaulle returned to Paris from a ten-day visit to Mexico and the French possessions of Guadeloupe, Martinique and French Guiana.

27. After being detained in East Germany, the last two members of the three-man crew of a United States Air Force RB-66 reconnaissance plane shot down over East Germany on March 10 were released by Soviet military authorities. The third crew member had been released on March 21.

APRIL

REVOLT IN BRAZIL. On April 1, units of Brazil's Second and Fourth armies marched on Rio de Janeiro, forcing President João Goulart to flee. As the revolt spread to other army units and gained the support of the governors of Brazil's states, Goulart went into exile in Uruguay. On April 11, Army Chief of Staff Humberto Castelo Branco was named president of Brazil.

The overthrow of Goulart was welcomed in Washington, for it was feared that he was leading Brazil toward communism. From the reaction of the thousands of Brazilians who joyously paraded through the streets, it was obvious that they too were pleased with Goulart's downfall.

Brazil is the fifth-largest country in the world. It has a population of 80,000,000 and a wealth of natural resources. But although its economic growth has been relatively high (6.5 per cent a year), the economy has been for many years plagued by inflation. Under Goulart, who took office in 1961, Brazil's economic situation worsened. He also wanted to take land away from the landowners and distribute it to the peasants. Without adequate planning this would have been disastrous to Brazil's economy. And although economic aid was available to him under the Alliance for Progress, Goulart remained aloof from this hemispheric organization.

As opposition to him increased, Goulart turned more and more to the Communists for support. He also talked of changing the constitution so that he could run for reelection when his term expired in 1966. Finally, in March, Goulart amnestied 1,425 Leftist sailors who had mutinied. This was the spark that set off the revolt and brought General Castelo Branco to power.

Wide World

RIGHTIST COUP IN LAOS. A coup by Right-Wing military forces overthrew the coalition Government of Prince Souvanna Phouma on April 19. The United States, however, moved to return the Prince to power, for it was feared that the coup would lead to an intensification of the fighting between Communists and Rightists in Laos. Pressure from the United States did indeed work. The Rightists could not afford to give up the $52,000,000 a year in military and economic aid they were getting from the United States. Prince Souvanna Phouma was restored to the premiership of a coalition Government of Rightists and neutralists. The Communists, however, refused to join. In fact they used the occasion to make further military advances against neutralist and Rightist forces.

UPI

Before President Goulart was ousted by a revolt, Brazilians marched through the streets of São Paulo demonstrating against his policies.

General MacArthur's body, on horse-drawn caisson, leaves the U. S. Capitol. He was later buried in Norfolk, Virginia.

UPI

		1	2	3	4
5	6	7	8	9	10	11
12	13	14	15	16	17	18
19	20	21	22	23	24	25
26	27	28	29	30		

1. Dr. François Duvalier had himself installed as president of Haiti for life.

3. The United States and Panama signed an agreement to restore diplomatic relations. Ties had been broken by Panama on January 10 after Panamanian rioters trying to enter the Panama Canal Zone had been fired on by United States troops. . . . In Moscow it was disclosed that three one time top Soviet leaders—Molotov, Malenkov and Kaganovich—had been expelled from the Communist Party.

5. General of the Army Douglas MacArthur, who led the Allied conquest of Japan in World War II and commanded the United Nations forces in the Korean war, died in New York City at the age of 84.

7. A Federal grand jury indicted eight major steel companies and two executives on antitrust violations for allegedly fixing carbon-steel-sheet prices.

14. Rachel Carson, biologist, writer and author of *Silent Spring*, died at the age of 56.

18. Writer Ben Hecht died at 70.

22. New York City's $500,000,000 World's Fair was opened by President Johnson.

26. The African states of Tanganyika and Zanzibar merged to form a single United Republic of Tanganyika and Zanzibar.

29. Princess Irene of the Netherlands and Prince Carlos Hugo of Bourbon-Parma were married in Rome.

MAY

NEHRU OF INDIA DIES. Jawaharlal Nehru, prime minister of India since 1947, died of a heart attack on May 27 at the age of 74. Known as the "maker of modern India," Nehru had led his country for 17 years, ever since it was granted independence by Great Britain. Before independence, Nehru was second only to Mahatma Gandhi in India's nonviolent independence movement.

When Gandhi was assassinated in 1948, the difficult task of welding India's more than 400,000,000 people of diverse ethnic backgrounds into a united nation fell on Nehru's shoulders alone. In this he succeeded. On the world scene Nehru made his mark by espousing neutralism. That is, he sided with neither the West nor the Communists in the cold war. His commitment to neutralism was, however, lessened when in October 1962 Communist China attacked India. Out of necessity Nehru had to call upon Britain and the United States for aid. India was still at odds with Communist China when Nehru died.

According to the rituals of the Hindu religion, Nehru was cremated, rather than buried, on May 28. More than 1,500,000 people watched the rites, paying last respects to their leader. Among the dignitaries at the services were United States Secretary of State Dean Rusk, British Prime Minister Sir Alec Douglas-Home and Soviet Vice-Premier A. N. Kosygin.

ASWAN HIGH DAM: STAGE I. Except for a few oases and the fertile strip of land along the Nile River and at the Nile Delta the United Arab Republic is desert. Only 3 per cent of its land is arable. The 28,000,000 people in the U.A.R. have a relatively low standard of living. To improve their economy they must industrialize. And they must irrigate more land so that more food can be grown. Toward this end, President Nasser, with Russian technical and financial aid, began building the Aswan High Dam. This enormous project will irrigate 2,000,000 acres of land. It will also produce 10,000,000,000 kilowatts of electricity a year for industrial projects. This will triple the U.A.R.'s power output.

Work on the dam was started in January 1960. On May 14, 1964, the first stage was completed. This milestone was marked by ceremonies at which President Nasser and Soviet Premier Khrushchev set off a dynamite charge that diverted the Nile waters through a newly constructed channel. When finally completed in 1970, the Aswan High Dam will have cost $1,000,000,000.

Egyptian laborers working on a canal to divert the waters of the Nile to permit further progress on the Aswan High Dam.

Henry Grossman

Above: Two deceased world leaders—President Kennedy and Prime Minister Nehru. Left: Nehru's funeral pyre.

Wide World

UPI

					1	2
3	4	5	6	7	8	9
10	11	12	13	14	15	16
17	18	19	20	21	22	23
24 31	25	26	27	28	29	30

2. Lady Astor, the first woman to sit in Britain's House of Commons (1919-44), died at 84. . . . The USNS *Card* was sunk at its dock in Saigon, South Vietnam, harbor by explosive charges placed by Vietcong terrorists.

11. After years of controversy, a 2,000-mile-per-hour B-70 experimental plane was unveiled by North American Aviation.

12. Missouri Democrat Clarence Cannon, 85, oldest member of the United States House of Representatives, died in Washington, D. C.

13. Panama's Electoral Tribunal announced that Marco A. Robles, the Government's candidate, had won the May 10 presidential election.

14. Defense Secretary Robert McNamara and General Maxwell D. Taylor, chairman of the Joint Chiefs of Staff, returned from a fact-finding mission in South Vietnam. They recommended increased economic and military aid to South Vietnam.

24. In Lima, Peru, at least 318 people were killed and 500 injured when a riot broke out at an Argentina-Peru soccer match.

25. The United States Supreme Court held unconstitutional the 1959 closing of public schools (to avoid desegregation) in Prince Edward County, Virginia. The court ordered "quick and effective" relief from the situation.

30. Physicist Leo Szilard, one of the developers of the atom bomb, died at the age of 66.

JUNE

SUPREME COURT DECISION ON STATE LEGISLATURE APPORTIONMENT. By a 6-3 majority, the Supreme Court on June 15 ruled that both houses of state legislatures "must be apportioned on a population basis." This historic decision will probably affect legislatures of 40 states. Gaining from the decision will be the cities and the suburbs. The losers will be the rural areas, which have dominated the legislatures of most states even though they have not had the population to warrant this domination.

CIVIL-RIGHTS BILL PASSED. On June 19, after 83 days of debate, the 1964 civil-rights bill was passed by the Senate by a vote of 73-27. The main provisions of the bill are:

TITLE I—Voting: Prohibits the application of different standards to Negro and white voters.

TITLE II—Public Accommodations: Prohibits discrimination or refusal of service because of race in hotels, motels, restaurants, gasoline stations and places of entertainment if their operations affect interstate commerce or if their discrimination "is supported by state action."

TITLE III—Public Facilities: Negroes are to have equal access to, and treatment in, publicly owned or operated facilities such as swimming pools, stadiums and parks.

TITLE IV—Public Schools: Gives the attorney general the right to bring school-desegregation suits. Authorizes technical and financial aid to school districts to assist in school desegregation.

TITLE V—Civil Rights Commission: Extends the life of the Civil Rights Commission until January 31, 1968.

TITLE VI—Federal Aid: States that no one shall be subjected to racial discrimination in any program that receives Federal aid. Federal agencies may take steps against such discrimination and even withhold money from state or local agencies that discriminate.

TITLE VII—Employment: Bans discrimination by employers or unions that have 100 or more employees or members the first year the act is effective. After four years this provision will be applied to employers and unions with 25 or more employees or members.

In Titles 1-4 and 7 the attorney general can bring suit to enforce the provisions of the law.

The passage of the civil-rights bill was widely applauded. CORE national director James L. Farmer said it "may well be the single most important act of our Congress in several decades."

Wide World

U. S. sailors start searching the Philadelphia, Mississippi, area for three missing civil-rights workers.

Ten thousand Korean students rioted in the streets of Seoul demanding ouster of President Chung Hee Park.

UPI

RIGHTS BILL ROLL-CALL VOTE

Listed below are the 73 U. S. Senators who voted for the civil-rights bill and the 23 Senators who voted against it on June 19.

FOR PASSAGE—73

Democrats—46

Anderson (N. M.)
Bartlett (Alaska)
Bayh (Ind.)
Brewster (Md.)
Bible (Nev.)
Burdick (N. D.)
Cannon (Nev.)
Church (Idaho)
Clark (Pa.)
Dodd (Conn.)
Douglas (Ill.)
Edmondson (Okla.)
Engle (Calif.)
Gruening (Alaska)
Hart (Mich.)
Hartke (Ind.)

Hayden (Ariz.)
Humphrey (Minn.)
Inouye (Hawaii)
Jackson (Wash.)
Kennedy (Mass.)
Lausche (Ohio)
Long (Mo.)
Magnuson (Wash.)
Mansfield (Mont.)
McCarthy (Minn.)
McGee (Wyo.)
McGovern (S. D.)
McIntyre (N. H.)
McNamara (Mich.)
Metcalf (Mont.)

Monroney (Okla.)
Morse (Ore.)
Moss (Utah)
Muskie (Me.)
Nelson (Wis.)
Neuberger (Ore.)
Pastore (R. I.)
Pell (R. I.)
Proxmire (Wis.)
Randolph (W. Va.)
Ribicoff (Conn.)
Symington (Mo.)
Williams (N. J.)
Yarborough (Tex.)
Young (Ohio)

Republicans—27

Aiken (Vt.)
Allott (Colo.)
Beall (Md.)
Bennett (Utah)
Boggs (Del.)
Carlson (Kan.)
Case (N. J.)
Cooper (Ky.)
Curtis (Neb.)

Dirksen (Ill.)
Dominick (Colo.)
Fong (Hawaii)
Hruska (Neb.)
Javits (N. Y.)
Jordan (Idaho)
Keating (N. Y.)
Kuchel (Calif.)
Miller (Iowa)

Morton (Ky.)
Mundt (S. D.)
Pearson (Kan.)
Prouty (Vt.)
Saltonstall (Mass.)
Scott (Pa.)
Smith (Me.)
Williams (Del.)
Young (N. D.)

AGAINST PASSAGE—27

Democrats—21

Byrd (Va.)
Byrd (W. Va.)
Eastland (Miss.)
Ellender (La.)
Ervin (N. C.)
Fulbright (Ark.)
Gore (Tenn.)

Hill (Ala.)
Holland (Fla.)
Johnston (S. C.)
Jordan (N. C.)
Long (La.)
McClellan (Ark.)
Robertson (Va.)

Russell (Ga.)
Smathers (Fla.)
Sparkman (Ala.)
Stennis (Miss.)
Talmadge (Ga.)
Thurmond (S. C.)
Walters (Tenn.)

Republicans—6

Cotton (N. H.)
Goldwater (Ariz.)

Hickenlooper (Iowa)
Mechem (N. M.)

Simpson (Wyo.)
Tower (Tex.)

JUNE 1964

1	2	3	4	5	6
7	8	9	10	11	12	13
14	15	16	17	18	19	20
21	22	23	24	25	26	27
28	29	30

1. The U. S. Supreme Court barred prayers and Bible reading in Florida public schools, reversing a decision of the Florida Supreme Court.

2. Arizona Senator Barry Goldwater upset New York Governor Nelson Rockefeller in the California Republican primary to move one step closer to the presidential nomination. . . . India's ruling Congress Party elected Lal Bahadur Shastri to succeed the late Jawaharlal Nehru as prime minister.

3. South Korean President Chung Hee Park declared martial law in Seoul after 10,000 students rioted against government policies.

12. Pennsylvania's Governor William Scranton entered the race for the Republican presidential nomination. . . . A 20-year treaty of friendship was signed by the Soviet and East German governments.

15. Governor Rockefeller, the first candidate to enter the Republican presidential race, withdrew in favor of Governor Scranton.

19. Albertville, capital of North Katanga Province in the Congo, fell to Leftist rebels. . . . Senator Edward Kennedy and Senator Birch Bayh were injured in the crash of a private plane.

22. Three civil-rights workers in Mississippi were reported missing and feared dead. President Johnson ordered the FBI and U. S. sailors to search for them.

23. Henry Cabot Lodge resigned as ambassador to South Vietnam and was succeeded by General Maxwell D. Taylor.

JULY

REPUBLICANS NOMINATE GOLDWATER. On July 15, at the 28th Republican National Convention, Arizona Senator Barry M. Goldwater was chosen as the Republican candidate for president. With the conservative Goldwater at its helm, the Republican Party moved further to the Right on the political spectrum.

Goldwater's first-ballot victory at the convention puzzled many observers. He had not made a very good showing in the early primary elections and polls. But behind the scenes, Goldwater had for years been working carefully toward his night of triumph. He began in earnest right after John F. Kennedy's election in 1960. He cultivated close friendships with state and city chairmen and influential party contributors. He spoke for state and local candidates and helped them raise money. By primary time, he had piled up support in state and district conventions. Finally, in June, Goldwater defeated New York Governor Rockefeller in the California primary. This put him within reach of the needed majority of delegates. The party moderates tried to organize a last-minute stop-Goldwater movement behind Pennsylvania Governor William Scranton. But it was too late.

By the time the 1,308 Republican delegates poured into the Cow Palace in San Francisco, it was all over but the shouting. The first-ballot tally: Goldwater, 883; Scranton, 214; other candidates, 211. As his running mate Goldwater chose conservative Representative William E. Miller from New York.

RACE RIOTS IN NEW YORK. Soon after the Republican convention ended, racial violence erupted in New York. The rioting and looting first started in Harlem. These were sparked by the killing of a Negro youth, James Powell, by an off-duty white policeman, Thomas Gilligan, on July 16 in mid-Manhattan. After four days the estimated toll in Harlem was one Negro shot to death, five other Negroes shot and wounded, 81 civilians and 35 policemen injured and 185 persons arrested. Damages to 112 stores and businesses were put at over $50,000. The rioting spread to the predominantly Negro Bedford-Stuyvesant section of Brooklyn, then broke out in Rochester on July 24. Most members of the Negro community deplored the violence, blaming it on young hoodlums. They added, however, that frustration caused by discrimination against Negroes was at the heart of the problem.

Arizona Senator Barry Goldwater and New York Congressman William Miller pose triumphantly after accepting the presidential and vice-presidential nominations at the 1964 Republican National Convention.

NEWS FLASHES

JULY 1964

				1	2	3	4
5	6	7	8	9	10	11	
12	13	14	15	16	17	18	
19	20	21	22	23	24	25	
26	27	28	29	30	31		

1. French-born orchestra conductor Pierre Monteux died at 89. . . . Heinrich Lübke was reelected president of West Germany.

2. President Johnson signed into law the Civil Rights Bill of 1964.

4. Soviet Premier Khrushchev and his wife ended a 19-day tour of Scandinavia.

6. Nyasaland became the independent state of Malawi, ending 73 years of British rule.

10. Moise Tshombe, who led the secession of Katanga Province from the Congo four years ago, was sworn in as the Congo's premier.

11. Maurice Thorez, chief of the French Communist Party from 1930, died at 64.

15. Anastas Mikoyan was named president of the Soviet Union. He succeeded Leonid Brezhnev, who became Premier Khrushchev's deputy in the Communist Party secretariat.

26. By a vote of 15-4 the Organization of American States condemned Cuba as an aggressor.

30. James M. Landis, a close adviser to Presidents Roosevelt, Truman and Kennedy, and former dean of the Harvard Law School, died at 64.

31. The spacecraft Ranger 7 sent back to earth via television over 4,000 still photographs of the moon. These were the first close-up shots of the earth's satellite. After relaying the photos, Ranger 7 crashed on the moon.

AUGUST

MURDERED CIVIL RIGHTS WORKERS FOUND. Though expecting the worst, people were still shocked when the bodies of the three missing civil-rights workers were found near Philadelphia, Mississippi, on August 4. Andrew Goodman, 20, and Michael Schwerner, 24, both white New Yorkers, and James Chaney, 21, a Mississippi Negro, had disappeared on June 21. The three had been part of a volunteer project aimed at increasing Negro voter registration in Mississippi. The presence of 1,000 such volunteers in that state had aroused the anger of die-hard segregationists. Local law officers, the FBI and hundreds of sailors ordered to the scene by President Johnson searched for the three young men. An informer told the FBI where the bodies of the murdered youths were buried.

Doyle in the Philadelphia "Daily News"

CAREFUL! LET'S NOT START A CHAIN REACTION.

GULF OF TONKIN. On August 2 and 4, North Vietnamese torpedo boats attacked United States ships of the Seventh Fleet. The ships were in international waters in the Gulf of Tonkin, miles from the North Vietnamese or Communist Chinese coasts. After the second attack, President Johnson ordered the Navy to retaliate. Carrier-based fighter planes then attacked North Vietnamese torpedo-boat bases, destroying or damaging at least 25 boats.

TURKISH PLANES ATTACK GREEK CYPRIOTS. As Greek Cypriots pressed their attacks against Turkish Cypriot villages, jet planes from Turkey, on August 8 and 9, strafed Greek positions in northwest Cyprus. Fears spread through the NATO countries that Greece would retaliate, plunging it and Turkey—two NATO allies—into war. Sensibly, Greece did nothing to worsen the situation. In fact the Greek Government put pressure on Cyprus President Makarios to find a solution to the crisis. And Turkey ended its flights over Cyprus.

DEMOCRATS NOMINATE JOHNSON AND HUMPHREY. On August 27 the delegates to the Democratic National Convention at Atlantic City, New Jersey, nominated Lyndon B. Johnson for the presidency. Johnson chose Minnesota Senator Hubert H. Humphrey as his running mate. The emotional highlight of the convention was a tribute to the late President Kennedy. The tribute consisted of a film of the highlights of his presidency. It was introduced by Robert F. Kennedy, who stood at the podium while the delegates applauded him—and the memory of his brother —for 16 minutes.

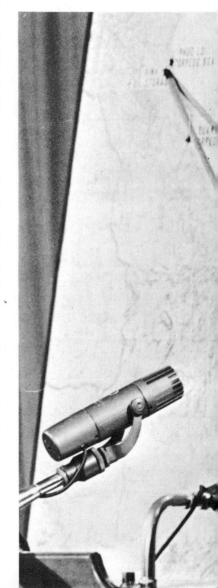

The burned-out remains of a Greek Cypriot gunboat which was attacked by Turkish Air Force planes. Six of the crew were killed and 15 wounded.

At the Pentagon, Defense Secretary McNamara announces that U. S. Navy planes destroyed or damaged 25 boats in an attack on North Vietnam bases.

NEWS FLASHES

AUGUST 1964

						1
2	3	4	5	6	7	8
9	10	11	12	13	14	15
16	17	18	19	20	21	22
23 30	24 31	25	26	27	28	29

4. For the third night, racial riots raged in Jersey City, N. J.

6. Sir Cedric Hardwicke, star of stage and screen, died at 71.

10. Pope Paul VI published his first encyclical, *Ecclesiam Suam* (His Church), which stated that the Church is ready to intervene between nations for peace.

11. The Government of Chile broke diplomatic relations with Cuba, following the recommendation of the Organization of American States.

12. Ian Fleming, 56, creator of James Bond, Secret Agent 007 of the British Secret Service, died of a heart attack. . . . Racial riots broke out in Paterson and Elizabeth, N. J.

18. Education Minister Charles Helou was elected president of Lebanon.

20. The $947,500,000 antipoverty bill was signed into law by President Johnson.

21. Bolivia broke diplomatic relations with Cuba. . . . Palmiro Togliatti, leader of the Italian Communist Party, died at 71.

22. It was announced that Malaysian forces had killed 7 and captured 30 to 35 Indonesian guerrillas.

27. Gracie Allen of the Burns and Allen comedy team died at 58.

28. Philadelphia, Pa., was hard hit by rioting and looting that began in the city's Negro section.

SEPTEMBER

WARREN COMMISSION REPORT. President John F. Kennedy was assassinated on November 22, 1963. Two days later his alleged assassin, Lee Harvey Oswald, 24, was himself murdered, by Jack Ruby, a Dallas, Texas, resident. These tragic acts raised many questions: Was Oswald really the assassin? If so, why did he do it? Did he have accomplices? Was the assassination part of a conspiracy? Was Oswald murdered to keep him quiet? The questions seemed endless.

To find the answers to these questions—insofar as was possible with Oswald, the star witness, dead—President Johnson set up the President's Commission on the Assassination of President John F. Kennedy, commonly called the Warren Commission after its head, Chief Justice Earl Warren.

On September 27, 1964, the findings of the commission were made public. The major conclusions were that three shots had been fired, all by Oswald. The commission also found that Oswald had acted alone, that there was no evidence of a conspiracy, foreign or domestic.

To the question, "Why did Oswald do it?" the commission found no easy answer. It saw Oswald's act as being influenced by many factors. He resented authority. He was unable to enter into meaningful relationships. He was capable of violence (in April 1963 he had tried to kill former Major General Edwin Walker). His life was a series of failures. And his belief in Marxism was expressed in antagonism to the United States. But while in Russia, Oswald was antagonistic to Communist Party members. In short, "he was never satisfied with anything."

The Warren Commission also criticized the FBI and the Secret Service for the way they handled security measures before and during the President's trip to Dallas. The commission called for an increase in the number of Secret Service agents and for a possible reorganization of the security forces. It also recommended that the President's doctor be with him at all times, and that assassination of a president or vice-president be made a Federal crime. A committee of four men was set up by President Johnson to advise him on carrying out the recommendations of the commission.

The response to the Warren Commission Report? There were still some doubters who felt that the assassination of John F. Kennedy was part of a conspiracy. But most people accepted the findings of the commission.

Above: Moments after President Kennedy's assassination. White arrow points to his foot, black arrow to wife of Texas Governor John Connally. Below: Lee Oswald, assassin. The commission found that he acted alone.

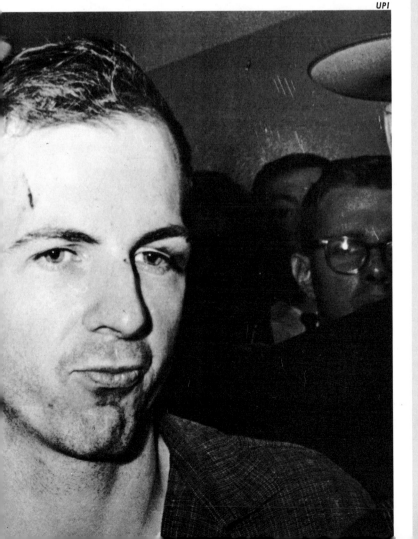

NEWS FLASHES

SEPTEMBER 1964

		1	2	3	4	5
6	7	8	9	10	11	12
13	14	15	16	17	18	19
20	21	22	23	24	25	26
27	28	29	30			

1. Robert Kennedy won the New York State Democratic senatorial nomination. . . . New York City Police Lieutenant Thomas R. Gilligan, who shot and killed 15-year-old Negro James Powell and set off the June riots in Harlem, was cleared of any wrongdoing by a grand jury.

2. Sergeant Alvin C. York, 76, World War I Medal of Honor winner, died after a long illness.

4. Eduardo Frei Montalva was elected president of Chile.

14. Government forces crushed a coup against South Vietnam Premier Nguyen Khanh. . . . The third session of the Ecumenical Council was opened by Pope Paul VI.

16. The Columbia River Treaty—a plan to develop hydroelectric power—was ratified by the United States and Canada.

18. King Constantine of Greece married 18-year-old Princess Anne-Marie of Denmark. . . . Two U. S. destroyers fired on what was believed to be North Vietnamese torpedo boats in the Gulf of Tonkin, destroying at least one. . . . Irish playwright Sean O'Casey died at the age of 84.

20. The Bolivian Army put down a revolt against the Government of President Victor Paz Estenssoro.

21. After 35 centuries of foreign rule, the island of Malta became independent. Dr. Georg Borg Oliver took office as prime minister.

28. Harpo Marx of Marx Brothers fame died at the age of 70.

OCTOBER

KHRUSHCHEV OUSTED AND CHINA EXPLODES A-BOMB.
The third week in October was a momentous one in the
East. The news that Russian Premier Nikita Khrushchev
had been ousted was followed by Communist China's announcement only hours later that it had exploded its first
nuclear bomb. Unlike the power switch in the Kremlin,
Red China's entry into the "nuclear club" was expected.
Although the October 16 blast was small and nuclear
rather than thermonuclear, its political repercussions were
far-reaching. In fact, the blast may very well have been
related to events in the U.S.S.R.

One of Premier Khrushchev's most pressing problems in
recent years had been the growing rift between Russia and
Red China. Many observers felt that the growing challenge
of Red China was one of the reasons for his ouster. As the
days passed, other reasons were suggested in the Soviet
press. It was noted that there had been friction between
Khrushchev and most of the other leaders of the Russian
Government and Communist Party. Khrushchev's agricultural and industrial programs were deemed unsuccessful.
He was accused of nepotism (his son-in-law Aleksei
Adzhubei was ousted as editor of *Izvestia*).

Khrushchev's two most important positions were taken
over by Leonid Brezhnev and Aleksei Kosygin. Brezhnev,
57, became first secretary of the Communist Party. This is
the most powerful position in Russia. Kosygin, 60, took
over as premier. The two new leaders announced that they
would continue Khrushchev's domestic and foreign policies, particularly his policy of peaceful coexistence with
the West. At the same time, they let it be known that they
would like to end Russia's bitter feud with Red China.

GREAT BRITAIN: LABOR PARTY ELECTED. On October 15,
British voters elected the first Labor Government in 13
years. Taking over from Sir Alec Douglas-Home as prime
minister was Labor Party leader Harold Wilson. The Labor
Party win reversed a trend to the Right evidenced in Britain's last four elections. However, the margin of victory
was very small. The Laborites have only a five-seat majority in Parliament.

Named as Wilson's new Cabinet members were George
Brown, secretary of state and minister of economic affairs
(the latter is a new post); Patrick Gordon Walker, foreign
secretary; James Callaghan, chancellor of the exchequer;
and Denis Healey, minister of defense.

U

Dr. Martin Luther King, Jr., winner of th
1964 Nobel Peace Prize.

Khrushchev's ouster paved the way fo
the November meeting of Chinese Premi
Chou En-lai and Soviet Premier Kosygi
Wide Wor

Herbert Clark Hoover (1874-1964), 31st president of the United States, died in New York City on October 30.

NEWS FLASHES

OCTOBER 1964

				1	2	3
4	5	6	7	8	9	10
11	12	13	14	15	16	17
18	19	20	21	22	23	24
25	26	27	28	29	30	31

10. Veteran comedian Eddie Cantor died in Hollywood at 72.

12. U. S. Air Force Lieutenant Colonel Michael Smolen was released unharmed by Leftist terrorists in Venezuela after being kidnaped and held for three days.

13. Queen Elizabeth returned to England after a week's tour of Canada. . . . The Soviet astronauts who orbited the earth 16 times in the *Voskhod*, the world's first three-man spaceship, returned to earth.

14. The 1964 Nobel Peace Prize was awarded to civil-rights leader Dr. Martin Luther King, Jr.

15. Composer and lyricist Cole Porter died at the age of 71. . . . The Nobel Prize in medicine or physiology was awarded to Professor Konrad E. Bloch of Harvard and Professor Feodor Lynen of the University of Munich.

20. Herbert Clark Hoover, 31st president of the United States (1929-33), died at the age of 90.

22. French writer and philosopher Jean-Paul Sartre was awarded the 1964 Nobel Prize for literature. However, he rejected the award and its accompanying $53,000.

24. Northern Rhodesia became the independent state of Zambia after 73 years of British rule.

29. The 1964 Nobel Prize for physics was awarded to an American, Charles H. Townes, and two Russians, Nikolai G. Basov and Aleksandr M. Prochorov. The chemistry prize went to Briton Dorothy C. Hodgkin.

NOVEMBER

DEMOCRATS WIN LANDSLIDE ELECTION. On November 3, over 70,000,000 Americans went to the polls and elected Lyndon Johnson president and Hubert Humphrey vice-president in one of the greatest landslide victories in United States history. The Democrats carried 44 states and the District of Columbia for a total of 486 electoral votes. The Republicans received 52 electoral votes while carrying only six states—Alabama, Arizona, Georgia, Louisiana, Mississippi and South Carolina. President Johnson received 43,100,000 votes to Goldwater's 27,100,000 votes. In winning his landslide victory, President Johnson carried with him a host of Democrats to increase the number of party Senate seats from 66 to 68 and the number of House seats from 257 to 295.

CONGO MASSACRE. On November 24, six hundred Belgian paratroopers dropped on the Leftist rebel capital of Stanleyville in the Congo. Their aim: to save hundreds of whites held hostage by the rebels. The paratroopers were fast but not fast enough, for by the time they arrived many whites—mostly Belgians—had already been murdered.

The Congo has been in a state of anarchy and chaos ever since it gained independence from Belgium on June 30, 1960. UN troops were sent to the country only a month later to help bring about order; but in four years little was accomplished. When the UN troops left in June 1964, communist-trained rebels challenged the Government of Premier Cyrille Adoula. To save the country from complete collapse, the leaders turned to Moise Tshombe, former premier of the Congo's Katanga Province. Tshombe replaced Adoula as Congo premier. To bolster the Congo's armed forces, Tshombe hired white mercenaries, who led the Congolese Army in a series of victories over the rebels. Then, as the mercenary troops advanced toward Stanleyville, the rebels threatened to execute the hundreds of whites held hostage in that city. After negotiations for the release of the hostages failed, the United States, Belgium and Britain decided to use force to free them. Belgian paratroopers were assembled on Britain's Ascension Island and then flown to the Congo in United States planes. The drop on Stanleyville was followed two days later by one on Paulis. After this operation, and the evacuation of hundreds of white civilians, the Belgian troops were withdrawn. Though the rescue operation had saved many lives, the rebels had still succeeded in killing more than one hundred whites.

All photos, "Paris Match"

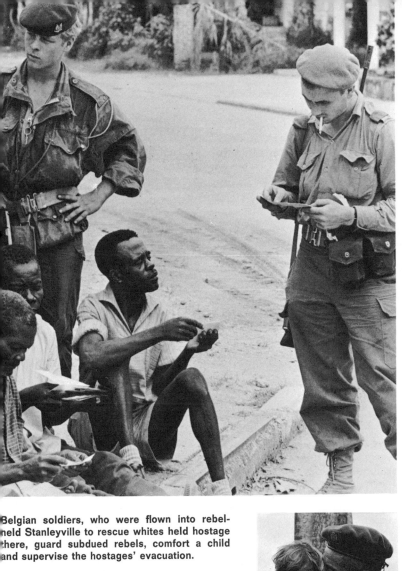

Belgian soldiers, who were flown into rebel-held Stanleyville to rescue whites held hostage there, guard subdued rebels, comfort a child and supervise the hostages' evacuation.

NEWS FLASHES

NOVEMBER 1964

1	2	3	4	5	6	7
8	9	10	11	12	13	14
15	16	17	18	19	20	21
22	23	24	25	26	27	28
29	30					

1. Communist guerrillas destroyed five B-57 bombers and killed five United States servicemen in a mortar attack on Bien Hoa air base in South Vietnam.

2. King Saud was dethroned and Crown Prince Faisal was proclaimed king of Saudi Arabia.

3. Roberto Sanchez Vilella was elected to succeed Luis Muñoz Marin as governor of Puerto Rico.

5. General René Barrientos Ortuño, leader of the military coup that ousted Victor Paz Estenssoro as president of Bolivia on November 4, was sworn in as president.

13-14. Israeli and Syrian forces clashed in bitter fighting north of the Sea of Galilee.

19. U.S. Secretary of Defense McNamara announced the closing of 95 military bases in 33 states and abroad for a predicted annual saving of $477,000,000.

20. The Roman Catholic hierarchy approved a text offering friendship and mutual respect to non-Christian peoples and specifically denying any special Jewish guilt in the crucifixion of Jesus.

21. Pope Paul VI adjourned the third session of the Ecumenical Council.

22. New York's Verrazano-Narrows Bridge, which has the world's longest suspended span, was opened.

26. The Israeli passenger liner *Shalom* and a Norwegian tanker collided off the New Jersey coast; 19 lives were lost.

DECEMBER

In December the Canadian Parliament approved the adoption of a new flag for Canada. The banner will have a red maple leaf on a field of white flanked by two vertical red stripes. In 1963 Lester Pearson, the Liberal candidate for prime minister, promised Canada a new flag if he were elected. Most French Canadians felt that the Red Ensign, the old Canadian flag derived from the British Union Jack, emphasized British influence over the French in Canada. Conservatives, led by then Prime Minister John Diefenbaker, attacked Pearson's position. However, Pearson won the election and saw to it that a new flag was approved by Parliament.

Canada's search for a distinctive flag of its own came to an end when Parliament adopted this maple-leaf design.

NEW CANAL. The year 1964 opened with fierce anti-American riots in Panama and the Panama Canal Zone. On December 18, President Johnson announced that the United States would build a new, sea-level canal in Central America or Colombia. Johnson also proposed to Panamanian President Marco Robles that the 1903 treaty, which gave the Panama Canal to the United States in perpetuity, be renegotiated. The present canal works too slowly and cannot accommodate many modern ships. Four sites were suggested for the new canal. It will take four years to decide where and how the canal can best be built.

FBI ARRESTS 21 IN CIVIL-RIGHTS MURDER CASE. On December 4, the FBI arrested 21 Mississippians in connection with the June 21 slaying of three young civil-rights workers—Michael Schwerner, James Chaney and Andrew Goodman. Among those arrested were Neshoba County Sheriff Lawrence Rainey and his Deputy, Cecil Price. The FBI announced that the Ku-Klux Klan had planned the crime, and that Price had set up the murders by unlawfully arresting and detaining the three youths, then turning them over to a mob of which he was a part. Nineteen of the 21 were charged with conspiring to violate the constitutional rights of the workers. Two were charged with refusing to disclose information about the crime. However, on December 10, at a preliminary hearing, U. S. Commissioner Esther Carter dismissed charges against 19 of the accused. The other two were later released. The Justice Department called for a grand-jury meeting as soon as possible. However, it remained up to the state of Mississippi to bring the men to trial for murder, since murder is not a Federal crime.

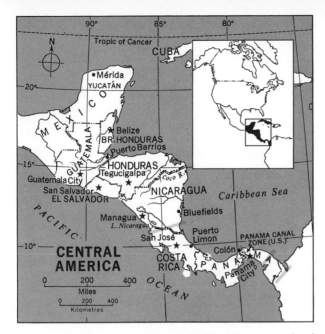

Map indicates routes being studied for the new, sea-level canal to be dug—either by conventional or nuclear means —through Central America or Colombia.

Police examine bazooka used to fire shell at the UN Building while Cuban Ernesto Guevara (above) addressed the General Assembly. On December 22, three anti-Castro Cubans were arrested and admitted firing the bazooka.

NEWS FLASHES

DECEMBER 1964

		1	2	3	4	5
6	7	8	9	10	11	12
13	14	15	16	17	18	19
20	21	22	23	24	25	26
27	28	29	30	31		

2. Pope Paul VI arrived in India for a three-day visit.

5. U.S. Army Captain Roger Donlon was awarded the Congressional Medal of Honor for gallantry in action in South Vietnam.

9. Dame Edith Sitwell, 77, writer and poet, died in London.

11. Movie star Percy Kilbride of Pa Kettle fame died at 76. . . . During a UN speech by Cuban Industry Minister Ernesto Guevara, a bazooka shell was fired at the UN Building from across the East River in Queens; the shell landed in the river and did no damage. The incident took place at the same time anticommunist Cubans were demonstrating against Guevara in front of the UN Building.

12. Kenya became a republic; it had been an independent dominion of the British Commonwealth. . . . Secretary of Defense McNamara announced plans to eliminate the Army Reserve and to reorganize the National Guard.

14. The U.S. Supreme Court upheld the public-accommodations section (Title II) of the 1964 Civil Rights Act. . . . Forbes Burnham became premier of British Guiana, replacing Cheddi Jagan, whose party lost its majority in the legislative election of December 7.

16. Secretary of Commerce Luther Hodges resigned and was replaced with drug executive John Connor.

19. South Vietnamese military leaders dissolved the country's civilian legislature and arrested many political figures—the Army thus became South Vietnam's most important political force.

Louis Goldman, Rapho-Guillumette

Joe Covello, Black Star

STATES

And so, my fellow Americans: ask not what your country can do for you—ask what you can do for your country....
John Fitzgerald Kennedy

Bruce Davidson, Magnum

Gene Daniels, Black Star

Fred Ward, Black Star

Review of the Year

By SAL FODERARO

POLITICS and prosperity highlighted the American scene during the presidential election year of 1964. The state primaries, the nominating conventions, the campaign, and finally the election itself all served to hold the public's attention on political affairs. Meanwhile, most Americans enjoyed the highest level of prosperity in their history. New income and production records continued to be set as the business boom moved well into its fourth year.

The growing civil-rights movement shared the national spotlight with politics. Passage of a historic civil-rights act by Congress marked a great forward step in the Negro's fight for equal opportunities. On the other hand, serious race riots in many northern cities upset Negroes and whites alike.

President Johnson's smashing victory over Senator Goldwater in the November election reached historic proportions. The outcome also revealed a deep split within the Republican Party. Many Republican moderates and liberals refused to support the kind of conservative philosophy represented by the Arizona Senator. In losing so decisively, Goldwater carried many state and congressional Republican candidates down to defeat with him.

Before the election, many important laws were written by the second session of the 88th Congress. This session passed more major legislation than had any Congress in recent years. For the first time, the Senate defeated a Southern filibuster to pass the civil-rights bill. Congress also approved a large cut in Federal income taxes and an antipoverty program.

Humphrey and Johnson at the LBJ Ranch in Texas after their landslide victory over Republicans Barry M. Goldwater and William E. Miller.

UPI

78

In foreign affairs, relations with the Soviet Union remained fairly good and at times seemed even friendly. The most serious problem facing the United States overseas continued to be the war in South Vietnam. There, the use of over 16,000 American troops and huge amounts of military and financial aid failed to halt the communist guerrillas.

Despite the lack of progress in South Vietnam, the United States was determined to prevent the Communists from taking over the country. This was clearly shown to the world in August when President Johnson ordered air raids against patrol-boat bases in North Vietnam. The President took this step after North Vietnamese boats attacked two U.S. Navy destroyers.

FOREIGN AFFAIRS

Trying to stop communism in southeast Asia was the biggest single problem for United States foreign-policy experts in 1964. United States aid to South Vietnam in the form of weapons, money and supplies was increased. But the communist forces (called the Vietcong) made further gains in their campaign to overthrow the South Vietnam Government in Saigon.

The role of the United States in South Vietnam caused disagreement at home. Many Republicans and some Democrats criticized the way the administration was handling the situation. But President Johnson and other government leaders believed that the United States must keep up its assistance to the anticommunist Government in Saigon. They warned that if South Vietnam fell, all of southeast Asia would be taken over by the Communists.

Secretary of Defense Robert S. McNamara was sent to South Vietnam in March and again in May to study the situation. After the March visit he reported that South Vietnam's Army would be increased by 50,000 men. In May he said that "excellent progress" was being made in South Vietnam. He added, however, that "It's going to be a long war."

United States Ambassador Henry Cabot Lodge, who had played a key role in South Vietnam for nearly a year, resigned in June. He returned home to help Pennsylvania Governor William Scranton seek the Republican nomination for president. President Johnson named General Maxwell D. Taylor, chairman of the Joint Chiefs of Staff, to replace Lodge in Saigon.

During the summer there were many demands that the United States carry the war into North Vietnam. The communist leaders of North Vietnam had been actively supporting the rebels in the South. However, the U.S. State Department did not want to widen the conflict. It was feared that such a move might bring the United States into a full-scale war with Communist China. President Johnson, however, warned the Communists that the United States would "risk war" to keep the peace. And he said that the United States would "use the force necessary" to defend South Vietnam's freedom.

A new crisis arose in early August when North Vietnamese patrol boats attacked two United States destroyers. The U.S. Navy warships were on a routine patrol in the Gulf of Tonkin, off North Vietnam, when the attack was made. The USS *Maddox* was attacked on August 2 and the USS *C. Turner Joy* two days later. Neither ship was hit by the attackers.

The United States quickly answered the challenge. On August 4, President Johnson told the nation in a television address that he had instructed U.S. Navy planes to hit certain targets in North Vietnam. The carrier-based aircraft bombed and strafed North Vietnamese patrol boats and their bases, as well as oil-storage tanks. Most of the patrol boats were destroyed and the bases were heavily damaged.

For days the world waited to see whether North Vietnam and its Chinese allies would reply with attacks of their own. The U.S. Seventh Fleet stood ready for battle. But the Communists took no military action, although they complained loudly.

Meanwhile, the United States had begun to build up its military forces in South Vietnam. The Government announced in July that more airplanes and training equipment would be sent to help the South Vietnamese. About 16,000 American troops were already in the country to train and advise the South Vietnam Army. It was expected that another 5,000 GIs would be placed on duty there.

The United States also continued to pour huge sums of money into the war effort. Military aid to South Vietnam was amounting to $200,000,000 yearly. Another $250,000,000 was being spent to pay the expenses of Americans stationed there. And $250,000,000 more was being given in nonmilitary aid.

New troubles also arose in neighboring Laos. On April 19, the head of the country's neutral Government, Prince Souvanna Phouma, was overthrown by a Rightist military group. The action was strongly criticized by the United States. In early May, Souvanna Phouma regained control as the head of the Rightists and Neutralists. The Communists refused to join the regime. A new crisis came in the summer when the Communists (known as the Pathet Lao) launched an offensive in the Plain of Jars section of Laos. At the request of the Laotian Government, unarmed United States planes began flying missions over the Plain of Jars to observe communist troop movements.

Relations with the Soviet Union were probably better in 1964 than at any time since World War II. There were many signs that the Russians, busy as they were with their own bitter quarrel with Communist China, wanted to avoid trouble with the United States.

The sudden downfall of Soviet Premier Khrushchev in mid-October, combined with Red China's first nuclear test explosion, posed new problems for the United States. The Johnson administration expressed the belief that the new Russian leaders would follow Khrushchev's policy of peaceful coexistence with the nations of the West.

Shiploads of American wheat began arriving in Soviet ports in February. The sale of wheat, which had been approved by President Kennedy in 1963, was a symbol of the better feelings existing between the two great powers.

Efforts toward ending the arms race continued, but no real progress was made. The 18-nation disarmament conference again met at Geneva, Switzerland, and the United States and the U.S.S.R. seemed to be moving closer to agreement on some points. American officials at the talks offered two main proposals. These were that no more atomic material be produced for weapons, and that each side destroy some of its old bombers.

Feelings between the United States and Cuba grew worse in February when Premier Fidel Castro cut off the water supply to the U.S. Navy base at Guantanamo. He said the action was taken because the United States had captured four Cuban fishing vessels in Florida waters.

The water stoppage was seen as part of Castro's efforts to expel the United States from the Cuban base. But the United States began shipping water to Guantanamo by tanker so that it would not have to depend on Castro for the water supply. It also planned to build a saltwater conversion plant at the base. This plant will turn seawater into drinking water.

United States efforts to bring pressure against the Castro regime were helped by a vote of the Organization of American States (OAS) on July 26. The twenty nations of the OAS passed a resolution calling on all members to break diplomatic ties with Cuba. Members were also asked to halt all trade with Castro (except for food and medicine) and to cut off all transportation to Cuba by sea. United States Secretary of State Dean Rusk said the conference proved that "Castro has no future in Cuba or this hemisphere."

A serious crisis involving the United States and Panama broke out in January.

Clashes between Panamanian crowds and United States troops in the Canal Zone left at least 23 persons dead (including 4 American soldiers) and 350 wounded. The fighting began at an American high school in the Canal Zone over the question of flying the United States and Panamanian flags side by side.

Panama quickly announced that it was breaking diplomatic ties with the United States. It also demanded changes in the treaty under which the United States operates the Panama Canal. With the help of OAS diplomats, the two countries reached an agreement on April 3. Diplomatic relations were restored. Both sides also agreed to work toward a settlement of the Canal question.

DOMESTIC AFFAIRS

Civil rights for Negroes was the most important problem facing Americans on the home front in 1964. Negro protest marches, which had begun on a large scale in 1963, were held again in several cities in the North and South. These demonstrations, intended to help the Negro win his full rights as a citizen, caused a great deal of argument. Many white people disliked this form of protest. They felt that Negroes should fight for their rights in the courts and not in the streets.

The fact that these demonstrations sometimes led to violence also worried many persons, including important Negro leaders. Oddly enough, most of the racial rioting in the summer of 1964 occurred not in the South but in the North. These northern riots made many persons realize that the so-called Negro "revolution" is a problem not only for the South but for the whole nation.

A milestone in the Negro struggle for equal rights was reached when Congress passed the Civil Rights Act of 1964. This legislation permits the Federal Government to help Negroes overcome discrimination in jobs, voting and schools. It also gives Negroes the right to use such public places

as hotels, restaurants, theaters and swimming pools.

A long, hard fight took place in Congress before the law was passed. The House of Representatives adopted the measure on February 10 by a vote of 290 to 130. In the Senate, however, the bill faced much tougher opposition. Senate rules place no limit on discussion. Thus a group of Southern senators was able to prevent the bill from coming to a vote by making lengthy speeches. This is known as a filibuster. Finally, on June 10, the Senate stopped the filibuster by voting for cloture (meaning a close of debate). It marked the first time that the Senate had taken this step in a debate on civil rights.

The final vote in the Senate was made on June 19. The act was passed by a vote of 73 to 27. Supporting the measure were 46 Democrats and 27 Republicans. Voting against it were 21 Democrats and 6 Republicans. The Senate galleries were filled with white and Negro spectators as the historic voting climaxed 83 days of debate. President Johnson signed the bill into law on July 2.

Coming in a presidential election year, the civil-rights contest was watched carefully for its effects on the political campaign. Actually, the votes of both Democrats and Republicans were needed to put the measure across. President Johnson gave it his full support, and Senator Hubert Humphrey led the bill's backers in the Senate. On the Republican side, Senator Everett M. Dirksen played a key role in the bill's success. As Senate Republican leader he worked with the administration in drawing up several compromise amendments (changes) of the original bill. He then urged his fellow Republicans to vote for the revised bill.

Among the six Republicans voting against the civil-rights bill was Senator Barry Goldwater. The vote took place shortly before he won his party's presidential nomination. Senator Goldwater explained that he was strongly against discrimination of any kind, but that he believed the bill was unconstitutional. He especially disliked the sections dealing with employment and public accommodations (hotels, dining places and so on).

The new law soon brought changes to the Southern way of life. Within a few days after the President signed the bill, Negroes were served in white restaurants in Birmingham and Montgomery, Alabama, as well as in many other cities throughout the South. Negroes also were admitted to theaters and swimming pools that had previously kept them out.

In some Southern cities, however, there were a few cases of Negroes being prevented from entering restaurants and bowling alleys. A number of court suits were begun to test the new law. Not until these cases are decided will the nation know just how much help the 1964 act will be in giving equal opportunities to Negroes.

Many persons had predicted that the civil-rights drive would bring a "long, hot summer" of disorder and violence. These forecasts largely came true.

The first major riot occurred in the Harlem section of New York City on July 18. Hundreds of Negroes, mostly teenagers and young men, went on a wild spree. They threw bricks and bottles at police, who fired shots over their heads in an attempt to quiet them. Dozens of stores were broken into and robbed of their merchandise.

The rioting in Harlem continued for several nights and then spread to a Negro section in Brooklyn. A few days later racial violence broke out in Rochester, New York. In August, Negro rioters fought with police in Jersey City, Paterson and Elizabeth, New Jersey, and in the Chicago suburb of Dixmoor. Another large-scale riot occurred on August 28 in Philadelphia, where damage to stores and property was very heavy.

All of these outbursts followed passage of the Civil Rights Act. They were not connected with the peaceful efforts of the major civil-rights groups. Police officials said that the rioters were mainly the "hoodlum" members of the community. However, in each of the cities where the disorder occurred there are thousands of Negroes living under conditions of terrible poverty. Poor housing, lack of jobs, and discrimination of all kinds created the anger and bitterness that finally exploded during the "long, hot summer" of 1964.

Earlier in the summer, the nation had been shocked by the murder of three young civil-rights workers in Mississippi. The three were taking part in a campaign to get Negroes in the state to vote. On June 21 they disappeared in the town of Philadelphia, Mississippi. An intense search was made for the missing men, two whites from New York City and a Negro from Mississippi. President Johnson ordered 200 unarmed Navy men to join in the hunt, along with the Federal Bureau of Investigation. The bodies were finally found after six weeks in an earth dam near where the young men had disappeared. While the search for them was on, the bodies of two other murdered Negroes were found.

The second session of the 88th Congress, beginning on January 7, completed action on several major bills in addition to the one on civil rights. The Democrats controlled both houses of Congress—by 66 to 34 in the Senate and by 254 to 176 (with 5 seats vacant) in the House.

In his first State of the Union Message, President Johnson gave most attention to matters at home. He called for a "war against poverty" in the United States. He also urged action in the fields of housing, education, civil rights, employment, and aid to elderly persons.

On January 21 the President outlined to Congress his budget for the fiscal year ending June 30, 1965. (The budget shows the total amount of money that the Government expects to receive and the amount it plans to spend.) President Johnson called for spending of $97,900,000,000 and receipts (or income) of $93,000,000,000.

The budget trimmed $1,100,000,000 in the money to be spent for defense, but the chief executive said the lesser amount would not weaken the nation's military power. More money was allowed for education, health and other domestic programs than in the previous year's budget.

Most of the legislation that President Johnson asked for had been originally presented by President Kennedy. The one major bill that was Mr. Johnson's own was the antipoverty measure, and he worked hard to win approval for it. As finally adopted by Congress on August 11, the antipoverty bill provided for spending $947,500,000 in the first year.

One of the chief features of the antipoverty bill is the Volunteers in Service to America (VISTA). It is a domestic version of the overseas Peace Corps. VISTA is designed to improve conditions at home by sending volunteers to work in areas suffering from poverty. The bill also set up a $340,000,000 fund to help communities get rid of slums, offer guidance to people in need and provide special schooling.

Other features of the antipoverty program include: (1) a Job Corps, in which young men and women would receive job training at special camps; (2) a plan to reduce the number of high school dropouts (students who quit school) by giving them part-time work at such places as hospitals and playgrounds; and (3) a system of loans for small farmers and businessmen to enable them to buy better equipment.

Other major legislation receiving Congressional approval included:

(1) A wilderness bill, which sets aside 9,000,000 acres of forest and mountain lands. These will be forever preserved in their natural state.

(2) A land and water conservation fund. The money will be used to obtain and develop parks and other outdoor recreational sites.

(3) Pay raises for members of Congress and about 1,700,000 other Federal employees, as well as for servicemen.

(4) The Urban Mass Transit Act of 1964. This law provides federal grants of $375,000,000 for improving transportation systems in and around cities.

(5) Several measures providing large-scale financial assistance in the fields of education (college, medical and vocational) and mental health.

In the closing days of the session, Congress again took up the argument on Medicare. The Medicare plan, first proposed by President Kennedy, is a way to provide health insurance for elderly persons through the Social Security program. The Medicare bill finally was passed in the Senate on September 2. Earlier the House had approved a Social Security bill without the Medicare feature. A Senate-House conference then failed to agree on a compromise bill, and the Medicare plan was dead for this session.

A bill to reduce Federal income taxes was signed into law by President Johnson on February 26. It reduced the taxes that both private persons and businesses pay to the Government. Part of the total cut of $11,500,000,000 took effect in 1964. The rest will take effect in 1965.

Most business and labor leaders agreed with the administration that lower taxes would help strengthen the economy. It was believed that if people had to pay less taxes they would spend more on consumer goods (such as cars, TV sets, refrigerators and the like). This would in turn create more jobs. To speed up this process, the withholding tax (which is taken out of each worker's paycheck) was reduced in March from 18 per cent to 14 per cent. It was figured that this step alone would put an extra $800,-000,000 into Americans' purses each month.

General prosperity continued throughout the nation in 1964. By September the rise in business and industrial activity had continued for 43 straight months and showed no signs of coming to an end. This marked the longest unbroken period of business growth in peacetime since 1933-

37, when the country began to recover from the Great Depression.

Nearly all types of businesses enjoyed the benefits of the boom. Industrial production rose in August for the 12th month in a row. Automobile manufacturing, which affects dozens of other industries, was heading for another record year. Steel production in July was 17 per cent higher than a year earlier. Both personal income and business profits showed considerable gains.

The employment picture improved a little but was still far from satisfactory. By July the number of persons out of jobs fell to 4.9 per cent of the total labor force—the first time the rate had dropped below 5 per cent in over four years. Employment in the same month reached a record high of 73,300,000, including the armed forces.

The rate of jobless persons among certain groups remained much greater than the national average, however. It was especially high among teen-agers and Negroes. This was mainly due to automation—the use of machinery and electronic devices to do the work of humans. Until ways can be found to train unskilled or partly skilled workers for the jobs required by modern industry, unemployment will continue to be a problem for the country.

Contributing to the healthy economy was the general labor peace that prevailed. A nationwide railroad strike that threatened serious damage to the economy was finally avoided on April 22. The dispute between 195 of the nation's 198 railroads and the five unions that operate the trains had lasted for five long years. The main question was whether the railroad companies should be allowed to end thousands of jobs that they considered no longer necessary. The settlement agreed to in April gave the companies the right to discontinue many of these jobs. At the same time it provided the workers with pay raises and other benefits.

In the automobile industry a threatened strike was avoided on September 11 when Chrysler Corporation and the United Auto Workers signed a new three-year contract. The agreement provides higher wages and other benefits adding up to more than 50 cents an hour for each worker. The Ford Motor Company reached a similar agreement. But the other member of the "Big Three" auto producers, General Motors Corporation, was hit by a nationwide strike of 350,000 workers. The union voted to end the month-long strike on October 25, but disputes at local plants delayed a return to full production.

A U.S. Supreme Court decision promised to have a great effect on state legislatures throughout the country. On June 15 the high court ruled that districts in both houses of the legislatures must be "substantially equal" in population. At least 40 states were affected by the decision. It was considered the most important action taken by the court since the 1954 ruling on school desegregation.

The basis of the Supreme Court decision is that the votes of all citizens should have equal weight. Each state is divided into voting districts. At present in most states they are set up so that the votes of small-town and farm citizens carry greater weight than those in the cities and suburban sections. This is because a small number of voters in a country district have the same representation in the legislature as do a much larger number of voters in a city district. The Supreme Court wants the boundaries of the districts changed so that each will contain about the same number of voters.

A loud outcry against the decision arose from the rural areas. Many members of Congress also were opposed to the court stepping into a field (the legislature) that it had always left alone. Bills were introduced in the House and Senate that would have overturned the Supreme Court ruling or at least delayed its taking effect. The most important of the delaying measures, offered by Senator Dirksen, finally was defeated after a hard fight.

A new voting machine in New York, showing the various candidates for the political parties in the state. New York was the scene of the bitterly contested Kennedy-Keating senatorial race.

ELECTIONS

The contest for the presidency overshadowed all other domestic news in 1964. The candidates for the two major parties were chosen during the summer. The Republicans, meeting at San Francisco in July, nominated Senator Barry M. Goldwater of Arizona on the first ballot. The convention named Representative William E. Miller of New York as the party's vice-presidential candidate. He had served as Republican national chairman.

Goldwater's nomination followed several months of political activity. Other leading contenders for the nomination were Governor Nelson A. Rockefeller of New York, Governor William Scranton of Pennsylvania, Ambassador Henry Cabot Lodge, and former Vice-President Richard M. Nixon. A woman, Senator Margaret Chase Smith of Maine, also entered the race.

The several state primaries did not produce a clear favorite. But while the primaries were making headlines, Goldwater had been picking up many delegates in the various state conventions. By scoring a narrow victory over Rockefeller in the big California primary, he just about clinched

his nomination. In a last-minute effort to stop Goldwater, Governor Scranton entered the race just a month before the convention. The move came too late to be effective.

The San Francisco convention revealed a sharp division between the Goldwater conservatives and the moderate wing of the Republican Party. A hot debate arose over such issues as civil rights and presidential control of nuclear weapons. The moderates also tried to have the convention condemn political extremism, in particular such groups as the John Birch Society, a far Right-Wing organization. But the Goldwater delegates easily beat down these challenges.

On the Democratic side, President Johnson won his party's nomination at Atlantic City in August without opposition. He personally appeared at the convention to announce his choice for the vice-presidency —Senator Hubert H. Humphrey of Minnesota.

The major issues that developed during the campaign included foreign policy, the role of the Federal Government, civil rights and morality. Goldwater charged that Johnson was "soft on communism." He urged a tougher attitude toward the Russians and

PRESIDENTIAL ELECTORAL VOTE DISTRIBUTION

WASH. 9 | MONT. 4 | N.D. 4 | MINN. 10 | N.H. | VT. 3 | ME. 4
ORE. 6 | IDAHO 4 | WYO. 3 | S.D. 4 | WIS. 12 | N.Y. 43 | MASS. 14
NEV. 3 | UTAH 4 | COLO. 6 | NEB. 5 | IOWA 9 | MICH. 21 | R.I. 4
CALIF. 40 | ARIZ. 5 | N.M. 4 | KAN. 7 | MO. 12 | ILL. 26 | IND. 13 | OHIO 26 | PA. 29 | CONN. 8
N.J. 17 | DEL. 3 | MD. 10
OKLA. 8 | ARK. 6 | KY. 9 | W.VA. 7 | VA. 12
TENN. 11 | N.C. 13 | WASH. D.C. 3
S.C. 8
TEXAS 25 | LA. 10 | MISS. 7 | ALA. 10 | GA. 12
FLA. 14
ALASKA 3
HAWAII 4

☐ DEMOCRATIC
■ REPUBLICAN

WINNERS

UPI · Wide World · Wide World

Gov. George Romney, Mich. (R) · Sen. Stephen Young, Ohio (D) · Sen. Robert Kennedy, N. Y. (D)

LOSERS

UPI · UPI · UPI

Charles Percy, Illinois (R) · Former Sen. Keating, N. Y. (R) · Former Sen. Salinger, Calif. (D)

Chinese. The Democrats in turn pictured the Senator as "trigger happy"—that is, they claimed that he would act recklessly in a crisis. They also attacked Goldwater for suggesting that the NATO commander be given authority to use nuclear weapons. The Democrats insisted that only the president should have this great responsibility.

In domestic affairs, Goldwater argued that the country was drifting toward socialism under the Democrats. He favored more power for the individual states. He also charged that corruption in Government was weakening the nation's moral standards. The civil-rights issue centered on Goldwater's vote against the 1964 Civil Rights Act. He repeatedly blamed the administration for permitting crime and "violence in the streets." This was generally understood to be a reference to Negro demonstrations.

On November 3, Americans went to the voting booths and gave President Johnson one of the greatest election victories in the nation's history. The President carried 44 states and the District of Columbia. The popular vote was: Johnson—43,100,-000; Goldwater—27,100,000. The electoral vote was: Johnson—486; Goldwater—52.

President Johnson's support came from all sections of the country except the Deep South. Goldwater carried Alabama, Mississippi, Louisiana, South Carolina and Georgia in the South, plus his home state of Arizona. Goldwater's strength in the South was clearly the result of the civil-rights issue.

Not since Franklin D. Roosevelt's re-election in 1936 had any candidate scored such a triumph. Roosevelt lost only Maine and Vermont that year. But even those Republican strongholds went for Johnson in 1964. His margin of 16,000,000 votes was the largest in history, and his share of the total vote stood at a record 61.3 per cent.

In forging his tremendous victory, President Johnson received strong backing from nearly every voting group—farmers, suburbanites, factory workers, businessmen, and various religious groups. Especially striking was the Negro vote. It was estimated that well over 90 per cent of the Negroes cast their ballots for Johnson.

As usually happens in a landslide vote, the President helped other candidates of his party to win office. The Democrats increased their already large majority in the House of Representatives by 38 seats (considering the 5 seats that were vacant as belonging to the party that had held them). The 89th Congress thus will have 295 Democrats and 140 Republicans.

Of the 35 Senate seats being contested, the Democrats won 28 for a net gain of two. The lineup in the new Senate will be 68 Democrats and 32 Republicans.

On the state level, the Democrats won 17 of the 25 races for governor. Since they had held 18 of these governorships, however, this represented a net gain of one for the Republicans. The national total stood at 33 Democratic governors to 17 Republicans.

Except in the South, most of the Republicans who managed to win were considered moderates. Even those who lost ran far ahead of Senator Goldwater in their states. Many Republicans refused to back Goldwater during the campaign, or gave him only token support.

A number of the U.S. Senate races attracted nationwide interest. Robert F. Kennedy, who had resigned as attorney general, captured the seat from New York. Robert A. Taft, Jr., son of the late "Mr. Republican," lost by a narrow margin in Ohio to Stephen Young. In California, Pierre Salinger, who served as press secretary to President Kennedy, was beaten by George Murphy, the former actor.

Probably the most impressive Republican victory was gained by Governor George Romney of Michigan. Although Johnson carried the state by over 1,000,000 votes, Romney won reelection by a margin of 300,000. The Governor, a leading moderate, had campaigned independently of Goldwater.

UNITED STATES
NATIONAL MONUMENTS

National monuments reflect the course of United States history. Presented on these pages is a selection that ranges from an ancient Indian cliff village to a Franciscan mission, founded in California in 1798. Here also are maps of mid-continental United States, Hawaii and Alaska.

…ns inhabited America long before Europeans arrived. The … Palace, in Colorado's Mesa Verde National Park, was built by …lo Indians in the 12th and 13th centuries. They abandoned it …in the 13th century because of prolonged drought in the area.

…oldest house in the oldest city of the United States, St. Augus-…Fla. Founded by the Spaniards as a military base in 1565, …ugustine has flown the flags of Spain, England, the United …s, and the Confederacy.

Ray Manley—Shostal

Winston Pote—Shostal

James Fort (reconstructed) was part of the Jamestown colony in Virginia. Founded in 1607, Jamestown was the first permanent English settlement in North America.

Statue of Massasoit, an Indian chief who was friendly to the Pilgrims, crowns Cole's Hill overlooking Plymouth Rock. The historic rock on the coast of Massachusetts is now protected by a granite portico.

colonial scene is enacted in front of the reconstructed Governor's
alace in Williamsburg. The original edifice, completed in 1720,
as built when Williamsburg was the capital of Virginia.

ort Niagara, in New York, was built by the French in about
726. The French were once powerful in large areas of
North America, but their attempt to rule the continent ended
n 1763 with British victory in the French and Indian Wars.

Minuteman statue stands in Lex-
ington, Mass. Here, on Apr. 19,
1775, a troop of British redcoats
and a small band of Yankee mili-
tiamen exchanged the first shots
of the American Revolution.

91

MID—CONTINENTAL
UNITED STATES

92

0   100   200   300   400

Lambert Conformal Conic Projection

☆ NATIONAL CAPITAL

⊛ STATE CAPITAL

TUNDRA AND PERMANENT

© 1963 JEPPESEN & CO., DENVER, COLO., U.S.A.
ALL RIGHTS RESERVED

EVERGREEN NEEDLELEAF FOREST

MID-LATITUDE MIXED FOREST

MEDITERRANEAN SCRUB WOODLAND

PRAIRIE

STEPPE

DESERT

IRRIGATED DRY LAND

TROPICAL WOODLAND AND SAVANNA

CULTIVATION

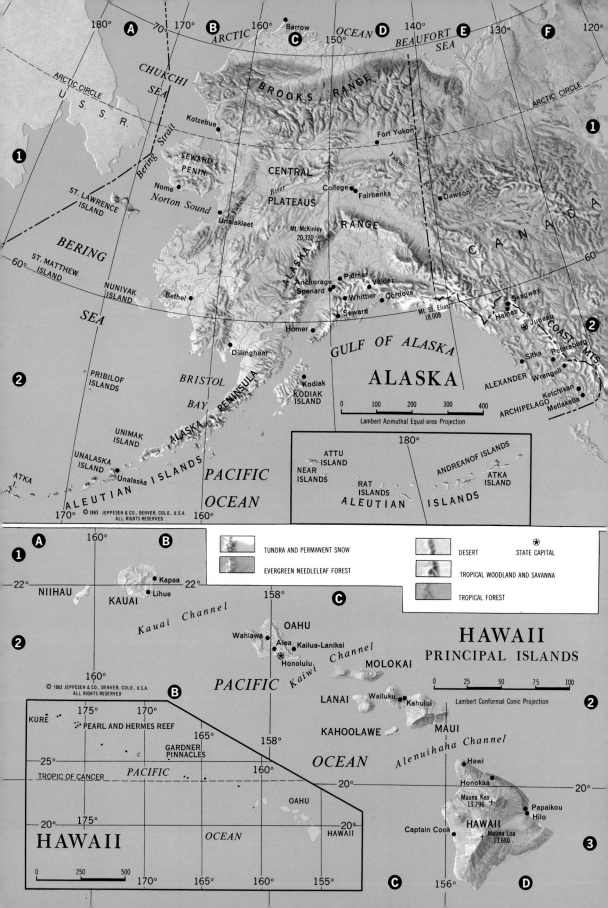

ALASKA

180° Ⓐ 70° 170° Ⓑ 160° Ⓒ Barrow 150° OCEAN Ⓓ 140° BEAUFORT Ⓔ 130° Ⓕ 120°

ARCTIC OCEAN

ARCTIC CIRCLE

CHUKCHI SEA

BROOKS RANGE

Ⓐ

U. S. S. R.

Bering Strait

Kotzebue

Fort Yukon

Yukon

SEWARD PENIN.

CENTRAL

College
Fairbanks

Dawson

CANADA

ST. LAWRENCE ISLAND

Nome

Norton Sound

Yukon
River

PLATEAUS

Unalakleet

RANGE

Mt. McKinley
20,320

ALASKA

Skagway

BERING

ST. MATTHEW ISLAND

60°

NUNIVAK ISLAND

Bethel

Anchorage
Spenard
Whittier
Palmer
Valdez
Cordova

Mt. St. Elias
18,008

Haines

Juneau

COAST MTS.

60°

Ⓑ

Seward

Sitka
Petersburg

SEA

Homer

GULF OF ALASKA

Wrangell

Dillingham

Kodiak

ALASKA

ALEXANDER

Ketchikan
Metlakatla

PRIBILOF ISLANDS

BRISTOL BAY

PENINSULA

KODIAK ISLAND

0 100 200 300 400

Lambert Azimuthal Equal-area Projection

ARCHIPELAGO

ATKA I.

UNIMAK ISLAND

ALASKA

PACIFIC

UNALASKA ISLAND

Unalaska

ALEUTIAN ISLANDS

OCEAN

180°

ATTU ISLAND

NEAR ISLANDS

ANDREANOF ISLANDS

ATKA ISLAND

RAT ISLANDS

170° © 1963 JEPPESEN & CO., DENVER, COLO., U.S.A.
ALL RIGHTS RESERVED 160°

A L E U T I A N   I S L A N D S

Ⓐ 160° Ⓑ

Ⓐ①

22°

NIIHAU

Kapaa
Lihue

KAUAI

Kauai Channel

158° Ⓒ

TUNDRA AND PERMANENT SNOW

DESERT

STATE CAPITAL ✪

EVERGREEN NEEDLELEAF FOREST

TROPICAL WOODLAND AND SAVANNA

TROPICAL FOREST

Ⓐ②

Wahiawa
Aiea
Kailua-Lanikai

OAHU

Honolulu

Kaiwi Channel

MOLOKAI

HAWAII
PRINCIPAL ISLANDS

© 1963 JEPPESEN & CO., DENVER, COLO., U.S.A.
ALL RIGHTS RESERVED

PACIFIC

LANAI

Wailuku

KAHOOLAWE

Kahului

0 25 50 75 100

Lambert Conformal Conic Projection ②

Ⓑ

KURĒ

175° 170°

PEARL AND HERMES REEF

165°

GARDNER PINNACLES

158°

160°

OCEAN

MAUI

Alenuihaha Channel

Hawi

20°

25°

TROPIC OF CANCER

PACIFIC

160°

20°

Honokaa

Mauna Kea
13,796

Papaikou
Hilo

OAHU

20°

175°

HAWAII

OCEAN

160°

155°

20°

HAWAII

Captain Cook

HAWAII

Mauna Loa
13,680

③

0 250 500

170° 165° 160° 155° Ⓒ 156° Ⓓ

The Betsy Ross House in Philadelphia. According to tradition, she sewed the first Stars and Stripes, adopted by Congress in 1777.

Log cabins at Valley Forge, Pa., are similar to those in which Washington's ragged army spent the terrible winter of 1777-78. The site of the army's encampment is now in Valley Forge State Park.

Life in Spanish California centered around the missions established by Franciscans. The Mission of San Luis Rey de Francia, in San Luis Rey, was founded in 1798.

Political Conventions

By HAROLD FABER

PRESIDENTIAL and vice-presidential candidates are nominated at national political conventions. These conventions are held every four years by the political parties. The first such conventions were held just before the elections of 1832. Before then, the political parties nominated their candidates in other ways. Usually they were chosen at caucuses, or secret meetings, of members of Congress or of the state legislatures. But many people did not like this system. They felt that choosing a presidential candidate at a secret meeting was not democratic. Thus, in 1831, one small party organized a national convention. The delegates met in Baltimore to choose—openly—their candidate for president. The party was the Anti-Masonic Party, a group opposed to secret societies. The delegates met on September 21, 1831, and nominated William Wirt of Maryland for president.

Both major parties of the time followed the example of the Anti-Masonic Party. They too held national conventions in Baltimore. Henry Clay was nominated by the National Republican Party in December 1831. (This party was a forerunner of the modern Republican Party.) President Andrew Jackson was renominated by the Democratic-Republican Party in May 1832. (This party later became the Democratic Party.) Andrew Jackson was reelected.

The Anti-Masonic Party soon died. But the system of political conventions it established has survived to this day. There have been some changes over the years. But the basic idea of a political party holding a national convention of delegates from the various states to select a presidential and vice-presidential candidate remains the same.

One of the first big changes in the form of conventions came in 1840. In that year, the Democratic-Republican Party renominated Martin Van Buren for president. At the convention, the delegates also adopted nine short "resolutions of purpose." This was the first true party platform. Before that each party had issued statements of praise for its candidate. But the party's program was never formally presented to the public.

In the years since, national conventions have become strange phenomena. They are unlike anything else in the world. In many other countries, the leader of a political party usually becomes the president or prime minister if his party wins the national election. The party leader usually does not run directly for the office. But in the United States, any citizen can become a candidate for the nomination. All he needs is the desire, the money and the political backing.

The first national convention—that of the Anti-Masonic Party—had 116 delegates. But through the years, the number of delegates to a convention has increased enormously. Today, more than 1,000 delegates go to the Republican or Democratic convention. At the convention these delegates try to overcome their differences and elect a candidate. But sometimes they cannot agree.

This happened in 1844, when the first dark-horse candidate was elected. A dark-horse candidate is one who is unexpectedly nominated. In 1844 the Democratic con-

FIRST REPUBLICAN CONVENTION HELD AT LAFAYETTE HALL, PITTSBURG, PA, FEB, 22ᴰ 1856.

The Bettmann Archive

A lithograph of the first Republican Party convention, at which
John Charles Frémont was nominated for president.

vention was deadlocked for seven ballots.
The delegates could not choose between
Van Buren and Senator Lewis Cass of
Michigan. Then, on the eighth ballot,
James K. Polk of Tennessee received 44
votes. On the next ballot there was a stam-
pede to support him. He was nominated
unanimously. Polk, the dark horse, went
on to win the presidential election.

The Republican Party, as we know it,
held its first convention in Pittsburgh in
1856. John C. Frémont was nominated for
the presidency. However, he lost the election to Democrat James Buchanan. Four
years later the Republican Party swept to
victory with Abraham Lincoln. In that
election, held on the eve of the Civil War,
there were four presidential candidates
representing four different parties.

In 1868 the Republicans had an obvious
candidate: Civil War hero Ulysses S.
Grant. The Democratic Party had no

obvious choice. At the Democratic convention, the names of 47 men were placed
in nomination. Twenty-one ballots were
held. Still no candidate was chosen. A
movement then developed to nominate
New York Governor Horatio Seymour,
who was permanent chairman of the convention. But Seymour did not want the
nomination. "Pity me," he cried, as he left
the hall in protest. But he was nominated
anyway. This is considered to be the first
genuine draft of a candidate in the history
of conventions.

The most quoted statement made in
connection with a convention was by a person who was not a candidate. In 1884,
General William Tecumseh Sherman sent
a telegram to the Republican convention.
He informed the Republican Party leaders
that he would not run for the presidency.
The General said, "I will not accept if
nominated and will not serve if elected."

Conventions haven't changed very much over the years. The 1888 Democratic convention and the 1964 Republican convention both had their noisy demonstrations. This 1964 demonstration was to no avail: Scranton lost to Goldwater. But in 1888, Allen Thurman, for whom the demonstration was held, won the Democratic vice-presidential nomination even though he was 75 years old.

Since then, any statement less firm has not been accepted as a real refusal to run.

Probably the most famous speech at a convention was made by William Jennings Bryan at the Democratic convention of 1896. Bryan was in favor of free coinage of silver. His convention speech ended with these words: "You shall not press down upon the brow of labor this crown of thorns. You shall not crucify mankind upon a cross of gold." Bryan's dramatic speech won him the nomination. But he later lost the election to Republican William McKinley. In fact this was the first of three Democratic nominations that Bryan won. He lost all three elections.

In 1920 the Republicans had no outstanding candidate. Several ballots were held at the convention, but no one was nominated. Finally the leaders of the party met in private to choose a candidate. They debated many hours before deciding on Ohio Senator Warren G. Harding. He was chosen primarily because nobody had anything against him. This long series of behind-the-scenes conversations gave rise to a new political phrase: the smoke-filled room.

The next day, the balloting continued. As the party leaders exerted pressure on the delegates, the votes shifted to Harding. He was nominated on the tenth ballot. And he went on to win the election. The 1920 Republican convention clearly showed the role of party leaders in selecting the candidate.

Who are the delegates to party conventions? Of course the party leaders from the various states are always at conventions. Other delegates include party workers. This is a kind of reward for party service. Sometimes people have been chosen as delegates just because they could afford the trip to the convention.

Some states have primary elections or state conventions to show their choice for president and vice-president. Delegates from these states sometimes are bound to vote in the convention according to the wishes of the people of their state. Once at the convention, delegates may be swayed by an impassioned speech by one of the nominees. Frequently they vote as their consciences dictate. More often, they vote as the party leaders dictate.

The longest national convention was held in the sweltering hot days of June 24 to July 9, 1924, in New York City's Madison Square Garden. New York Governor Alfred E. Smith and William G. McAdoo of California were the leading contenders for the Democratic nomination. However, neither could get enough votes to win. Finally, after 100 ballots, McAdoo withdrew. The delegates who supported him were then able to vote for other nominees. With the shift in votes, the nomination went to John W. Davis of West Virginia on the 103d ballot. He lost the election to Republican Calvin Coolidge.

Recent conventions have been shorter than in the past. This is basically because the parties want to present a united front to the public. With television, the public can see almost everything that goes on at a convention. Long, drawn-out affairs with bitter fighting can lose votes.

There has been much debate over the years about whether the national-convention system is the best way to nominate the presidential and vice-presidential candidates. Many people feel that the delegates often do not vote the way the people of their state want them to vote. The conventions also tend to have the atmosphere of a circus. Some observers have called them vulgar, stupid, tedious, nonsensical and fraudulent. One critic has said, "party conventions resemble tribal rituals; almost everything about them is phony." But conventions have their defenders too. These people admit that the convention system has its faults. But they also say, "It works." Joseph Martin, Republican Congressman from Massachusetts, presided over five conventions. He has said, "I always ask 'What system could be better?' and I have yet to hear a convincing answer."

An unemployed coal miner, one of the 30,000,000 Americans living in poverty.

Poverty: U.S.A.

By OSCAR ORNATI

POVERTY is the condition of persons who have and earn less money than they need to satisfy just their basic needs. Everyone has to have food, housing, clothing, medical care in illness, and some entertainment. People who do not have enough to pay for these minimum needs are said not to have enough to sustain themselves. They live "below minimum subsistence."

It is not easy to agree on a definition of minimum subsistence. There is no scientific way to establish what a person must have to live on. Generally speaking, the people of a country increase the subsistence minimum as their country gets richer and produces more. Thus the minimum that an Indian or an African feels is necessary for survival is less than what Americans have

Because coal mining in West Virginia is a dying industry, these skilled workers are now unemployed.

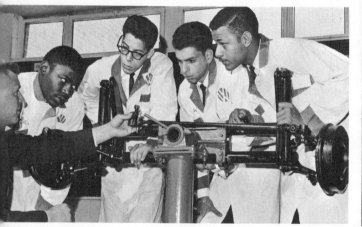

One method of combating poverty: qualified school dropouts are being taught specialized skills.

Many migrant farm workers live below the level of minimum subsistence.

decided is necessary. And what Americans a hundred years ago felt they needed to survive was less than what Americans of today require. It is for this reason that many people say that poverty is relative.

Most students of poverty in 1964 agree that there are three levels of minimum needs. It is generally felt that for a family of four—a father, a mother and two children —the subsistence minimum is at least $2,500 in income per year. To reach a level of minimum adequacy, $3,500 is needed. And $5,500 is necessary for a level of minimum comfort. These different levels make it hard to decide how many Americans may be considered poor. But most people think that there are about 30,000,000 poor people in the United States today. There is agreement that for a rich country like the United States this is too large a number.

It is true that poverty is relative. However, you cannot view poverty as only a relative matter. Such a view tells us what poverty is only as compared to other standards of living. It says nothing about the condition itself. It also suggests that the United States need not do anything to wipe out poverty. For many people in the United States the conditions of the past have disappeared. But to know this is of very little use. It is like telling a man working in a poorly lit room that a hundred years ago even the very rich had to use candlelight. The man still works in the dark.

POVERTY IN THE UNITED STATES—A PROFILE

Families living in poverty are defined by the U.S. Government as those having less than $3,000 a year. Map and charts show where poverty is and whom it affects.

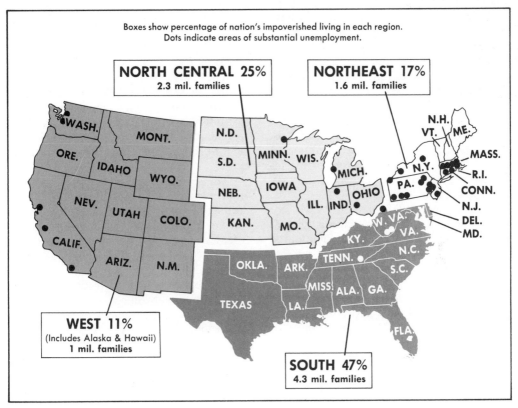

Boxes show percentage of nation's impoverished living in each region.
Dots indicate areas of substantial unemployment.

NORTH CENTRAL 25%
2.3 mil. families

NORTHEAST 17%
1.6 mil. families

WEST 11%
(Includes Alaska & Hawaii)
1 mil. families

SOUTH 47%
4.3 mil. families

FOUR CHARACTERISTICS

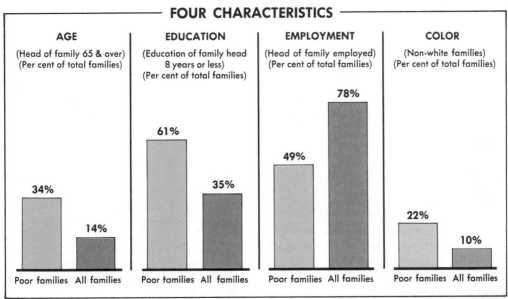

AGE
(Head of family 65 & over)
(Per cent of total families)

34% — Poor families
14% — All families

EDUCATION
(Education of family head 8 years or less)
(Per cent of total families)

61% — Poor families
35% — All families

EMPLOYMENT
(Head of family employed)
(Per cent of total families)

49% — Poor families
78% — All families

COLOR
(Non-white families)
(Per cent of total families)

22% — Poor families
10% — All families

It is often said that no matter how productive and rich a country is some people will always have more and others will have less. The people of any country can be ranked comparatively by the wealth or the income that they have. Such ranking gives what is called the income distribution. The lower fifth, or the lower tenth, for example, can be said to make up the country's poor. In this sense it is true that the poor are always with us and always will be with us. But what is important is the condition of life of the people at the bottom of the income distribution. In other words, do they have enough to live on?

Until recently the United States was not a rich enough country for all those living at the bottom of the income distribution to have enough. In fact, poverty was the fate of a large part of the population. All kinds of people—the old and the young, men and women, farmers and city-dwellers, blacks and whites, northerners and southerners— faced, nearly equally, the possibility of being poor.

The postwar situation is a different story. The United States has become so productive and well-off materially that even those living at the bottom of the income distribution need not be poor. However, despite the general improvement, their lot is no better. Instead, as the overall impact of poverty has lessened, poverty has become increasingly the burden of certain individuals. Now poverty in the United States is, for the most part, limited to specific people. The personal and social conditions of their lives must be changed or they will remain poor.

Since 1960, partly because of President Kennedy's interest in the American economy and in the problems of the poor, we have found new ways of looking at poverty. Available statistics tell us what kinds of people are poor and how many poor people there are. For example, we know about how many of the 30,000,000 poor are old, whether they are white or Negro, where they live and so on. We also know how many of each group in our total population are poor.

Census statistics have enabled us to find out three important things about the kinds of people who are most likely to be poor. Particularly handicapped are nonwhite families with a female as head of the family, aged families living on farms, aged Negro families living anywhere, Negro farm families, and farm families headed by a female. Three out of four such families are likely to earn less than $4,500 per year.

The second thing we have found out is that except for the family whose breadwinner is over 65 the risk of poverty for any of those in the above groups has increased since 1947. And thirdly, the risk of poverty has remained almost the same regardless of the ups and downs of the national economy. For those living at levels of minimum subsistence, economic expansion did not reduce the risk of poverty. Nor did economic contractions increase it by very much.

From such studies, American economists and legislators have learned that their country needs more than rapid economic growth and a high level of employment to do away with poverty. It also needs more than unemployment insurance, sickness benefits and old-age pensions. These all help people who are employed. The poor of the 1960's are outside the American economy. For these reasons the United States Congress passed, in 1964, the Economic Opportunity Act. It aims to bring people on the bottom of the ladder back into the national economy by providing a Job Corps for young people, work training for teen-age dropouts, community social service activities and loans for small businessmen. Other programs in the act provide for needy college students and a domestic peace corps known as VISTA.

Doing away with poverty is not easy. It clearly will take a long time. But the Economic Opportunity Act is a step in the right direction.

History of Negro Protest

... after 350 years, the struggle for equality is bearing fruit

By LOUIS E. LOMAX

THE American Negro has never been satisfied with his lot. From the day the first slaves landed in the future United States (1619), the Negro, with strong aid from his white friends, has maintained an ever increasing protest movement. And it was this protest movement that culminated in the passage of the 1964 Civil Rights Bill. This new act is the most detailed and precise spelling-out of the rights of the minority citizen ever adopted by a nation.

The history of the Negro protest movement is a complex thing. First, the Negro did not want to destroy the majority society. He sought to become a part of it. Thus, unlike any other revolutionary movement, the Negro revolt was carried out by men—Negro and white—who were committed to finding nonviolent ways of integrating the Negro into the American mainstream. This meant that the Negro had to use new techniques. He resorted to legalism, not guns; to peaceful demonstrations, not ruin and pillage.

The Negro protest movement actually began along the shores of West Africa, where the tribesmen fled from the white slave hunters only to be captured by their fellow Africans who often sold them into

The two most important documents in the Negroes' struggle for equal rights: the Emancipation Proclamation, which freed the slaves in 1863, and the 1964 Civil Rights Act, which spells out the rights of American Negroes.

105

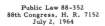

By the President of the United States of America:

A Proclamation.

Whereas, on the twenty-second day of September, in the year of our Lord one thousand eight hundred and sixty-two, a proclamation was issued by the President of the United States, containing, among other things, the following, to wit:

"That on the first day of January, in the year of our Lord one thousand eight hundred and sixty-three, all persons held as slaves within any State or designated part of a State, the people whereof shall then be in rebellion against the United States, shall be then, thenceforward, and forever free; and the Executive Government of the United States, including the military and naval authority thereof, will recognize and maintain the freedom of such persons, and will do no act or acts to repress such persons, or any of them, in any efforts they may make for their actual freedom.

"That the Executive will, on the first day

Public Law 88-352
88th Congress, H. R. 7152
July 2, 1964

An Act

78 STAT. 241.

To enforce the constitutional right to vote, to confer jurisdiction upon the district courts of the United States to provide injunctive relief against discrimination in public accommodations, to authorize the Attorney General to institute suits to protect constitutional rights in public facilities and public education, to extend the Commission on Civil Rights, to prevent discrimination in federally assisted programs, to establish a Commission on Equal Employment Opportunity, and for other purposes.

Be it enacted by the Senate and House of Representatives of the United States of America in Congress assembled, That this Act may be cited as the "Civil Rights Act of 1964". Civil Rights Act of 1964.

TITLE I—VOTING RIGHTS

SEC. 101. Section 2004 of the Revised Statutes (42 U.S.C. 1971), Operation and as amended by section 131 of the Civil Rights Act of 1957 (71 Stat. enforcement. 637), and as further amended by section 601 of the Civil Rights Act of 1960 (74 Stat. 90), is further amended as follows:

(a) Insert "1" after "(a)" in subsection (a) and add at the end of subsection (a) the following new paragraphs:

"(2) No person acting under color of law shall—

"(A) in determining whether any individual is qualified under Voting quali- State law or laws to vote in any Federal election, apply any fications. standard, practice, or procedure different from such law or laws to other individuals within the same county, parish, or similar political subdivision who have been found by State officials to be qualified to vote;

"(B) deny the right of any individual to vote in any Federal Registration, election because of an error or omission on any record or paper etc. relating to any application, registration, or other act requisite to voting, if such error or omission is not material in determining whether such individual is qualified under State law to vote in such election; or

"(C) employ any literacy test as a qualification for voting in Literacy tests. any Federal election unless (i) such test is administered to Records. each individual and is conducted wholly in writing, and (ii) a certified copy of the test and of the answers given by the individual is furnished to him within twenty-five days of the submission of his request made within the period of time during which records and papers are required to be retained and preserved pursuant to title III of the Civil Rights Act of 1960 (42 U.S.C. 1974- 74c; 74 Stat. 88): *Provided, however,* That the Attorney General Attorney General. may enter into agreements with appropriate State or local author- Agreements with ities that preparation, conduct, and maintenance of such tests in State and local accordance with the provisions of applicable State or local law, authorities. including such special provisions as are necessary in the preparation, conduct, and maintenance of such tests for persons who are blind or otherwise physically handicapped, meet the purposes of this subparagraph and constitute compliance therewith.

"(3) For purposes of this subsection—

"(A) the term 'vote' shall have the same meaning as in subsec- "Vote." tion (e) of this section;

"(B) the phrase 'literacy test' includes any test of the ability "Literacy test." to read, write, understand, or interpret any matter."

(b) Insert immediately following the period at the end of the first sentence of subsection (c) the following new sentence: "If in any such proceeding literacy is a relevant fact there shall be a rebuttable

This 1864 engraving shows a Union soldier reading the Emancipation Proclamation to a group of slaves.

The Bettmann Archive

slavery. During the Middle Passage, the journey by ship from Africa to America, hundreds of slaves rebelled and were killed. Others pretended to cooperate with their capturers until the slave boat docked. They then made a dramatic dash for freedom. Many of the slave women made their protest by refusing to have children. They knew full well that slavery would soon die out if the Negro women failed to have offspring.

The first Africans brought to this country were not actually slaves. They were *indentured servants*. That is, they were bound to the white master who paid the slave hunters for capturing the Africans and bringing them to this country. But as indentured servants, the Negroes could buy their freedom by working an agreed-upon number of years for their owners. Indeed, many Negroes took on extra jobs off the plantation after their daily work for their owners was finished. In this way they earned more money to help buy their freedom. The early American white settlers had tried to indenture both the Indians and their fellow white Europeans. But the white Europeans would run away. And they could not be identified as they mingled among free white citizens. The Indians simply refused to do the hard work the hot farm climate of the deep South demanded. Thus it was that Africans were imported.

They were easily identifiable. And they were also accustomed to life and work in a hot climate.

Many Negroes were able to earn their freedom, but most of them remained on the plantations. Gradually, but surely, the Negro sank from indentured servitude into chattel slavery. This means that the white owners assumed full and total ownership of the Negroes, just as you own your bicycle or model airplane. Though a human being, the slave could no more buy his freedom than could a mule or an ox.

Once chattel slavery became a common American practice, the Negro protest movement really began in earnest. It was spearheaded by free Negroes and fiercely supported by white liberals. (There were more than half a million free Negroes in the United States by the end of slavery.) The Negro protest movement based its arguments on moral grounds. Its leaders argued that it was unchristian for one man to hold another in slavery. The proslavery forces argued back that slavery was not immoral unless the person held in slavery was also a Christian. But even as they were making this argument, the slaveowners were busily converting their slaves to Christianity. This is how, and when, the American Negro joined the Christian tradition. This is one of the main reasons slavery eventually collapsed.

Free Negroes like Frederick Douglass and white liberals like Harriet Beecher Stowe took to the platform and to the pages of every major publication to preach their antislavery theme. Douglass even toured Europe to drum up money and support against that "peculiar institution"—slavery. Miss Stowe's book, *Uncle Tom's Cabin,* told a story of human despair that shocked the world as much as we were shocked by the dogs and fire hoses of Birmingham, Alabama. In the pulpit, in the press and in the forums of world opinion, the clamor for the end of slavery mounted.

It is all but impossible to tell just what one thing brought on the end of slavery. The work of the antislavery forces was one thing. World opinion was another. And the invention of the cotton gin, which displaced thousands of Negroes from the cotton fields, was certainly a third factor. The immediate cause of the end of slavery was, of course, the Civil War. This war between the states was fought over whether the Federal Government had the right to regulate life and freedom within the several states. This was the beginning of the *States' Rights Doctrine* we hear so much about today. Slavery—particularly the extension of slavery to new states—was the key matter under dispute. But the Civil War broke into flames, as President Abraham Lincoln put it, over the preservation of the Union. Regardless of the mixed motives involved, the result of the Civil War was the Emancipation Proclamation. At this turning point, the Negro protest movement took on a new form.

From the Emancipation Proclamation (1863) until the turn of the century, the Negro protest movement evolved on two levels. On one level, there were those, such as Booker T. Washington (1856-1915), who felt that education would leapfrog the Negro over centuries of slavery and handicaps. On another level there were those who felt that education would be of little value to the Negro if the Negro were not guaranteed such constitutional rights as

Brown Brothers

Frederick Douglass, a leader in the struggle to free the slaves, had himself escaped from slavery. From 1889-91 he was U. S. minister to Haiti.

the franchise and freedom from bodily harm as he moved about in pursuit of work and happiness. Both arguments proved to be correct. Without an education, the Negro could not take advantage of American freedoms and compete with white men even if allowed. But by the same token, education alone was not enough to guarantee the Negro the freedoms promised by the Constitution. In the latter part of the nineteenth century, the Negro had gained considerable power at the polls. He was also beginning to make some headway in the job market. Then the white South struck back. Negroes were lynched, flogged and beaten. Former slaves and their children were frightened away from the polls. The deep South went on to pass the infamous *Black Codes*—now known as segregation laws. These state statutes call for separate public accommodation facilities, from water fountains to schools. Near the close of the century, Negro protest organizations asked the United States Supreme Court to strike down these laws. The court, however, ruled that separate but equal facilities *were* constitutional.

107

Negro leaders. Left to right: Bayard Rustin; Jack Greenberg (NAACP); Whitney Young, Jr. (National Urban League); James Farmer (CORE); Roy Wilkins (NAACP); Martin Luther King, Jr.; John Lewis (Student Nonviolent Coordinating Committee—SNCC); A. Philip Randolph (Negro-Amercan Labor Council); Courtney Cox (SNCC).

The Negro protest movement acquiesced in the ruling but never really accepted it. Meanwhile thousands of Negroes fled the deep South to get away from the lynch mobs and low wages. These Negroes poured into the North. But they had little training or skill to aid them in adjusting to urban life. It was in this context that the two best-known Negro protest organizations, the National Urban League (established 1910) and the National Association for the Advancement of Colored People (established 1909), were born. The Urban League set as its goal the training of Negroes to enter the urban way of life. League officials not only found Negroes work in northern industry, but went on to give the migrants some guidance in how to adapt to their new way of life. The NAACP sought to end lynchings, denial of the ballot, and restrictive covenants that forbade Negroes to live in certain sections of both northern and southern cities.

A lynching is a murder and is thus covered by state laws. But Negroes were never able to get Congress to make lynching a Federal crime. However, the protest movement created such a public consensus that this ghastly practice has all but passed from the American scene. Efforts to gain the Negro more freedom at the polls met with slow but mounting success. The Civil Rights Act of 1964 gives the Negro his strongest weapon to date against voter discrimination. Every evidence is that the American Negro will have complete voter freedom by 1970. The fight against restrictive covenants was won in the late 1940's. Such covenants were declared unenforceable in a court of law.

So, the Negro protest movement can best be charted in terms of the two great wars. It got under way just as World War I was coming upon us and reached its point of major intensity just after World War II.

The young Negro teen-agers of the early 1950's were war babies. Their fathers and mothers had suffered and died for the United States. Neither they nor their leaders were in a mood to endure further denial of basic American freedoms.

Under the leadership of the NAACP, the Negro protest movement made its boldest strike in 1952. It went before the United States Supreme Court and argued that segregation of the public schools was unconstitutional. After two years of deliberation, the court agreed with the Negroes. It issued orders that all public schools admit students without regard to color or religion. School desegregation has proceeded slowly. In the South, Negroes entering previously all-white schools have been beaten and stoned. But by 1964 school desegregation was proceeding without bloodshed. The best estimates predict that the process will be completed in about ten years. In the North, where the Negro has been plagued by housing segregation, the schools fell heir to *de facto*—that is to say by fact of the neighborhood being all Negro—segregation, rather than *de jure* segregation, which is school segregation by law as practiced in the South prior to the 1954 Supreme Court decision. Northern school desegregation is still a matter of hot dispute. But when the dust settles it will be clear that once the Negro father can get a job equal to his abilities and is free to buy or rent outside the Negro ghetto, the problem of northern school segregation will vanish.

School desegregation was but one of the major thrusts of the Negro protest movement during the 1950's. The second was an all-out assault on segregation in public accommodations. This included everything from segregation on buses and trains, to the right of a Negro to eat in any restaurant or stay in any hotel.

While the NAACP was embroiled in the legalism of the school desegregation decision, other protest organizations came to the fore and undertook the fight to desegregate public facilities. The first blow was struck by Dr. Martin Luther King, Jr., in 1955 when he led the Montgomery bus boycott. This led to a Federal ruling ordering the desegregation of both intrastate (within the state) and interstate (between the states) travel. Dr. King then went on to form his own Negro protest organization, the Southern Christian Leadership Conference. At about the same time CORE, the Congress of Racial Equality (established 1942), made its major move as a Negro protest group and instituted the freedom rides of 1961-62. These civil-rights demonstrations sought to establish the right of Negro travelers to be served at all bus, train and airline depots. They met with bitter violence, but after several months of litigation the courts ruled in favor of the freedom riders.

Despite these court rulings many southern cities refused to comply. Birmingham was one of the more reluctant. During the late spring and summer of 1963, Dr. King led a series of public demonstrations to break down discrimination in public facilities in that Alabama city. The city officials responded by releasing savage police dogs on the demonstrators, many of whom were white. Other demonstrators were doused with water from fire hoses. The nation—indeed, the world—reacted in horror. A few small concessions were won in Birmingham, but the national consensus forced President John F. Kennedy to introduce the Civil Rights Bill.

Congress was slow to act on the Kennedy measure. His assassination ended the conflict between the late President and Congress over the bill. President Lyndon B. Johnson came to power and one of his first public acts was to call for the enactment of the Kennedy Civil Rights Bill. On July 2, 1964, the Civil Rights Bill became the law of the land.

The new Civil Rights Act restates the right of the Negro to use all forms of public transportation and to sit where he pleases. He may eat in any restaurant that in any way profits from interstate commerce. And since every restaurant gets at least some of its supplies from out of state, this means that the Negro can eat in freedom in about any restaurant in the nation. The act also reaffirms the Negro's rights at the polls and provides punishment for those who would deny him that right—or any other civil right, for that matter.

The Negro protest movement has come a long way. Its basic goals have been realized; implementation will not be easy nor will it occur overnight. But every evidence suggests that the Negro has carried out the first nonviolent revolution in history. Every evidence suggests that the American system is working, that democracy does respond to proper protest. And all this is a matter of credit to both the Negro and the nation.

PEOPLE IN

THE NEWS

No great man lives in vain. The history of the world is but the biography of great men....
Thomas Carlyle

Magnum

Ludwig Erhard

By LORRAINE ABELSON

LUDWIG ERHARD became chancellor of West Germany on October 16, 1963. He was elected to this position primarily because he is the man most responsible for his country's prosperity. Onkel Ludi, as the people laughingly call him, is a roly-poly man with bulging, apple-red cheeks. He is strong willed, yet open and warm in his dealings with people.

The Chancellor and his wife live in a modest house in Bonn, the capital of West Germany. There is no official residence for the head of the West German Government. The Erhards never entertain more than 10 or 12 guests at one time. A quiet game of cards—with the music of Bach, Beethoven or Brahms playing in the background—is their idea of a perfect evening at home.

112

Henri Cartier-Bresson, Magnum

Erich Lessing, Magnum

Under Erhard's guidance, a thriving economy and bustling streets and cities have replaced the shambles left by World War II.

West German Chancellor

...the reins of West German government have been passed to Der Dicke

Erhard loves music and he once dreamed of becoming an opera director. He still plays the piano very well. When official duties allow, the Erhards like to spend some time in a cottage in southern Germany. There Mrs. Erhard cooks up a pot of Bavarian stew, her husband's favorite dish. Sometimes they visit their only child, Elisabeth, who is a housewife in Stuttgart.

Chancellor Erhard was born on February 4, 1897, in Furth-in-the-Forest, Bavaria. This city is near Nuremberg in southern Germany. His family was from the middle class. The senior Mr. Erhard ran a clothing store. Everyone thought that young Ludwig would one day follow in his father's footsteps. But the first World War decided that he would not. During that war Erhard was

113

badly wounded. One leg was seriously shattered. And after seven operations his left arm is still shorter than his right. Today the Chancellor must wear special high-button shoes because of his war injuries.

Erhard was educated at the Nuremberg School of Commerce and the University of Frankfurt. At Frankfurt he studied economics under the well-known economist Franz Oppenheimer. Oppenheimer was a firm believer in free enterprise and free trade.

Erhard obtained a doctorate in economics and political science in 1924. In 1923 he had married Luise Lotter, a fellow Frankfurt University economics student. After graduating, they returned to Nuremberg to live. Erhard went to work for the government-controlled Institute for Market Research. In a short time he was made deputy director. Meanwhile, World War II began. Ludwig Erhard refused to join any Nazi organizations, and he was forced out of the institute by Julius Streicher, an important Nazi. Dr. Erhard then started his own small market-research company. He lived a quiet life for the rest of the war.

If Streicher had known what Erhard was up to in his spare time, the economist's career would have come to an end abruptly. By the winter of 1944, Erhard knew what fate had in store for Germany. One afternoon he sat outside his house, holding a briefcase. His neighbor, Theodor Eschenburg, emerged from his house and stopped to chat. Erhard handed him a thick manuscript and told him to read it when he got back inside.

The opening words of this manuscript would have been enough to hang Erhard. The long work began with these words: "Now that it is clear that Germany has lost the war, it is absolutely essential that we decide upon our postwar economic program immediately."

Erhard also sent a copy of his proposal for rebuilding Germany after the war to Carl F. Goerdeler, mayor of Leipzig. Goerdeler was later executed for being one of the organizers of the plot against Hitler's life in July 1944. To this day Erhard does not know why he himself was not executed.

Before he was killed, Goerdeler managed to send a message to his friends. He told them that Erhard must become a minister in the postwar German Government. But it was not Goerdeler who was responsible for Erhard's government position. As the Chancellor himself says, "I am an American creation." In the summer of 1945, when a knock on the door still made a German's heart pound, a U.S. Army jeep drove up to Erhard's house. The men asked Erhard to come with them. Only after several hours of interviews—and fears of some unknown destiny—did Erhard find out that the United States Military Governor had appointed him Bavarian minister of economics. Three years later, in 1948, Erhard was made economic administrator of the United States and British zones of occupied Germany.

The Americans liked Erhard's economic policies. He believes in a graduated income tax. And he believes in a far-reaching social-security system.

Erhard also believes that only incentives such as higher wages and better living conditions can urge the worker on to greater productivity. He feels that government controls on business and industry should be avoided. As he explains it: "Political freedom loses its meaning if we pay for it with increased control and collectivization, retreating into a complete welfare state."

Just how strongly Erhard believes in economic freedom is shown by the following incident, which Erhard considers his "finest hour." In 1948, goods sold in Germany were rationed and their prices were controlled. Dr. Erhard felt that these policies should be ended. Thus in June 1948, when currency reforms were made in Germany, Erhard also wanted to end the Government controls on prices and supply. But Erhard was unable to convince the Americans and British that his plan was best for the German economy. So one Sunday afternoon he took matters into his own hands. Dr. Erhard went to the main radio station and announced that the rationing of most goods was ended. "Turn the people loose," he said, "and they will make the country strong."

At first Erhard's plan did not work. Prices went up. Goods were scarce. "Erhard to the gallows" signs appeared. But Erhard believed strongly that, given time, supply and demand would meet and that prices would drop. And they did. By late 1948, German production was increasing at a rapid pace, and the cost of most goods dropped.

The recovery of the German economy proved Erhard's theories. He had offered more goods to the hungry German people. He asked only that the worker toil long hours and not ask for immediate wage increases. Erhard became West German economics minister in 1949. Under his guidance the country became the industrial leader of Europe. Erhard was vice-chancellor from 1957 to 1963.

Ludwig Erhard is very popular with the people of West Germany, for he is the symbol of their prosperity. He enjoys this image and even pokes fun at himself about being overweight. The chubby Chancellor is affectionately called Der Dicke (the fat one) by some people.

Erhard's success with West Germany's economic problems and his personal popularity brought him to the attention of those who sought to replace the aging Chancellor Konrad Adenauer. In earlier years, Erhard had let it be known that he wanted to stay out of politics. It was no secret that Adenauer wanted Erhard to stay out of the political arena. Adenauer struggled for years to keep Erhard from becoming his successor; he feels that Erhard is an economist and not a politician. And he questions Erhard's ability to withstand the pressures of the East-West struggle. But when necessary Erhard has a lion's courage and an unyielding will.

Adenauer and Erhard differ in many ways. Konrad Adenauer held tremendous personal, almost dictatorial, power. This is not Erhard's way of governing. There is no doubt that Erhard's administration is one of teamwork and flexibility. The members of the Cabinet already have more individual power and freedom to express their opinions than they did under Adenauer.

Another important difference between the two men is their attitude toward the rest of Europe. Adenauer agrees with French President de Gaulle's idea of a "Little Europe." That is, a Common Market without Great Britain. This would mean that France would have a strong voice in the Common Market, and an independent nuclear force. It might also mean that Germany would eventually have an independent nuclear force too. Erhard and other members of the Christian Democratic Union (West Germany's ruling party) want Britain in the Common Market. They also want a strong Atlantic Alliance with the United States taking an important role.

As chancellor, Erhard must deal with some very difficult problems. One such problem is that Germany is still a divided nation. East Germany is dominated by the Soviet Union. But short of war with the Soviet Union there seems to be no immediate solution to this problem. In answer to the charge that the division of Germany must be accepted as reality, Chancellor Erhard has replied: "Of course, it is a reality, but it is an unbearable one. An illness, too, is a reality, but no one would think of blaming someone who tries to cure the disease."

The problem of German reunification is very complicated. If the Germans tried to make a deal with the Soviet Union, they would lose the protection of the United States. On the other hand, the Germans feel that the easing in tensions between Russia and the United States might bring about a deal that would permanently divide Germany. All Chancellor Erhard can do is sit tight and see what happens.

Alberto Giacometti

...renowned painter, sculptor and winner of the 1964 Guggenheim International Award

By JAMES LORD

This hound, thin and gnarled, is typical of Giacometti's style.

Caroline, a Giacometti oil painting done in 1961.

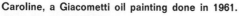

THE Swiss sculptor and painter Alberto Giacometti has now won the three most important prizes available to artists. In 1961 he was given the Carnegie International. In 1962 he received the Venice Biennale first prize. And in 1964 he won the Guggenheim International Award for his painting *Large Nude*. Giacometti is well on the way to being recognized as one of the old masters of modern art, like Picasso, Braque and Matisse. More and more articles about his work are appearing in magazines and newspapers. In the past dozen years there has been a growing demand for his sculptures and paintings. And the prices of his work have increased by about twenty times.

Alberto Giacometti was born in 1901 in Stampa, Switzerland. Stampa is a small town not far from the Italian border. It is surrounded by high Alpine peaks. In such a landscape a man might feel that he is a very small part of nature. This feeling seems to have had an important influence on the development of Giacometti's later work.

Giacometti's father, Giovanni, was a well-known and successful landscape painter. Alberto and his two brothers grew up in a home where the arts were not only appreciated but practiced. Giacometti became interested in painting, drawing and sculpture at an early age. Unlike many other artistic youngsters, he received en-couragement from his father. At the age of 18 he went to the School of Fine Arts in Geneva. But the traditional views of the teachers there did not appeal to him. He left after only three days. His strong and creative personality was already showing itself. The School of Arts and Crafts in Geneva proved to be more to his liking. There he learned the working methods of his calling.

During a stay in Italy, Giacometti admired and studied the works of the Renaissance masters. At the age of 21, he felt ready to face Paris. In the 1920's, Paris was the center of the world of art. It was in Paris and only in Paris that a young artist could hope to make a major reputation for himself. Many tried, but few succeeded. Giacometti was to labor in Paris for more than 25 years before the power and originality of his talent began to be felt. During these years, he knew the moments of doubt and despair that all artists know so well. But he never let anything interfere with his work.

After three years of formal study at the Académie de la Grande-Chaumière in Paris, Giacometti became dissatisfied. He left school. Feeling his work was too close to nature, he experimented by working from memory, then from imagination. These experiments led him to join the surrealists. During the late 1920's the most original work in Paris was being done by this group of painters and writers. The works that Giacometti produced at this time are strange and haunting. They look like figures and objects seen in dreams.

Toward 1935, however, Giacometti felt a need to sculpture and paint things more closely related to everyday life. He began to work again directly from a live model. Suddenly he felt overwhelmed by the difficulty of finding a new approach to art. He did not want to copy what had been done by the painters and sculptors of the past five centuries. Soon Giacometti left the surrealist group. For years he worked alone day in, day out. He was trying to achieve a result that would satisfy his ideal vision of reality. Of this period of searching he has said, "It became impossible for me to grasp the totality of a figure. The distance between one side of the nose and the other became like the Sahara, limitless." And yet he worked on. But he did not feel that his work was satisfactory. He destroyed everything that he produced. From the work of over eight years nothing is left.

At one point, Giacometti's sculptures became so small that he was able to carry them around with him in matchboxes. In relation to their surroundings these works certainly seemed no larger than a lone man on the big mountainside near Stampa.

But at least the artist did not destroy them.

And so it was that by the end of World War II, in 1945, Giacometti had begun to find his way. His work was starting to look like the work we today think of as typical of him. The figures in his sculptures and in his paintings are similar. They are very thin, gnarled and stretched out. The women are still. The men are always in motion.

From 1946 on, Giacometti's works were in this style. Little by little, art collectors and dealers on both sides of the Atlantic began to realize that he was an important, very talented artist. The first major showing of Giacometti's work in his mature style took place in New York City in 1948. It was held at the Pierre Matisse Gallery. In 1955 the Guggenheim Museum in New York gave a show of his work. And there have been many other shows.

Now Giacometti's paintings and drawings and his tall, thin sculptures are admired by art critics and art lovers everywhere. But Giacometti himself is not too interested in his growing fame. Nor does he care that his work now brings high prices. He wants only to keep on trying to paint and sculpture the human figure in a way that will make it seem more real. He works on several sculptures at the same time. This way, each one helps him to see the other. If he is not pleased with the results, he smashes the pieces.

Giacometti still works in the same small, simple, cluttered studio in Paris that he has occupied for over 35 years. But every year he returns to Stampa for a visit. In the village where the Giacometti family has lived for six centuries, he can relax away from the pressures of his life in Paris. In Stampa or in Paris his wife Annette and his brother Diego are always with him. He uses them as models. They pose for him almost daily. Most of his work represents one or the other of them. "There is nothing more exciting," he has said, "than trying to see, as if for the first time, a human face that is absolutely familiar."

Lal Bahadur Shastri

By LLOYD and SUSANNE RUDOLPH

Marilyn Silverstone, Magnum

. . . *a biography of India's new Prime Minister*

ON June 2, 1964, Lal Bahadur Shastri was chosen to succeed Jawaharlal Nehru as prime minister of India. As prime minister, he is the leader of India's 460,000,000 people. Yet many Westerners know very little about him.

Shastri was born in 1904 at Benares, one of the holy cities of Hinduism. Benares is near Nehru's birthplace, and Shastri occasionally visited Nehru as a youth. But the two men grew up very differently. Nehru was the son of a high-caste prominent lawyer. Shastri's family was of the Kayastha caste. Members of this caste are traditionally minor clerks and scribes. In addition, Shastri's father died when his son was only a year and a half old. The grandfather supported the family. He saw to it that Shastri was educated at a local school. But it was not an easy life. As a boy Shastri used to wade a river to school, carrying his books on his head to save the ferry fare.

Still, these years of poverty have paid one dividend. Many poor and suffering Indians now feel that he can understand their sufferings perhaps better than Nehru could.

The new Prime Minister is a frail man. Only about five feet tall, he weighs hardly more than a hundred pounds. Strangers have trouble picking him out from his office staff. He wears simple, homespun Indian clothes. They consist of a cloth known as a dhoti loosely draped around the legs. The dhoti is topped by a loose shirt and vest or a fairly long jacket. Shastri is much less like the elegant Nehru in his appearance and habits than he is like Mahatma Gandhi, the man who led India to independence. Like Gandhi, Shastri lives and dresses as an ordinary villager, inspiring Indians by his simplicity. He sleeps on a rope cot and eats plain food. And like many Kayasts, he is a teetotaler and a vegetarian.

119

He turns his salary over to the Servants of the People Society, which was founded by Gandhi. It is run by devoted nationalists who live simply and serve their country. From the society, Shastri receives just enough for himself and his family to live on. He is married and has four sons, two daughters and many grandchildren. His workday, before a recent heart attack made him more careful, regularly lasted from 7 A.M. to 11 P.M.

Shastri's education and experience could also hardly be more different from Nehru's. Rather than going to school and college in England, he studied Indian philosophy at Kashi Vidyapith, a nationalist college dedicated to reviving Indian learning. Except for a brief trip to the neighboring state of Nepal in 1963, he has never been abroad. Nor can he be considered an intellectual, as Nehru certainly was. Still, Shastri is well-read, broad-minded and has many interests. For example, he translated a biography of Madame Curie into Hindi when he was young. He also has criticized some aspects of the Hindu faith. In a country where some believe their language, their religion or their caste to be more important than public peace or the common good, Shastri stands out as a tolerant man.

His first brush with politics came in the nationalist movement to free India from British colonial rule. In 1920, when Shastri was 16, Mahatma Gandhi called on students to leave schools and colleges that were financially supported by the British Government. Shastri responded and with other students joined Gandhi in his nonviolent campaign for India's independence. He was first arrested for anti-British activities in 1930. By 1942 he had been arrested five more times and had spent a number of years in jail, as did Nehru and other Indian patriots.

During this time he was working in his home state, the United Provinces of northern India (now Uttar Pradesh), for the state committee of the Indian National Congress. Congress was the nationalist political party. Because Uttar Pradesh today has over 70,000,000 people—more than many independent nations have—this was important work. It was also good training for higher office.

In 1947, when India finally did gain its independence, Shastri became minister for police and transport in the state government. India's first general elections in which everyone could vote were held in 1952. The Indian National Congress Party was one of several parties running. Since Shastri had worked so well for Congress, Nehru called him to Delhi to help manage the party's campaign. When Congress won, Shastri promptly received a cabinet post. He became minister for transport and railroads in the first postelection Cabinet. During this time he spent 18 hours at his office nearly every day and managed to accomplish a great deal for his branch of the Government. Later, Shastri held other important cabinet posts, including minister for commerce and industry and home minister. As home minister he worked hard and effectively to unify India's clashing interests. He also became a very close adviser to Nehru and was able to strengthen his own position in the party.

Shastri is best known as a peacemaker. His talents as a conciliator are notable. He wins men by patience and persuasion rather than by the force of his personality. When hostile groups in any of the state parties threaten the party's and state's welfare, Shastri often travels to the scene. Because he himself is so calm he manages to persuade angry men to listen to each other and find compromises. His steadfast honesty and justness also help restore peace in troubled situations.

When Nehru died on May 27, 1964, the Indian National Congress had no man of his stature to replace him. Among the possible successors were men at the far Left and the far Right politically. But choosing such a man might have divided the party. It might also have cost it the majorities it had won in the national legislature. These

Shastri's main task as prime minister is to raise the living standard for India's millions of people.

majorities have been one reason that India, unlike many other new nations, has remained politically stable. What India needed to replace Nehru was a moderate, a person whose views were unlikely to divide the party. Shastri is such a person.

Although Shastri is usually found in the Center politically, he considers each problem independently. For example, on economic issues he has welcomed government regulation or ownership where private enterprise has failed to do the job. However, he does not by any means think that nationalizing industries or other enterprises is a cure-all. It is his strong belief that India must give social and economic justice to her underprivileged people. Thus he favors whatever economic and legislative measures he thinks will make this belief a reality.

Dozens of languages are spoken in India. A controversial issue is whether Hindi or English should be the official language. Here, too, Shastri is a moderate. Hindi is the mother tongue of most north Indians, including the people of Shastri's home state. However, the language that south In-

dians speak is very different. Thus, while most northerners would prefer Hindi as the official language, southerners would rather have English. Some southerners even threatened to secede from India if Hindi won out. In 1963, however, Shastri offered a compromise bill, which was accepted. It makes Hindi the official language of India but also allows English to be used.

In foreign affairs Shastri generally continues the policies of Nehru. Like Nehru, he believes in keeping friendly relations with both the United States and Russia. And he believes that India must strengthen its defenses against the Chinese.

Indians who admired Nehru feared that Shastri might lack imagination and firmness. But he has shown that he has both. Just before Nehru's death, a hair of the Prophet Mohammed was mysteriously stolen from the Hazratbal Mosque in Kashmir. This theft set off angry riots between Muslims and Hindus. Some Muslims suggested that Muslim shrines and relics were unsafe as long as Kashmir remained tied to India. The hair was recovered, but the Muslims suspected that it was a substitute. They demanded that it be inspected by Muslim divines. Shastri's advisers felt that such an inspection might be too risky. However, displaying cool nerves and good political sense, Shastri overruled his advisers and arranged the inspection. It was decided that the relic was real, and peace was restored.

Less than a month after his election as prime minister, Shastri was stricken with what was believed to be a mild heart attack. It was his second attack in five years. Indians had been pleased that a successor to their beloved Nehru had been found so peacefully. Now they again became worried. But Shastri acted quickly to quiet their fears. He appointed a foreign minister instead of trying to combine the work of a foreign minister with his own duties. He also placed more responsibilities in the hands of his cabinet members. Shastri's new system seems to be working very well.

Hubert Horatio Humphrey, Jr.

...Minnesota's senior Senator is elected 38th Vice-President of the United States

By NANCY ABOLIN HARDIN

. . . the first Vice-President from Minnesota.

LIKE the rags-to-riches heroes of the Horatio Alger stories, Hubert Horatio Humphrey, Jr., had all the odds against him when he started out in politics. He had no money. He was a Democrat in a solidly Republican state. And he knew little about the art of political persuasion. Yet he proved to be such a good pupil that on August 26, 1964, President Lyndon B. Johnson personally nominated him as the Democratic vice-presidential candidate of the United States.

The future vice-president was born and bred in South Dakota. His father, Hubert H. Humphrey, and his mother, Norwegian-born Christine (Sannes) Humphrey, lived in an apartment over their drugstore in Wallace, South Dakota. It was in this apartment that Hubert Humphrey—one of four children—was born on May 27, 1911.

Even as a child Humphrey was exposed to politics. His father was a Republican who became a Woodrow Wilson Democrat.

He often took his son with him to Democratic rallies and conventions. By the time Humphrey was in high school he was using his now-famous gift for public speaking to win debating prizes. When he graduated from high school in 1929, he entered the University of Minnesota. But the depression forced him to leave college at the end of his sophomore year. Humphrey's family had moved from Wallace to Doland and then to Huron, South Dakota, where his father opened another drugstore. Humphrey spent the next six years helping out in this drugstore, except for a brief period in 1932-33 when he took a six-month course in the Denver School of Pharmacy. It was in Huron that Humphrey met Muriel Fay Buck, the daughter of the local butter-and-egg dealer. They married in 1936.

By this time, Humphrey had made up his mind to enter public life. As a first step in this direction, he returned to the University of Minnesota. There he majored in political science. Student life was difficult for the

1664

1964 DEMOCRATIC NATIONAL CONVENTION

The Humphrey and Johnson families at the 1964 Democratic convention.

Humphreys, but they were resourceful. Home was a one-room apartment. Muriel helped out by working. Humphrey took a job as a janitor and worked part time in a drugstore. In spite of all this, he managed to win a medal for debating and a prize for an essay on political science. He also graduated with honors and was elected to Phi Beta Kappa.

In 1939, Humphrey entered graduate school at Louisiana State University on a fellowship. While working on the Master's degree he received in 1940, he taught political science. Next he returned to the University of Minnesota on a teaching fellowship to study for a Ph.D. Muriel, by now housebound with the first of their children, helped out by typing papers and making sandwiches for her husband to sell for ten cents to other poor students.

But Humphrey was becoming impatient with studying. He was anxious to get into politics. Entering public service, he took a job in the Works Progress Administration.

Later he held posts in the field of adult education. During World War II, he directed Minnesota's War Production Training and Reemployment, becoming chief of Minnesota's War Service Program in 1942. He was also well known locally as a forceful speaker for President Roosevelt's New Deal. So, in 1943, he ran for mayor of Minneapolis. He lost his first bid for elective office by 4,900 votes.

Temporarily discouraged and in debt, Humphrey went back to teaching. He took a post as visiting professor in the political-science department of Macalester College in St. Paul. He also worked as a radio news commentator, lectured as often as possible and managed the apartment building where he and Muriel lived. After a little more than a year he was able to pay off his campaign debts. He then set himself to figuring out how he could make Republican Minneapolis elect a Democrat. Before long he had the solution. He formed a new coalition of liberal Democrats with farmers and

123

Hubert Humphrey in 1940 when he graduated from the University of Louisiana. He received a Master's degree in political science.

laborers. As leader of this coalition, he won his second bid for mayor by 31,000 votes in 1945. An active and progressive term followed, and in 1947 he was reelected with a 52,000-vote majority—the largest in Minneapolis history. That same year he and other liberal New Dealers founded the Americans for Democratic Action. Later he served as the organization's chairman for many years. The next step up the political ladder was obvious: in 1948 Humphrey defeated Republican Senator Joseph H. Ball to become the first Democratic senator ever to be elected by Minnesota.

Humphrey's first taste of the national limelight actually came several months before he was elected to the Senate. As mayor of Minneapolis he went to the Democratic National Convention as a Minnesota delegate in July 1948. While there he fought for a strong civil-rights plank in the platform. "The time has arrived in America," he told the convention, "for the Democratic Party to get out of the shadow of states' rights and to walk forthrightly into the bright sunshine of human rights." This dramatic speech touched off a floor demonstration and the plank was adopted. But Humphrey paid dearly for this early success. The delegates from Mississippi and Alabama walked out of the convention and formed the States' Rights, or Dixiecrat, Party. This was his first exposure to the complexities and pitfalls of national politics. Today there are still Southerners who hold that 1948 speech, and the split in the Democratic Party that resulted from it, against Humphrey.

Senator Humphrey was reelected in 1954. In 1958 he came once again into the national limelight with his highly publicized eight-hour talk with Soviet Premier Nikita Khrushchev in Moscow. In 1960 he was reelected to a third term. The following year he became Majority Whip of the Senate. This role brought him more than ever into the public eye.

During his first term it seemed as though Humphrey would never learn the ways of the Senate. In his very first speech he informed the Senate that "what the people want is for the Senate to function." Other fiery speeches and criticisms of his fellow senators followed. Most of his indignant colleagues promptly wrote him off as a brash and gabby upstart. But they underestimated his capacity to learn and the extent of his ambitions. With the help of Senator Lyndon B. Johnson, one colleague who did recognize his potential, Humphrey changed his tactics and started mending his political fences.

Important committee assignments began to come his way. His growing abilities as a conciliator gradually were recognized, even by his Southern enemies. So was his legislative foresightedness. He fought hard for the nuclear-test-ban treaty, the Peace Corps abroad and at home, Food for Peace, urban renewal, Federal aid for education, the Wilderness Bill, Medicare and trade expansion. He eventually became one of the most effective legislative leaders in the Senate.

Humphrey is cheered by well-wishers after his nomination as a candidate for the United States Senate in 1948.

The tireless and skillful senator who floor-managed the Civil Rights Act in 1964 was a far cry from the fiery delegate who provoked the Dixiecrat split. In 1948 he had been unwilling to compromise. Through years of hard experience he learned to settle for what he could get rather than demand all or nothing.

But during the years in which his political talents were steadily growing, Humphrey also suffered some great political letdowns. Twice—in 1958 and in 1960—he sought a place on the national ticket, and both times he met defeat. Humphrey was confident that he was to be Adlai Stevenson's running mate in 1956. He was caught unprepared when Stevenson decided to let the delegates to the Democratic convention nominate the vice-presidential candidate. Bitterly disappointed, he watched John F. Kennedy and Estes Kefauver struggle for the spot that Kefauver finally won. However, four years later Humphrey was back in the political arena, this time fighting for the top spot. But the superior forces and appeal of Kennedy defeated Humphrey in the Wisconsin and West Virginia primaries and once again he had to bow out. After Johnson became president, however, the tide of events turned in Humphrey's favor. Soon his name was high on the list of vice-presidential prospects. But the President, with his flair for drama and his desire to bring excitement to the 1964 Democratic National Convention, kept his choice a secret for as long as possible. Even at the convention, Humphrey was fitting personal politicking in between negotiating a settlement of the Mississippi and Alabama credentials fight and doing television commentaries on the proceedings. This time, however, his patience paid off in full.

During the weeks before the November 3 election, Humphrey tirelessly stumped the country. Muriel, now 52, proved, as always, a political asset to her husband. Throughout his political career she has been an active and effective campaigner in a class with Lady Bird Johnson. For years the Humphreys have maintained two homes (one in Minnesota and one near Washington) for themselves and their four children. The two younger children—Robert, 20, and Douglas, 16, are in school in Minnesota. The two eldest are married. Nancy, 25, lives in Minnesota with her husband and their two small daughters. Hubert, 22, lives with his wife in Virginia.

Lyndon Baines Johnson

... thirty-sixth president of the United States

By CHARLES J. JONES

Lyndon B. Johnson and his family. Left to right: Luci Baines, the President, Lynda Bird and Mrs. Lady Bird Johnson.

AT 12:30 P.M., CST, Friday, November 22, 1963, President John Fitzgerald Kennedy was assassinated in Dallas, Texas. Less than two hours later Vice-President Lyndon Baines Johnson was sworn in as the 36th president of the United States. Almost a year later, on November 3, 1964, the people of the United States voted their approval of President Johnson and his policies. They elected him to a full four-year term.

Lyndon Johnson's interest in politics started at an early age. Both his father and grandfather had been members of the Texas legislature. When Lyndon Johnson was born, on August 27, 1908, his grandfather told everyone who would listen that a future United States senator had just been brought into the world.

Lyndon Johnson's father, Samuel Ealy Johnson, Jr., was a farmer and schoolteacher as well as a state legislator. The life of the man who was to become America's president in a tragic hour began in a small house on his father's farm. The house is still there, near Johnson City, Texas, the first settlement in the area. Johnson's family on both sides is of pioneer stock.

They were among the earliest settlers of central Texas. Lyndon Johnson's grandfather founded Johnson City.

The young boy's family had a heritage of public service. In addition to being a state legislator, his grandfather had been secretary of state of Texas. One relative was a signer of the Texas Declaration of Independence. Another had been a governor of Kentucky.

Lyndon's mother, Rebekah (Baines) Johnson, was a good-natured but determined woman. She had once taught elocution, and she saw to it that her son learned his school lessons. Young Lyndon didn't have much time for books though. He was a bright young man, quick and alert, but not too enthusiastic about reading.

He graduated from high school in 1924, president of a class of seven. At that time he had no thought of going to college. After graduation Lyndon and a group of friends took a trip to California. The boys soon ran out of money and had to hunt for jobs. For a few months Lyndon supported himself with odd jobs, such as waiting on tables. Then he decided to hitchhike back to Texas. But he still had no plans for col-

lege. Instead he got a job as a laborer doing road construction near Johnson City. His mother and father continued to talk of college. Eventually he saw that he would get nowhere beyond his job on the road without more education.

So in February of 1927 he entered Southwest Texas State Teachers College in San Marcos. Here he began in earnest to hew out a career for himself. He organized a campus political group, edited the school paper and became an accomplished debater. During 1928-29 he took a year off to teach elementary school in Cotulla, Texas. Despite this, he was able to graduate in 3½ years at the age of 22.

Now, with college behind him, Johnson began teaching debating and public speaking at a high school in Houston. True to the family tradition, he was also becoming interested in politics and public service. He worked on the campaign of Richard M. Kleberg, one of the owners of the gigantic King Ranch. Kleberg was elected to the House of Representatives. In 1932 Lyndon Johnson became Kleberg's secretary.

In Washington the young Texan found not only an exciting city but a challenge.

There he began the work that was to be a lifelong career. He learned his way around Washington very quickly. He talked to people, asked endless questions, listened and absorbed. After only one year there he was elected speaker of the "Little Congress." This is an organization made up of secretaries to Congressmen. His election, after only one year in Washington, was quite a remarkable feat.

At the same time, Lyndon Johnson was observing how Congress was run and who ran it. He worked hard at Kleberg's office. But he also found time to attend classes at Georgetown Law School for a year. He was lucky, too, in that he was befriended by the powerful Congressman Sam Rayburn and Vice-President John N. Garner. From them Johnson learned lessons he could not have learned elsewhere.

On a visit to Austin, Texas, in 1934, Johnson met Claudia Alta Taylor, whom a childhood nurse had nicknamed Lady Bird. A recent graduate of the University of Texas, she had grown up in Karnack, Texas, a tiny community near the Louisiana border. After a whirlwind courtship Lyndon Baines Johnson and Lady Bird Taylor were married. They now have two daughters—Lynda Bird, who was born in 1944, and Luci Baines, who was born in 1947. All three of the Johnson women help out in politics at times. And Lady Bird has made a reputation for herself as an excellent businesswoman.

As newlyweds, the Johnsons returned to Washington after a honeymoon in Mexico. Not long after their return, Lyndon Johnson was given one of his most important and satisfying jobs. President Franklin D. Roosevelt's New Deal included a program to get young people off the streets and into school and jobs. Just before he became 27, Johnson was made head of the National Youth Administration for Texas. Being young himself and interested in education, Johnson did an outstanding job. His state program was so good that it was copied in other states.

In 1937 a Texas member of the House of Representatives died. Johnson decided to run for the unexpired term. Except for the young people he had helped, he was almost unknown to Texas voters. He decided to stake his campaign on support of Roosevelt's New Deal. He won a landslide victory. At the age of 29, Lyndon Johnson became a congressman.

From the first day he took office, Lyndon Johnson was aware of his responsibility to the people who elected him. He got through legislation for power projects, housing projects and other works for the area he represented. The Texans he represented reelected him four times.

Then, at Roosevelt's urging, Johnson ran for another seat vacated by death— this time in the Senate. One of his campaign issues was preparedness for war. He urged citizens to be ready for any emergency. It was June 1941 and Johnson lost. But he continued to serve in the House of Representatives.

In December 1941 Johnson volunteered for active duty in the Navy one hour after he voted for the declaration of war against Japan. He served in New Zealand and Australia until President Roosevelt called all congressmen back to work in July 1942.

In May 1948 Johnson decided to run again for the Senate. This time he made it—although he had won the Democratic primary by only 87 votes.

The new Senator worked hard, just as he had in the House. He went from majority whip to minority leader to majority leader. He became known and respected as a skillful organizer and an effective Senate leader. But the hard work and long days took a toll on his health. In 1955 he had a serious heart attack. He was laid up for more than six months. His recovery was complete, however, and soon he was as active as ever in the Senate.

During these years, he served on the Senate Armed Services Committee, the Interstate and Foreign Commerce Committee, the Finance Committee and the Appropriations Committee, among others He worked for economy in military and government spending, preparedness in the Korean conflict, and aid for underprivileged areas and citizens. He never stopped working for Texas interests too.

Johnson has close ties with conservative interests and leaders. But he is credited with liberal efforts, such as the passage of the first civil-rights bills (1957 and 1960) of this century. In the late 1950's he became very active on committees dealing with space programs.

In 1960 Johnson made a losing bid for the presidential nomination. He was then asked to run for vice-president in John F. Kennedy's campaign. The proud leader who had ruled the Senate for so long surprised many people by accepting the second spot on the Democratic ticket.

As vice-president, Johnson worked hard on space, defense and employment problems. He traveled to more than twenty countries and learned as much as he could about foreign affairs. President Kennedy kept in constant touch with him and conferred with him on many important policy decisions.

Thus Johnson was well trained for the office he was to assume so sadly on November 22, 1963. During his first few months in office, the new President stressed the continuity between his administration and Kennedy's. But it wasn't long before Johnson had put his own stamp on the office. He worked, with a great deal of success, for the passage of legislation on civil rights, aid to education, tax reduction, foreign aid, and employment for youth.

In his first State of the Union Message he promised more economy in government spending. He also launched the now-famous "war against poverty." Johnson rapidly gained the confidence of the American people. The firmness with which he handled both domestic and foreign problems was responsible for his victory at the polls in November 1964.

Photo, Wide World→

POPE
PAUL VI

By ROBERT NEVILLE

. . . the 262d Pontiff of the
Roman Catholic Church.

Roma's Press, PIX

WHEN Cardinal Giovanni Batista Montini of Milan was elected Pope in June 1963, he chose for himself the name of Paul VI. His choice suggested that, like St. Paul, he would stress evangelism and Christian unity. So far, he has.

John XXIII, the Pope before Paul VI, also stressed these things. A very popular pontiff, Pope John gave world Catholicism a new face during a reign of less than five years. It was he who, early in 1959, issued the call for the Second Vatican (Ecumenical) Council. And it was he who gave the council the guiding theme of Christian unity.

When Montini became Pope after Pope John died, he let it be known that he considered his first and most important job the completion of the work of the Ecumenical Council. "Can we," he asked, "turn aside from the path that John XXIII so boldly opened to future religious history, that of Roman ecumenicism, that of the universality of the Catholic faith?" The council's second session was held in the autumn of 1963. A third session was opened by the Pope in September 1964. The Ecumenical Council promises to be one of the most important religious events of the twentieth century.

At the Vatican, Paul VI is known more for his scholarship and intellect than for his pastoral qualities. No one who knows him was surprised when he delivered his coronation sermon in nine languages. Of medium height with a spare build, he has the pale skin of a man who has spent most of his life indoors. He can usually be found either at his office or in his library. His working hours are very long. And for relaxation he reads. It took more than 95 fair-size cases to ship the newly elected Pope's books from Milan to Vatican City. Newspapermen who have looked over his library have noted that besides the usual volumes on religion and the Church, there are also many books on modern society.

To the papacy, Paul VI brings a high degree of intellectual training. In many ways the Pope has in fact spent much of his life preparing himself for the position he now holds.

He was born near Brescia in northern Italy on September 26, 1897. His upper-middle-class parents were very devout Catholics who named their second son after John the Baptist. Giovanni Battista's father was a lawyer and the editor of a progressive Catholic newspaper. One of his two brothers is now a member of Italy's Senate, and the other is a physician. He also has four sisters. The Montini family has lived near the Po River for five centuries. During this time, various mem-

With his January trip to the Holy Land—where he met with Athenagoras I—Pope Paul became the first Pope to leave Italy since 1809 and the first Pope ever to travel by air or to visit Jordan and Israel.

LeGoubin, Black Star

St. Peter's is filled during the third session of the Ecumenical Council, begun in September 1964.

bers of the family have been prelates or priests.

Giambattista, as he was called, was so frail as a child that he had to leave the Jesuit school he attended in Brescia to be tutored at home. Nonetheless he managed to qualify for a degree from the Arnaldo Lyceum in Brescia in 1916. Since he was physically unable to do military service in World War I, he then began to study for the priesthood. In 1920 he was ordained at the Church of St. Mary of the Graces in his hometown.

In the fall of that year he went to Rome to study philosophy at the Gregorian University of the Holy See and letters at the University of Rome. There his outstanding work caught the eye of an influential monsignor. The monsignor had him admitted to the Pontifical Ecclesiastical Academy. This academy trains priests for the diplomatic service of the Vatican.

Montini won degrees in theology, civil and canon law, and philosophy. Then, in 1923, he was sent by the Church to Poland. However, Warsaw's climate turned out to be bad for his health. He returned to Rome after only a few months. There he became a document writer in the Vatican Secretariat of State. He was to remain at the Vatican in an administrative capacity for nearly twenty years.

At about this time he also became spiritual adviser to the Catholic students' club in Rome. The Catholic students often clashed openly with Mussolini's Fascists. Montini befriended many anti-Fascists and for ten years defied the Fascists, to work with the students. Eventually, however, growing pressures against nonfascist groups plus his heavy load of duties at the Vatican forced him to leave the students' club.

When his friend Eugenio Cardinal Pacelli became Pope Pius XII in 1939,

Montini became the new Pope's close adviser. During and after the difficult years of World War II, he played an increasingly important role at the Vatican. In 1954, however, he left Rome. The Pope had chosen him to succeed the Archbishop of Milan, who had just died. He became archbishop of the biggest archdiocese in Italy on December 12, 1954.

While in Milan, Montini developed a big-business technique rare for diocesan government. He set up a team of assistants. They formed an ecclesiastical board of directors which he consulted regularly. His constant concern was to see that in a rapidly expanding city like Milan enough new churches were built to serve new districts. Tirelessly he persuaded contractors to attach chapels to big apartment houses. In his seven years in Milan, he visited more than 800,000 workers, referring to himself as "the workers' Archbishop." He also became an expert manager of the Church's large real-estate holdings in Milan.

At the end of 1958, Pope John made Montini a cardinal. During the next few years the Pope occasionally sent Montini on diplomatic missions abroad. In 1960 he visited the United States. Later that year he went to South America, and in 1962 he toured Africa. Early in 1964, after he had become Pope, he undertook the most meaningful trip to be made by a Pope in many centuries. Traveling by air, he went to the Holy Land, visiting places associated with Jesus. The high point of his trip was his cordial and dramatic meeting with Athenagoras I, the ecumenical patriarch of Constantinople (Istanbul), representative of the whole Catholic Church in the East.

It is too early to tell exactly what kind of Pope Montini will turn out to be. In Rome, however, Paul VI is regarded as a combination of the last three Popes. He has the firmness of Pius XI, especially toward totalitarian societies. He has the scientific approach and the diplomacy of Pius XII. And he has the great abundance of goodwill of the late Pope John XXIII.

In general it can be said that the new Pope is a very hard worker. He is a master of diplomacy, and he is an expert and impassioned speaker. He knows how to express his ideas. In the past, papal language has often been vague and clumsy, but Paul VI is very clear as well as graceful in his phrasing.

He is especially expressive in his discussions of Christian unity. "Our spiritual attitude toward non-Catholics must change," he has said. "We must no longer consider them irreducible and foreign enemies but rather brothers who have been painfully detached from us." In one of his most remarkable speeches the Pope addressed this appeal to the Eastern Orthodox Church: "Come! Let fall the barriers that separate us. Let us seek to join and fit together our hierarchical union. We do not want either to absorb or mortify that great flowering of the Eastern Church but only to reinstate it on the single tree of unity of Christ."

133

SAN FRANCISCO 18400 K

TERREADELIE 6950 K

TAHITI 11600 Km

HONOLULU 14900 K

MELBOURNE 6000 K

BIKINI 11300 K

TOKIO 11700 K

SAIGON 7500 K

MISRA 1300 Km

MOSCOU 13000

PARIS 12700 K

BRAZZAVILLE 7200 Km

NEW-YORK 17000 Km

MARION 2400 Km

THE WORLD

Wide World

UPI

Middle East Features Service, Black Star

Camera Press, PIX

News-making Flags

In January, Panamanians rioted when United States students tore down a Panamanian flag that was being flown alongside the U. S. flag in front of a Canal Zone school.

Turkish Cypriots, with a Turkish flag flying from their position, watch for attacking Greek-Cypriot forces. The Cyprus crisis almost brought about a war between Greece and Turkey.

In 1964, Canada faced a political crisis over the adoption of a new flag. This design was submitted to Parliament by Prime Minister Pearson but was rejected. A flag with one maple leaf was finally approved.

137

In March, French President de Gaulle visited France's Caribbean
possessions and Mexico, where he received this musical welcome.

"Paris Match," Pictorial Parade

BIENVENIDO

SEÑOR PRESIDENTE
GRAL. CHARLES DE GAULLE

AFRICA

By THOMAS M. FRANCK

THE great decolonization of Africa began just ten years ago. The years since have been years of feverish activity. Africa is now the focus of worldwide interest. The former colonial powers, and other nations, have been pouring in money and technical assistance. France, for example, has been spending more than one per cent of its total income on helping its former African possessions. With such aid, new universities have sprung up everywhere. Kenya, Tanganyika, Northern Rhodesia (now called Zambia), the Sudan, Nyasaland (Malawi) and Basutoland all have new universities. In Ghana two new universities have opened; in Nigeria, four. Even the troubled Congo has found time and money to start new colleges at Leopoldville and Elisabethville.

What is true of education is equally true of hospitals, housing and roads. Youthful and idealistic Americans, in the Peace Corps, in university programs operated by Harvard, Syracuse, Columbia, MIT and others, have gone to Africa. Sometimes they stay for the summer, sometimes for as long as three years. They have taught at village schools and at fine universities. They have coached school athletes and have helped draft laws.

Working with these Americans are many British, Canadians, French and Belgians. There are also some Chinese Communists, Russians, Czechs and East Germans. This is because Africans are so anxious for help they will generally take it wherever it is freely offered.

Economic development, too, has leaped forward. Africa would like to catch up with Western standards of living in twenty-five years. The continent has the minerals, the farmlands and the electric potential to do this. More than that, it has a vast unsatisfied consumer market. Imagine opening a shop in a town where almost nobody had yet bought a radio, a typewriter, books, or even shoes and suits.

The most important ingredient in achieving the African dream is, of course, the African himself. To buy shoes and typewriters, to harness the great rivers for electricity, to get the most out of his soil, the African must educate himself. And he must be willing to work hard. Since Africans have started to run their own countries, they have shown greater enthusiasm for education and work.

Even more than education and hard work, Africa needs political stability. Unhappy people do not work hard or well. A frightened government cannot plan ahead with confidence. A shaky political climate produces a shaky economy and frightens away investment.

In 1964 Africa made good progress in education, social services, housing and industrial growth. But it was only a mixed year for political stability. Developments in any one year should not be taken as setting a trend. Yet it is also true that since civil war erupted in the Congo in 1960, the political stability of other governments in Africa has increasingly been under attack by the forces of revolution, tribalism and chaos.

In the Congo itself, fighting broke out again even before the last UN soldier had boarded his plane for the trip home. The UN had for almost four years stood guard with up to 26,000 troops at a cost of $433,000,000 and 235 lives. In all, 93,-000 men from 22 countries had seen action in the Congo under the UN banner. But as the international army began to leave, the cold war began anew.

Communist China, which had been training certain Congolese leaders for this moment, supplied the means for a new round in the civil war. Under the leadership of Gaston Soumialot and Christophe Gbenye, a People's Republic was proclaimed in the eastern Congo. China's role in supporting the Congolese rebels was made easier when the relatively well-

In January, at the request of the Tanganyika Government, British troops put down a mutiny in the armed forces.

"Paris Match," Pictorial Parade

Congo Premier Moise Tshombe receives a jubilant welcome from residents of Albertville after his troops liberated the city from Leftist rebels.

liked and respected Cyrille Adoula was replaced as prime minister by Moise Tshombe. The new Congolese premier is regarded throughout Africa with disfavor.

Tshombe took office on July 10. To make matters even worse, he began to recruit white mercenaries from South Africa and Southern Rhodesia. For high pay and adventure, these men were willing to fight for him against the rebels. Southern Rhodesia and South Africa are two hotbeds of white supremacy. Other Africans feel that no self-respecting African should accept help from them. Therefore many African states reluctantly began to side openly with the rebels.

The United States had little choice but to back him against the communist-backed rebels.

In November, as Tshombe's troops neared Stanleyville, the rebel capital, the rebels threatened to slaughter hundreds of white hostages. To save these people, Belgian paratroopers were flown to the Congo in American planes. They dropped on Stanleyville and the smaller city of Paulis, rescuing hundreds of people from the rebels. However, almost one hundred whites had already been murdered.

In other parts of Africa, instability also threatened economic and social progress. In Ghana, the Chief Justice, Sir Arku Korsah, and a number of other members of the Supreme Court, ruled against the Government in an important treason case. As a result they were fired by President Nkrumah. On January 2, 1964, still another attempt was made on the life of Nkrumah. And on February 2, after a plebiscite that no neutral observer considered even remotely honest, the country was declared a one-party state.

A revolt broke out on February 17 in the tiny but very rich country of Gabon.

142

President Nyerere of Tanganyika (now Tanzania) inspects troops sent by Nigeria to aid him in the wake of a mutiny in his country's Army.

On April 27 the former British colonies of Tanganyika and Zanzibar merged to become the United Republic of Tanganyika and Zanzibar. In October the name was officially changed to Tanzania.

Quickly, at midnight, a handful of troops took control of the main cities and arrested the Cabinet of President Léon M'Ba. Next morning, however, troops of the former colonial power, France, were flown in. They broke the rebellion and restored the lawful Government. As elsewhere, the unsuccessful attempt at revolution did not strengthen democracy by testing it. Indeed, it caused the victor to tighten up political controls. The next time, M'Ba argued, rebels might not make the fatal mistake of leaving the airport runways unblocked.

The most dramatic case of political instability took place in Zanzibar, for a brief while Africa's smallest independent state. Here, however, few African experts were surprised. Zanzibar has an area almost exactly that of Rhode Island and a population the size of Omaha's. It has a history of violence and hatred between the small but wealthy Arab minority and the poor African majority. This history goes back 200 years to the Arab slave trade. So it was generally expected, when Britain on December 10, 1963, gave independence to Zanzibar under Arab leadership, that trouble lay ahead.

Few, however, would have guessed how fast and furiously that trouble would arise. On January 12, 1964, a bloody revolution overthrew the Government. Hundreds of people were killed. The Arab Sultan fled into exile aboard his official yacht. The revolution appeared to be led by self-styled Field Marshal John Okello, a religious mystic, bricklayer and genius-madman from northern Uganda.

After his victory, the Field Marshal began a reign of terror. After two months, during which the people stood in mixed admiration and horror of their eccentric benefactor, he was exiled from the country by the very Government that he had himself installed. The new Government was headed by President Abeid Karume.

Between January 20 and 24, army mutinies broke out in all three of the newly independent nations of East Africa: Kenya, Uganda and Tanganyika. Two of Africa's most popular leaders, President Julius Nyerere of Tanganyika and Prime Minister Jomo Kenyatta of Kenya, were forced by a small discontented minority to the humiliation of having to be rescued from some of their own people by the troops of the former colonial power, Britain.

It is very much to the credit of these countries that they took the return of the British troops calmly. It is to Britain's credit that its troops quickly defeated the rebels (in the case of Tanganyika, in 18 minutes) and then left. Yet the three East African nations could not emerge from these experiences unaffected. In Tanganyika, hundreds of people were arrested and held without trial. And in all three countries there was talk about the need for a one-party state. The rebel-

lions had failed, but they succeeded in destroying political confidence and peace.

Later in the year, in October, there was an attempted revolt in Niger. And in the Sudan, rioting brought about the ouster of the six-year-old military regime of General Abboud. A civilian Government under Premier Sir-el-Khatim el-Khalifa was set up on October 30.

Political developments in Africa in 1964 were not all on the negative side. Among the more hopeful elements was the growth of African unity. The Organization of African Unity (OAU) held an important meeting of heads of state in Cairo during July.

Perhaps the best example of this cooperation is the Special Arbitration Commission set up on November 18, 1963. Its purpose was to deal with the Moroccan-Algerian border dispute. The commission brought about the end of the fighting and set up a demilitarized zone between the two countries. It even demanded that Algeria and Morocco stop making hostile public comments about each other. As a result, this explosive situation has at least for the present been calmed.

Also very much on the credit side is the union of Tanganyika and Zanzibar. This took place on April 27. As usual, unity came about through a mixture of common interests and common troubles. Among the latter was the series of revolutions that wracked East Africa, and the revolution in Zanzibar, which many thought to be communist-inspired.

Encouraging too was the spirit of cooperation with which Nigeria and Ethiopia went to the aid of Tanganyika after the military mutiny. For four months after the British were withdrawn, Nigeria gave Tanganyika troops; Ethiopia provided an air force. This gave Tanganyika time to rebuild its shattered military forces.

Also among the brighter events of the year in Africa were the coming to independence of two new states: Malawi on July 6, and Zambia on October 24.

ASIA

By ARNOLD C. BRACKMAN

A Malaysian sentry in Sarawak watches carefully for an attack by Indonesian guerrillas. Sarawak is part of Malaysia and is on the island of Borneo. The distant ridge is in Kalimantan, which is the Indonesian part of Borneo.

Christa Armstrong, Rapho-Guillumette

THE most ominous event in Asia during 1964 was the explosion of a nuclear test bomb by Communist China on October 16. Experts felt that it would be some time before the Chinese could build up a nuclear arsenal. Nevertheless, the atomic blast firmly established Communist China, with its 750,000,000 people, as a power to be reckoned with on the world scene. It also raised tensions in the world, particularly in already tense Asia.

In 1964 violence and crises swept Asia from the tip of the Indian subcontinent to the tip of the Korean peninsula. The gravest crisis came in midyear when the United States and Communist China veered briefly on a collision course in the Tonkin Gulf.

In *southeast Asia* the situation was especially serious. In Vietnam the United States was still embroiled in a conflict that goes on without prospect of victory. In nearby Laos the Communists made new military gains. In Indonesia a communist-backed, neofascist regime stepped up its terror campaign against the Federation of Malaysia. In *northeast Asia* there were more riots by Korean students. In *central Asia,* tensions increased along the Russian-Chinese border as Moscow and Peking vied for the leadership of the communist world. In *south Asia,* Jawaharlal Nehru, one of the political giants of this century, died. In disputed Kashmir there was fighting between Indian and Pakistani troops. Clearly, for Asia, 1964 was a year of grave trial.

The most critical spot in Asia in 1964 was South Vietnam. In January the military situation was worsening rapidly. For the second time within three months a coup was staged in Saigon, the capital city. General Nguyen Khanh, an able field commander, was swept into power. He, in turn, was nearly ousted in September. Student and Buddhist pressure finally brought about a civilian regime in November, with Tran Van Huong as premier. Khanh became commander in chief of the armed forces. But at year's end, political discontent and rioting still plagued South Vietnam.

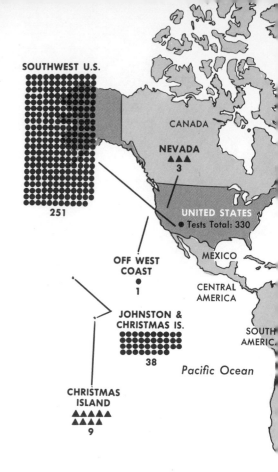

The train of events in Vietnam in 1964 confronted the United States with four choices. The first was to withdraw and forget about southeast Asia. This, however, would adversely affect the entire course of the East-West cold war. Withdrawal would mean a worldwide loss of confidence in the will of the United States to resist the Communists. In the view of Secretary of State Dean Rusk, "it would also bring us much closer to a major conflagration" since it would embolden the Communists.

A second choice was to expand the war. General Khanh, for example, sounded the cry, *"Bac Tien!"* ("To the North!"). His view, which some Americans shared, was that the communist guerrillas (the Vietcong) should be deprived of their sanctuary in North Vietnam. He argued that by carrying the war to North Vietnam, communist pressure on South Vietnam would be eased. President Johnson, how-

Arctic Ocean

NOVAYA ZEMLYA

NOVAYA ZEMLYA
SIBERIA

SOVIET UNION
■ Tests
Total: 126

126

MONGOLIA

CHINA
◆ Test
Total: 1

ENIWETOK-
BIKINI
37

UNITED
KINGDOM
Tests
Total: 24

FRANCE
Tests
Total: 5

ALGERIA

AFRICA

SINKIANG
◆
1

SAHARA
★★★★★
5

Indian Ocean

WOOMERA-
MARALINGA
▲▲▲▲▲
▲▲▲▲
9

SOUTH
ATLANTIC
●●●
3

MONTEBELLO
ISLANDS
▲▲▲
3

AUSTRALIA

NEW
ZEALAND

AS CHINA EXPLODES ITS BOMB—
THE PERIODS OF TESTING SO FAR

Members of "atomic club"—
nations that have tested nuclear weapons.

Adapted from "The New York Times"

ever, did not want to expand the war. He feared that this would throw the quarreling Russians and Chinese together. Attacking North Vietnam could also lead to a general war in southeast Asia, which would engulf peaceful and prosperous Thailand, a United States ally. An expanded war might also lead to "another Korea," that is, a second Chinese–United States conflict.

A third choice was to negotiate for the purpose of making all of Vietnam neutral. This idea was pushed by French President Charles de Gaulle. But the United States believes that a new agreement of this sort is not needed. What is needed is good faith on the part of the Communists to live up to the agreement of 1954. Washington said that when the Communists stop their aggression, United States forces in South Vietnam will be withdrawn. "Our forces in southeast Asia are there solely in response to the threat and reality of communist ag-

gression from the North," the Johnson administration declared.

The fourth choice for the United States was to give South Vietnam more aid and try to defeat the communist guerrillas. President Johnson chose this path. He announced in July that the United States was sending 5,000 more military "advisers" to help the South Vietnamese. He also committed the prestige of the United States by appointing General Maxwell D. Taylor as ambassador to South Vietnam. But despite the increased aid, the war went poorly for the South Vietnamese Government.

On August 2 the USS *Maddox,* a destroyer of the U. S. Seventh Fleet, was on patrol in international waters in the Gulf of Tonkin off the coasts of North Vietnam and Communist China. Suddenly the ship was attacked by three North Vietnamese torpedo boats. The *Maddox* drove off the attackers. In Washington, President John-

General Maxwell D. Taylor, United States ambassador to South Vietnam, talks to Vietamese strong man General Nguyen Khanh.

son announced that the Navy had been instructed to destroy future attackers. On August 4 the Communists launched a second attack. They fired on the *Maddox* and the destroyer USS *C. Turner Joy*. United States response was immediate but limited. In a dramatic midnight television appearance, President Johnson ordered a "positive reply." As he spoke, carrier-based U. S. Navy jet planes attacked torpedo-boat bases in North Vietnam. They knocked out 25 boats. Dock and harbor facilities were destroyed and oil depots were blown up. "There can be no peace by aggression," President Johnson declared, "and no immunity from reply." Congress quickly backed the President by passing a resolution that asserted that the United States regards southeast Asia as "vital to its national interest and to world peace." The President was authorized "to take all necessary measures to repel any armed attack against the forces of the United States." In September, North Vietnamese boats again attacked United States ships. They were driven off and at least one was destroyed.

Under the terms of a 1962 agreement the Communists and the West agreed to respect an "independent and neutral" Laos. A coalition Government was then set up. It was made up of the three warring factions: neutralists, Communists and anti-Communists (Rightists). The head of the neutralists, Prince Souvanna Phouma, was named premier. In 1963, however, the Communists withdrew from the coalition. In 1963 and 1964 they fought against the Government. Because of this situation, the anti-Communists, in 1964, overthrew the neutralist Government. They hoped to prevent the Communists from taking over the country. But, upholding the 1962 agreement, the United States put pressure on the Rightists to restore the neutralists to power. This they did. However, the Pathet Lao Communists then began a military drive against the neutralist forces on the strategic Plain of Jars. Premier Souvanna Phouma asked the United States to send reconnaissance planes over the area to determine the size and scope of the communist offensive. In June two United States planes were shot down by the Communists. The United States retaliated by bombing and strafing communist gun positions and a field headquarters. At year's end the neutralist Government was still in trouble: the Communists refused to withdraw from their newly won positions and threatened to overrun more of Laos.

Indonesian President Sukarno continued his campaign against the Federation of Malaysia. On the island of Borneo—where Malaysia and Indonesia share a 900-mile jungle border—Indonesian terrorists were at work. Indonesian terrorists were also landed in Malaya; most were quickly captured. These raids came about at a time when Malaysia had internal troubles: in midyear, Chinese and Malay citizens rioted in Singapore.

Many observers believe that Sukarno has launched his "crush Malaysia" campaign for domestic reasons. In Indonesia, where Sukarno is "president for life," there is an uneasy balance of power between a large Communist Party and a large military machine. The Indonesian economy is in a shambles. Sukarno is dependent on food shipments from abroad to survive. And the once-free Indonesian press is strictly controlled by the Government.

In the Malaysia-Indonesia struggle, the Malaysians have received aid from Britain. Australia, too, has helped. The British have provided helicopters and Gurkha jungle fighters. Indonesia has received military aid from Russia. This aid includes warships and jet fighters and bombers. It has also received economic, diplomatic and propaganda support from Communist China.

A potentially dangerous situation in Asia has developed along the Russian-Chinese border. In 1964 the split between Russia and China widened. This has divided the communist movement in Asia and around the world.

In the spring of 1964, for the first time, Communist China hinted that it had moved large units of its Army into Sinkiang Province in northwest China. The Russians were also reported to be fortifying their side of the border. In October, however, Russian Premier Khrushchev was ousted from power. Russia's new leaders promptly tried to work out their differences with the Communist Chinese. Toward this end, Chinese Premier Chou En-lai went to Moscow in November. At year's end it was still too early to tell whether a reconciliation would be possible.

This century has known two great Indian leaders: Mohandas K. Gandhi and Jawaharlal Nehru. Gandhi guided India to independence and was enshrined as a saint after his assassination in 1948. Nehru was known as "the maker of modern India." In January Nehru suffered a stroke. In May, at the age of 74, he had a fatal heart attack. His death posed a severe test for India.

Nehru's greatest achievement was to give India a sense of unity and purpose after independence. But when he died India was at odds with its two major neighbors —Communist China and Pakistan. This was the situation inherited by Nehru's successor, Lal Bahadur Shastri. Shastri was named prime minister on June 9 and he immediately tried to ease the tension between India and Pakistan over Kashmir. However, fighting between Indian and Pakistani troops in Kashmir continued throughout the latter part of the year.

The south Asian scene was further clouded by Pakistan's growing friendliness with Communist China. Pakistan is an ally of the United States. But it was angered by American arms shipments to India when Communist China attacked northern India in the fall of 1962. The Pakistanis feel that India will not fight China and that the United States military aid will be used against Pakistan.

At the other end of Asia, in Korea, there were serious student riots led by ultrapatriotic groups. The riots were sparked by talks of a reconciliation between South Korea and Japan, which once ruled Korea. President Chung Hee Park was forced to proclaim martial law in Seoul, Korea's capital, after the riots had spread to 11 other cities.

The economy of Japan continued to boom during 1964. But most of the news was about the Olympics, held in Tokyo in October. On the political scene, Hayato Ikeda was sworn in for a third term as premier in July. In November, however, he resigned because of ill health. Finance Minister Eisaku Sato became premier.

AUSTRALIA

By GEOFFREY L. GRIFFITH

THE Liberal-Country Party coalition Government, led by Prime Minister Sir Robert Menzies, continued in power in 1964. Australia's prosperity continued too. Imports totaled $2,372,000,000 for the 1963-64 fiscal year. Exports reached the record level of $2,768,000,000. Since World War II, the Australian economy has grown at a greater rate than that of most other countries. Its yearly average growth from 1945 to 1964 was 4.3 per cent. One million new jobs have been created in the past five years. Steel production has tripled. The mileage of rural roads has doubled, and automobile production increased to 1,000 a day.

Australia is the world's leading wool producer. It has more sheep—158,000,-000—than any other nation. Although it has only one sixth of the world's sheep, Australia produces one third of the world's wool. In 1964, Australia's wool yielded a record $760,000,000.

Australia's oil industry made a great stride forward in 1964 with the opening of the pipeline from Moonie field to Brisbane, capital of Queensland. Oil and gas were discovered in other parts of Queensland. Natural gas was discovered in the northeast corner of South Australia and near Alice Springs in the center of the continent. These gave promise of rich oil yields. The Government and oil companies (mainly American) have spent a total of $246,-000,000 looking for oil. Most of this was spent in 1964 as the search for oil was intensified in all states. In 1964, too, Australia became self-sufficient in bauxite, the basic raw material for making aluminum.

In 1964, Japan drew ahead of Great Britain as Australia's best export market. Sales of manufactured goods and raw materials also increased to other parts of Asia.

Before World War II, about 9 per cent of Australia's exports went to Asia. In 1964 nearly one third went to Asia.

Australia's interest in Asia was also political and military. The Menzies Government supported United States policy in southeast Asia, sending Australian military advisers to join Americans in troubled South Vietnam.

Australia's search for oil continued in 1964. Here, workers drill for black gold in the Surat Basin in Queensland, the Commonwealth's northeastern state and site of the oil-rich Moonie field.

Australia's population rose to 11,090,455 in 1964. This was an increase of 97,644 over 1963. The Government announced plans to encourage 127,000 new settlers to come to Australia. It is particularly interested in getting skilled workers. Australia has a shortage of skilled workers. But it hopes to gain 8,000 metal tradesmen and 5,000 building workers by 1966.

The Australian Government announced that decimal currency would be introduced into Australia in 1966. Denominations of the note issue will be $20, $10, $2.00 and $1.00. A $5.00 bill may be introduced later. The coins will bear the imprint of Australian animals and wild flowers.

The tourist industry became increasingly important to Australia in 1964. More than $60,000,000 was spent by tourists across the continent. Most visitors to Australia came from the United States, New Zealand and Great Britain.

The construction of Sydney's opera house, now world famous for its unique design of billowing white sails rising from the harbor, progressed slowly in 1964. The latest estimate is that it will be completed in 1967 at a total cost of $34,000,000.

In 1964 the territory of Papua and New Guinea made its single greatest advance toward nationhood since the first white man settled along the shoreline of the territory more than seventy years ago. In February and March, elections were held for the new 64-seat House of Assembly. For the first time, elected Papuans and New Guineans have a majority. They won 38 of the seats. The other seats are held by 16 elected Australians and 10 appointed Australians.

The people of Nauru, an island administered by Australia under the UN trusteeship system, elected to stay on their island. Because Nauru's phosphate deposits, almost the sole basis of the island's economy, will be worked out in about 25 years, Australia offered them Curtis Island, off the Queensland coast, as a future home. But the 2,700 islanders are asking for a legislative council as a traditional step toward independence, which they seek by 1967.

Queen Elizabeth visits Canada's National War Memorial in Ottawa.

CANADA

By R. D. HILTON SMITH

THE year 1964 was Canada's fourth boom year in a row. Industry after industry reported higher output. Dividends paid by most corporations ran well ahead of 1963's record totals. And sales of practically everything from aspirin to yachts were greatly increased.

Among the major mining events of the year was the discovery of a tremendous ore bed near Timmins, Ontario. This bed is estimated to hold some 25,000,000 tons of copper, zinc and silver worth at least $850,000,000. The financial speculation touched off by this find gave the Toronto stock exchange the wildest few days in its history.

There was welcome news for the Atlantic Provinces in the announcement that the world's first large-scale commercial heavy-water plant would be built at Glace Bay, Nova Scotia. The economic growth of western Canada was shown by the granting of charters to two new banks. One has its head office in Winnipeg, the other in Vancouver.

In Parliament, 1964 is likely to be remembered as "the year of the flag." The question of a distinctive national flag for Canada has been debated for generations. At different times more than 1,500 designs for a new flag have been put forward. But until 1964 no clear-cut proposal had ever been submitted to Parliament.

Prior to 1964, the Canadian Red Ensign had been accepted as Canada's flag. The Red Ensign is the traditional flag of the British merchant marine. When it was adopted by Canada, the shield from the

Canadian coat of arms was added. In 1924 the Red Ensign was authorized for display on Canadian government buildings abroad. In 1945 its use was extended to public buildings within the country. This flag emphasized Canada's link with Great Britain. And it meant a great deal to many of the men and women who had served under it in two world wars. Thus any suggestion for a change was bound to meet with an emotional response. On the other hand, many citizens, especially French-Canadians, felt that the time had come for the country to have a flag that would be truly Canadian.

During the election campaign of 1963, the Liberal Party promised to introduce a distinctly Canadian flag if it won the election. The Liberals did win the election, and Prime Minister Lester B. Pearson presented his Government's design for a new flag to Parliament. The flag has a cluster of three red maple leaves on a white background flanked by blue bars. These bars symbolize Canada's dominion from sea to sea. The merit of the design is a matter of personal taste. But the proposed change from the familiar Red Ensign proved too drastic for those who were devoted to it. The veterans' associations and other groups called for a national vote on the flag issue. They were backed by the Progressive Conservative opposition in Parliament, led by former Prime Minister John Diefenbaker. But Prime Minister Pearson did not yield to this pressure. Finally, after weeks of bitter debate, the matter was turned over to a committee, which was given six weeks to find a new design.

Another major decision by Parliament had to do with Canada's defense system. Canada's Army, Navy and Air Force will be integrated under one commander. The man selected for this post is Air Chief Marshal Frank R. Miller.

Parliament also approved a pension plan for the entire working population. This scheme will be financed by contributions from employers and employees. It will take a few years to get into full operation. But when fully working it will offer the best returns—proportionate to contributions—of any similar national pension plan in the world.

A surprising political upset occurred in Saskatchewan in 1964. The Cooperative Commonwealth Federation, led by Premier Woodrow Lloyd, had been in power for twenty years. It was the only socialist government in North America. But in 1964 the Liberal Party, under the leadership of Ross Thatcher, won 33 of the 59 seats in the provincial legislature. The CCF won 25 seats and the Progressive Conservatives one.

Canada's smallest province, Prince Edward Island, had a year of festivity. It was at PEI's capital, Charlottetown, that Canada's founding fathers first met in September 1864. Their meeting, followed by another conference in Quebec City, led to the confederation of Ontario, Quebec, Nova Scotia, New Brunswick and Prince Edward Island in 1867. To mark the 1864 meeting, the province, aided by contributions from other parts of the country, built a Memorial Building in Charlottetown. The Memorial Building houses a theater, art gallery, museum, library and meeting hall.

Throughout 1964, Prince Edward Island was the scene of pageants, meetings, festivals and the like. High point of the celebrations came in October with the arrival of Queen Elizabeth and the Duke of Edinburgh. After officiating at ceremonies in Charlettetown, the Queen and Prince went to Quebec City for similar ceremonies there. They then visited Ottawa before returning to England.

For several centuries the control of education in the province of Quebec was in the hands of the church. A very important and far-reaching change was made in 1964. The Quebec legislature approved a bill that created a ministry of education. Thus control of education was transferred from the church to the government.

LATIN AMERICA

By JOHN L. HOCHMANN

Argentine police quell a demonstration by followers of ex-president Peron during a visit by French President de Gaulle.

IN Latin America, 1964 opened on a note of crisis. In January, anti-American demonstrations took place in Panama and the Panama Canal Zone. By a treaty of 1903, the United States controls the Canal and a five-mile-wide belt of land on each side of it. More than 36,000 Americans live and work in the Canal Zone. These Americans, and United States control of the area, have long been a source of irritation to many Panamanians. They say that they receive lower wages than Americans for similar jobs. They also feel that by occupying part of their country the United States is violating Panama's sovereignty. One very touchy issue was which flag—Panama's or the United States' or both—should fly in the Canal Zone. Finally, it was agreed that both flags would be flown, side by side. In some places, such as schools, neither flag would be flown.

In January, however, a group of United States teen-agers raised the American flag at their high school in Balboa. Soon mobs of Panamanians were rioting, burning American buildings and shooting at United States troops. The rioting went on for several days. Four American soldiers and at least 20 Panamanians were killed.

Panama then broke diplomatic relations with the United States. It accused American soldiers of brutality. However, an impartial group of lawyers—the International Commission of Jurists—investigated the case. The United States was absolved of the charge. The commission stated that "the tempo and violence of the disturbances were such that there is little doubt that they held out a real threat to life and security, which could only be met by strong measures. In these circumstances, Zone authorities and United States military forces were entitled to use force."

Nevertheless the squabble dragged on. Panama demanded that the United States renegotiate the treaty of 1903. The United States refused to negotiate under pressure. In April diplomatic relations were finally resumed. And on May 10 Marco A. Robles was elected president of Panama. He had campaigned on the promise to "rescue for our country the commerce of the Canal Zone." It was clear that the Canal Zone issue was far from settled.

In April a military uprising overthrew João Goulart, the president of Brazil. During Goulart's 31 months in office the cost of living had soared 300 per cent. The country's foreign debt rose to $3,700,000,000. And the value of the cruzeiro dropped 83 per cent. Goulart made many promises to reform the economy, but he did little. As Brazil's economic situation went from bad to worse, Goulart turned to the far Left for support. He threatened to rewrite Brazil's constitution, which forbids a president to succeed himself.

In March some sailors and marines staged a sit-down strike. They were fully pardoned by Goulart's Navy Minister. This weak handling of the situation angered the Opposition. Finally, a Brazilian Army corps rose against Goulart. When he sent an infantry division to put down the uprising, it joined the Opposition. The revolution spread and Goulart fled into exile. The head of the Chamber of Deputies was named interim president. Soon after, General Humberto Castelo Branco was sworn in as president. He will serve until 1967. Elections will be held in December 1966.

The change of presidents in Venezuela in 1964 was less dramatic than in Brazil. When President Romulo Betancourt left office he was the first elected president in Venezuela's 134 years as a republic to complete his term. In March 1964 Betancourt handed over his sash of office to Raul Leoni. The new President warned the outlawed Communists and supporters of Cuba's Fidel Castro that "they must leave the road of violence and incorporate themselves into democratic life." He also promised to develop the country's interior, stimulate private enterprise and create 20,000 new jobs.

Despite Leoni's offer of peace to Leftist groups, violence flared again. In July, Castroite terrorists killed three policemen in Caracas. They also attacked national-guard posts and blew up a highway bridge.

These attempts to overthrow the Venezuelan Government finally resulted in action by the Organization of American States. Venezuela claimed that Cuba had smuggled arms to pro-Castro revolutionaries. It demanded that the OAS take action to prevent further Cuban aggression. In July the foreign ministers of the American states voted 15-4 to brand Cuba as an aggressor. The OAS called on all member states to cut diplomatic ties with Cuba and to cut off all trade except in food and drugs. By year's end all member states except Mexico had severed diplomatic ties with Cuba. Most important of all was the OAS threat to use force against Cuba if it continued attempts to overthrow any Latin American government.

In Cuba itself the economic situation became worse. Because of hurricanes and bad management, Cuba's sugar crop was

Jubilant, flag-waving Brazilians weave through heavy traffic in downtown São Paulo, April 2, celebrating the overthrow of Leftist President João Goulart.

UPI

the lowest in twenty years. Industrial production was off 16 per cent. And the country was badly in need of basic consumer goods. Castro continued to blame the United States for his difficulties. In February four Cuban fishing vessels drifted or sailed into United States territorial waters. They were detained at Key West, Florida. In retaliation, Castro turned off the water supply of the U.S. naval base at Guantanamo. The United States began shipping water to the base by tanker. And a saltwater conversion project was started.

Meanwhile Russian troops were gradually pulling out of Cuba. By midyear there were only about 2,000, as compared with 30,000 in 1962. Despite Castro's protests, the United States continued to send reconnaissance flights over the island.

As embarrassing to Castro as his country's worsening economy was the defection of his sister Juanita Castro in June. She flew from Havana to Mexico City and issued the following statement: "My brothers Fidel and Raul have made Cuba an enormous prison surrounded by water."

Though a democracy, Mexico has only one major political party—Institutional Revolutionary Party. Its candidates almost always outpoll those of the token Opposition. In July, as President Adolfo Lopez Mateos' term neared its end, voters went to the polls to approve his successor. As expected, Gustavo Diaz Ordaz won a six-year term, which began on December 1.

Argentina spent 1964 trying to recover its economic balance. Thanks to high beef prices and a good wheat crop, exports were expected to exceed imports in 1964. Argentina's industrial production also increased during the year.

In Peru a major land-reform project was started. Its aim is to help the 6,000,000 Indians who live in the highlands. These people, who speak the language of their Inca ancestors, earn only $110 per family per year.

In May, fans rioted at a soccer game in Lima. Fifty thousand people were watching a match between Peru and Argentina that would help decide who would represent Latin America in the Olympic Games.

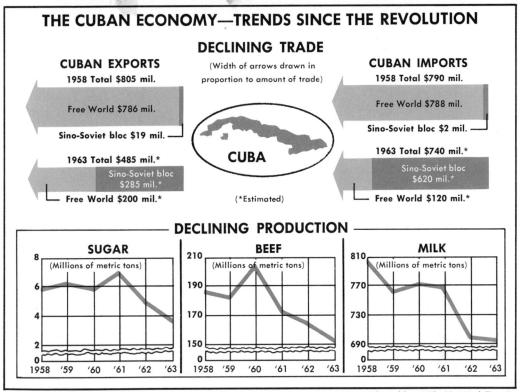

THE CUBAN ECONOMY—TRENDS SINCE THE REVOLUTION

DECLINING TRADE

CUBAN EXPORTS
1958 Total $805 mil.

(Width of arrows drawn in proportion to amount of trade)

CUBAN IMPORTS
1958 Total $790 mil.

Free World $786 mil.

Free World $788 mil.

Sino-Soviet bloc $19 mil.

Sino-Soviet bloc $2 mil.

1963 Total $485 mil.*

1963 Total $740 mil.*

CUBA

Sino-Soviet bloc $285 mil.*

Sino-Soviet bloc $620 mil.*

Free World $200 mil.*

(*Estimated)

Free World $120 mil.*

DECLINING PRODUCTION

SUGAR
(Millions of metric tons)

8
6
4
2
0
1958 '59 '60 '61 '62 '63

BEEF
(Millions of metric tons)

210
190
170
150
0
1958 '59 '60 '61 '62 '63

MILK
(Millions of metric tons)

810
770
730
690
0
1958 '59 '60 '61 '62 '63

Adapted from "The New York Times"

During 1964 the economic situation in Cuba, handicapped by hurricanes and management problems, grew steadily worse. The sugar crop was Cuba's smallest in the last two decades. Industrial production showed a sharp decline, and there were acute shortages of basic consumer goods.

When a referee disallowed a tying goal shortly before the end of the game, the fans rioted. In the crush, about 300 people were killed and 500 injured.

Since 1952, when Victor Paz Estenssoro first became president of Bolivia, the Government has run the tin mines on which Bolivia's economy depends. Over his years in office (1952-56; 1960-64), in the face of widespread economic decline, Paz became increasingly dictatorial. In May 1964 he was reelected president. But in September he exiled 34 political opponents and declared martial law. A month later, disgruntled tin miners and Leftist students rioted against him, setting the stage for the military coup that occurred November 4. Vice-President René Barrientos Ortuño, who had previously broken with Paz, became president, promising to call for new elections.

Luis Giannattasio became president of Uruguay on March 1; in September Eduardo Frei Montalva defeated Salvador Allende Gossens, a communist-backed candidate, in Chile's national elections.

In Haiti there was an election too. Dictator François Duvalier held a "popular referendum" in June to name him president for life. Ninety per cent of the Haitians are illiterate and could not read the ballot. They could only hope that Duvalier would help increase their extremely low per capita income.

In 1964 the Bahamas became semi-independent. Great Britain will continue to handle defense, internal security and foreign affairs. Bahamians will run the rest of their affairs.

Perhaps the highlights of the year in Latin America were French President de Gaulle's two trips there. In March he visited Mexico and some islands in the Caribbean. In September and October he toured ten South American countries, hoping to increase French influence in the area.

157

THE MIDDLE EAST

By HARRY J. PSOMIADES

Heavily armed with rifles and automatic weapons, Turkish Cypriots guard St. Hilarion Castle, their main stronghold in north Cyprus.

Camera Press, PIX

THE Middle East continued to attract worldwide attention in 1964. The year began with the historic pilgrimage of Pope Paul VI to the Holy Land and the divided city of Jerusalem. The high point of his trip was his meeting with the Orthodox Patriarch of Constantinople (Istanbul), Athenagoras I, on Jerusalem's Mount of Olives. For the first time in more than five hundred years the heads of the Roman Catholic and Greek Orthodox churches met and talked. But all was not peace in the Middle East. The Arab-Israeli dispute remained. The two-year-old civil war in Yemen continued to take its toll of lives. And the struggle between Greek and Turkish Cypriots continued despite the dispatch of a United Nations peace-keeping force to Cyprus.

In January, 13 Arab heads of state met in Cairo. They discussed a common approach to Israel's plan to divert water from the Jordan River. Israel has completed a $150,000,000 pipeline stretching over 100 miles from the Sea of Galilee in the north to the parched Negev in the south. The pipeline will bring more water to Israel's central plains. And it will open up new land in the Negev. An earlier plan for sharing the waters of the Jordan among Jordan, Syria, Lebanon and Israel was turned down by the Arabs in 1955.

At the January Cairo conference, the Arabs agreed to set up a permanent joint military command. They talked of ways to restore "occupied Palestine" (Israel) to the Palestinian Arab refugees. But they did not support Syria's plan to use force to stop Israel from diverting Jordan waters. In fact, President Nasser's main reason for calling the conference was to prevent Syria from starting a war with Israel. The Arab world did not want to be dragged into a war for which it was unprepared. The Arabs then talked of their own plans to use Jordan headwaters before they reached Israel. They feel that this will damage Israel's project. The Hasbani and Baniyas rivers, tributaries of the Jordan, originate in Lebanon and Syria.

In May, Israel completed the first full-scale tapping of the Jordan waters. The Arabs did nothing. But the danger of war over the water issue is not over. The Arabs still plan to stop the Hasbani and Baniyas rivers from reaching the Jordan. Israel has warned that it would consider such action as "aggression."

Cyprus, strategically situated in the eastern Mediterranean, is 40 miles south of Turkey.

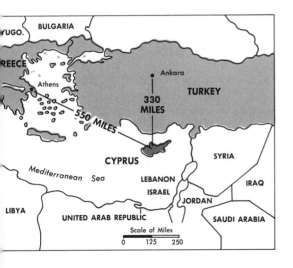

The distribution of Greeks and Turks on Cyprus. Greeks make up 80 per cent of the population.

Adapted from "The New York Times"

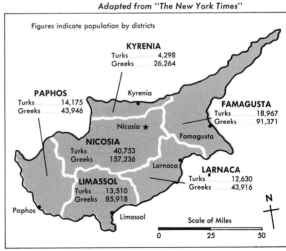

The Cairo conference was also a victory for Nasser on another front. Diplomatic relations with Jordan were resumed. Relations had been broken in 1961 when Jordan recognized the secession of Syria from the United Arab Republic. In March, normal diplomatic relations were also restored between the U.A.R. and Saudi Arabia. More important, Nasser convinced King Hussein of Jordan and Crown Prince Faisal of Saudi Arabia to slow up aid to the Royalist tribesmen of Imam Mohammed al-Badr of Yemen. In July, Hussein recognized the Republic of Yemen and its President, Abdullah al-Salal. And although Faisal continued to supply the Imam with money, his support for the Royalists was temporarily reduced.

This streak of success has strengthened Nasser's position in Yemen where 30,000 to 40,000 Egyptian soldiers have been fighting Royalist tribesmen. By August, Egyptian forces had gained control of the Yemeni lowlands.

A second Arab summit meeting was held in Alexandria in September. There the Arab leaders tried to find a solution to the conflict in Yemen. They were seemingly successful, for a cease-fire was put into effect in November.

During the summer months, Nasser tried to stir up the tribes of the British-supported South Arabian Federation. His efforts were met with stiff British resistance. Royal Air Force planes bombed the rebel tribesmen and destroyed many of their villages. In March, British planes had attacked the military fort of Harib in Yemen. This was in response to attacks on the South Arabian Federation by the Republic of Yemen.

There were two important domestic developments in Nasser's United Arab Republic. Efforts were made to create new and permanent political institutions. And the first stage of the Aswan High Dam project was completed.

Elections were held on March 10 and 19 for a 350-seat National Assembly. The deputies were selected from a government-supported list of 1,748 candidates. All the candidates were members of the only political party allowed in the country—the Arab Socialist Union. On March 25 a new Government was sworn in as a new provisional constitution went into effect. The prime minister of the new Government is Ali Sabry. Under the constitution President Nasser will remain in office until March 26, 1965. Two months before that date the deputies to the National Assembly will nominate one candidate for president by a majority vote. His name will then be submitted to a national vote. If the candidate is elected by the people, he becomes president for a full six-year term. But before the presidential election in 1965, a new permanent constitution must be drafted by the present National Assembly.

On May 14, President Nasser and Russian Premier Khrushchev pressed a button setting off a dynamite charge. This charge diverted the Nile River from its regular course so that the Aswan High Dam could be completed. When the $1,000,000,000 dam project is finished in 1967-70, it will increase Egypt's arable land by one third.

In Iraq, President Abd al-Salam Arif tried to model his regime after that of the U.A.R. In July, all private banks and insurance companies, and 30 industrial and commercial firms were nationalized. Also, all political parties were replaced by a new political organization, the Arab Socialist Union—Iraqi Region.

In 1964, President Arif brought about an end to the long war with the Kurds of Iraq. About one out of every seven Iraqis is a Kurd. The Kurds of Iraq live in the northern highlands. On February 10, Arif and Mulla Mustafa al-Barzani, chief of the Kurdish rebels, broadcast orders to cease fire, over the Baghdad radio. The Iraqi Government promised to carry out some of the Kurdish demands for self-government. However, it evidently did not go so far as the Kurds would have liked, for in early November, after negotiations failed, it was reported that the Kurds had established an autonomous government in northern Iraq.

The Arif Government is in trouble because it is opposed by Iraq's powerful minority groups—the Shia Muslims and the Kurds. It is also unpopular with other segments of Iraqi society. The Baath Socialists, whom Arif ousted from power in November 1963, tried unsuccessfully to regain power in September and have pledged themselves to the overthrow of his regime.

The Baath Socialists continued to maintain a precarious hold on the Syrian Government. Indeed, several plots to overthrow the Government were discovered. In April, a revolt at Hama was backed by Iraq and the U.A.R. The Baathist Government of Major General Amin el-Hafez seemed to be torn between a pro-Nasser and an anti-Nasser policy. The weak position of the Syrian Government and its cool relations with the other Arab governments seemed to account for its aggressive attitude toward Israel.

In Lebanon, it was business as usual. The economy continued to develop in a favorable manner. Elections were held in April and May. The new Parliament includes 71 former deputies. Fifty-seven had been in the Parliament dissolved in February. Twenty-eight deputies were elected for the first time. Hussein al-Oweini had become interim prime minister in February. He won a strong vote of confidence in May. In the same month the Chamber passed a motion calling for an amendment to the Constitution to allow the reelection of General Fuad Chehab for a second term as president. But the General refused to run for a second term. His action created some anxiety in Lebanese politics.

On August 18, however, the Lebanese Parliament by a vote of 92 to 7 elected Charles Helou as president. He succeeded General Chehab in September.

Under Prime Minister Levi Eshkol, Israel continued to enjoy stable government. But problems with the Arab states continued. In November at least ten people were killed when Israeli and Syrian armed forces clashed. Each side accused the other of starting the incident. More skirmishes were reported in December.

In Iran in 1964 the problems of putting into effect the Shah's social and economic reform programs remained. About 90 per cent of the Iranians are farmers who do not own the land they cultivate. A few large landowners still dominate the political, economic and social life in Iran. Many of them continue to oppose the reform programs which the country needs. On March 7, Premier Assadullah Alam resigned. The Shah appointed Hassan Ali Mansour to replace him. The new premier is expected to handle with greater vigor Iran's economic and social problems.

By far the most dangerous event in the Middle East was the threat of war between two NATO allies, Greece and Turkey. The area of dispute was Cyprus. The Cyprus constitution of 1960 gave the 18-20 per cent Turkish minority an absolute veto over the Greek majority of the island. In December 1963, when the Greeks tried to change the constitution and do away with the Turk veto, violence broke out between the two communities. After attempts to restore peace failed, Cypriot President Makarios took the matter to the UN Security Council. Meanwhile Greece and Turkey threatened to intervene on opposing sides. Finally, in March, the Security Council agreed to send a UN peace-keeping force to Cyprus.

Even with UN troops on the island, tension remained high. The Turks demanded partition of the island; the Greeks insisted on majority rule. The most critical moment came in August. Turkey felt that the Turkish minority on Cyprus was in grave danger. So it sent several dozen jet airplanes to bomb Greek Cypriot villages and military positions. As a result of this action it was expected that Greece and Turkey would soon be at war. Greece, however, withheld its military forces. War was avoided. But the threat of war was still there at year's end.

SOVIET UNIO

By HARRISON E. SALISB

ON October 15 the communist world—indeed, the entire world—was shaken by news of Nikita Khrushchev's fall from power. Leonid Brezhnev replaced Khrushchev as Communist Party first secretary. This is the most powerful position in Russia. The Russian premiership was taken over by Aleksei Kosygin.

According to observers of the Russian scene, Khrushchev's ouster came about for at least three reasons. First, under Khrushchev's rule, Russia entered into a bitter feud with Communist China. This feud split the communist world apart. The Eastern European communist nations became more independent of Russia. Secondly, during Khrushchev's reign Russian agricultural and industrial production did not increase as predicted. Some observers also attributed Khrushchev's ouster to the Russian military. Many military leaders were angry with him for reducing the size of Russia's armed forces.

Once in office, Russia's new leaders announced that they would continue Khrushchev's policy of peaceful coexistence with the West. At the same time, however, they promptly attempted to bring about an end to the split with Communist China.

On November 7, delegates from the communist nations of the world went to Moscow for celebrations of the 47th anniversary of the Russian Revolution. Premier Chou En-lai of Communist China was also invited. While in Moscow he held talks with Russia's new leaders with an aim to ending their bitter feuding; however, no real progress was made.

In 1964 Soviet economic problems were intensified. The pace of economic growth, which had been slowing down for several years, became even slower. Early in the year a Central Intelligence Agency report put the Soviet growth rate at about 2.5 per cent. In previous years it had been 7.5 per cent. It also set the Soviet gross national product for 1963 at $260,000,000,000. This is about half the GNP of the United States.

The CIA figures were challenged by Russian economists as well as some specialists in the United States. It was conceded that due to the crop failure of 1963 overall production figures were down. But Soviet economists said the expansion rate was about 5 per cent, not 2.5 per cent.

nd EASTERN EUROPE

Missiles in Red Square during 47th anniversary celebrations of Russian Revolution.

In 1964 the Soviet Union continued to import huge amounts of grain from the Western world. However, the 1964 Soviet grain harvest came back to more or less normal figures. Before his ouster, Premier Khrushchev stressed that greater emphasis must be given to the needs of the Soviet consumer. At the same time he called for an expansion of the chemical industry, so that more fertilizer could be produced for farm use.

Diplomatic activity between the United States and Russia was at a minimum in 1964. But Russian and American diplomats did complete one major piece of business. They negotiated a treaty governing consular relations between the two nations. It was the first such treaty since 1934.

Death took from the scene a number of prominent communist leaders. Among them were O. V. Kuusinen, the oldest member of the Soviet Party Presidium. Kuusinen was once head of the Comintern and of a short-lived "Soviet" Finland. Palmiro Togliatti, the Italian communist chief, and Maurice Thorez, the French communist leader, both died in Russia while under treatment for illnesses. Elizabeth Gurley Flynn, head of the American Communist Party, also died in Russia.

Throughout 1964 there was angry controversy over Soviet policy on its Jewish population. Charges of anti-Semitism have often been made against the Soviets. These charges were strengthened by the publication in the Ukraine and Moldavia of two very anti-Semitic books. Indignation was aroused when the Soviet Government placed restrictions upon Jewish observance of religious holidays. The Soviets also continued a campaign against "speculators" who appeared to be generally of Jewish origin. Many were executed.

The continuing Soviet policy brought forth angry denunciations by Jewish communities and public bodies in the United States and by foreign communist parties. Lord Russell and a group of 11 other well-known Britons sent a protest letter to Premier Khrushchev in February. The Soviets insisted that anti-Semitism as a policy did not exist.

Eastern Europe was quiet except for repercussions of the Russian-Chinese dispute and Khrushchev's fall from power. Eastern European leaders were almost always on the go, back and forth to Moscow, for conferences and consultations on the two issues.

During the year the Rumanian Communist Party, under Gheorghe Gheorghiu-Dej, continued to chart an independent course. Gheorghiu-Dej broke with Moscow because Russia tried to subordinate Rumania's economy to that of the other communist countries. Moscow wanted Rumania to be basically agricultural. The Rumanians wanted to industrialize their country. To show its independence, Rumania began to break off trade contacts with other communist countries. At the same time, it increased its dealings with Britain, France and West Germany. The Hungarians also began to flirt with Communist China and to stay away from meetings sponsored by the Soviet Union.

The United States sought to strengthen Rumanian independence. It entered into diplomatic negotiations with Rumania, and

UPI

All that wheat just wasn't enough: Russia's poor grain harvest was one of the reasons for the ouster of Premier Khrushchev.

164

SUCCESSION IN THE SOVIET LEADERSHIP SINCE 1917

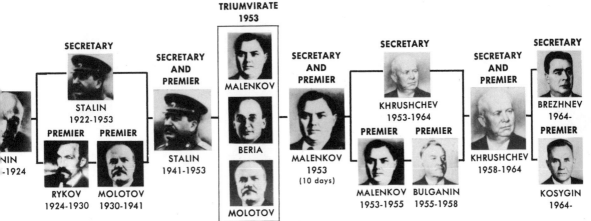

Adapted from "The New York Times"

in June signed the most extensive trade pact yet negotiated with a communist state. The pact was designed to help Rumania become less dependent on Russian economic aid.

The Rumanians also moved to strengthen ties with Yugoslavia. Marshal Tito and Gheorghiu-Dej met to consider possibilities for joint action in the Balkans. This project was started in 1957 but had been put aside because of Russian opposition.

Marshal Tito played a cautious diplomatic game in 1964. He met with Premier Khrushchev in Leningrad and gave him support in the conflict with Communist China. However, he took care not to place too great a strain on his ties with the West. Yugoslavia had a serious grain failure in 1964 and once again was hoping for United States aid.

Premier Khrushchev traveled to Hungary in April. While there he strongly defended his argument that world communism could best be advanced by improving the material conditions of life in communist countries. He ridiculed arguments that revolution should come ahead of raising living standards. He also said that only "a child or a fool does not fear war." He made scornful references to the Chinese and praised the good judgment of United States leaders.

Mr. Khrushchev's trip to Hungary was made at a time when that country was becoming increasingly liberal and standards of living were improving. The United States and Hungary engaged in diplomatic talks with the hope of regularizing relations. Negotiators also hoped to arrange a way for Cardinal Mindszenty to leave the United States Embassy in Budapest. He had taken refuge there at the time of the October-November 1956 uprising. Vatican representatives also took part in these negotiations.

In 1964, Polish liberals watched with concern as tough-line Stalinists tried to gain greater influence in the Polish Communist Party. Warsaw's event of the year was the visit of Attorney General Robert Kennedy. He was mobbed and cheered, especially when talking to Warsaw University students.

East Germany began a serious effort to improve relations with the West after signing a new treaty with Russia. An agreement was made with West Germany for easier transit through the Berlin Wall. And an effort to expand trade with Western Europe was also begun. The veteran East German communist leader Otto Grotewohl died in September. His place as chairman of the Council of Ministers was taken by Willi Stoph.

WESTERN EUROPE

By MARSHALL PECK

Great Britain's new Prime Minister, Labor Party leader Harold Wilson.

THE political event of the year in Western Europe took place in Britain. On October 15 the Labor Party defeated the Conservatives at the polls. Labor Party leader Harold Wilson became prime minister. However, the Laborites' victory was a narrow one: a five-seat majority in Parliament. Out of power since 1951, the Labor Party won votes with a sharp attack on the Conservative record and a pledge to "get Britain moving again." Ousted by the election was Conservative Prime Minister Sir Alec Douglas-Home.

There were two major trends in Western Europe in 1964. Nationalism was becoming so strong that it threatened the harmony of the North Atlantic Treaty Organization (NATO). And the danger of inflation threatened Europe's growing prosperity. However, neither threat was a death thrust—or appeared to be insurmountable. In fact, both nationalism and the signs of inflation were results of Western Europe's healthy economy. Still, they tended to put a drag on the area's political and economic forward motion. Also, they affected Europe's dealings with the rest of the Western world.

The trend toward nationalism was natural enough. It has been 25 years since World War II broke out and shattered Europe. Now these old and proud nations are seeking to reassert themselves.

At the same time, as NATO marked its 15th birthday, there was a feeling in Europe that world tensions had eased. Europeans felt that Soviet pressure against the

West was muted, if not resolved. The iron curtain still divided Eastern and Western Europe. But more and more, Western European nations were seeking trade and cultural outlets to the east.

Europe has worked hard, with the help of the United States, to rebuild its spirit and economy. Now it wants to reap the harvest of good times. West Germans were buying vacation homes in Ireland. French travelers could be found throughout Spain. France, Belgium and the Netherlands no longer had colonial problems. For Europe, prospects for peace appeared to be excellent.

Whether others liked it or not, President

Charles de Gaulle of France made himself the foremost personality in Europe. Typical of De Gaulle's growing independence was his attempt to build up French influence in Latin America. In March he took a successful ten-day tour of Mexico and French possessions in the Caribbean. And in September and October, De Gaulle made a 27-day goodwill tour of ten South American countries.

Although firmly behind the Western alliance, De Gaulle has often challenged United States leadership in Europe. For example, in January he recognized Communist China. This move was frowned

While other escapees wait their turn, an East German woman is swung into a West Berlin cellar in a dramatic escape under the Berlin wall.

167

upon by Washington. And it caused Nationalist China to break diplomatic relations with France. General de Gaulle then came out for the neutralization of southeast Asia, where United States soldiers are fighting communist guerrillas. President Johnson quickly rejected De Gaulle's plan. De Gaulle has also criticized NATO although he made no move to drop out of the organization at the annual NATO spring meeting.

General de Gaulle believes that France should control its own atomic force. In his opinion France should cooperate with but not be reliant on the United States for European defense. Thus French policy is opposed to the United States-supported attempt to organize a multilateral nuclear force (MLF) made up of men from all NATO nations. De Gaulle also wants to limit European union to a confederation of the Common Market countries—France, West Germany, Italy, Belgium, Luxembourg and the Netherlands.

Unlike De Gaulle, West German Chancellor Ludwig Erhard is against lessening Europe's ties with the United States. Nor does he want any great change in the political and military arrangements that link Europe and the United States in the NATO alliance. He feels there is great danger in decreasing the unity of the West. And he emphasizes that Western Europe's future depends largely on its ability to cooperate with the United States as a bloc—not as individual states each following its own course.

In 1964 NATO had other, more serious problems. Two NATO members—Turkey and Greece—almost went to war over Cyprus. The United Nations and the United States were hard pressed to keep these two countries apart when fighting erupted between Greeks and Turks on Cyprus.

Rising wages and cost of living brought an inflationary trend to Western Europe in 1964. In Italy, where the problem was most acute, the Government approved heavy tax increases to cut consumer spending. Con-

PIX

The inaugural fleet of boats on the Moselle River in 1964 when it was made navigable from the North Sea to the Ruhr-Lorraine Basin.

tinuing governmental crisis, plus the stroke suffered by President Antonio Segni in August, added to Italy's woes.

In April, 2,000 delegates from more than 120 nations met at Geneva for the three-month United Nations Conference on Trade and Development, the largest trade conference ever held. It met at the insistence of the underdeveloped nations of the world. These nations, which were in a majority at the conference, joined together to demand trade and aid concessions from the industrialized nations. They had the votes but not the treasuries, and were unable to get much support. However, they did manage to get the industrialized nations to agree to some of their proposals, including the creation of a Trade and Development Board which will meet every three years. Moreover, they moved toward forming a new alliance—built on economics rather than politics—against the richer nations, whether Western or Communist.

The failure of the UN conference to come up with immediate solutions to world-trade problems strengthened the 60-odd-nation General Agreement on Tariffs and Trade (GATT). GATT is dominated by the wealthy nations and excludes communist nations. At a conference in Geneva,

PIX

At the inauguration of the new route: French President de Gaulle, Luxembourg's Grand Duchess Charlotte and West German President Lübke.

GATT's members tried to lower international trade barriers. These negotiations were known as the Kennedy Round, since the conference had been envisioned by the late President Kennedy. He had hoped that tariff cuts of up to 50 per cent could be made and extended to underdeveloped countries. But no immediate results came of this conference either.

There was little labor unrest of importance during 1964. However, the 18-day Belgian doctors' strike in August caused widespread disorders in that country. The strike took place after the Government proposed a new health plan. Doctors charged that the plan was a step toward socialized medicine. They felt it would be bad for the people and the medical profession. After both houses of Parliament voted for the bill, the doctors went on strike and refused to treat patients. Many doctors left the country for a while to escape the wrath of angry citizens. The Government then ordered 3,600 medical reserve officers and 3,000 civilian physicians to duty, to provide emergency service. The strike ended with some yielding on both sides, and agreement for amendments to the bill.

September elections in Sweden and Denmark showed opposite results. Although the Swedes reelected Premier Tage Erlander's Social Democrats for four more years, the Communists increased their representation from 5 to 8 seats in the same election. Danish voters, on the other hand, moved to the Right. They upset Premier Jens Otto Krag's coalition and forced him to form a minority administration. Earlier in the year the Scandinavian countries played host to Russian Premier Khrushchev during an 18-day visit.

Two royal marriages caught Europe's fancy in 1964. One of them, the marriage of King Constantine II of Greece to Princess Anne-Marie of Denmark, was in the finest tradition. Constantine had become king of Greece in March, after the death of his father, King Paul. The September 18 wedding in Athens was attended by many members of the leading royal families of Europe.

The marriage of Spain's Prince Carlos of Bourbon-Parma to Princess Irene of the Netherlands caused dissension in Holland. Carlos' Roman Catholic faith, to which Irene had been converted, and his desire to assume the Spanish throne if it is reestablished after Franco's death, combined to make him unacceptable to the Dutch people. They could not forget their sixteenth-century war of independence against Spain. Thus, while Irene was blessed by her parents, Queen Juliana and Prince Bernhardt, the couple was married in Rome in April without her family in attendance.

A less-publicized royal act was the abdication of Grand Duchess Charlotte of Luxembourg. After 45 years as head of state of the Grand Duchy, Charlotte, 68, gave way in favor of her 43-year-old son, Prince Jean.

The year also marked the completion of the 160-mile canalization of the Moselle River. The canal, started in 1957, goes through France, West Germany and Luxembourg. It provides a practical transportation link between the French steel basin of Lorraine and the German coal fields in the Ruhr.

TO THE NEWS

FOCUS: MIDDLE EAST, CARIBBEAN AND CANADA

THREE areas of the world very much in the news in 1964 were the Middle East, the Caribbean and Central America, and Canada. News reports from the Middle East concerned an island, a dam and water. The island of course was Cyprus. The fighting there between Greek and Turkish Cypriots threatened constantly to erupt into a larger war between Greece and Turkey. The dam was the United Arab Republic's Aswan High Dam, which will cost about $1,000,000,000. Because two fifths of it is being financed by the Soviet Union, Soviet Premier Khrushchev traveled to the U.A.R. in May to celebrate with U.A.R. President Nasser the completion of the first stage of the project. Another Middle Eastern irrigation scheme caused friction between Israel and the Arab states. Israel wants to irrigate its vast, arid desert lands and build farms. So in 1964 the Israelis began diverting water from the Jordan River and piping it south. The Arabs strongly objected and the bitter dispute is still unsettled.

Water also caused problems in the Caribbean in 1964. In February, some Cubans were arrested when their boats drifted into Florida waters. To retaliate, Cuban Premier Castro ordered the water supply to the United States naval base at Guantanamo cut off. The United States averted an immediate crisis by shipping water to Guantanamo. Another crisis in the Caribbean was not averted. In January, riots in Panama and the Panama Canal Zone, by Panamanians who resented the raising of the United States flag by American students there, brought about a new low in U.S.-Panamanian relations.

A flag was at issue in Canada too. Prime Minister Lester Pearson sought to replace Canada's Red Ensign with a more distinctively Canadian flag. This issue raised tempers already near the boiling point over the demands by many French-Canadians that Quebec become independent of the rest of Canada.

Full reports of these events are given elsewhere in the *Annual*. On the following pages, pictorial coverage takes you to the places where these newsworthy events occurred.

THE MIDDLE EAST

OIL AND WATER IN A DRY LAND

The birthplace of urban civilization, the Middle East has served for centuries as a bridge between the three continents of Asia, Europe, and Africa. In the 20th century the area's importance has been further enhanced by the discovery of vast reserves of oil and, to a lesser degree, by the application of modern methods of irrigation, whereby arid land is converted to productive soil.

Pipeline junction at Kuwait, a port of export for the rich oil fields of the Middle East. British- and American-trained Arabs comprise much of the work force.

J. B. Charbonnier — Photo Researchers

Israel's vast irrigation projects have made possible the reclamation and settlement of once arid acres. Below, Kibbutz Givat Brenner, a thriving collective farm community.

Jerry Cooke — Photo Researchers

George Holton — Photo Researchers

Interior of the Church of the Nativity, Bethlehem, Palestine. The present basilica was erected by Justinian I in the 6th century.

George Holton — Photo Rese

Interior of the Umayyad Mosque in Damascus, Syria. Origina Cathedral of St. John the Baptist, it was converted to a m during the reign (705-15) of the Umayyad Caliph al-Walid.

THREE GREAT FAITHS: JUDAISM, CHRISTIANITY, ISL/

A church, a mosque, and a temple—old and new—emblems of the world's three great monotheistic religions, all of which originated in the Middle East.

Synagogue, built in 1957, is on the campus of Hebrew University in Jerusalem.

Jerry Cooke — Photo Resec

INDEX TO MAP OF THE MIDDLE EAST

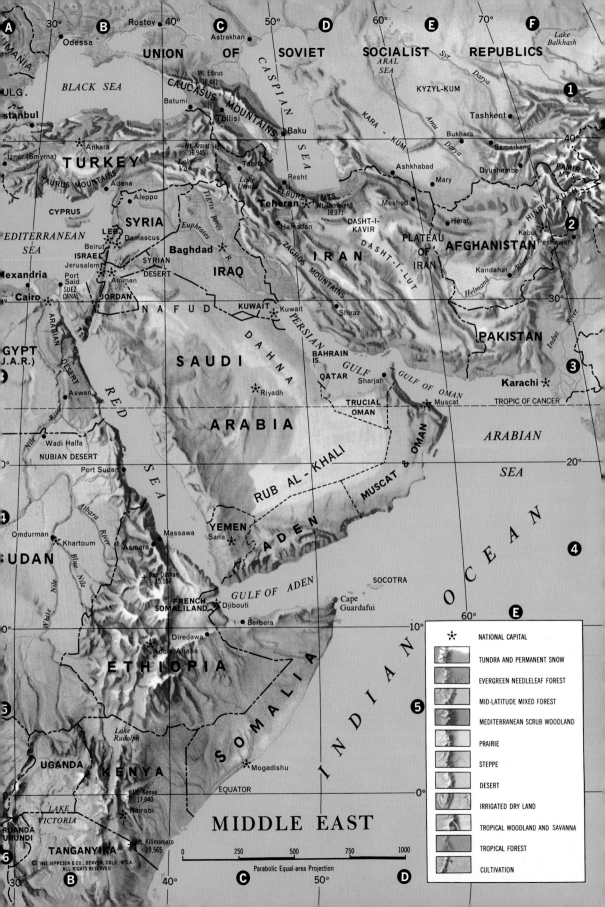

MIDDLE EAST

A 30° **B** Rostov 40° **C** Astrakhan **D** 50° **E** 60° 70° **F** Lake Balkhash

UNION OF SOVIET SOCIALIST REPUBLICS

Odessa
ULG.
stanbul
BLACK SEA
CAUCASUS MOUNTAINS
Batumi
Mt. Elbrus 18,481
CASPIAN SEA
ARAL SEA
Syr Darya
KYZYL-KUM
Tashkent
1
Ankara
Tbilisi
Baku
KARA - KUM
Amu Darya
Bukhara
Samarkand
40°
Izmir (Smyrna)
TURKEY
Mt. Ararat 16,945
Lake Van
Tabriz
Lake Urmia
Resht
ELBURZ MTS.
Ashkhabad
Mary
Dyushambe
PAMIR MTS.
TAURUS MOUNTAINS
Adana
Aleppo
Tigris River
Teheran
Mt. Demavend 18,371
Meshed
Herat
HINDU KUSH
Kabul Peshawar
2
CYPRUS
SYRIA
Damascus
Euphrates R.
DASHT-I-KAVIR
PLATEAU OF IRAN
AFGHANISTAN
EDITERRANEAN SEA
LEB.
Beirut
Baghdad
ZAGROS MOUNTAINS
IRAN
DASHT-I-LUT
Kandahar
Helmand River
ISRAEL
Jerusalem
Amman
SYRIAN DESERT
IRAQ
Hamadan
30°
lexandria
Port Said
SUEZ CANAL
JORDAN
KUWAIT
Kuwait
Shiraz
PAKISTAN
Indus River
3
Cairo
NAFUD
DAHNA
PERSIAN GULF
BAHRAIN IS.
GYPT
(J.A.R.)
SAUDI
Aswan
QATAR
GULF
Sharjah
GULF OF OMAN
Karachi
ARABIAN
TRUCIAL OMAN
Muscat
TROPIC OF CANCER
ARABIAN SEA
RED
ARABIA
MUSCAT & OMAN
20°
Nile River
Wadi Halfa
NUBIAN DESERT
SEA
RUB AL-KHALI
A D E N
4
Omdurman
Khartoum
Atbara River
Massawa
Asmara
YEMEN
Sana
SOCOTRA
SUDAN
Blue Nile
Ras Dashan 15,157
GULF OF ADEN
Cape Guardafui
5 60° **E**
White Nile
FRENCH SOMALILAND
Djibouti
Berbera
NATIONAL CAPITAL
TUNDRA AND PERMANENT SNOW
ETHIOPIA
Diredawa
Addis Ababa
EVERGREEN NEEDLELEAF FOREST
MID-LATITUDE MIXED FOREST
MEDITERRANEAN SCRUB WOODLAND
5
UGANDA
KENYA
SOMALIA
Lake Rudolph
Mt. Kenya 17,040
Nairobi
Mogadishu
I N D I A N   O C E A N
PRAIRIE
STEPPE
DESERT
IRRIGATED DRY LAND
LAKE VICTORIA
EQUATOR
5
0°
RUANDA URUNDI
TROPICAL WOODLAND AND SAVANNA
TROPICAL FOREST
CULTIVATION
6
TANGANYIKA
Mt. Kilimanjaro 19,565
30°
B 40°

0   250   500   750   1000
Parabolic Equal-area Projection

C 50° **D**

İstanbul, Turkey — a modern metropolis touching two continents, Europe and Asia. It is divided by the Bosporus.

TURKEY:
ON THE EDGE OF EUROPE

More highly developed technologically than most her Middle Eastern neighbors, Turkey contains extremes of industrialized cities, such as İstanbul, a countryside where modern technology is alm unknown.

Women of a village in central Turkey labor under the hot sun preparing apricots for drying.

Dan Page

Raw sugar is poured into a hopper at the large Guánica mill, Ensenada, Puerto Rico. Later, it will be refined on the United States mainland.

CARIBBEAN
AND CENTRAL AMERICA

Sugar, coffee, bananas—the nations of the Caribbean and Central America depend on these export crops. The production of sugar in the Caribbean and coffee and bananas in Central America employs most of the region's labor force and accounts for almost all of its foreign trade.

Resort area east of Montego Bay, Jamaica, has sandy beaches, shallow bathing waters.

Hunting Survey Corp.—Annan

100°   Ⓐ   **95°**   Ⓑ   **90°**   Ⓒ   **85°**   Ⓓ   **35°**   80°

35°

U N I T E D   **S T A T E S**

Mississippi River

⓵

Mobile

Jacksonville

30°

Houston •

New Orleans •

San Antonio

• Galveston

Rio Grande

⓶

• Corpus Christi

Key West •

Florid

G U L F

• Brownsville

Havana ✦   C

25°

TROPIC OF CANCER   **O F**

M E X I C O

Yucatan Channel

I. OF PINES
(CUBA)

⓷

Tampico •

Mérida •

20°

Mexico City ✦

GULF
OF
CAMPECHE

Veracruz •

Puebla •

Belize ✦

M   • Orizaba
(Citlaltepetl)
18,696

**BRITISH
HONDURAS**

⓸

E   **X**   **I**   **C**   **O**

Usumacinta

Oaxaca •

GUATEMALA

HONDURAS

GULF
OF
TEHUANTEPEC

SIERRA MADRE

Tajumulco
13,814

Tegucigalpa ✦

15°

P A C I F I C

Guatemala
City ✦

San Salvador ✦

Matagalpa •

EL SALVADOR

NICARAGUA

Managua ✦   Lake

⓹

Nicaragua

COSTA

O C E A N

San José ✦
RICA   ✦ Chirripo
Grande
12,467

10°

© 1962 JEPPESEN & CO., DENVER, COLO., U.S.A.
ALL RIGHTS RESERVED

100°   Ⓐ   **95°**   Ⓑ   **90°**   Ⓒ   **85°**   D

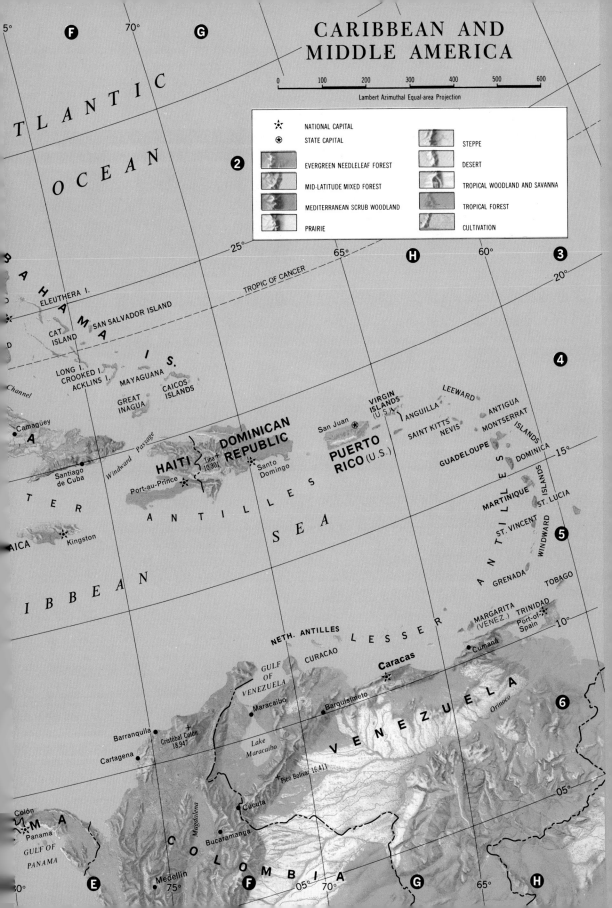

CARIBBEAN AND MIDDLE AMERICA

Lambert Azimuthal Equal-area Projection

NATIONAL CAPITAL
STATE CAPITAL
EVERGREEN NEEDLELEAF FOREST
MID-LATITUDE MIXED FOREST
MEDITERRANEAN SCRUB WOODLAND
PRAIRIE
STEPPE
DESERT
TROPICAL WOODLAND AND SAVANNA
TROPICAL FOREST
CULTIVATION

ATLANTIC OCEAN

BAHAMA IS.

ELEUTHERA I.
SAN SALVADOR ISLAND
CAT ISLAND
LONG I.
CROOKED I.
ACKLINS I.
MAYAGUANA
GREAT INAGUA
CAICOS ISLANDS

Channel

TROPIC OF CANCER

Camagüey

Santiago de Cuba

Windward Passage

HAITI
Port-au-Prince
Tiña 10,301

DOMINICAN REPUBLIC
Santo Domingo

San Juan
PUERTO RICO (U.S.)

VIRGIN ISLANDS (U.S.)
ANGUILLA
SAINT KITTS
NEVIS
LEEWARD
ANTIGUA
MONTSERRAT
GUADELOUPE
DOMINICA
ISLANDS

GREATER ANTILLES

AICA
Kingston

CARIBBEAN SEA

LESSER ANTILLES

MARTINIQUE
ST. LUCIA
ST. VINCENT
WINDWARD ISLANDS
GRENADA
TOBAGO

MARGARITA (VENEZ.)
TRINIDAD
Port-of-Spain
Cumaná

NETH. ANTILLES
CURAÇAO

GULF OF VENEZUELA
Caracas
Maracaibo
Barquisimeto
Orinoco

VENEZUELA

Barranquilla
Cartagena
Cristóbal Colón 18,947
Lake Maracaibo
Pico Bolívar 16,411

Cúcuta
Bucaramanga

COLOMBIA
Magdalena

Colón
PANAMA
Panama
GULF OF PANAMA

Medellín

CENTRAL AMERICA

The church of Santo Tomás, which dominates the market place of Chichicastenango, recalls the Spanish empire that once ruled the Caribbean and Central America. A trading center near Guatemala City, Chichicastenango has been the "capital" of the Quiché Indians for centuries. The Quiché, descendants of the ancient Mayas, work on nearby coffee plantations.

Dandalet—Shostal

INDEX TO MAP OF THE CARIBBEAN AND CENTRAL AMERICA

CANADA

Malak—Annan

Royal Canadian Mounted Police on parade. The scarlet jacket, symbol of courage, honesty, and justice since the organization of the force as the North West Mounted Police in 1873, is reserved for ceremonial occasions.

"FROM SEA TO SEA"

At one and the same time a constitutional monarchy, a democracy, a federation, and the oldest dominion of the Commonwealth of Nations, Canada is completely independent of British rule in the conduct of its affairs, domestic and foreign.

High on a promontory overlooking the Ottawa River at Ottawa, the federal Parliament buildings, center, Library, left, and memorial Peace Tower, right, with its 53-bell carillon dominate a predominantly level river-bottom area.

Malak—Annan

181

FROM THE WILDERNESS
NEWSPRINT FOR THE WORLD

The primarily coniferous "great northern" forest, extending from coast to coast, covers almost 40% of Canada. Most of the accessible timber is in British Columbia, Ontario, and Quebec. Western operations, which contribute more than half of the production, are year-round; but east of the Rockies cutting begins in August and continues until snowbound. The spring floods carry the logs downstream to the mills.

Logs pile up behind a restraining boom in the Manicouagan River in Quebec. A maneuverable batch has been cut out for towing downstream to a pulp mill.

A roll of pulp paper receives final inspection in an Ontario mill before being cut to shipping weights. Canada produces the raw material for 60% of the world's newsprint.

Malak—Annan

Hunting Survey Corp.—Annan

INDEX TO MAP OF CANADA

183

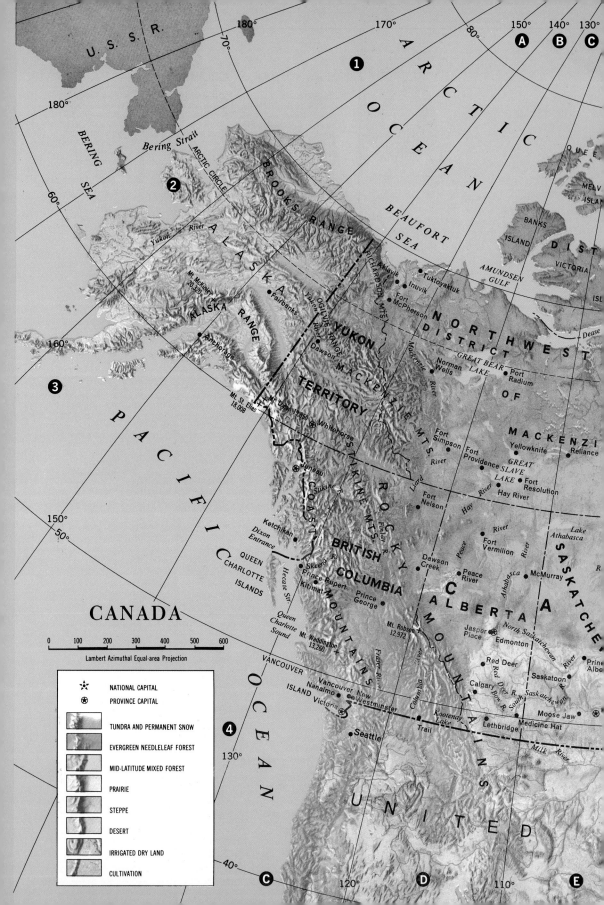

CANADA

Lambert Azimuthal Equal-area Projection

0 100 200 300 400 500 600

☆ NATIONAL CAPITAL

⊛ PROVINCE CAPITAL

TUNDRA AND PERMANENT SNOW

EVERGREEN NEEDLELEAF FOREST

MID-LATITUDE MIXED FOREST

PRAIRIE

STEPPE

DESERT

IRRIGATED DRY LAND

CULTIVATION

GREENLAND

ICELAND

H J K

70° 60° 50° 80° 30° 20° 20°

①

ELLESMERE
ISLAND

Thule

BAFFIN

BAY

②

ARCTIC CIRCLE 60°

VON ISLAND

SLANDS

Davis

F

Godthaab

BAFFIN ISLAND

ISLAND

DON ISLAND

GULF
OF
BOOTHIA

FRANKLIN

ORIES

RITORIES

DISTRICT

MELVILLE
PENIN.

FOXE

Strait

Cape Farewell 40°

③

FOXE
BASIN

Frobisher
Bay

Hudson Strait

O C E A N

50°

Chesterfield
Inlet

SOUTHAMPTON
ISLAND

Foxe
Channel

Hudson

Strait

Cape Chidley

TORNGAT MTS.

UNGAVA

KEEWATIN

HUDSON

UNGAVA
PENINSULA

BAY

George

Hebron

Nain

LABRADOR

NEWFOUNDLAND

Eskimo
Point

Leaf River

River

Hopedale

Michikamau
Lake

L. Melville

Churchill

BAY

Great Whale R.

Schefferville

Hamilton R.

Goose
Bay

50°

River Port Nelson

Fort
George

A

Moisie

LAURENTIANS

Sept-Iles

Strait of Belle Isle

Corner
Brook

Gander

St. John's

OBA

Severn River

JAMES

Eastmain River

Manicouagan

ANTICOSTI
ISLAND

GULF OF
ST. LAWRENCE

Cabot Str.

Glace Bay ST. PIERRE

④

D

Albany River

Fort
Albany

BAY

Rupert
House

Lake
Mistassini

QUEBEC

Gaspe

PRINCE
EDWARD
ISLAND

Sydney CAPE BRETON MIQUELON
ISLAND (FR.)

ONTARIO

Moosonee

Nottaway R.

Abitibi R.

Lake
St. John
Jonquière
Chicoutimi

Saguenay R.

Charlottetown

NEW
BRUNSWICK

Fredericton Moncton

Dartmouth

Boniface

Lake
Nipigon

Rouyn

La Tuque

Shawinigan Falls
Trois-Rivières
Joliette

Quebec

Lévis

Thetford Mines

St. John

NOVA
SCOTIA

Halifax

Lake of
the Woods

LAKE SUPERIOR

Sault
Ste. Marie Sudbury

Ottawa
River

St. Hyacinthe

St. Lawrence R.

Bay of Fundy

MANITOULIN
IS.

North
Bay

Montréal

Sherbrooke

Yarmouth Cape
Sable

LAKE HURON

Georgian
Bay

Ottawa

Cornwall

40°

Minneapolis

Owen Sound
Peterborough
Toronto
Kitchener
Hamilton
Sarnia
Windsor London

Belleville

Kingston

L. ONTARIO

St. Catharines

Buffalo

Boston

60°

LAKE MICHIGAN

ATES

Detroit

LAKE ERIE

Cleveland

ATLANTIC

© 1962 JEPPESEN & CO., DENVER, COLO., U.S.A.
ALL RIGHTS RESERVED

F 90° **G** 80° **H** 70° **J**

BIG COUNTRY
BIG FUTURE

The second-largest country in the world, Canada combines vast and varied natural resources with an energetic population.

An oil refinery at Montreal, Quebec, symbolizes Canada's industrial growth. Crude petroleum is the most valuable of Canada's mineral fuel resources, which also include natural gas and coal.
Malak—Annan

The Sault Ste. Marie locks, in Ontario and Michig overcome a 22-ft. difference in level between la Huron and Superior. This is the easternmost lif the mighty St. Lawrence-Great Lakes waterway.

Truck farms supply rapidly expanding urban markets as well as a booming canning industry in Ontario and Quebec. Almost two-thirds of Canada's population is concentrated in these two provinces.

187

CANADA'S CITIES AND INDUSTRIAL POTENTIAL

In recent years Canada has experienced a great incre[ase] in urban population, most of it occurring around the ci[ties] and giving rise to widespread metropolitan areas suc[h as] Greater Montreal and Greater Toronto. At the same ti[me] industry has overtaken agriculture as the leading e[co]nomic activity, with the greatest concentration (ab[out] 80%) located in the Great Lakes-St. Lawrence lowla[nds] in southern Ontario and Quebec.

View of downtown Montreal, Quebec, as seen from Mount Royal, with the St. Lawrence River visible beyond the skyscrapers.

Donald T. Sanders

Potline of an aluminum reduction plant at Kitimat, British Columbia. This is one of many industries attracted to the area by the availability of cheap and dependable electric power.

Annan Photo Fea[tures]

Quebec Separatism:
Canada Faces a Crisis

By BLAIR FRASER

. . . tensions between English- and French-speaking Canada may disrupt that country's federal system

SEPARATISM in Quebec means two different things. It is a political movement and a public mood. The movement has been a failure. The mood, however, has been felt in almost every aspect of life in Quebec. This mood is still gaining in strength. It is now recognized as a threat to the present structure and even the existence of Canada as a united federal state.

Outright separatists want the French-speaking province of Quebec to become an independent country. They hope to accomplish this by peaceful means if possible, by outright rebellion if necessary. These extremists are the ones who make up the organized separatist movement. They are still few in number. Much more numerous and much more dangerous are the Quebeckers who say "I'm not a separatist, but. . . ." What they often seem to mean is "I'm not a separatist *yet,* but I'm becoming one." They are to be found in all political parties in Quebec. They are among the rank and file as well as the leadership. These separatists are pushing Quebec into a general policy of withdrawal from all-Canadian projects and plans. This trend may have very grave effects on Canada's capacity for national decision.

However, neither the mood nor the political movement is truly represented by the occasional outbreaks of violence. In 1963, homemade bombs were placed in mailboxes and other places by members of the Quebec Liberation Front (FLQ). One man was killed and another maimed for life. Some of the guilty terrorists were caught and jailed.

Early in 1964, young men of another terrorist group, the Army of Quebec Liberation (ALQ), raided some armories of the militia in Quebec. They stole large quantities of arms and ammunition. Soon afterward there were many bank robberies in Quebec towns.

For a time it seemed that the ALQ might really be a considerable force. Then, in early April 1964, Quebec police captured some half dozen youths after a $5,000 holdup in a rural bank. They had with them some of the weapons stolen from the militia armories. More of the weapons were found in a cache near the home of one of the youths. One of the boys turned out to be the younger brother of a lad now in prison for his part in the 1963 bombings. Police were cautious about claiming to have wiped out the ALQ. They still had not found all the stolen weapons nor all the young conspirators. But at least they were strengthened in their belief that the so-called Army of Quebec Liberation is not an army, hardly even a gang. The police believe that the ALQ consists almost entirely of the few dozen young lawless individuals who actually carried out the raids and the robberies. There is no evidence, so far, that they represent anyone except themselves.

189

No doubt this made it easier for the government to defy, or rather ignore, certain threats against Queen Elizabeth II when it was announced that she would visit Quebec and other parts of Canada in the autumn of 1964. All three authorities concerned—Ottawa, Quebec and Buckingham Palace—agreed that Her Majesty and her ministers should not be intimidated by this kind of bluster. Only the memory of Dallas in November 1963, when a single unsuspected madman was able to kill President Kennedy, caused any misgiving about this decision. At any rate, the security precautions for the Queen were very strict. They were probably out of all proportion to the true seriousness of the threats.

The most widely publicized of these threats came from Dr. Marcel Chaput. This French-Canadian scientist had given up his job with the Federal Government to found a separatist party in Quebec a few years ago. Speaking to the Young Men's Canadian Club in Toronto, Dr. Chaput said that if the Queen were to visit Canada again, "some of our own people are prepared to let her know, even brutally, that she is not welcome."

This statement raised two quite different storms, one in English and one in French Canada. English Canadians were outraged at the insulting threat to the Queen. French Canadians were outraged that anyone should have given Dr. Chaput a respectable platform, let alone paid attention to anything he said. They all called Dr. Chaput a discredited eccentric who speaks for nobody anymore except himself. He no longer leads the party he founded or any other group. Twice he had embarked upon "fasts unto death," Mahatma Gandhi style, as a means of raising money for his party. He announced that he would not eat until a certain amount had been raised by public donations. Neither time did he get the sum he had specified. But both times he broke his fast anyway. Since then, no separatist group has shown any desire to have Dr. Chaput as a leader or even a member. He

is now disclaimed by almost all separatists.

Of the separatist organizations that still exist, the most important is called the Assembly for National Independence (Rassemblement pour l'Indépendance Nationale, or RIN). Another separatist party is so secret that its leader is known only as Mr. X. Its name is known only to its members. This party communicates with the newspapers by anonymous messages. Whether or not it really has any members is also a secret. None of these separatist groups has any real political strength. It seems unlikely that they will ever amount to anything.

The serious aspect of Quebec separatism is not the political movement but the public mood. Quebec is in a mood to demand maximum control of its own affairs and minimum interference from the Federal Government. It also wants minimum collaboration with Ottawa on shared projects. Quebec wants the Canadian constitution

Canada Wide

The Assembly for National Independence (Rassemblement pour l'Indépendance Nationale), the most important of the separatist groups in Quebec, holds a demonstration on Victoria Day.

and public welfare. They involve a total contribution from the Federal treasury of nearly $1,000,000,000. At the conference, Quebec served notice that it wishes to withdraw from almost all of these joint projects. Instead Quebec wants an equivalent amount of tax money, which it will then decide for itself how to spend. These demands are within Quebec's constitutional rights. However, many Canadians fear that if Quebec continues to insist upon every provincial right being scrupulously observed, and eventually expanded, Canada will become a weak confederation of self-governing provinces rather than a strong and unified nation.

Many English Canadians admit that English Canada bears a large share of blame for this unhappy situation. Quebeckers have genuine grievances. French Canadians feel, with reason, that their language has never enjoyed the equality in Canada to which it is entitled. They also feel they have been the victims of economic discrimination and, in some cases, even exploitation by English-Canadian capital and management. They are also resentful because the nine English-speaking provinces have never given their French-speaking minorities the same fair treatment that Quebec has always given to its English-speaking minority. For example, in Quebec the English-speaking minority controls its own schools. But in the other provinces, the French-speaking minority does not have the right to control its own schools.

These grievances are real. Lately they have been recognized far more widely than ever before. Some of them are being redressed. Unfortunately, there is much reason to fear that the redress has come too late to ease the tensions that exist, and seem to be increasing, between Quebec and the rest of Canada.

rewritten to give more power, and more taxing authority, to the provincial governments and less to the national Government. Meanwhile Quebec is insisting on all the rights given to it under the British North America Act, 1867, which is Canada's constitution. This constitution gives a great deal of power to the provinces. In fact, it gives more power than most of the provinces now wish to exercise.

The separatist mood in Quebec has been developing for several years. It emerged most clearly at a Federal-provincial conference in Quebec City during the first week of April 1964. In recent years Federal and provincial governments have been sharing the costs of more than fifty types of joint programs. These programs fall mainly within provincial authority. But the poorer provinces cannot afford them without massive Federal assistance. The projects include highway construction, hospital insurance, various kinds of aid to education

E. Bradley Davis, DPI

Young and old, modern and old-fashioned—side by side on the Ginza, Japan's Fifth Avenue.

Japan's Twin Revolutions

By WALTER BRIGGS

...economic boom and female emancipation have transformed Japan

BEFORE World War II, Japan ranked only twelfth among the nations in industrial output. Today it ranks fourth. Only the United States, the Soviet Union and West Germany produce more goods than Japan.

In prewar days, Japanese women were among the most downtrodden in the world. The Japanese housewife was treated as though she were just a cleaning woman and a childbearer. She even had to walk behind her husband on the few occasions when he would consent to be seen out with her. Today she and her daughters have achieved a new status. Japanese women no longer think of themselves as inferior. Men can no longer treat the women as they have in the past. Still, Japanese women are not content. They are grasping for more rights.

Interestingly enough, these twin revolutions are related. The soaring economy has helped Japanese women gain their new position in life. And Japanese women have had a great deal to do with making the economy boom.

A visitor's first impression of Japan is likely to be gained as much by ear as by eye. Everywhere there are the sounds of building. The visitor becomes aware of new or nearly finished factories, houses, harbor facilities and highways. He sees new trains that rocket along at 125 miles an hour. Frequently he sees blue-gowned Shinto priests hurrying down the street. They are off to wave their sacred twigs in dedication of still another school. Japan has one of the highest literacy rates in the world.

Japan's economy has grown by almost 10 per cent a year since 1950. By comparison the United States and Russian growth rates have been wobbling between 2 and 6 per cent a year. Also, Japan's national income has tripled since 1953. Even after taking rising prices into account, wage earnings for Japanese workers increased by 15.2 per cent in 1961.

Japan has little iron ore and only limited reserves of poor-quality coking coal. Thus it must import these minerals for its industries. Yet its steel output has risen 655 per cent in the last 12 years. Steel production was expected to reach 36,000,-000 tons in 1964. This would threaten West Germany's position as the world's third-biggest steel producer.

Japanese shipbuilders raised their output 530 per cent in the same period. They turned out some 2,000,000 tons of shipping in 1963 to lead the world for the eighth straight year. This tonnage included some of the biggest ships ever built—tankers grossing more than 130,000 tons.

So it has gone, industry by industry. About 25 per cent of the profits from Japan's economic growth is put back into new industry. By comparison, only 15 per cent of profits is put back into industry in the United States. Still, much has gone to the Japanese worker.

For every 100 yen the Japanese worker received five years ago, his real wages are 150 yen today. His real income rose 5 per cent in 1963 to about $1,150. This is nearly as much as the average Italian worker earns. His savings crept close to $2,000. He took his family to the beach and nearby mountains on four weekends. Four out of every five Japanese families own a television set, making Japan second only to the United States in this respect.

There are almost no jobless Japanese. The big firms have scouts roaming the college campuses. Like American ball clubs, they sign up promising seniors even before graduation. They attract young women to the workbenches with offers of free flower-arranging and tea-ceremony lessons. In fact, 54 per cent of Japanese women 15 years of age or older have jobs. Two fifths of Japan's workers are women. One of every three doctors, teachers and professors is now a woman. But most

women work in the offices and factories. Few rise to high positions there, to be sure. Their salaries, despite a Labor Standard Law, lag behind men's. But they remain workers only four years on the average. In truth, their work is usually just a prelude to marriage.

No longer do many Japanese young women accept marriages arranged by their parents. They are not interested in young men who may have old-fashioned views about the male being superior to the female. Having a job of her own, the young Japanese worker can wait for the right man to come along. What is more, with the skills learned on the job, she knows she can always make a living. Thus she can leave the groom if he doesn't measure up to her standards.

So bad has become the lot of the Japanese male that more than half of the younger husbands questioned by a Tokyo magazine confessed that they "fear" their wives. Among 2,000 interviewed, four out of five admitted they hand over all of every paycheck to their wives. About 85 per cent said they shine their own shoes. And 75 per cent said they give their wives notice when planning to stay out after 10 P.M. How the mighty have fallen!

And Japanese women press ahead. In another poll, three out of every five women said they still felt so downtrodden they would rather have been born men. Many quoted a proverb out of Japan's feudal past: "The saddest thing in life is to be born a woman."

The freeing of the Japanese woman, which began twenty years ago right after World War II, is still being resisted by the male population. The battle of the sexes probably provides more material for Japan's publications, TV and movies than any other subject.

When a move was made to increase the number of holidays, Tokyo's powerful newspaper *Asahi Shimbun* wrote a humorous editorial in protest. Its housewife readers would "not welcome the idea of having hard-to-please creatures in the house all day," the newspaper said.

Premier Hayato Ikeda took his wife along on an official visit to the United States. This in itself is, something entirely new. After their return to Japan, he helped Madame Ikeda into his limousine. The entire nation was startled at TV shots of this.

The constitution of 1947 gave Japanese women the vote and promised equal education and "equal rights of husband and wife." Equality of the sexes included many new female rights involving divorce, child custody, family property and inheritance. Japanese women were delighted with these new privileges. Women elected 50 of their number to the first postwar Diet (parliament). Girls enrolled in universities from which they were formerly barred. Now one of every three students in higher-educational institutions is a woman.

There are currently 717 members of the two houses of the Diet. The number of female members has come down to 23. This is still a higher proportion than is in the United States Congress. In 1963, Madame Aki Fujiwara, a TV question-game panelist, was overwhelmingly elected to the Diet's upper house. She placed first in a field of 107 candidates for the 51 nationally elected seats in this house. Her 1,652,022 votes came to about 250,000 more than the closest male candidate's.

On the family front, women begin three out of every four divorce actions. This is remarkable when you consider that once a wife could not divorce a husband at all.

Yet Madame Fujiwara, ever the champion of female rights, asks indignantly, "Do you know the position of the divorced woman?" Twice divorced herself, the 64-year-old legislator knows what she is saying. "A woman who lives alone cannot rent an apartment in a municipally constructed building. . . . Did you know that there is nothing, just nothing, that a divorced woman can do to force her husband to pay alimony ordered by the

René Burri, Magnum

Japanese women have joined the men on the job. They account for 40 per cent of the work force.

courts?" Naturally, Madame Fujiwara means to do something about these grievances.

Everyday items cost very little in Japan. The typical housewife, who usually handles the family budget, pays about 5½ cents for streetcar fare, 40 cents for a dozen eggs, 45 cents for a first-run movie and $2.80 for a first-rate pair of high-heeled shoes. She is now able to serve meat, eggs and dairy products regularly. Before, rice was the only staple in Japan. As a result, her high-school daughter stands 3¼ inches taller than she, is an inch larger around the chest and has slimmer, unbowed legs.

Japan has always had "three divine treasures"—the imperial sword, jewel and mirror. These days the joke goes that each family dreams of its own "three divine treasures"—automobile, air conditioner and hi-fi set. Newly independent women have been buying many timesaving appliances for their homes. Vacuum cleaners, washing machines and self-timing rice cookers are now within reach of most families. This means that the housewife is freed from much boring housework.

The Japanese people want much the same things that most people want: higher incomes and a rising standard of living.

Farmers, in particular, have come a long way toward realizing these goals. In spite of its frequent typhoons, Japan has had eight straight years of bumper crops. Only one sixth of mountain-ribbed, Montana-sized Japan can be cultivated. Still, very concentrated methods of farming have achieved the "impossible." After years of depending on imported rice, Japan now provides enough rice for its people.

A new look has come to Japan's farm villages. The women no longer wear baggy, patched trousers. They are more likely to appear in the latest fashions from Tokyo. Electricity is available in the smallest towns. Village shops gleam with electric appliances. Two thirds of farm housewives have sewing machines.

Indeed Japan's farmers are no longer peasants, Japanese sociologists contend. They are now middle class. Another sign of the times is that the farm population is becoming smaller. Mechanization is reducing the need for farmhands, and daughters and second sons are flocking to city jobs. In 1945, half of Japan's population lived and worked on farms. Today only 30 per cent of the country's 96,000,-000 people are on farms. By 1970, this figure should be down to about 25 per cent.

The march to female freedom has been slower in the usually conservative villages and among the older urban generation. Still, a 72-year-old rural wife showed the new spirit by suing to end half a century of marriage. The reason? Her husband spent too much money on the town.

Dawdling in bars and teahouses after work is, in fact, a popular form of male revenge against women for taking over in the home. Eighty per cent of Japanese husbands "go home slowly," a poll showed.

President Takeshi Mitarai of the huge Canon Camera Company felt this practice probably slowed down workers. So he started the GHQ ("go home quickly") movement with loans for new houses and automobiles as encouragement. His male employees, while having nothing against these things, were amazed how eagerly their wives fell in with this scheme.

The Japanese woman's struggle has not been easy. Neither has Japan's economic recovery. Japan ended World War II with nearly half of its industry bombed out. Its empire was taken away. The nation had to depend only on what its home islands could provide. American aid saved the Japanese worker and his family from starvation and helped them get to their knees. The Korean war, which required large amounts of industrial equipment, helped get them back on their feet.

But much of the credit for Japan's remarkable comeback must go to the worker himself. The Japanese are a hardworking people and they are thrifty. They are not afraid of changes. Thus the business leaders were not confined to the old pattern of doing things when they started to rebuild Japan's economy. The very rapid growth of Japan's industry owes a great deal to their adventuresome attitude.

UPI
Chou En-lai

UPI
Hussein

Wide World
Nyerere

Wide Wor
Makarios

HEADS OF GOVERNMENT *

COUNTRY	NAME AND OFFICE	INSTALLED	COUNTRY	NAME AND OFFICE	INSTALLE[
Afghanistan	Mohammed Zaher Shah, king	1933	Dahomey	Sourou Migan Apithy, president	196
	Mohammed Yusuf, prime minister	1963	Denmark	Frederik IX, king	194;
Albania	Enver Hoxha, first secretary of the Al-			Jens Otto Krag, prime minister	196
	banian Labor (Communist) Party	1954	Dominican	J. Donald Reid Cabral, head of civilian	
	Haxhi Lleshi, chairman of the presidium	1953	Republic	directorate	196
	Mehmet Shehu, premier	1954	Ecuador	Ramon Castro Jijon, head of military	
Algeria	Ahmed ben Bella, premier and president	1963		junta	196;
Argentina	Arturo Illia, president	1963	El Salvador	Julio Adalberto Rivera, president	196;
Australia	Sir Robert Gordon Menzies, prime		Ethiopia	Haile Selassie I, emperor	193(
	minister	1949	Finland	Urho Kaleva Kekkonen, president	195(
Austria	Adolf Schärf, president	1957		Reinho Lehto, prime minister	196;
	Josef Klaus, chancellor	1964	France	Charles de Gaulle, president	195'
Belgium	Baudouin I, king	1951		Georges Pompidou, premier	196
	Théodore Lefèvre, prime minister	1961	Gabon	Leon M'Ba, president and prime	
Bolivia	René Barrientos Ortuna, president	1964		minister	196(
Brazil	Humberto Castelo Branco, president	1964	Germany, East	Walter Ulbricht, president	196(
Bulgaria	Georgi Traikov, president of the pre-			Willi Stoph, premier	196₄
	sidium	1964	Germany, West	Heinrich Lübke, president	195'
	Todor Zhivkov, premier	1962		Ludwig Erhard, chancellor	196;
Burma	Ne Win, prime minister and chairman		Ghana	Kwame Nkrumah, president	196(
	of the revolutionary council	1962	Great Britain	Elizabeth II, queen	195;
Burundi	Mwambutsa IV, king (mwami)	1962		Harold Wilson, prime minister	196₄
	Pierre Ngendandumwe, premier	1963	Greece	Constantine, king	196;
Cambodia	Prince Norodom Sihanouk, chief of			George Papandreou, premier	196;
	state	1960		George Athanassiades Novas, presi-	
	Prince Norodom Kantol, premier	1962		dent	196₄
Cameroun	Ahmadou Ahidjo, president	1960	Guatemala	Enrique Peralta Azurdia, chief of state	196;
	Charles Assale, premier	1960	Guinea	Sékou Touré, president	195₈
Canada	Lester B. Pearson, prime minister	1963	Haiti	François Duvalier, president	1957
Central African			Honduras	Osvaldo Lopez Arellano, chief of state	196;
Republic	David Dacko, president	1960	Hungary	Istvan Dobi, president of the presiden-	
Ceylon	Mme. Sirimavo Bandaranaike, prime			tial council	195.
	minister	1960		Janos Kadar, prime minister	196'
Chad	François Tombalbaye, president	1960	Iceland	Asgeir Asgeirsson, president	195;
Chile	Eduardo Frei Montalva, president	1964		Bjarni Benediktsson, prime minister	196;
China,	Chou En-lai, premier	1949	India	Sarvepalli Radhakrishnan, president	196;
Communist	Mao Tse-tung, chairman of the Commu-			Lal Bahadur Shastri, prime minister	196
	nist Party	1949	Indonesia	Dr. Sukarno, president (1949) and	
	Liu Shao-chi, chairman of the people's			prime minister	196;
	republic	1959	Iran	Mohammad Reza Pahlavi, shah	194'
China,	Chiang Kai-shek, president	1943		Hassan Ali Mansour, premier	196₄
Nationalist	Yen Chia-kan, premier	1963	Iraq	Abd al-Salam Arif, president	196;
Colombia	Guillermo Leon Valencia, president	1962		Taher Yahya, prime minister	196;
Congo	Alphonse Massamba-Debat, president	1963	Ireland	Eamon de Valera, president	195₉
(Brazzaville)	Pascal Lissouba, premier	1963		Sean F. Lemass, prime minister	195₉
Congo	Joseph Kasavubu, president	1960	Israel	Schneor Zalman Shazar, president	196;
(Léopoldville)	Moise Tshombe, premier	1964		Levi Eshkol, prime minister	196;
Costa Rica	Francisco Jose Orlich Bolmarcich, presi-		Italy		
	dent	1962		Aldo Moro, premier	196;
Cuba	Osvaldo Dorticos Torrado, president	1959	Ivory Coast	Felix Houphouet-Boigny, president and	
	Fidel Castro, premier	1959		premier	196(
Cyprus	Archbishop Makarios III, president	1960	Jamaica	Sir Alexander Bustamente, prime minister	196;
Czechoslovakia	Antonin Novotny, president	1957	Japan	Hirohito, emperor	192(
	Josef Lenart, premier	1963		Eisaku Sato, prime minister	1964

* As of December 21, 1964

	UPI		UPI		Wide World		UPI
Shastri		**Wilson**		**Johnson**		**Frei**	

COUNTRY	NAME AND OFFICE	INSTALLED	COUNTRY	NAME AND OFFICE	INSTALLED
..rdan	Hussein I, king	1952	Poland (cont.)	Edward Ochab, chairman of the council of state	1964
	Bahjat Abdul Khadr Talhouni, prime minister	1964		Jozef Cyrankiewicz, premier	1954
..nya	Jomo Kenyatta, president	1964	Portugal	A. D. Rodrigues Tomas, president	1958
..rea, North	Kim Il Sung, premier	1948		Antonio de Oliveira Salazar, premier	1932
..rea, South	Chung Hee Park, president	1963	Rumania	Gheorghe Gheorghui-Dej, president of the state council	1961
	Choi Doo Sun, prime minister	1963			
..wait	Abdullah al-Salim al-Sabah, sheik	1950	Rwanda	Gregoire Kayibanda, president and premier	1962
..os	Savang Vatthana, king	1959			
	Souvanna Phouma, premier	1962	Saudi Arabia	Faisal ibn Abdul Aziz, prime minister (1962) and king	1964
..banon	Charles Helou, president	1964			
	Rashid Karami, prime minister	1961	Senegal	Leopold Senghor, president	1960
..eria	William V. S. Tubman, president	1943		Mamadou Dia, premier	1960
..ya	Mohammed Idris et Senussi, king	1951	Siérra Leone	Albert N. Margai, prime minister	1964
	Mahmud Muntasser, premier	1964	Somali Republic	Aden Abdulla Osman, president	1960
..chtenstein	Franz Josef II, prince	1938		Abdirizak Haji Hussein, prime minister	1960
	Gerard Batliner, head of government	1962	South Africa	Charles R. Swart, president	1961
..xembourg	Jean, prince	1964		Hendrik F. Verwoerd, prime minister	1958
	Pierre Werner, prime minister	1959	Spain	Francisco Franco, chief of state	1939
..alagasy Rep.	Philibert Tsiranana, president	1960	Sudan	Sir-el-Khatim el-Khalifa, prime minister	1964
..alawi	H. Kamazu Banda, prime minister	1964	Sweden	Gustaf VI, king	1950
..alaysia	Putra Ibni Al-Marhum Syed Hassan Jamalullail, king	1963		Tage Erlander, prime minister	1946
	Tunku Abdul Rahman, prime minister	1963	Switzerland	Willy Spühler, president	1963
..ali	Mobido Keita, president and premier	1960	Syria	Amin el-Hafez, president and premier	1963
..auritania	Moktar Ould Daddah, president and premier	1960	Tanzania	Julius Nyerere, president	1964
			Thailand	Bhumibol Adulyadej, king	1950
..exico	Gustavo Diaz Ordaz, president	1964		Thancm Kittikachorn, prime minister	1963
..onaco	Ranier III, prince	1949	Togo	Nicolas Grunitzky, president	1963
	Jean Raymond, minister of state	1963	Trinidad and		
..ongolia	Yumzhagin Tsedenbal, premier	1952	Tobago	Eric Williams, prime minister	1962
	Zhamsarangin Sambu, president of the presidium	1950	Tunisia	Habib Bourguiba, president	1957
			Turkey	Cemal Gursel, president	1962
..orocco	Hassan II, king	1961		Ismet Inonu, prime minister	1961
	Ahmed Bahnini, premier	1963	Uganda	Mutesa II, president	1963
..epal	Mahendra Bir Bikram Shah Deva, king	1955		Milton Obote, prime minister	1962
	Tulsi Giri, prime minister	1963	U.S.S.R.	Leonid Brezhnev, Communist Party first secretary	1964
..etherlands	Juliana, queen	1948			
	Victor Marijnen, prime minister	1963		Aleksei Kosygin, premier	1964
..ew Zealand	Keith J. Holyoake, prime minister	1960		Anastas I. Mikoyan, president of the presidium	1964
..icaragua	Rene Schick Gutierrez, president	1963			
..iger	Hamani Diori, president and premier	1960	United Arab	Gamal Abdel Nasser, president	1958
..igeria	Nnamdi Azikiwe, president	1963	Republic	Ali Sabry, premier	1962
	Sir Abubakar Balewa	1960	United States	Lyndon B. Johnson, president	1963
..orway	Olav V, king	1957	Upper Volta	Maurice Yameogo, president and premier	1960
	Einar Gerhardsen, prime minister	1955			
..akistan	Mohammad Ayub Khan, president	1958	Uruguay	Luis Giannattasio, president	1964
..anama	Marco A. Robles, president	1964	Vatican City	Paul VI, pope	1963
..araguay	Alfredo Stroessner, president	1954	Venezuela	Raul Leoni, president	1963
..eru	Fèrnando Belaunde Terry, president	1963	Vietnam, North	Ho Chi Minh, president	1945
..ilippines	Diosdado Macapagal, president	1961	Vietnam, South	Phan Khac Suu, head of state	1964
..oland	Wladyslaw Gomulka, first secretary of the Polish United Worker's (Communist) Party	1956		Tran Van Huong, premier	1964
			Yemen	Abdullah al-Salal, president	1962
			Yugoslavia	Josip Broz Tito, president	1953
			Zambia	Kenneth D. Kaunda, prime minister	1964

197

SPORTS

In the name of all competitors I swear that we will take part in these Olympic Games, respecting and abiding by the rules which govern them, in the true spirit of sportsmanship, for the glory of sport and the honor of our team.

Olympic Oath

U.S. runner Bob Hayes (right) dashes across the finish line in 10 seconds to win the gold medal for the men's 100-meter dash.

Summer Olympics

By HARVEY GINSBERG

SOME 5,500 athletes from 94 nations competed in 20 different sports in the 1964 Olympics, held in Tokyo. This XVIII Olympiad was particularly successful for the United States team, which gained the most victories, 36, and for Russia, which won the most total medals—for first, second and third place—96.

Beyond doubt the outstanding group of athletes was the swimming team from the United States. They captured 16 of the 22 swimming events and set 11 world records in the process. Pacing the United States swimmers was Don Schollander. He tied an Olympic record by winning four gold medals, the most ever received by any swimmer in Olympic competition. Schollander was a member of the 400- and 800-meter relay teams that set new world records with times of 3:33.2 and 7:52.1 respectively. He also set a new world record of 4:12.2 in the 400-meter freestyle and an Olympic record in the 100-meter freestyle. Right behind Schollander came Steve Clark and

15-year-old Sharon Stouder of the women's team, who picked up three gold medals each. Credit for the most courageous swimming performance went to Dick Roth, also of the United States. Ignoring an attack of appendicitis, he rose from bed to set a world mark of 4:45.4 in taking the 400-meter individual medley.

Almost as impressive was the United States' showing in the track-and-field competition. In the men's contests Americans won 12 of the 24 events. Some of the victories were not unexpected, including those of Hayes Jones in the 110-meter high hurdles, Bob Hayes in the 100-meter and Henry Carr in the 200-meter race, Dallas Long in the shot put, Fred Hansen in the pole vault, and Rex Cawley in the 400-meter hurdles. Bob Schul's win in the 5,000-meter run made him the first United States athlete to take this event. Another

Ethiopia's Abebe Bikila hits the tape in a precedent-breaking running victory.

In the Olympic open judo competition Anton Geesink, representing the Netherlands, triumphed over his Japanese opponent to win a gold medal.

United States Olympic first was achieved by Marine Lieutenant Billy Mills. He became the only person from his country ever to win the 10,000-meter run. Mills' victory was one of the major upsets of the Tokyo games. Other upsets were scored by Willi Holdorf of Germany in the decathlon, Mike Larrabee of the United States in the 400-meter race, and Lynn Davies of Great Britain in the broad jump. For the ninth time in ten meetings, Valeri Brumel of Russia defeated the United States' John Thomas in the high jump. Neither jumper could do better than 7'1¾". But Brumel was judged the victor when he missed fewer tries.

Abebe Bikila of Ethiopia, who captured the hearts of Rome as well as the Olympic marathon in 1960 when he raced barefoot, shod himself in 1964 to earn the distinc- tion of being the only man to win the marathon twice. And Peter Snell of New Zealand chalked up his own double by winning both the 800- and 1,500-meter runs. Two track and field competitors who, in very different ways, exemplified the spirit and pride of the Olympic games were Al Oerter of the United States and Ranatunge Karunananda of Ceylon. Oerter, suffering from internal bleeding and torn muscles as a result of a training injury, took his third gold medal in the discus throw despite overwhelming pain. Karunananda, lapped four times in the 10,000-meter run, gamely finished the race all alone on an otherwise deserted track.

Another fine example of the Olympic amateur spirit was the accomplishment of the Vesper Boat Club of Philadelphia, the United States representative in the 2,000-

meter race for eight-oared shells. The Vesper crew was a pickup team that was forced to train at odd hours. They were given almost no chance of making the Olympics. Fourth seeded in the trials, they upset previously undefeated Harvard in the semifinals. They repeated their victory over the Eastern Champions in the finals. This earned them the right to go to Tokyo, thereby becoming the first club team to be the United States Olympic entry since 1904. The Vespers were considered sure to lose to the defending champions, the Ratzeburg eight from Germany. But once again they confounded the experts by crossing the finish line 1¼ lengths ahead of the favorites.

An amazing record was kept untarnished by the United States basketball team. Never since the sport had become part of the Olympics in 1936 had the United States entry been defeated or failed to win the championship. 1964 proved no exception. Meeting the Soviet Union five in the finals, the United States, after trailing early in the game, came back to win with little trouble, 73–59.

As the Olympics drew to a close, almost everyone agreed that at no time in history had a more spectacular group of athletes ever been assembled in one place. In all, 22 world records were broken by gold-medal winners alone. The official ending

to the games came with these appropriate words of address from Avery Brundage, president of the International Olympic Committee: "I call upon the youth of all countries to assemble four years from now at Mexico City, there to celebrate with us the games of the XIX Olympiad. May they display cheerfulness and concord so that the Olympic torch will be carried on with ever-greater eagerness, courage and honor for the good of humanity through the ages."

OLYMPIC MEDALS

FINAL STANDINGS

	Gold (1st)	Silver (2nd)	Bronze (3rd)	Total
United States	36	26	28	90
Soviet Union	30	31	35	96
Japan	16	5	8	29
Germany	10	22	18	50
Italy	10	10	7	27
Hungary	10	7	5	22
Poland	7	6	10	23
Australia	6	2	10	18
Czechoslovakia	5	6	3	14
Britain	4	12	2	18
Bulgaria	3	5	2	10
Finland	3	0	2	5
New Zealand	3	0	2	5
Rumania	2	4	6	12
Netherlands	2	4	4	10
Turkey	2	3	1	6
Sweden	2	2	4	8
Denmark	2	1	3	6
Yugoslavia	2	1	2	5
Belgium	2	0	1	3
France	1	8	6	15
Canada	1	2	1	4
Switzerland	1	2	1	4
Ethiopia	1	0	0	1
Bahamas	1	0	0	1
India	1	0	0	1
South Korea	0	2	1	3
Trinidad-Tobago	0	1	2	3
Tunisia	0	1	1	2
Cuba	0	1	0	1
Argentina	0	1	0	1
Pakistan	0	1	0	1
Philippines	0	1	0	1
Iran	0	0	2	2
Ireland	0	0	1	1
Kenya	0	0	1	1
Mexico	0	0	1	1
Brazil	0	0	1	1
Ghana	0	0	1	1
Nigeria	0	0	1	1
Uruguay	0	0	1	1
Total	163	167	174	504

France's Joseph Gonzales lost the light-middleweight event to Russian Boris Lagutin (in white).

PIX

Winter Olympics

By JIM BECKER

THE 1964 Winter Olympic Games were held at Innsbruck, Austria, from January 29 to February 9, 1964. These games ran into trouble long before the 1,100 athletes from 37 countries arrived for the opening ceremonies. There was no snow. Thousands of Austrian soldiers brought in snow by the truckload from valleys as far away as Germany on the other side of the mountain ranges. They packed it on the barren slopes by hand. When they were finished, the ski trails snaked through trees and rocks like silver rivers. The trails were fast—and dangerous.

Then, a week before the games started, a 58-year-old British tobogganist named Kazimierz Kay-Skrzypeski hurtled down the course on his tiny sled and flew off a curve into a grove of trees. He died in a hospital 24 hours later.

Three days after this, Ross Milne, a 19-year-old Australian skier, flew off the man-made path of the downhill ski run. He skidded on bare rocks and grass and crashed head on into a tree. He was killed instantly. These were the first deaths to overshadow the Winter Games since a bobsledder was killed in 1932.

Accidents continued to plague practice sessions. A German tobogganist was seriously hurt. Then French, Czech and Greek skiers suffered injuries. Safety gates were installed on the runs, but a feeling of tragedy dampened final preparations.

These games were the ninth to be held since the first ones in 1924. When they were over, the Soviet Union had won the most medals. It has done so ever since it first entered the Winter Games in 1956.

The United States managed to stave off its worst-ever finish only through some last-minute heroics.

The Russians won a total of 25 medals in the 34 events. They received 11 gold medals, 8 silver and 6 bronze. The host Austrian team was runner-up to the Russians, with 4 golds, 5 silvers and 3 bronzes. Five countries won 3 gold medals each. They were Norway, Finland, France, a combined East-West German team and Sweden. The United States was eighth in the unofficial scoring table, with 1 gold medal, 2 silvers and 3 bronzes.

Impressive as it was, the Soviet performance was nonetheless lopsided. Women won 15½ of the 25 medals (the half was for figure-skating pairs). And 9 of these medals came in women's speed skating alone. This is a sport indulged in by about 2,500,000 Russians, nearly every living Scandinavian, about 250 Americans, and no Latins at all.

Mrs. Lidiya Skoblikova, a young schoolteacher from Siberia, won 4 gold medals in speed skating. She was the first person ever to win 4 golds at the Winter Games. However, some observers were catty enough to point out that the 4 races involved—500, 1,000, 1,500, and 3,000 meters—were so much alike that the feat was somewhat akin to winning the 70-, 80-, 90- and 100-yard dashes at a track meet.

Another rugged young lady from Russia, Mrs. Claudia Boyarskikh, won both of the women's cross-country ski races. She also anchored the winning ski relay team. That made seven gold medals be-

...opening ceremonies of the IX Winter Olympics. Athletes from 37 nations take the Olympic oath.

Donald Moss for ''Sports Illustrated''© 1964 Time Inc.

More than 1,000 athletes competed in the 1964 Winter Olympics held at Innsbruck, Austria, against the majestic backdrop of the Austrian Alps.

PATSCHERKOFEL

Men's Downhill

Olympic Village

Ice Arena

Bobsled Run

Toboggan Run

NOCKSPITZE

Speed-Skating Oval

NNSBRUCK

Special Jump Bergisel Stadium

IGLS

MUTTERS

BIRGITZKOPFL

Men's Giant Slalom

Men's Slalom

Ladies' Slalom

LIZUM

An Olympic jumper sails through the air, his body almost parallel to his skis.

"Life" magazine © 1964 Time Inc.

Russian speed-skating champion Mrs. Lidiya Skoblikova won gold medals in the 500-, 1,000-, 1,500- and 3,000-meter races.

James Drake

tween the two Soviet women. The Soviet Union's other gold medals came in hockey, men's speed skating and men's cross-country skiing.

The only gold medal to be won by the United States also came in speed skating. Terry McDermott, a 23-year-old barber from Essexville, Michigan, won it in the 500-meter event. His victory was the first for the United States in a race since 1952. McDermott was promptly invited to tour Scandinavia, where his skating would have been more properly appreciated than in the United States. But his newlywed wife suggested he come home to Michigan right after the races, and he did. McDermott received a telegram of congratulations from President Johnson and appeared on television. Within a week, however, he was back behind the third chair in his uncle's barbershop in Bay City.

Jean Saubert, a husky 21-year-old college girl from Oregon State University, won two skiing medals for the United States. The girl with the urchin haircut and shy smile took a silver medal in the giant slalom and a bronze in the slalom. Miss Saubert led all the skiers but the Goitschel sisters from France.

Christine Goitschel, at 19 the elder sister by a year, won the slalom. Her sister Marielle came in second. As the event progressed, Marielle was the only one left in the field with a chance to beat Christine's time. In the end, she was content to come down the hill just fast enough to finish second. "I wasn't going to break my leg to beat my own sister," she said. It was Marielle's turn in the giant slalom. She won the event with a time of 1:52.24, compared to 1:53.11 for Christine. Miss Saubert also was timed in 1:53.11, so the two girls each got a silver medal for second.

Jean Saubert's performance had been anticipated, since American girls frequently had done very well in the slalom. But American men had never won a medal of any kind in Olympic skiing. This year, however, they were expected to win. Their coach, Bob Beattie, told everyone who would listen that his young men were as good as the veteran European skiers. He also made a very public fight for good starting times. He wanted his team to ski before the snow was too badly chopped up. He got good times, but at first they did not seem to help. In the first Alpine skiing event—the downhill—the best American finish was 14th. In the giant slalom, Billy Kidd of Stowe, Vermont, managed a seventh place. But seventh was far from the promised placings.

There was only the slalom left. And then, on the next-to-last day of action, the breakthrough came. The world's greatest skiers flashed down the two runs of the slalom. Josef Stiegler of Austria was the winner, but Kidd was second and Jimmy Heuga of Tahoe City, California, third.

The names of the two 20-year-old Americans went up on the Olympic scoreboard in medal-winning positions in men's skiing. It had never happened before. Kidd wrapped his arms around Heuga at the finish line, pointed up at the big board and shouted:

"Do you see that, Jimmy? Do you see that? That's us up there."

The team celebrated for several hours. It may have been the first time that victory-conscious Americans ever found cause for so much rejoicing over anything other than a first-place finish.

Another major cause of United States cheering came when Scott Allen of Smoke Rise, New Jersey, won the bronze medal in men's figure skating. The victory came two days before his 15th birthday. He became the youngest medal winner in Winter Olympics history.

United States teams have done better, and they have done worse, in the Olympics. For example, in 1960, when the games were at Squaw Valley, California, the United States won three gold medals. However, the one that came in hockey was widely regarded as a freak. The other two were in figure skating. A few months later the entire American figure-skating team died in an airplane crash. Scott Allen is a member of the fresh young crop of skaters that hopefully will restore American supremacy in this field.

Despite the problems and accidents that took place before the games began, the games themselves were free of serious injuries. Crowds were large and enthusiastic. The organizers announced that a total of 936,000 people watched the various events. Some of these events were held a dozen miles from the city at sites that could be reached only by narrow mountain roads. At times the traffic jams stretched almost to the Brenner Pass, 18 miles away. Police had a great deal of trouble untangling the mess.

OLYMPIC MEDALS
FINAL STANDINGS

	Gold (1st)	Silver (2d)	Bronze (3d)
Soviet Union	11	8	6
Austria	4	5	3
Norway	3	6	6
Finland	3	4	3
France	3	4	0
Germany	3	3	3
Sweden	3	3	1
United States	1	2	3
Netherlands	1	1	0
Canada	1	0	2
Britain	1	0	0
Italy	0	1	3
North Korea	0	1	0
Czechoslovakia	0	0	1

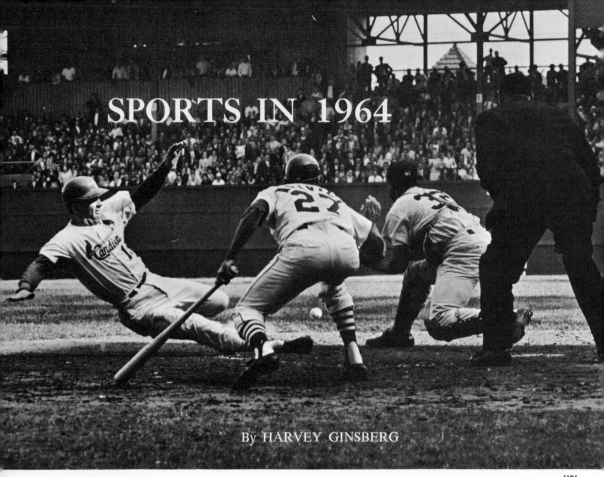

SPORTS IN 1964

By HARVEY GINSBERG

Cardinal Tim McCarver skids across home plate during a 4th-inning double steal in the final game of the New York-St. Louis World Series.

BASEBALL

IN late August 1964 the New York Yankees, playing for the first time under the managership of Yogi Berra, were in third place, 6 games out of first. Hank Bauer's Baltimore Orioles and Al Lopez' Chicago White Sox were engaged in a dogfight for the top spot. Over in the National League, the Philadelphia Phillies enjoyed a 6½-game lead with two weeks of play left.

But it was the Yankees and the Cards who met in the World Series. The New Yorkers came to life in September. They surged past Chicago and Baltimore to beat out the White Sox by one game. The Phillies, with the flag seemingly wrapped up, had a 10-game losing streak. The Cincinnati Reds took over first place with

only a week to go. The Reds, however, gave up the top spot two days later to the Cards, who were managed by Johnny Keane. On the last day of the season, Cincinnati and St. Louis were tied for first. The Phils were one game back. St. Louis beat the New York Mets 11–5 while the Reds were losing to the Phillies 10–0. Thus the Cards, who had been 7½ games behind with only 15 games left, clinched first.

In the World Series, the Yanks and the Cards battled it out to the full seven games before St. Louis finally won. The Cards took the opener 9–5 behind the pitching of Ray Sadecki. The Yanks, with rookie Mel Stottlemyre on the mound, bounced back for an 8–3 victory in the second game. After that, home runs proved decisive.

1964 WORLD-SERIES RESULTS

GAME	R.	H.	E.	BATTERIES
1. NEW YORK	5	12	2	FORD, Downing (6), Sheldon (8), Mikkelsen (8) and Howard
ST. LOUIS	9	12	0	SADECKI, Schultz (7) and McCarver
2. NEW YORK	8	12	0	STOTTLEMYRE and Howard
ST. LOUIS	3	7	0	GIBSON, Schultz (9), G. Richardson (9), Craig (9) and McCarver
3. ST. LOUIS	1	6	0	Simmons, SCHULTZ (9) and McCarver
NEW YORK	2	5	2	BOUTON and Howard
4. ST. LOUIS	4	6	1	Sadecki, CRAIG (1), Taylor (6) and McCarver
NEW YORK	3	6	1	DOWNING, Mikkelsen (7) and Howard
5. ST. LOUIS	5	10	1	GIBSON and McCarver
NEW YORK	2	6	2	Stottlemyre, Reniff (8), MIKKELSEN (8) and Howard
6. NEW YORK	8	10	0	BOUTON, Hamilton (9) and Howard
ST. LOUIS	3	10	1	SIMMONS, Taylor (7), Schultz (8), Richardson (8), Humphreys (9) and McCarver
7. NEW YORK	5	9	2	STOTTLEMYRE, Downing (5), Sheldon (5), Hamilton (7), Mikkelsen (8) and Howard
ST. LOUIS	7	10	1	GIBSON and McCarver

MAJOR-LEAGUE STANDINGS

AMERICAN LEAGUE

	WON	LOST	P.C.	GAMES BEHIND
NEW YORK	99	63	.611	
CHICAGO	98	64	.605	1
BALTIMORE	97	65	.599	2
DETROIT	85	77	.525	14
LOS ANGELES	82	80	.506	17
CLEVELAND	79	83	.488	20
MINNESOTA	79	83	.488	20
BOSTON	72	90	.444	27
WASHINGTON	62	100	.383	37
KANSAS CITY	57	105	.352	42

NATIONAL LEAGUE

	WON	LOST	P.C.	GAMES BEHIND
ST. LOUIS	93	69	.574	
CINCINNATI	92	70	.568	1
PHILADELPHIA	92	70	.568	1
SAN FRANCISCO	90	72	.556	3
MILWAUKEE	88	74	.543	5
LOS ANGELES	80	82	.494	13
PITTSBURGH	80	82	.494	13
CHICAGO	76	86	.469	17
HOUSTON	66	96	.407	27
NEW YORK	53	109	.327	40

MAJOR-LEAGUE LEADERS

AMERICAN LEAGUE

BATTERS	A.B.	R.	H.	P.C.
Oliva, Minnesota	672	109	217	.323
B. Robinson, Baltimore	612	82	194	.317
Howard, New York	550	63	172	.313
Mantle, New York	465	91	141	.303
Robinson, Chicago	525	83	158	.301
Freehan, Detroit	520	69	156	.300
Bressoud, Boston	566	86	166	.293
Kaline, Detroit	525	77	154	.293
Yastrzemski, Boston	567	78	164	.289
Mantilla, Boston	425	69	123	.289

NATIONAL LEAGUE

BATTERS	A.B.	R.	H.	P.C.
Clemente, Pittsburgh	622	95	211	.339
Carty, Milwaukee	455	72	150	.330
Aaron, Milwaukee	570	103	187	.328
Torre, Milwaukee	601	87	193	.321
Allen, Philadelphia	632	125	201	.318
Brock, St. Louis	634	111	200	.315
Santo, Chicago	592	94	185	.313
Williams, Chicago	645	100	201	.312
Flood, St. Louis	679	97	211	.311
Robinson, Cincinnati	568	103	174	.306

AMERICAN LEAGUE

RUNS BATTED IN		HOME RUNS	
B. Robinson, Baltimore	118	Killebrew, Minnesota	49
Stuart, Boston	114	Powell, Baltimore	39
Mantle, New York	111	Mantle, New York	35
Killebrew, Minnesota	111	Colavito, Kansas City	34
Colavito, Kansas City	102	Stuart, Boston	33

NATIONAL LEAGUE

RUNS BATTED IN		HOME RUNS	
Boyer, St. Louis	119	Mays, San Francisco	47
Santo, Chicago	114	Williams, Chicago	33
Mays, San Francisco	111	Callison, Philadelphia	31
Torre, Milwaukee	109	Cepeda, San Francisco	31
Callison, Philadelphia	104	Hart, San Francisco	31

SPORTS

Mickey Mantle hit a towering blast into the right-field stands in the bottom of the ninth to give New York a 2–1 win in the third game. On the next day, St. Louis third baseman Ken Boyer hit a grand-slam home run in the sixth inning to account for all the Cardinal's runs. They beat the Yankees 4–3.

Even more dramatic was the homer of Cards' catcher Tim McCarver. This one came with two men on in the top of the tenth inning of the fifth game, which St. Louis won 5–2. Home runs by Roger Maris and Mickey Mantle and a grand slammer by Joe Pepitone accounted for six of New York's eight runs in the sixth game as Jim Bouton recorded an 8–3 win for his second Series victory.

Starting with only two days rest, pitchers Bob Gibson and Mel Stottlemyre faced each other for the third time in the seventh game. Five home runs were hit by the two teams. But the real turning point in the Cards' 7–5 victory came as a result of Yankee errors in the fourth inning when St. Louis broke up a scoreless game by putting across three runs.

Several records were broken or tied during the Series. Mantle had entered the Series tied with Babe Ruth at 15 for the most home runs in Series play. His three homers set a new record of 18. Mantle also tied Yogi Berra's mark of 39 runs batted in in Series play and broke Berra's old mark of 41 runs scored. Bobby Richardson, Yankee second baseman, got 13 hits, a new high for a single Series. Two Cardinals also got into the record books. Gibson's 31 strikeouts were a Series high. And Carl Warwick's three pinch hits tied the old mark.

A strange ending to an unusual season came when, within a week after the end of the Series, both pennant-winning managers were out of their jobs. Berra was relieved of his post by Yankee brass. Keane resigned from the Cards and signed to manage the Yanks in 1965. He became the first pilot to leave a winning World

Series team to join the club he defeated.

The National League, after having won only 4 of the first 16 All-Star games, finally drew even with the American League by scoring its seventeenth victory in the midseason classic. Trailing 4–3 going into the bottom of the ninth, the Nationals put across four runs to win 7–4. Honors were divided between Willie Mays of the San Francisco Giants and Philadelphia Phillie outfielder John Callison. Mays' lead-off walk and brilliant baserunning were responsible for the tying run. Callison's two-out homer with two runners on base provided the margin of victory. Phillie Jim Bunning hurled two scoreless innings to become the first player to pitch

212

The Constellation races ahead of the Sovereign in the America's Cup Race.

for both leagues in All-Star competition. The winning pitcher was Juan Marichal of the Giants. Red Sox relief ace Dick Radatz was the loser.

During the year Jim Bunning was traded from the Detroit Tigers to the Phillies. Thus when he pitched a 6–0 no-hitter against the New York Mets he became the first modern-day player to toss a perfect game in both leagues. The victory made him the first Senior Circuit hurler and the eighth in either league ever to pitch a perfect game. Sandy Koufax of the Dodgers shut out the Phillies 3–0 and allowed only one man to reach base (by means of a walk) in tying Bob Feller's major-league record of three no-hit games.

The hard-luck loss of the year went to Ken Johnson of the Houston Colts. He pitched a no-hit game of his own but was defeated 1–0 when an unearned run was scored against him in the ninth inning.

BOATING

The big news in the world of boating was the rather easy triumph of the United States yacht *Constellation* over the British challenger *Sovereign* in the 113-year-old America's Cup. The *Constellation,* skippered by Bob Bavier, Jr., swept four consecutive races.

In the 58th Newport-Bermuda Race, Milton Ernstof's *Burgoo,* one of the small-

213

est boats entered, finished the 635-mile contest almost 20 hours behind the scratch boat *Stormvogel* but won by 30 minutes on corrected time.

The United States captured three titles and shared a fourth at the Henley Regatta in England. Seymour Cromwell became the first American since 1949 to take the Diamond Sculls. The Eliot-House Crew of Harvard won the Thames Cup. And Washington-Lee High of Virginia won the Princess Elizabeth Cup for schoolboy eights. John Roche Kiely of Florida paired with John Lecky of Canada for a two-length victory in the Silver Goblets for pairs. The big race of the regatta, the Grand Challenge Cup, went to a Lithuanian crew representing the Soviet Union.

At home, the University of California became the Intercollegiate Rowing champions by registering a 1¾-length victory over the University of Washington.

RACING

With a record average of 147.35 mph, A. J. Foyt crossed the finish line first in the 48th running of the Indianapolis 500. A second-lap accident involving seven cars caused the death of two drivers.

TRACK AND FIELD

During the 1964 indoor season, American or world records were tied or broken in every standard running event except the 1,000-yard race and the two-mile run. Tom O'Hara ran the mile in 3:56.4. Hayes Jones ran the 50- and 60-yard high hurdles in 0:05.9 and 0:06.8. Wendell Mottley finished the 440- and 600-yard races in 0:48 and 1:09.2. And Bob Hayes sprinted 60 yards in 0:05.9. The NCAA indoor championships were divided into two regional meets. The University of Oregon won in the Western Division. Maryland State took Eastern honors. Oregon also won the NCAA outdoor tourney. Another double victor was Villanova,

which took both the indoor and outdoor IC4A competition. The Southern California Striders won the AAU outdoor meet; the New York Athletic Club won the AAU indoor championship. Several world records were established in the field events, including a toss of 67' 10" by Dallas Long in the shot put and a pole vault of 17' 4" by Fred Hansen. In November, Peter Snell ran the mile in a record 3:54.1. And in December, Ron Clarke ran 3 miles in a record time of 13:07.6.

SWIMMING

Never before did so many people swim so fast over so many different distances using so many different strokes as they did in 1964. During just a single five-month period (exclusive of the Olympics), 26 world records were set. United States swimmers set 17 of them. In most sports age and experience are invaluable. But swimming offered teen-agers great opportunity for fame in 1964. Among those not yet twenty who set world records for men were Kevin Berry and Ian O'Brien of Australia in the 200-meter butterfly and the 110-yard breaststroke respectively. Dick Roth of the United States set a record in the 400-meter individual medley. Don Schollander set records in the 200- and 400-meter freestyle. Equally impressive was the performance of the girls under twenty. Many of them also set world records. These included United States stars Donna de Varona in the 400-meter individual medley; Sharon Stouder in the 100- and 200-meter butterfly; Cathy Ferguson in the 200-meter backstroke; and 13-year-old Patty Caretto in the 800- and 1,500-meter freestyle.

The West Coast dominated the major American swimming meets. The Santa Clara Swim Club won the men's AAU outdoor and the women's AAU outdoor and indoor championships. The University of Southern California won the men's AAU indoor title and the NCAA crown.

Cassius Clay, new heavyweight champion, after his victory over Sonny Liston.

BOXING

The most ballyhooed boxing match of the year was between Cassius Clay and Sonny Liston. Clay, the challenger, was given little, if any, chance to lift the world heavyweight championship from the massive titleholder. An 8-1 underdog when he went into the ring, Clay pulled one of the greatest upsets in the history of boxing. He led all the way and then scored a technical knockout when Liston was unable to answer the bell for the 7th round because of a dislocated shoulder. Their scheduled November rematch was postponed just three days before the bout when Clay was rushed to the hospital for an emergency hernia operation.

In his two title defenses during the year, light-heavyweight-champion Willie Pastrano TKO'd Gregorio Peralta in 6 rounds and Terry Downes in 11 rounds. Lightweight-titleholder Carlos Ortiz and welterweight-king Emile Griffith also defended their respective crowns twice during the year. Neither was defeated. Ortiz won a unanimous 15-round decision over Kenny Lane and a 14th-round TKO over Flash Elorde. Griffith eked out a 15-round split decision over his old rival Luis Rodriguez and outpointed Brian Curvis.

Sugar Ramos had a far more hectic year. It started off normally enough when he kept his featherweight title with a 6th-round TKO of Mitsunori Seki. However, it ended in disappointment when fellow Mexican Vicente Saldivar dethroned him with a 12th-round TKO. The real hoopla came in between these two matches, when Ramos went to Ghana for the first championship bout ever held in that country. Pitted against him was Ghanian Floyd Robertson. Even though he was knocked down twice, Ramos was awarded the decision. The verdict so enraged the Ghana Boxing Authority that they reversed it and declared Robertson the victor. Their action left Ramos the world featherweight champion except in Ghana, and Robertson the world featherweight champion of Ghana.

Pone Kingpetch regained the flyweight championship from Hiroyuki Ebihara. And in December, in the first defense of his middleweight title, Joey Giardello outpointed challenger Rubin Carter.

Kenny Washington of UCLA outjumps Jeff Mullins of Duke. The Bruins were the top team of 1964, ending the season with a 26-0 record.

BASKETBALL

TWO teams dominated basketball in 1964. On the collegiate level it was the Bruins of UCLA. In professional basketball it was the Boston Celtics. The Bruins finished the season with a 26-0 record. It was the first time since 1961 that a major college team won every game in a season. In 1961 Ohio State had a perfect season. But the Bruins went the Buckeyes one better. They won all their postseason games as well.

The major conference winners, with their conference records, were: UCLA (13-0) in the Big Six, Princeton (12-2) in the Ivy League, Kentucky (11-3) in the Southeastern Conference, Duke (14-1) in the Atlantic Coast Conference, Davidson (9-2) in the Southern Conference, Kansas State (11-2) in the Big Eight, Wichita (11-2) in the Missouri Valley, and Texas A. & M. (13-1) in the Southwest.

The nation's top-ten teams, according to the Associated Press poll, were (season's records are given): UCLA (26-0), Michigan (20-4), Duke (23-4), Kentucky (21-4), Wichita (22-5), Oregon State (25-3), Villanova (22-3), Chicago Loyola (20-5), De Paul (21-3) and Davidson (22-4).

The all-American team, named by the National Association of College Basketball Coaches, included Gary Bradds of Ohio State, Walt Hazzard of UCLA, Dave Stallworth of Wichita, Cotton Nash of Kentucky and Bill Bradley of Princeton. Bradds was named Player of the Year.

Taking their place beside UCLA's NCAA champions were other winners of postseason tournaments. The Bradley Braves beat New Mexico 86-54 in the National Invitation Tournament finals. Rockhurst defeated Pan American in the NAIA.

And Evansville defeated Akron 72-59 for its third NCAA small-college championship in the past eight years.

The Boston Celtics have been longtime rulers of the National Basketball Association. In 1964 they earned the right to call themselves the Team of the Century. They defeated the San Francisco Warriors 4 games to 1 for their sixth NBA crown in a row.

During regular season play, the two finalists led their divisions. The Celtics finished in the East with a 59-21 record. The Warriors captured first place in the West with a 48-32 year.

Oscar Robertson of the Cincinnati Royals was named the Association's Most Valuable Player by the widest margin in the history of the balloting. Alex Hannum of the San Francisco Warriors received the UPI's Coach of the Year Award. Wilt Chamberlain, also of the Warriors, was the Association's top scorer for the fifth straight year. He scored 2,948 points for a per-game average of 36.9.

HOCKEY

THE 1964 hockey season was highlighted by the first-place finish of the Montreal Canadien team. Coach Hector (Toe) Blake was named Coach of the Year for guiding the Canadiens to the top. For the Chicago Black Hawks, 1964 was the second year in a row in which they missed first place by only one point.

FINAL NHL STANDINGS

	W	L	T	Pts.	GF	GA
Montreal	36	21	13	85	209	167
Chicago	36	22	12	84	218	169
Toronto	33	25	12	78	192	172
Detroit	30	29	11	71	191	204
New York	22	38	10	54	186	242
Boston	18	40	12	48	170	212

The Toronto Maple Leafs won the Stanley Cup for the third time in a row. This made them the first team in NHL history to win it three times in a row on two different occasions. The Maple Leafs took the cup by defeating the Detroit Red Wings 4 games to 3. The Toronto team won a 4-0 victory in the seventh and deciding game.

Two Red Wing stars established enviable league records. Goalie Terry Sawchuck, playing his 11th NHL season, gained his 95th shutout. This topped George Hainsworth's old mark. Sawchuck also set another record for goalies by playing in his 804th regular-season game. His teammate Gordie Howe scored his 545th goal. This beat Maurice Richard's record for goals scored during total years of play. Andy Bathgate of the Toronto Maple Leafs made 58 assists. This matched the previous all-time high of Jean Beliveau of the Canadiens. Bathgate had been traded to the Toronto team by the New York Rangers toward the end of the season.

Beliveau came in for his share of honors by winning the Hart Trophy as Most Valuable Player. He got 102 out of 180 possible points in the voting. Beliveau had previously won the Hart Trophy in 1956. Other Canadiens also received awards. Goalie Charlie Hodge won the Vezina Trophy. This is given to the goalie who allows the fewest goals during the regular season. Hodge allowed only 151 goals and had 8 shutouts in 62 games played. Jacques Laperriere won the Calder Trophy as Rookie of the Year. Remaining honors were divided among three members of the Chicago Black Hawks. Stan Mikita edged teammate Bobby Hull by two points, 89 to 87, for the Art Ross Trophy. This award is given to the league's leading scorer. Mikita made 39 goals and 50 assists. However, Hull's 43 goals were high for the league. Meanwhile, Ken Wharram became the first Black Hawk in 19 years to win the Lady Byng Memorial Trophy. This award is given to the player best combining good sportsmanship and outstanding play. Wharram scored 71 points and served only 18 penalty minutes. For the second year in a row, Pierre Pilote of Chicago received the James Norris Trophy. This award is given to the best defenseman.

GOLF

Some of the most emotion-filled moments in the history of golf took place on the final day of the U.S. Open championship. Ken Venturi was six strokes behind leader Tommy Jacobs going into the final 36 holes of play. Then Venturi scored a 66 and a 70 to win with a 72-hole total of 278. His victory marked one of the greatest comebacks in sports annals.

Only slightly less dramatic was the triumph of Bobby Nichols in the PGA championship. Nichols started off with a PGA record round of 64 and went on to chalk up a final score of 271.

Arnold Palmer set a record by becoming the first player to win the Masters golf title four times. After ending the first day of play in a five-way tie for the lead, Palmer finished six strokes ahead of Jack Nicklaus and Dave Marr, with a 276.

Tony Lema took the fourth part of golfing's Grand Slam by winning the British Open championship. He won by five strokes with a 279. In a play-off with Venturi, Nichols and Palmer in the $75,000 World Series of Golf, Lema won with a 36-hole total of 138.

In the Canada Cup International Tournament, Palmer and Nicklaus teamed to give the U.S. its fifth straight win.

Bill Campbell defeated Ed Tutwiler to win the U.S. amateur golf championship. However, Campbell and his teammates finished a disappointing fourth in the world amateur-golf-team championship. They ended 13 strokes behind the winning British entry.

Mickey Wright racked up an unprecedented fourth U.S. Women's Open championship. One of the few tournaments Miss Wright lost all year was the Ladies' PGA championship in which Mary Mills, with a 278, won by two strokes.

On the ladies' amateur circuit, Barbara McIntire took her second U.S. women's amateur crown. In amateur-team competition, United States women batted .500.

They won their last three singles matches to retain the Curtis Cup with 10½ points to England's 7½. But they lost the first Women's World Amateur Team championship to France by one stroke.

HORSE RACING

Ridden by Bill Hartack, Northern Dancer held off a strong closing threat by the favored Hill Rise to win the 90th Kentucky Derby by a neck in the record time

Bill Hartack rides Northern Dancer to victory in the 90th Kentucky Derby.

of two minutes flat. For Hartack, the triumph was his fourth in six Derby tries. Northern Dancer was the first Canadian-bred horse to win the Derby.

With Hartack again in the saddle, Northern Dancer scored a far easier victory in the 88th Pimlico Preakness. He finished 2¼ lengths in front of The Scoundrel. Although racing's Triple Crown was now within reach, Northern Dancer just could not come through over the longer distance in the 96th running of the Bel-

mont Stakes. He finished third, six lengths behind Quadrangle, ridden by Manuel Ycaza. Returning to Canada, Northern Dancer delighted the welcoming crowd by breezing to a 7½-length victory in the running of the Queen's Plate at Toronto.

In 1964, Kelso, Horse of the Year from 1960 to 1963, and Gun Bow carried on what amounted to a personal feud. Seven-year-old Kelso suffered a 12-length defeat at the hands of Gun Bow in the Brooklyn Handicap. At this point he was thought by many to be too old to be taken seriously. Then, in what was probably the most popular victory of the racing season, he beat Gun Bow in the Aqueduct Stakes. The two horses then met for a third time, in the Woodward Stakes. Gun Bow was judged the winner by a hair.

In October, Kelso won the Jockey Club Gold Cup at Aqueduct to become the greatest money-maker in racing history. He then beat Gun Bow again in the Washington, D.C., International and clinched Horse of the Year honors for 1964.

In England, Team Spirit, ridden by Willie Robinson, came from behind in the last 100 yards to become the first American-owned horse to win the Grand National Steeplechase since 1938. In the English Derby, Santa Claus earned a record $201,787 by winning the event.

In the Hambletonian for three-year-old trotters, Ayres, driven by John Simpson, Sr., registered straight-heat victories in times of 1:56⅘, which was a Hambletonian record, and 1:58⅕ for the mile.

TENNIS

Australia regained top place in the world of tennis during 1964. And Australian Roy Emerson established himself as the best amateur player. Only a loss to Nicola Pietrangeli of Italy in the semifinals of the French championships stopped him from scoring a Grand Slam. Emerson met and defeated his countryman Fred Stolle in the Australian singles, at Wimbledon and at Forest Hills. As for Pietrangeli in the French finals, he was aced 23 times by winner Manuel Santana of Spain.

Emerson was most responsible for the return of the Davis Cup to Australia. He won his singles matches against both Chuck McKinley and Dennis Ralston, who were defending the trophy for the United States. Earlier, McKinley had teamed with Ralston to defeat Emerson and Stolle in doubles. McKinley had also downed Stolle in their singles match. Stolle defeated Ralston in what was probably the most exciting match of the competition.

McKinley and Ralston won the U. S. doubles championships at Brookline, Massachusetts. Billie Jean Moffitt and Mrs. Karen Hantze Susman upset Margaret Smith and Lesley Turner of Australia in the women's finals. That Misses Smith and Turner had been undefeated in 48 straight matches going into the finals at Brookline is some indication of the size of the upset. En route, they had captured the French and Italian doubles titles. And they had defeated Miss Moffitt and Mrs. Susman for the Wimbledon crown.

Emerson and fellow-Australian Ken Fletcher appeared in the finals of the other three major men's doubles championships. They beat Tony Roche and John Newcombe for the French title but lost to Stolle and Bob Hewitt in the Australian finals and at Wimbledon.

In women's singles, Miss Smith and Maria Bueno of Brazil divided honors. At the Wimbledon finals, Miss Bueno spoiled Miss Smith's bid for a Grand Slam, thus avenging her defeat at the hands of Miss Smith in the French championships. Earlier, Miss Smith had taken her fifth Australian singles crown in a row by defeating Miss Turner. In the ladies' finals at Forest Hills, Miss Bueno defeated Mrs. Carole Caldwell Graebner in 25 minutes of play.

Nancy Richey and Billie Jean Moffitt helped the United States gain its fourth Wightman Cup victory in a row. They racked up two triumphs apiece as the United States defeated England 5–2 in match play. The United States did not fare so well in its defense of the world women's team championship. It lost 2–1 to Australia in the finals.

The iron-man feat of the year was turned in by Chuck McKinley. He played 184 games of tennis in 24 hours in the United States National Indoor competition, where he beat defending champion Dennis Ralston in the singles finals.

FOOTBALL

Notre Dame's bid for a perfect season was spoiled in its final game when it was upset 20-17 by the Trojans of Southern California. But 1964 will still be remembered as the year that the Irish once again became a collegiate-football power. In his first year as coach, Ara Parseghian took essentially the same team that had won only two games in 1963 and almost turned it into a national champion. Led by quarterback John Huarte (winner of the Heisman Trophy), Notre Dame climbed to the top of the rankings after its sixth victory in a row. It remained there until the upset.

The final ratings in both the AP and UPI polls were identical (season records in parentheses): Alabama (10-0-0), Arkansas (10-0-0), Notre Dame (9-1-0), Michigan (8-1-0), Texas (9-1-0), Nebraska (9-1-0), Louisiana State (7-2-1), Oregon State (8-2-0), Ohio State (7-2-0), and Southern California (7-3-0). Princeton was the only major team besides Alabama and Arkansas to be undefeated and untied at the end of its schedule.

Conference champions included Michigan in the Big Ten; Oregon State and Southern California (tie) in the Pacific Athletic; Arkansas in the Southwest; Nebraska in the Big Eight; Utah, New Mexico and Arizona (tie) in the Western Athletic; Alabama in the Southeastern; Princeton in the Ivy; West Virginia in the Southern; and North Carolina in the Atlantic Coast.

Army ended five years of Navy dominance by turning back the Middies 11-8 in their annual clash at Philadelphia.

In professional football, the Baltimore Colts won the Western Division championship of the National Football League. The Cleveland Browns won in the Eastern Division. Cleveland triumphed in the NFL title game. In the American Football League the San Diego Chargers took Western honors, while the Buffalo Bills won in the East. Buffalo downed San Diego 20-7 in the AFL title game.

UPI

Florida's Larry Dupree picks up two yards before being downed by Alabama's Dan Kearly (76) and Creed Gilmer.

NATIONAL FOOTBALL LEAGUE

FINAL STANDING OF CLUBS

Eastern Conference

	W.	L.	T.	PC.	Points For	Agst.
Cleveland	10	3	1	.769	415	293
St. Louis	9	3	2	.750	357	331
Philadelphia	6	8	0	.429	312	313
Washington	6	8	0	.429	307	305
Dallas	5	8	1	.385	250	289
Pittsburgh	5	9	0	.357	253	315
New York	2	10	2	.167	241	399

Western Conference

	W.	L.	T.	PC.	Points For	Agst.
Baltimore	12	2	0	.857	428	225
Green Bay	8	5	1	.615	342	245
Minnesota	8	5	1	.615	355	296
Detroit	7	5	2	.583	280	260
Los Angeles	5	7	2	.417	283	339
Chicago	5	9	0	.357	260	379
San Francisco	4	10	0	.286	236	330

AMERICAN FOOTBALL LEAGUE

FINAL STANDING OF CLUBS

Eastern Division

	W.	L.	T.	PC.	Points For	Agst.
Buffalo	12	2	0	.857	400	242
Boston	10	3	1	.769	365	297
New York	5	8	1	.385	278	315
Houston	4	10	0	.286	310	355

Western Division

	W.	L.	T.	PC.	Points For	Agst.
San Diego	8	5	1	.615	341	300
Kansas City	7	7	0	.500	366	306
Oakland	5	7	2	.417	303	350
Denver	2	11	1	.154	240	438

THE ARTS

Art is not a handicraft, it is the transmission of feeling the artist has experienced....
Leo Tolstoy

G. Schirmer, Inc.

Wide World

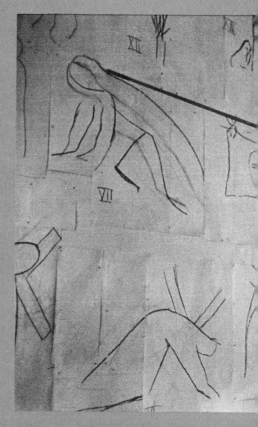

Wayne J. Shilkret, Hurok Inc.

Fundamental Photographs

Robert Capa, Magnum

Warner Bros.

Jewelry through the Ages

JEWELRY—in one form or another—has been around since the Old Stone Age. Even before he learned to work with metals, the caveman decorated himself with whatever he found handy. He put fishbones through his nose. And he dangled bits of wood or iron from his ears. His bracelets and necklaces were made from strings of teeth, pebbles or shells. Even animal hair was used in primitive jewelry.

As people's tastes and their ideas of beauty changed, jewelry also changed. And as metals and gems were discovered, new forms of jewelry were created. By Babylonian times, jewelry making had become a craft that required great skill. And in ancient Egypt, jewelry was considered an important part of the costume. Religious themes often appear in Egyptian jewelry. Gold and silver were widely used.

With the conquests of Alexander the Great (356-323 B.C.), precious stones became available to the Greeks. These were soon widely used by them, and later by the Romans, for their jewelry. The Greeks worked a great deal in enamel and filigree (metal shaped into lacy openwork).

Enamel and detailed designs are characteristic of Byzantine jewelry too. Like Byzantine art, Byzantine jewelry showed the influence of the Orient. The technique of cloisonné enameling was often used. In cloisonné work, a design is made and outlined with strips of metal. These strips are then set on edge and joined to a flat metal base. The compartments formed by the strips, or *cloisons,* are filled with colored enamels. The result looks somewhat like a tiny stained-glass window.

During the Dark Ages (fifth-ninth centuries) the barbarians of northern Europe patterned their jewelry after animals and beasts. The more civilized south of Europe produced jewelry with filigree gold designs, cloisonné garnet work and cabochon (unfaceted) gems. In the seventh century, Christian elements began to appear in designs.

During the early part of the Middle Ages, jewels were scarce. Very few were worn. By the early fourteenth century, however, precious stones were again being obtained from the East. Many noblemen began to wear thickly jeweled robes and gloves.

During the Renaissance, even the greatest of artists, such as Dürer in Germany and Botticelli, Ghiberti and Cellini in Italy, designed jewelry. The wearing of jewels became a sign of high rank. As a result, for a time only certain people were allowed by law to wear jewelry.

By the late fifteenth century, elaborate gem cutting had become a factor for the first time in the art of jewelry making. Many of the same techniques and designs used in the sculpture, painting and architecture of the period were also used, in small scale, in the jewelry being made. In fact, since Italian artists of the time were often first trained as goldsmiths, jewelry often tended to be miniature gold sculpture. In the seventeenth century, the emphasis in European jewelry shifted from enameled gold to gems.

The eighteenth-century passion for light and lightness produced lighter jewelry designs. Pieces that featured sparkling gems to glitter by candlelight were also popular. In the last decade of the nineteenth century, some jewelry was mass-produced. This lowered the standard of jewelry making as an art. Only a few artists, such as Peter Carl Faberge, still hand-made beautiful jewelry.

The twentieth century, too, has produced its own distinctive jewelry. It is an age of synthetics and alloys and of simple design. Not surprisingly, modern jewelry tends to be very plain. And it is often made of metals such as platinum, aluminum and palladium.

JEWELRY

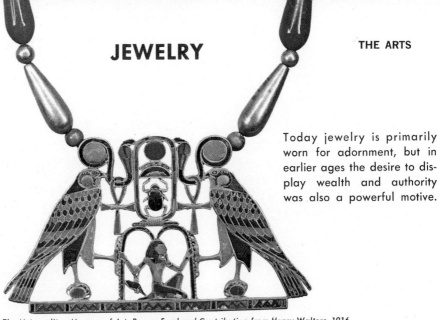

Today jewelry is primarily worn for adornment, but in earlier ages the desire to display wealth and authority was also a powerful motive.

Courtesy, The Metropolitan Museum of Art, Rogers Fund and Contribution from Henry Walters, 1916
Egyptian gold pectoral, inlaid with lapis lazuli, turquoise, garnet, and carnelian, belonged to a 12th Dynasty princess.

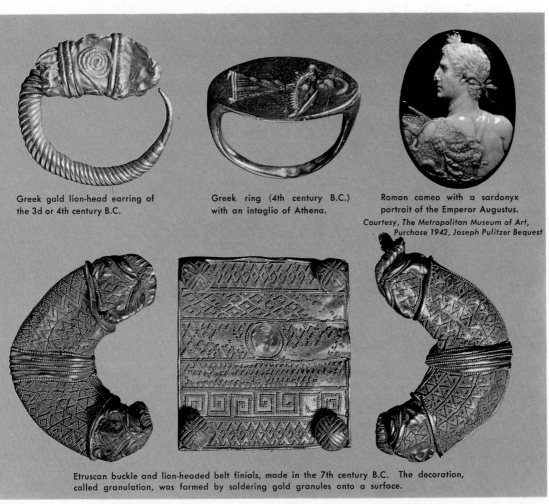

Greek gold lion-head earring of the 3d or 4th century B.C.

Greek ring (4th century B.C.) with an intaglio of Athena.

Roman cameo with a sardonyx portrait of the Emperor Augustus.
Courtesy, The Metropolitan Museum of Art, Purchase 1942, Joseph Pulitzer Bequest

Etruscan buckle and lion-headed belt finials, made in the 7th century B.C. The decoration, called granulation, was formed by soldering gold granules onto a surface.

Unless otherwise indicated, all photos are from Melvin Gutman Loan Collection of Ancient and Medieval Gold, Allen Memorial Art Museum, Oberlin College, Ohio—A. E. Princehorn

Byzantine ring (c.11th century) with cloisonné enamel of Christ.

Medieval gold ring (12th century) is set with a large cabochon, or unfaceted, stone.

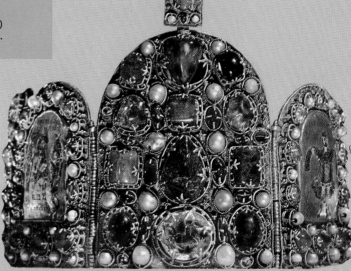

T. Moore—Shostal
The Old German Imperial crown, made about 960 for the Holy Roman Emperor Otto the Great. The band consists of eight gold plates, four ornamented with cabochon emeralds and sapphires set in filigree and four bearing enameled scenes. A cross and band are mounted on the central plate.

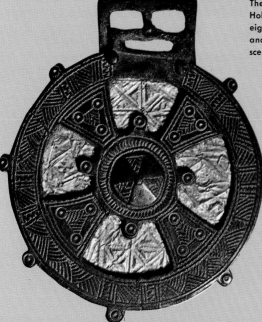

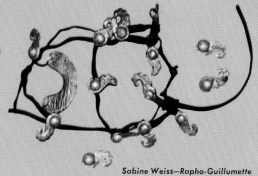

Sabine Weiss—Rapho-Guillumette
Bridle trappings of the Scythians. These pre-Christian nomads used simple schematized forms, many based on animals, as did the Visigoths and other semicivilized peoples of the Dark Ages.

Bronze chatelaine with gold underlay, made c.450-550 A.D., is an example of Visigothic workmanship.

...enaissance Italian 15th-century endant showing an Annunciation.

German 16th-century pendant in the form of the Lamb of God (Agnus Dei).

French 16th-century pelican pendant. The bird's body is a baroque pearl.

Neoclassic topaz mourning ring (18th or 19th century) with intaglio scene of a woman contemplating a funerary urn.

...enaissance gold necklace adorned with pearls, pre-...ous stones, and enamel, made in Eastern Europe in the ...te 16th century.

227

Necklace, comb, and earrings of gold and amethyst, from a parure made c.1820 and said to have belonged to one of the Bonaparte family.

Despite the widespread use of costume jewelry, the art of making personal ornaments with precious stones and metals continues to attract many skilled craftsmen. Design trends of the 20th century show both traditional and modern influences.

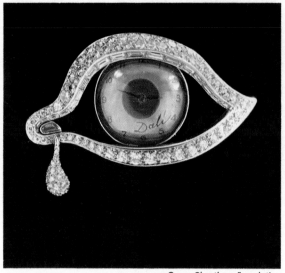

Owen Cheatham Foundation

"The Eye of Time," an imaginative timepiece of enamel with diamonds and a ruby, designed by Salvador Dali.

Glen C. Leach—Sho

Hope Diamond (Smithsonian Institution, Washington), a 44.5-c blue gem, is believed to have once belonged to Louis XIV of Fran

Robert Doisneau—Rapho-Guillumette

The influence of modern sculpture is reflected in a gold clip of a bird with a diamond for a head, designed by the French artist Georges Braque.

Courtesy, Art in Americ

Owl with sapphire eyes, diamond feathers, an shell body, designed by Rudolph von Rippe

Young People's Books

By CLAUDIA LEWIS

Reproductions of Eastern art enhance "The Moment of Wonder," Richard Lewis' collection of Oriental poems. Publisher, The Dial Press.

The Metropolitan Museum of Art, Gift of Annette Young, 1956, in memory of her brother, Innis Young.

MANY wonderful books of interest to young readers were published in 1964. At the very top of the list is Sterling North's *Rascal.* This warmhearted memoir tells about the author's boyhood in Wisconsin during the years of World War I. It was written for adults, but all ages from ten up can enjoy it. On the surface this is the story of a country boy's adventures with a pet raccoon. But a great deal more is said between the lines, particularly about the strength of family bonds in a household where father and son were getting along after the death of the mother.

Among the stories written especially for readers of about 9 to 12, two stand out. *Out of Hand* by Emma Smith is a delightful story about the escapades of four spirited children. These youngsters are bent on saving themselves and their beloved old Cousin Polly from unwelcome intruders during a summer holiday in an old Welsh farmhouse. *The Return of the Twelves* by Pauline Clarke is one of those rare stories that can almost make the reader believe the impossible. In this book, the 12 wooden soldiers that belonged to the famous Brontë children over a century ago are discovered in an attic. They come to life in the presence of Max, the little English boy who adores them.

Among the other fine books that are sure to interest the younger readers are two horse stories. *Stormy: Misty's Foal* by Marguerite Henry is the latest in the author's popular series about Misty of Chin-coteague Island. *A Horse Called Mystery* by Marjorie Reynolds is a most satisfying story about a horse, a doctor, a mysterious island and a lame boy. This young boy makes some important discoveries about accepting his own handicaps and those of others.

Readers who want to know more about the daily life of children in other countries will enjoy *Taiwo and Her Twin* by Letta Schatz. This is a story about the coming of a school to a village in Nigeria. Here you will read about a little girl's frustration when her father says, "What need has a girl for schooling?" *Little Plum* by Rumer

Godden is especially for girls who enjoyed the author's *Miss Happiness and Miss Flower.* Here is a chance to meet the Japanese dolls again. And here again is Belinda, that "rough, tough little girl" whose accidents and quarrels fill this story with life and suspense. A book to please everyone is William O. Steele's *The Year of the Bloody Sevens.* This story is packed with suspense, danger and valor. It tells of an 11-year-old boy's trek from Virginia to Kentucky in 1777, through perilous Indian country. Also for everyone is *The Moment of Wonder* edited by Richard Lewis. This beautiful book of short Japanese and Chinese poems is illustrated with black-and-white reproductions of Japanese and Chinese paintings.

For older readers Leonard Wibberley has completed two volumes of his planned four-volume biography of Thomas Jefferson: *Young Man from the Piedmont* and *A Dawn in the Trees.* These books tell the dramatic story of a great man's part in the making of the United States. If this is the kind of book you enjoy most, you will also want to read *The Amazing Alexander Hamilton* by Arthur Orrmont. Two other fine life stories are *Girl with a Pen: Charlotte Brontë* by Elisabeth Kyle, and *The Young Leonardo da Vinci* by E. M. Almedingen.

Three of the year's best fiction books have a theme in common: in all of them a boy in his teens begins to find himself. The hero of *It's Like This, Cat* by Emily Neville is a 14-year-old New York City boy. His story, told in his own words, deals with his gradually maturing feelings toward his lawyer father, his neighborhood friends and a girl companion. In Elspeth Bragdon's *There Is a Tide,* a 15-year-old boy who has been "fired" from several boarding schools discovers new ambition and understanding during the year he spends with his father in a small village on an island off the coast of Maine. The hero of *The Loner* by Ester Wier is a 14-year-old orphan boy who finds something to live for among the Montana

Illus. by Edward Osmond

In Charles Paul May's "Animals of the Far North," an Eskimo child proudly displays a leveret (a baby hare) he has caught. Publisher, Abelard-Schuman.

sheepherders. They take him in and teach him the importance of caring about people. This story is rich in values. And it is especially interesting for its details about sheepherding.

For older girls there are two junior novels of unusual quality. *The Rock and the Willow* by Mildred Lee is the most moving of all the books mentioned in this review. Though it is about an Alabama girl and her family back in the 1930's, it is much more than a regional story. Enie and her family are universal: their troubles are yours and mine. *Time of Trial* by Hester Burton is a rousing story of a courageous bookseller, Mr. Pargeter, and his 17-year-old daughter Margaret. The story takes place in the London of 1801, a time when it was dangerous to protest on behalf of the poor. The theme here is the struggle to speak the truth.

In 1964, other books combined interesting historical background with exciting story. In *The Skies of Crete* by James Forman a young girl learns with her soldier cousin something about the realities of war at the time of the nazi invasion. *Tiger Burning Bright* by Theodora DuBois is full of suspense and adventure. It tells about an escape flight across a desert in India at the time of the Sepoy Rebellion of 1857. The little caravan of people fleeing for their lives is made up of an odd assortment of children and adults. The details about food and clothing and Indian life are fascinating. In *Strangers in Africa* by Russell Davis and Brent Ashabranner, two young men, one Negro and one white, work together on sleeping-sickness prevention in the African bush. They are on a Peace Corps assignment.

Those of you who find that adult books offer you the best reading should not miss Michel Siffre's *Beyond Time*. Here is a thrilling account of the 23-year-old author's two-month stay in a deep ice cavern in the French Alps. He went there to explore the effects of such isolation on man's sense of time. Thrilling also, but in another way, is Dorothy Clarke Wilson's *Take My Hands: The Remarkable Story of Dr. Verghese*. This is a biography of a young woman doctor of south India who was paralyzed from the waist down in a bus accident, yet managed to rebuild her life and become a famous surgeon. For space lovers there is Jeff Sutton's *Apollo at Go*. This story of the first flight to the moon is a work of fiction yet seemingly realistic.

The best-seller lists of 1964 included *The Burden and the Glory* edited by Allan Nevins. This interesting volume contains a

Lee Samuels

"A Moveable Feast," Ernest Hemingway's recollections of his early life in Paris, came out three years after his death. Publisher, Scribners.

selection of the addresses and public statements made by President Kennedy from the fall of 1961 until his assassination in November 1963. Also a best seller was *A Tribute to John F. Kennedy,* a beautiful collection of tributes edited by Pierre Salinger and Sander Vanocur. Topping the best-seller list was *The Spy Who Came In from the Cold* by John Le Carré.

The 1964 National Book Award went to Aileen Ward's *John Keats: The Making of a Poet*. The Pulitzer Prize was awarded to *John Keats* by Walter Jackson Bate.

High on the fiction list was the suspenseful war-refugee story *The Night in Lisbon* by Erich Maria Remarque. William Golding's *The Spire* was not so well received as his *Lord of the Flies,* but it did offer a reading experience of intensity and depth.

Last but not least 1964 was the year of Ernest Hemingway's *A Moveable Feast*. This book is to be cherished not only for its picture of a young man's life in Paris in the 1920's, but for the freshness, charm and vitality of its writing. As Hemingway says in this book, he tried not to "describe" when he wrote, but to "make." The result is that unmistakable, remarkable Hemingway prose.

William Shakespeare
400th Anniversary

Shakespeare's birthday, April 23, is celebrated each year at Stratford-on-Avon. But during 1964, the quadricentennial of Shakespeare's birth, celebrations extended far beyond the British Isles. Festivals took place in Italy, Austria, West Germany, Canada and the United States. And in England nearly 60 towns offered special programs to the tourists who flocked to the Shakespeare shrines pictured here.

This engraving reveals Shakespeare's London, as seen from the south bank of the Thames. In the foreground is Southwark, the entertainment district. There flags fly from the Globe (36) and the Swan (38) theaters, indicating that performances are scheduled for the day. A flag also flies at the Bear Garden (37). Across the river, St. Paul's Cathedral (1) dominates the scene. Whitehall Palace (2), where Queen Elizabeth lived, is to the left; on the right is the Tower of London (30).

Bettmann Archive

232

Ewing Galloway

Shakespeare was born in this comfortable half-timbered house on Henley Street in Stratford.

A portrait bust of Shakespeare looks down over his tomb in the chancel of Holy Trinity Church, where he was baptized.

Anne Hathaway's cottage, which is about a mile from Stratford, has been restored and is now a museum.

Holy Trinity Church, where Shakespeare and his family are buried.

Model of the Globe Playhouse by John Cranford Adams and Irwin Smith

Scale model of the Globe Theater, where many of Shakespeare's plays were first presented.

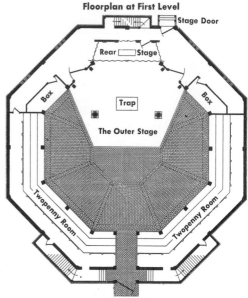

From Shakespeare's Globe Playhouse by Irwin Smith, copyright © 1956 Charles Scribner's Sons

Floor plan of the Globe Theater, showing how the galleries faced the actors on three sides.

Tourists who visit Stratford from April through November can see Shakespeare's plays at the Royal Shakespeare Theater.

Robert Graves

...a versatile writer who is famous as a poet, novelist, essayist, critic and translator.

By RUSSELL J. SULLY

AT the age of 15 Robert Graves vowed to devote his life to poetry. Both Robert Graves himself and the people who know him can vouch that he has never gone back on that oath.

Today Robert Graves is an active 70. He is an impressive-looking man, tall, with gray hair. He has a boxer's nose and a firm jaw. Graves lives in a small olive-producing village in the northwestern mountain area of the Spanish island of Majorca. There he built his house in 1932. The money for the house came from sales of his autobiography, *Goodbye to All That*.

Robert Graves is one person who *must* write. He spends most of his time at the worktable in his study. He refuses to use a typewriter, and he dislikes ball-point pens. So he puts words to paper with a steel nib. Each page is rewritten many times. Eventually he selects three or four versions. His secretary then types them up. These too are reworked until the final version is achieved.

When not at his worktable, Robert is often in his garden. There he busies himself weeding and watering the plants or digging holes for new ones. For relaxation he goes down to the cove for a swim.

Robert has a diverse background. Before giving a poetry reading in Boston, he introduced himself in this way: "I am British by birth. My father was from Dublin, my mother from Munich. The Graves family is of French origin. I have close ties with Wales and have lived in Spain—apart from wartimes—since 1929. My conditioning is Protestant; my chief obsession, poetry; my

chief study, the English language." He has married twice and has seven children. (The eighth, his eldest son, was killed in World War II.) Their ages range all the way from 46 down to 11.

Robert Graves came to the attention of the public as a war poet during World War I. He went through the horror of trench warfare as a frontline infantry officer of the Royal Welsh Fusiliers. At the Somme he was so badly wounded that he was officially listed as having "died of wounds." He decided on the very day that he got out of the army never to be under anyone's orders again. He would live by his writing.

In the United States, Robert Graves is most widely known as a writer of prose. He is the author of best-selling novels, brilliant essays and translations. But he has written some of the most beautiful lyrical poetry of our century. I once asked Robert at what age he felt he was writing true poetry. He answered simply, "I was born a poet." He had to learn to write prose to earn a living. In his opinion, poets are not usually good prose writers. He himself has had to work hard at it in order, as he says, "to be very kind to my readers." To him, poets and prose writers use words in very different ways. As he explains it: "In commercial, scientific and newspaper prose there is an increasing tendency to use words as mere counters—stripping them of their content, history, association and force—as one might use a box of old foreign coins in a card game, without regard for their country of origin, date, face value or intrinsic value. The creative side of writing consists in

235

Graves' renown as a writer is the result of half a century of hard work at his craft.

treating words as though they were living things—in coupling them and making them breed new life."

Robert Graves was named Professor of Poetry at Oxford University in 1961. In his inaugural address he said that the Tudor poet John Skelton was a good example of the dedicated poet. In fact Skelton has had a greater influence on Graves' work than any other poet. Skelton's fixed rhyme, irregular syllable count and simplicity of style can all be found in Graves' poetry. His terse and earthy language also reflects the earlier poet's influence. The similarities are seen here in a comparison of Skelton's intense lines:

> Woefully arrayed
> And shamefully betrayed
>   My blood, man
>   For thee ran
> It may not be nayed:
>   My body blue and wan
> Woefully arrayed . . .

with some lines from Graves' poem *The Devil at Berry Pomeroy:*

> Snow and fog unseasonable,
> The cold remarkable,
> Children sickly;
> Green fruit lay thickly
> Under the crab tree
> And the wild cherry.
> I heard witches call
> Their imps to the Hall . . .

Robert Graves is a generous man. I have known many young writers whom he has helped financially. If he thinks they have talent he encourages them and even helps them get their work published. In addition, he has given young poets some valuable advice. For example, Graves does not feel that there are poetic prodigies, as there are musical prodigies. He would advise a young poet to work hard because it is only through years and years of experience with language that good poetry can be written. To write good poetry, a poet must also read as much poetry—and prose—as pos-

By ROBERT GRAVES

Good-bye to All That
I, Claudius
Claudius the God
Count Belisarius
Sergeant Lamb's America
Wife to Mr. Milton
King Jesus
Hercules, My Shipmate (The Golden Fleece)
The White Goddess
The Common Asphodel: Collected Essays on Poetry
The Golden Ass (translation from Latin)
Occupation: Writer
The Nazarene Gospel Restored (with Joshua Podro)
Homer's Daughter
The Crowning Privilege
Suetonius' Twelve Caesars (translation from Latin)
The Greek Myths
5 Pens in Hand
The Anger of Achilles: Homer's Iliad (translation from Greek)
Food for Centaurs
Collected Poems

sible. Through the work of other writers the poet can learn his own powers and limitations.

Words are the heart of poetry. So Graves suggests that you always have at hand a good historical dictionary, such as the unabridged Oxford English Dictionary. He looks up four or five words a day, not only to find out their meaning but to find their derivation, when the word first appeared, how it has changed throughout the years and in what contexts it can be used. Knowing these things is very important in choosing a particular word for a poem. A copy of *Roget's Thesaurus* can also be helpful, although Graves uses it only for writing prose. But remember that even though certain words may be called synonyms, there are shades of difference between them that a poet must know.

Never, says Graves, try to write a poem in a particular meter. This is just a game. A poem should suggest its own meter. To try to fit words to a rhythm will result in bad poetry. The technical devices used in creating a poem should never stand out or in any way call attention to themselves. They are just the skeleton upon which the flesh of the poem—words and their meanings—is strung.

Latin-American Poetry

Translations and Introduction
By ROBERT LOSADA, JR.

POETRY is at least as old as speech itself. Indeed some people think that language developed because of an inborn human drive to make rhythmic sounds. Even babies make noises—sometimes, it seems, simply for the fun of it. Tribes so primitive that they do not even plant their own food or use any but the crudest tools will still have many songs. Among such people songs are sung during work, play and worship.

The invention of writing made it possible for people to communicate with one another without speaking. However, many people still feel the urge to make language more musical than ordinary conversation requires. But now that poetry is no longer sung, the forms of language used by poets today are often very complicated. Unfortunately this has caused some poetry to become meaningless to people who do not have the time or special education to study it carefully.

It is interesting that although South America has a much higher rate of illiteracy than the United States, writers and poets are much more important there. South American ambassadors, senators and even presidents are often also very good writers. Like poets everywhere, South American poets write about their feelings, the people they love and their religious experiences. But a South American poet will write more often than a North American poet about his country. The history and geography of his native land and the problems that his country faces today are often reflected even in the most personal poems written by a

South American poet. Such poems are interesting not only because some of them are very good poetry but also because they may help us to understand conditions in Latin America.

Although he is not too well known in the United States, Pablo Neruda is one of South America's finest poets. In the Spanish-speaking world, his books have sold millions of copies. Neruda was born in Chile in 1904. Like many South Americans, he is part Indian and very proud of it. He has served his country as a diplomat and in 1945 was elected a senator. Though he is most famous for his love poetry, his real subject—often even in his love poems —is the geography of South America: the jungles, the Andes Mountains and the Pacific Ocean. Latin America's rugged landscape and the effect it has had on the lives of the people, especially the poor, have influenced the other writers translated here.

Carlos Castro Saavedra is from Colombia. His fame as a poet has been growing steadily throughout Latin America and Europe for the last 15 years. Efraín Barquero is one of the finest young poets in South America, but he is not yet widely read outside his native Chile.

César Vallejo was a Peruvian Indian who died in Paris in 1938. He was a friend of many of the famous artists and writers who lived in Paris in the 1920's and 1930's. The poem translated here is part of a series that he wrote after seeing the bloody battlefields of the Spanish Civil War (1936-39). Like all of his poems, it is rich in love and compassion for his fellowmen.

UNA HOJA NO MAS

Por CARLOS CASTRO SAAVEDRA

Una hoja no más. Esto es el hombre.
¿Dónde su rama original?
Una hoja cayendo eternamente
sobre la tierra y sobre el mar.
El agua es infinita,
las llanuras son vastas.
El viento pasa por los pueblos
lleno de muertas esperanzas.

Una hoja no más, pequeña, deshojada,
de tumbo en tumbo, sola, desolada.
¿Dónde el sitio en que va a caer?
La tempestad tala los árboles
que han empezado a florecer.
A lo lejos se escuchan gritos.
Sobre la hierba verde y madre
está pariendo una mujer.

Una hoja no más. La noche avanza.
El tiempo apaga el fuego de las cosas.
La muerte sopla sobre los hogares.
Al misterio se llega del misterio.
Se padece, se vuelve a padecer.
Una hoja cayendo hacia el olvido
para luego volverse a desprender.

A LEAF, NO MORE

By CARLOS CASTRO SAAVEDRA

A leaf, no more. That is man.
Where is the branch he fell from?
A leaf eternally falling
over the earth, over the sea.
The water is infinite,
the plains are vast.
The wind moves through villages
heavy with dead hopes.

A leaf, no more, small, falling,
tumbling, lonely, desolate.
Where is the spot it will land?
The storm prunes the trees
as they begin to blossom.
Far off the sound of screams.
Upon the green, mother grass
a woman is bearing a child.

A leaf, no more. Night advances.
Time puts out the fire of things.
Death blows on the hearths.
Mystery leads to mystery.
One suffers, and suffers again.
A leaf falling toward oblivion
to break off and fall again.

ODA DE INVIERNO AL RIO MAPOCHO

Por PABLO NERUDA

Oh, sí, nieve imprecisa,
oh, sí, temblando en plena flor de nieve,
párpado boreal, pequeño rayo helado
quién, quién te llamó hacia el ceniciento valle,
quién, quién te arrastró desde el pico del águila
hasta donde tus aguas puras tocan
los terribles harapos de mi patria?
Río, por qué conduces
agua fría y secreta,
agua que el alba dura de las piedras
guardó en su catedral inaccesible,
hasta los pies heridos de mi pueblo?
Vuelve, vuelve a tu copa de nieve, río amargo,
vuelve, vuelve a tu copa de espaciosas escarchas
sumerge tu plateada raíz en tu secreto origen
o despéñate y rómpete en otro mar sin lágrimas!
Río Mapocho cuando la noche llega
y como negra estatua echada
duerme bajo tus puentes con un racimo negro
de cabezas golpeadas por el frío y el hambre
como por dos inmensos águilas, oh río,
oh duro río parido por la nieve,
por qué no te levantas como inmenso fantasma
o como nueva cruz de estrellas para los olvidados?
No, tu brusca ceniza corre ahora
junto al sollozo echado al agua negro,
junto a la manga rota que el viento endurecido
hace temblar debajo de las hojas de hierro.
Río Mapocho, adónde llevas
plumas de hielo para siempre heridas,
siempre junto a tu cárdena ribera
la flor salvaje nacerá mordida por los piojos
y tu lengua de frío raspará las mejillas
de mi patria desnuda?
                    Oh, que no sea,
oh, que no sea, y que una gota de tu espuma negra
salte del legamo a la flor del fuego
y precipite la semilla del hombre!

240

WINTER ODE TO THE RIVER MAPOCHO

By PABLO NERUDA

Oh, yes, oh indefinable snow,
yes, oh trembling in full flower of the snow,
boreal eyelid, tiny ray of frozen light,
who, who called you to the valley of ashes,
who, who dragged you from the eagle's beak
down to where your pure waters touch
the terrible rags of my country?
River, why do you bring down
the freezing, secret water,
water which the hard dawn of the stones
kept in its inaccessible cathedral,
down to the wounded feet of my people?
Go back, go back, oh bitter river, to your cup of snow,
go back, go back to your cup of spacious frost,
sink your silver root in your secret spring
or plunge, break into another, tearless sea!
River Mapocho, when night comes
and like a tumbled, black statue
sleeps beneath your bridges with a black cluster
of heads beaten by the cold and hunger
as by two immense eagles, oh river,
oh hard river born of the snow,
why don't you rise like a vast phantom
or a new cross of stars for all forgotten men?
No, now your harsh ashes run
beside the sob thrown to the black water,
beside the tattered sleeve whipped and shivering
in the hardened wind beneath the iron leaves.
River Mapocho, where do you take
those feathers of ice forever wounded,
along your purple shores will wild flowers
always be born bitten by lice
and your tongue of cold forever scrape
the cheeks of my naked country?
                         Oh, let it not be so,
let it not be so; let a drop of your black foam
leap from the mud into a flower of fire
and precipitate the seed of man!

MASA

Por CESAR VALLEJO

Al fin de la batalla,
y muerto el combatiente, vino hacia él un hombre
y le dijo: "¡No mueras; te amo tanto!"
Pero el cadáver ¡ay! siguió muriendo.

Se le acercaron dos y repitiéronle:
"¡No nos dejes! ¡Valor! ¡Vuelve a la vida!"
Pero el cadáver ¡ay! siguió muriendo.

Acudieron a él veinte, cien, mil, quinientos mil,
clamando: "¡Tanto amor, y no poder nada contra la muerte!"
Pero el cadáver ¡ay! siguió muriendo.

Le rodearon millones de individuos,
con un ruego común: "¡Quédate hermano!"
Pero el cadáver ¡ay! siguió muriendo.

Entonces todos los hombres de la tierra
le rodearon; les vió el cadáver triste, emocionado;
incorporóse lentamente,
abrazó al primer hombre; echóse a andar . . .

PUREZA

Por EFRAÍN BARQUERO

Blancura de los hombres,
junto a la oscuridad que los circunda.

Blancura de la madre con su hijo.
Del niño que aún no ha despertado
y sueña con dos manos blancas.
Y de la mujer que lo alimenta,
humillada por la tos y por el hambre.

Blancura de aquellos que no duermen.
De los ojos que conocen el mundo
y recuerdan la menor alegría.

Blancura de los que saben morir,
envueltos en su propia desnudez,
bajo el sueño más blanco.

Blancura de mis palabras,
por olvidarme de mí mismo.

Blancura de mí corazón,
por encontrarlo tan oscuro.

MASSES

By CÉSAR VALLEJO

At the end of the battle
when the soldier was dead, a man came toward him,
saying: "Do not die, I love you so much!"
But the body, ah!, it went on dying.

Two approached him, repeating over and over:
"Do not leave us! Courage! Return to life!"
But the body, ah!, it went on dying.

Twenty came, a hundred, a thousand, five hundred thousand,
clamoring: "So much love, powerless against death!"
But the body, ah!, it went on dying.

Millions of individuals gathered around him
with a common prayer: "Stay with us brother!"
But the body, ah!, it went on dying.

Then all the men on earth gathered there;
the sad corpse saw them and was moved;
slowly he rose,
embraced the first man, and began to walk . . .

PURITY

By EFRAÍN BARQUERO

Whiteness of men,
beside the darkness around them.

Whiteness of a mother with her child.
Of the child not yet awake
and dreaming of two white hands.
And of the woman who nourishes it,
humbled by a cough and by hunger.

Whiteness of those that do not sleep.
Of the eyes that know the world
and remember the smallest joys.

Whiteness of them that know how to die,
wrapped in their own nakedness,
beneath the whitest dream.

Whiteness of my words,
forgetting myself.

243

Whiteness of my heart,
finding it so dark.

Nursery Rhymes

By PHILLIP BENNETT SHEPPARD

HAVE you ever been on a fat-free diet, or sat on a tuffet, or had a great fall? No? Well, Jack Sprat, Little Miss Muffet and Humpty-Dumpty have. And they've been doing these things for hundreds of years, bringing delight to millions of children.

Today, children know the names of these nursery-rhyme heroes long before they know such names as Lyndon B. Johnson, Nikita Khrushchev or U Thant. But it may surprise you to learn that nursery rhymes were not originally for children. They were composed by adults for their own enjoyment. But young people love to imitate their elders. So, while dancing and playing games, children, all through the ages, have copied their parents and made nursery rhymes of the grownups' songs.

The songs were originally folk songs, ballads, cries of street vendors, rhyming riddles, political satire or jokes, and songs sung in taverns. There are many different kinds of nursery songs. But we can put most of them into six main groups. There are lullabies and riddles. There are play rhymes, number rhymes and accumulative rhymes. And there are rhymes that tell about people and events in history.

Long, long ago, in the fourteenth century, lullabies were called cradle songs or lullynges. One lullaby that is at least two hundred years old and is still very popular is:

> Hush-a-bye, baby, on the tree top,
> When the wind blows the cradle will
>   rock;
> When the bough breaks the cradle will
>   fall,
> Down will come baby, cradle, and all.

This is the best-known of all the lullabies. It was first written down in the eighteenth century, but it was probably sung to children long before then. Some people believe that this song was originally meant as a warning to overly ambitious people. It told them in effect that

if they climbed too high they were in danger of falling.

Riddles have long been among the most popular of the nursery rhymes. Can you figure out this one?

> Four stiff-standers,
> Four dilly-danders,
> Two lookers,
> Two crookers,
> And a wig-wag.

Cow

or this?

> As I was going to St. Ives,
> I met a man with seven wives,
> Each wife had seven sacks,
> Each sack had seven cats,
> Each cat had seven kits:
> Kits, cats, sacks and wives,
> How many were there going to St. Ives?

None or One

or this?

> Two bodies have I,
> Though both joined in one.
> The stiller I stand,
> The faster I run.

Hourglass

The third group is made up of play rhymes. Parents often play these with their children. Some are played by children themselves. With these, actions go along with the words. How many of you haven't played pat-a-cake? This is probably the most famous of the play rhymes. It was known as far back as 1698. Another famous play rhyme is "This little pig went to market."

Little babies have long been delighted by this play rhyme:

> Ring the bell, (*tug the baby's hair*)
> Knock at the door, (*tap his forehead*)
> Peep in, (*look into his eyes*)
> Lift the latch, (*pull up his nose*)
> Walk in, (*open his mouth*)
> Go way down cellar
>   and eat apples. (*tickle his throat*)

Number, or counting-out, rhymes were once used by the Druids to count out people who were to be sacrificed to the gods. Now they are used in games, such as tag, to count out the one who is "it."

The most widely used of all the number rhymes is:

> Eenie, meenie, minie, mo,
> Catch a monkey by the toe;
> If he hollers, let him go,
> Eenie, meenie, minie, mo.

As with most other nursery rhymes, counting-out rhymes are found in other

"This is the House that Jack Built"—as shown in an early-nineteenth-century illustration.

languages. For example, in Germany we find:

Ene, tene, mone, mei,
Pastor, lone, bone, strei,
Ene, fune, herke, berke,
Wer? Wie? Wo? Was?

The fifth type of nursery rhyme is the accumulative rhyme. In these, the verses get longer and longer—and the action gets more and more complicated. "This is the House that Jack Built" is an accumulative rhyme. It has been recited for at least 150 years:

This is the house that Jack built.

This is the malt
That lay in the house that Jack built.

This is the rat,
That ate the malt
That lay in the house that Jack built.

and so on to

This is the farmer sowing his corn,
That kept the cock that crowed in the
  morn,
That waked the priest all shaven and
  shorn,
That married the man all tattered and
  torn,
That kissed the maiden all forlorn,
That milked the cow with the crumpled
  horn,
That tossed the dog,
That worried the cat,
That killed the rat,
That ate the malt
That lay in the house that Jack built.

The last type of nursery rhyme is about people and events in history. One such rhyme that you probably know quite well is:

Little Jack Horner
Sat in the corner,
Eating his Christmas pie;
He put in his thumb,
And pulled out a plum,
And said, What a good boy am I!

Jack Horner, according to one story, was steward to an abbot in Glastonbury, England. One Christmas, the abbot sent Jack to London with a gift for King Henry VIII. The gift was a pie, and in the pie were deeds for 12 manors. But the King never got the gift because on the way to London, Jack decided to taste the pie. "He put in his thumb, and pulled out a plum." The plum, of course, was the deeds—and Jack kept them. Jack's descendants still live in England. They say that this story is not true.

Nursery rhymes have brought joy to children—and adults—for centuries. Many of them are pure poetry. They will no doubt continue to delight people for centuries to come.

United Artists

Sidney Poitier and Lilia Skala scored acting triumphs in "Lilies of the Field."

Motion Pictures

By ROBERT SALMAGGI and ROBERT HAWK

MOST of the 150 or more American films released during 1964 were not worth seeing. Still, there were several that needed no apologies. The most encouraging film trend was the desire to take a topical look, both serious and comic, at the United States. *The Best Man* and John Frankenheimer's *Seven Days in May* showed backstage political wheeling and dealing effectively. And, of course, there was Stanley Kubrick's savagely comic *Dr. Strangelove or: How I Learned to Stop Worrying and Love the Bomb.* The atomic bomb, the Pentagon, the presidency, fluoridation and Russian premiers were among the targets it treated with satiric originality.

Eleanor and Frank Perry did not duplicate the success they had with *David and Lisa* in their new film *Ladybug, Ladybug.* This film, about the terror children might undergo in the atomic age, was admirable more for its theme than its execution, as was Shirley Clarke's *The Cool World.* This motion picture was a cry of outrage at the world that society has created for Harlem's young people. More successful artistically was *One Potato, Two Potato.* It treated the problems of a young white divorcée and a Negro co-worker who marry.

There were only three superior dramas of a more general nature. Elia Kazan's *America America* was the story of a young Greek boy and his struggle to immigrate to the United States. Tennessee Williams' play, *The Night of the Iguana,* an intense study of loneliness, was brought to the

United Artists

Tom Jones (Albert Finney) with his long-lost father in the "year's best movie."

Paramount Pictures Corp.

Patricia Neal, Melvyn Douglas and Brandon de Wilde in a scene from "Hud," which also starred Paul Newman.

screen effectively. All three of its stars—Deborah Kerr, Richard Burton and Ava Gardner—gave top-notch performances. Miss Kerr also starred in *The Chalk Garden,* a drama about a teen-age girl (Hayley Mills) with emotional problems.

Other than the films mentioned, there was little to recommend of the more serious American films. *Love with the Proper Stranger,* starring Steve McQueen and Natalie Wood; *The Prize,* with Paul Newman and Edward G. Robinson; and *Captain Newman, M.D.,* with Gregory Peck playing a sort of Ben Casey/Dr. Kildare in soldier's garb, all fell short of the mark. Equally disappointing were Alfred Hitchcock's *Marnie* (very *un*suspenseful) and Otto Preminger's *The Cardinal.*

Even worse were the big box-office sensation and shock films that came out during the year. *Dead Ringer* with Bette Davis,

Straitjacket with Joan Crawford, and *Lady in a Cage* with Olivia de Havilland were all regrettable films, as were *The Carpetbaggers* and *A House Is Not a Home.*

In the field of comedy, film makers also tried to get away with as much as possible. There was a parade of tasteless "romantic" comedies: *Good Neighbor Sam, Sunday in New York, Honeymoon Hotel* and *What a Way to Go!*

However, comedy was not all bad in 1964. For in the spring along came *The World of Henry Orient.* Peter Sellers was delicious in the title role. But two teenage girls, played by newcomers Tippy Walker and Merrie Spaeth, stole the movie with their captivating performances. Peter Sellers also was responsible for much of the fun of two lesser but nonetheless amusing comedies: *The Pink Panther* and *A Shot in the Dark.* In both he played that

ACADEMY AWARD
WINNERS

Motion Picture: **Tom Jones**
Foreign-Language Motion Picture: **8½**
Actress: **Patricia Neal** (*Hud*)
Actor: **Sidney Poitier** (*Lilies of the Field*)
Supporting Actress: **Margaret Rutherford** (*The V.I.P.s*)
Supporting Actor: **Melvyn Douglas** (*Hud*)
Director: **Tony Richardson** (*Tom Jones*)
Story and Screenplay: **James R. Webb** (*How the West Was Won*)
Song: **Call Me Irresponsible** (*Papa's Delicate Condition*)
Documentary Feature: **Robert Frost: A Lover's Quarrel with the World**
Documentary Short: **Chagall**
Film Editing: **Harold F. Kress** (*How the West Was Won*)
Costume Design (black and white): **Piero Cherardi** (*8½*)
Costume Design (color): **Irene Sharaff** (*Cleopatra*)
Short-Subject Cartoon: **The Critic**
Live-Action Short: **An Occurrence at Owl Creek Bridge**
Cinematography (black and white): **James Wong Howe** (*Hud*)
Cinematography (color): **Leon Shamroy** (*Cleopatra*)
Screenplay: **John Osborne** (*Tom Jones*)
Special Effects: **Cleopatra**
Sound: **How the West Was Won**
Sound Effects: **It's a Mad, Mad, Mad, Mad World**
Musical Score: **John Addison** (*Tom Jones*)
Film Editing: **How the West Was Won**
Art Direction (color): **Cleopatra**
Art Direction (black and white): **America America**
Scoring of Music: **Irma La Douce**

bungling French police inspector Clouseau.

Musicals were practically nonexistent till the latter half of the year. *The Unsinkable Molly Brown,* based on Meredith Willson's Broadway show, was a popular success. However, this loud, brassy production starring Debbie Reynolds robbed *Molly* of much of its original charm. Two of the biggest and best Hollywood musicals were released in the fall. One, naturally, was *My Fair Lady.* Rex Harrison re-created his Henry Higgins, with Audrey Hepburn as his lady fair, and all was as it should be. But the big surprise was Walt Disney's *Mary Poppins.* Combining live action with animation, it had a lively score and an enchanting script. It also introduced Julie Andrews, Broadway's charming Fair Lady, to the screen.

As always, Mr. Disney led in the field of children's films. Except for *Mary Poppins,*

however, only his full-length cartoon, *The Sword in the Stone,* was exceptional. Robert B. Radnitz, creator of the excellent *Misty* and *A Dog of Flanders,* put out the equally first-rate *Island of the Blue Dolphins* in 1964. And MGM's dolphin reappeared in *Flipper's New Adventure.*

As usual, many of the year's outstanding films came from foreign countries. Probably the biggest surprise was England's *A Hard Day's Night,* the screen debut of the Beatles. This film was fresh in its ideas and exciting in its brisk photography and marvelous editing. As comedians, the Beatles compared favorably with the Marx Brothers. Peter O'Toole and Richard Burton added great distinction to *Becket,* a rather good adaptation of Anouilh's play. From Britain, too, came *Girl with Green Eyes,* starring Rita Tushingham and Peter Finch. This moving film was about a young girl's first encounter with love.

France gave us two deft spoofs. Both of them starred Jean-Paul Belmondo. The first, *That Man from Rio,* was a dazzling mixture of every plot device and hairbreadth escape from Tarzan to Bogart. The other, *Cartouche,* concentrated on swashbuckling epics.

Among Italy's best was *Seduced and Abandoned.* This was a funny but acid look at the hypocrisies maintained in the name of honor, family and society by the Sicilian people. Sicily was also the locale for *Mafiosa,* a documentary-style account of the underworld there. From Italy, too, came *The Organizer* and *Yesterday, Today and Tomorrow,* both starring Marcello Mastroianni. Sophia Loren costarred in the latter.

Notable films from other countries included Sweden's *The Silence.* This was the last of Ingmar Bergman's trilogy, which began with *Through a Glass Darkly* and *Winter Light.* Japan's best offerings were *Harakiri,* a samurai film, and *High and Low,* a dandy detective thriller. *Los Tarantos* was a primitive Spanish film with echoes of *West Side Story.*

A melancholy Richard Burton, playing Hamlet, listens to Alfred Drake (Claudius) while Hume Cronyn (Polonius) and Eileen Herlie (Gertrude) look on.

Theater Review

By GORDON ROGOFF

FOR years anyone who wanted to be a success in the theater dreamed of coming to New York and conquering Broadway. It has been "Broadway or bust" for every young hopeful. And in many ways it still is. But theater in New York no longer means just Broadway. Now, in addition to the Great White Way itself, there are two other kinds of theater: off-Broadway and repertory. Off-Broadway theater has been growing and spreading at a great rate for about ten years. And the 1963-64 theater season marked the opening of two important repertory companies—the Lincoln Center Repertory Theater and the Actors Studio Theater.

Even on Broadway, times are changing. Compared to the old days, very few plays are put on. What plays do get on are nearly always from the same few countries. Either they run for months and even years, or they disappear after only one night.

For a while this season it seemed as if Broadway had turned into the off-London theater. The British sent over wave after wave of their plays and players. Their biggest success with New York audiences was Albert Finney in the title role of John Osborne's *Luther*. Playing Martin Luther from youth to old age, Finney showed remarkable talent. His performance gave *Luther* a stirring power that was not always present in Osborne's play.

A more interesting production was *Chips with Everything*. This play was written by Arnold Wesker, another young British playwright. The title refers to Wesker's somewhat angry view that the

WINNERS

Musical: **Hello, Dolly!**
Play: **Luther**
Dramatic Actor: **Sir Alec Guinness** (*Dylan*)
Dramatic Actress: **Sandy Dennis** (*Any Wednesday*)
Male Musical Star: **Bert Lahr** (*Foxy*)
Female Musical Star: **Carol Channing** (*Hello, Dolly!*)
Supporting Actor in a Drama: **Hume Cronyn** (*Hamlet*)
Supporting Actress in a Drama: **Barbara Loden** (*After the Fall*)
Supporting Actor in a Musical: **Jack Cassidy** (*She Loves Me*)
Supporting Actress in a Musical: **Tessie O'Shea** (*The Girl Who Came to Supper*)
Scenic Designer: **Oliver Smith** (*Hello, Dolly!*)
Producer of Play: **Herman Shumlin** (*The Deputy*)
Director of Play: **Mike Nichols** (*Barefoot in the Park*)
Producer of Musical: **David Merrick** (*Hello, Dolly!*)
Director of Musical: **Gower Champion** (*Hello, Dolly!*)
Author of Musical: **Michael Stewart** (*Hello, Dolly!*)
Costume Designer: **Freddy Wittop** (*Hello, Dolly!*)
Choreographer: **Gower Champion** (*Hello, Dolly!*)
Composer and Lyricist of a Musical Play: **Jerry Herman** (*Hello, Dolly!*)
Musical Director-Conductor: **Shepard Coleman** (*Hello, Dolly!*)
Special award for distinguished contribution to the theater: **Eva Le Gallienne** (for her work with the National Repertory Theater)

Carol Channing charmed critics and public alike as the wily widow in the hit musical "Hello, Dolly!"

For his portrayal of the Welsh poet Dylan Thomas, Alec Guinness won a Tony.

working classes in England accept too easily the hard work and boredom of their daily lives. Wesker's symbol of this is that they eat fried potatoes (chips) with every meal. The playwright got his message across by showing the conflict between officers (upper class) and young recruits (working class) during training for the Army. A large cast was drilled by its young director, John Dexter, into giving a painfully real account of army life. The play was a success with the critics. But it found only a limited audience during its four-month run. Perhaps this was because Americans do not feel the pressure of the class issue as much as the British do.

The English also gave Broadway two evenings of light and bittersweet comedy. These were Peter Shaffer's one-act plays, *The Private Ear* and *The Public Eye,* and an English production of *The Rehearsal* by France's Jean Anouilh. Shaffer's short fables were charming and often sad. In the first, a shy young man who loves serious music tries to entertain a sweet, but silly, young girl in his apartment. They have little in common, and he loses her to his more aggressive friend. Brian Bedford was particularly touching in the leading role. *The Public Eye* was more of a farce. But it was also about people who find it hard to communicate with one another. A comical private detective, armed with yoghurt in his briefcase, manages to bring together a quarreling husband and wife.

Anouilh's play had a touch of cruelty. The innocence of a young girl is placed against the worldly ways of older people. In one long, difficult scene the harder truths of life are brought home very dramatically to the girl by a bitter middle-aged man well played by Alan Badel.

Americans on Broadway had greater success with musicals and comedies than they did with serious plays. For the second season in a row, no American drama received the Pulitzer Prize. It was also a season in which stars from Hollywood and Broadway had several failures. They found

Henry Grossman

A new star—Funny Girl Barbra Streisand.

that their names and personal charms were not always strong enough to make people forget the weakness of the shows in which they were appearing. Hollywood's Kirk Douglas in *One Flew Over the Cuckoo's Nest* and Lee Remick in the musical *Anyone Can Whistle* did not find favor with large audiences. Broadway veterans such as Mary Martin (in *Jennie*), Helen Hayes (in *The White House*), Julie Harris (in *Marathon '33*), Charles Boyer (in *Man and Boy*) and Margaret Leighton (in *The Chinese Prime Minister*) were other stars who failed to garner big box-office returns.

But people did save their money for the biggest successes. With two exceptions these were either extravagant musicals or very light comedies. Carol Channing, playing the title role of *Hello, Dolly!* to the hilt, was the popular favorite of the year. For her performance, she won Broadway's Tony Award. Not far behind her was Barbra Streisand. This young singer had a huge personal success in her first starring vehicle, *Funny Girl*. In the part of Fanny Brice, Miss Streisand showed that she was gifted with more than a sweet, powerful voice. She is a truly funny girl, a bright comic spirit who can change instantly from rough clowning to gentle sadness.

The most popular new comedies were *Barefoot in the Park* by Neil Simon and

Any Wednesday by Muriel Resnik. The first caught reviewers' fancies mostly because of the clever, smooth direction of comedian Mike Nichols in his first directing job. And the second won a Tony Award for its star Sandy Dennis. At the same time it offered a good performance by Rosemary Murphy. This talented dramatic actress showed her gifts as a comedienne for the first time.

The two exceptions to the rule of comedies and musicals were *Hamlet* and *The Deputy*. Shakespeare's tragedy, thought by many to be the greatest play ever written, had the longest run in its 400-year-old history. This was largely because Hamlet was played by Richard Burton. Directed by British actor Sir John Gielgud, who was once a great Hamlet himself, the production as a whole was very disappointing. Most of the cast surrounding Burton did not have his life or intelligence. His was a colorful and passionate performance. He painted a portrait of a brilliant young prince cut off from the harsh Danish court because of his poetic wit and his genius for high moral feeling.

Rolf Hochhuth's *The Deputy* came from Germany in a cloud of controversy. It suggested that Pope Pius XII, as leader of the Roman Catholic Church, should have taken a stronger moral stand against the Nazis' treatment of the Jews during World War II. The author's greatest mistake was in bringing the Pope onstage for one scene. Despite the best efforts of actor Emlyn Williams, the Pope seemed more like a puppet than a man. This made many people feel that Hochhuth was not doing justice to both sides of the argument. Even so, the play proved to be a moving document for a large audience.

For the most part, off-Broadway theater and (to a lesser extent) the new repertory companies seemed more in touch with the world of drama and the drama of the world. Off-Broadway's Obie Awards were given to Samuel Beckett's difficult and beautiful short play called *Play* and to Le-Roi Jones' *Dutchman,* a powerful one-acter dealing with racial tension. Judith Malina and Julian Beck were also honored for their very realistic production about man's inhumanity to man, *The Brig.* Actress Gloria Foster captured an Obie for her deeply moving performance in *In White America,* a documentary play about two centuries of injustice to Negroes.

Meanwhile, in its temporary home in Greenwich Village, the long-awaited Lincoln Center Repertory Theater opened with Arthur Miller's *After the Fall.* This was the famous playwright's first new play in nine years. A long drama, it was seriously flawed because Miller was unable to draw back far enough from his characters to give a fair account of their actions. Directed without focus by Elia Kazan, it nevertheless offered a sharp and biting performance by Barbara Loden. She played the hero's blonde, tragically damaged second wife. The play first ran in repertory with a revival of Eugene O'Neill's *Marco Millions* and S. N. Behrman's *But for Whom Charlie.* But when these two rather dull productions failed to attract many people, the Repertory Theater gave *After the Fall* a long summer run.

The Actors Studio Theater continued to produce plays in several Broadway theaters. While it failed with *Marathon '33* and *Dynamite Tonight,* it had some success commercially with *Baby Want a Kiss* starring Paul Newman and Joanne Woodward. At modest prices, the Studio succeeded in keeping James Baldwin's *Blues for Mr. Charlie* running. This was a controversial play, which many found less moving than Baldwin's essays.

Kim Stanley's richly emotional performance as Masha in the revival of Chekhov's *The Three Sisters* was the high point of the Studio's last production of the season. The casting and direction of this superb play were uneven. But Miss Stanley reminded us that the gestures and emotional power of a great actress can often say more than a thousand words.

NBC

Chet Huntley and David Brinkley outrated all other TV newscasters in reporting the Republican and Democratic national conventions.

Television during the Year

By MARIE TORRE

REALITY is often more exciting than make-believe. This led television networks to stress news even over entertainment during the 1963-64 season. Broadcasters were given expanded newscasts. Producers sought to fill these news programs with more and more of the information found in newspapers, such as features, commentary, and book and theatrical reviews. And by the end of the year there was no sign that the news bubble would burst.

While it was a meaningful year for television news, it was a routine year for entertainment. In September 1963, 34 new weekly series turned up on the networks' nighttime schedule. Of these only 13 were invited back for a second round. And the percentage was even lower for the number of show business "names" that survived.

Before the season started, many people had high hopes for the shows of Judy Garland, Jerry Lewis, Danny Kaye and

Richard Boone. Only Danny Kaye, whose giant talent provided a consistently charming hour each Wednesday night, won a renewal. Miss Garland's weekly effort was seldom entertaining.

The Jerry Lewis Show, on ABC, was heralded as the boldest experiment in TV programing since the introduction of the spectacular. The Lewis innovation was a two-hour show, all live, on Saturday nights. According to the ABC drumbeaters, the show would put no stopwatches on any phase of the comedian's performance. If the short-lived venture (it folded long before the season's end) proved anything, it was that Jerry Lewis *needs* a stopwatch.

There were other show-business lights that went into darkness during the year. Phil Silvers attempted to revitalize Sergeant Bilko in civilian clothes. He took on the role of Harry Grafton, foreman of a small factory and operator of a number of side

EMMY AWARDS WINNERS

Program of the Year: **The Making of the President, 1960,** ABC
Comedy Program: **The Dick Van Dyke Show,** CBS
Dramatic Program: **The Defenders,** CBS
Musical Program: **The Bell Telephone Hour,** NBC
Variety Program: **The Danny Kaye Show,** CBS
Children's Program: **Discovery '63/'64,** ABC
Documentary: **The Making of the President, 1960**
News Reports: **Huntley-Brinkley Report,** NBC
Actor: **Jack Klugman** ("Blacklist" on *The Defenders*)
Actress: **Shelley Winters** ("Two is the Number" on *Bob Hope Presents the Chrysler Theater*), NBC
Actor (series): **Dick Van Dyke** (*The Dick Van Dyke Show*)
Actress (series): **Mary Tyler Moore** (*The Dick Van Dyke Show*)
Supporting Actor: **Albert Paulsen** ("One Day in the Life of Ivan Denisovich" on *Bob Hope Presents the Chrysler Theater*)
Supporting Actress: **Ruth White** ("Little Moon of Alban" on *Hallmark Hall of Fame*), NBC
Outstanding Performance in Variety, Musical or Series: **Danny Kaye** (*The Danny Kaye Show*)
Director (drama): **Tom Gries** ("Who Do You Kill?" on *East Side/West Side*), CBS
Director (comedy): **Jerry Paris** (*The Dick Van Dyke Show*)

ABC

Frank Buxton and Virginia Gibson on award-winning "Discovery '64."

lines. But like most imitations, this Bilko was inferior to the original. In *Grindl,* a Sunday evening comedy series, Imogene Coca was presented as a maid-of-all-trades who blunders around from employer to employer solving mysteries. Neither show was invited back for the new season.

A few well-intentioned series were unable to survive in the commercial world of television. Among these were *The Great Adventure,* dramatizations based on American history; *Arrest and Trial,* a 90-minute court series; and *East Side, West Side.* In this, the enormously talented George C. Scott played a social worker in a private welfare agency in Manhattan. The show dealt forcefully with current social problems. Although *East Side, West Side* had enough fans among viewers, it did not attract enough sponsors. So CBS decided to replace it with one of the happy-type shows favored by sponsors.

The lengthy list of unrenewed shows also contained a number of long-run series, including *The Garry Moore Show.* Moore did not take kindly to the CBS rejection and asked to be released from his moderator's role on *I've Got a Secret* as well as his CBS radio chores. The network reluctantly agreed. Mitch Miller was another disappointed personality when he could not get a new TV lease for his *Sing Along With Mitch. The Joey Bishop Show* also faded, along with *Route 66, The Eleventh Hour, Du Pont Show of the Week, 77 Sunset Strip,* Rod Serling's *The Twilight Zone* and the weekly boxing telecasts.

The American Broadcasting Company had the largest number of holdover shows among the new series: six, in all. The most interesting of these, from a critic's standpoint, was *The Fugitive,* which starred David Janssen in a tale of hunter and hunted. ABC's other surviving shows in-

255

cluded two situation comedies, *The Patty Duke Show* and *The Farmer's Daughter*. There was also a girly-girly detective show, *Burke's Law,* and a country music variety program known as *The Jimmy Dean Show*. In addition, a well-produced science-fiction effort called *The Outer Limits* was kept.

NBC kept only four of the shows it introduced during the 1963-64 season. *Mr. Novak,* offering low-key dramatizations of life in a contemporary high school, proved popular enough to be brought on again, as did *The Bill Dana Show,* an occasionally amusing series about a mixed-up bellhop. *Kraft Suspense Theater* and Bob Hope's anthology series, a mixture of variety, comedy, mystery and drama, also remained.

CBS, which introduced fewer new shows than either of the other two networks, kept three. One was *Petticoat Junction,* which was obviously inspired by the season's top-rated show, *The Beverly Hillbillies,* and is just as silly. *My Favorite Martian,* about a Martian anthropologist gone wrong, and the always-delightful *Danny Kaye Show* were also presented again.

Two late starters, ABC's *The Hollywood Palace* and NBC's *That Was The Week That Was,* both of which debuted in mid-season, were deservedly held over. *The Hollywood Palace* offers a different variety bill each week with names from all sections of show business in a guest-emcee position. *That Was The Week That Was* takes its scripts from the week's headlines and laces them with satire. The satire is not always biting but neither is it dull.

And if the year's new ventures did not satisfy the viewer, there were enough "old" television friends on the scene to fill his leisure hours at home. Among the familiar programs were Jackie Gleason and his *American Scene Magazine, The Defenders,* Ed Sullivan's show, *What's My Line,* Walt Disney's *Wonderful World of Color, Candid Camera, Bonanza, The Lucy Show* with Lucille Ball, *The Dick Van Dyke Show, Ben Casey* and *Dr. Kildare.* Familiar faces

included Danny Thomas, Red Skelton, Jack Benny, Jack Paar, Perry Como and Andy Williams.

The year's specials (once called spectaculars) did not create the excitement they once did, largely because few were really special. Carol Burnett starred in an undistinguished *Calamity Jane* on CBS, and Sid Caesar and Edie Adams teamed up for an uninspired ABC special. Andy Williams regularly provided pleasant hours on NBC. Robert Goulet joined his bride Carol Lawrence on CBS for a nice musical interlude. Classical music was well represented on TV by the *Bell Telephone Hour,* the *NBC Opera Company,* the *Young People's Concerts* with Leonard Bernstein at the helm. *Lincoln Center Day* was the title for an hour of music and dance from New York's new cultural Center. There was also an impressive performance on CBS by London's Royal Ballet with Dame Margot Fonteyn and Rudolf Nureyev.

The dramatic specials were confined mainly to adaptations of the classics. Ingrid Bergman appeared as *Hedda Gabler.* Richard Burton and Maurice Evans starred in *The Tempest.* Charlton Heston played Thomas Jefferson in *The Patriots.* Jason Robards, Jr., was *Abe Lincoln In Illinois.* And *A Cry of Angels,* a play with music based on Handel's *The Messiah,* was seen.

Significantly, the specials that created the most talk were those out of the news-public-affairs departments. *CBS Reports* came up with a number of worthwhile shows. Also first-rate were the Chet Huntley specials and David Brinkley's *Our Man on the Mississippi. The Making of a President,* about the presidential campaign of John F. Kennedy, was a stirring piece. It won the Emmy for Program of the Year.

In nonprograming areas of television, color television had yet to get off the ground in spite of a drop in retail prices. And pessimism also prevailed over the prospects of pay-TV, despite plans on the west coast for a big pay-television operation that would eventually go national.

Television and Radio Ratings

...rating services determine the fate of our favorite TV and radio shows

By SANFORD R. WHITE

FOR IMMEDIATE RELEASE
(CURRENT UNTIL JUNE 5)

NATIONAL NIELSEN-RATINGS

TOP SPONSORED NETWORK TELEVISION PROGRAMS

BASED ON NIELSEN ESTIMATES IN FIRST NTI REPORT FOR

MAY 1964 (TWO WEEKS ENDING MAY 10) *

NIELSEN AVERAGE AUDIENCE (†)

RANK		RATING % U.S. TV HOMES	NO. HOMES (000)
1.	BEVERLY HILLBILLIES	35.6	18,260
2.	BONANZA	34.2	17,540
3.	DICK VAN DYKE SHOW	29.9	15,340
4.	ANDY GRIFFITH SHOW	29.4	15,080
5.	PETTICOAT JUNCTION	29.3	15,030
6.	DANNY THOMAS SHOW	25.6	13,130
7.	LUCY SHOW	25.5	13,060
8.	JACK BENNY SHOW	23.7	12,160
9.	CANDID CAMERA	23.5	12,060
9.	ED SULLIVAN SHOW	23.5	12,060

* SUBJECT TO DEFINITIONS & REMINDERS IN THE NTI REPORT.
(†) Homes reached during the average minute of the program.

MANY American television viewers have been puzzled about one thing. Just what affects the fate of a TV show? Why is one show kept on the air and another show "killed"? The research departments of advertising agencies and the sponsors of TV shows decide which shows will continue. But they base their decisions on information given to them by companies called rating services.

Rating services play a very important role in radio and television programing. But in 1963 many people wondered whether these services were effective. The methods of the largest radio and television rating service, the A. C. Nielsen Company, were questioned. An investigation was even conducted by the Congress of the United States. After this investigation, Congress and the Federal Communications Commission were convinced that the rating system used by Nielsen was legitimate and effective.

How does Nielsen rate a television show? Usually an electronic device called an audimeter is used. This machine is attached to the television set. It records what channels are turned on during a certain period of time. It also records the length of time each channel is turned on. In this way, the rating service can find out which programs are the most popular.

In principle this system would seem accurate. But some people did not think so. They felt that too few audimeters were used. Out of nearly 60,000,000 television sets that were in the United States as of January 1, 1962, audimeters were placed in only 1,200 of them. This seems to be a very small number. But Nielsen argued that audimeters are very carefully placed. The families or individuals are chosen to represent different social and economic backgrounds. And the audimeters are placed in different areas of the country. Therefore, Nielsen feels that these people, though few in number, do represent the viewing public accurately. The audimeters automatically record all the programs that are seen in the homes in which they are installed. Thus Nielsen is convinced that the ratings are accurate.

The American Research Bureau (ARB) is the second-largest rating service. It concentrates more on the local level. Nielsen emphasizes the national, or network, level. In addition to using audimeters, Nielsen and the ARB have also used personal interviews for researching program ratings. Interviewers visit people in their homes. They ask them all kinds of questions about the various shows. Closed-circuit television is another way for researchers to find out viewers' reactions. They ask people to view TV shows or commercials, either on tape or film, in a special theater. Each person is then given a questionnaire to fill out. He is asked to write down his opinions and comments. Here, too, the researchers try to choose a varied group of people. It is best if they have different social and economic backgrounds, and if they come from different parts of the country. This system is less accurate than the audimeter system. For one thing, very few people can be questioned at one time. And seeing a TV show in a theater is not the same as viewing it in your own home.

When is the best time of the year to determine ratings of radio and television programs? For the most accurate results, ratings should be made during the last two weeks in February and the first two weeks in March. By this time, all the programs have been on the air for six months—since September. Before that, during the summer, reruns were seen. After the February-March period, the advertising agencies and the companies that sponsor the shows (you see their commercials) decide the fate of the programs.

The Nielsen ratings are based on surveys done in the 32 largest cities of the United States and the areas that surround them. Ratings are made every week. The weekly ratings are then combined into what is called a "four-week cumulative audience." A National Nielsen Television Index (NTI) is issued twice a month. These go to subscribers, such as advertising agencies and television and radio stations or networks. These booklets are sent out about 15 days after the report period. They tell about weekly ratings for the television programs, television trends, and how different types of programs compare in the ratings. Finally, Nielsen also issues a Comprehensive Audience Composition Report four times a year. This gives the number of viewers-per-set in the homes tested. It also tells the age and sex of the television audience.

Similar reports are sent out by Nielsen for radio ratings. The National Nielsen Radio Index (NRI) is issued twice a month. This report covers sponsored network radio programs. It shows the number of United States radio homes reached per minute and per broadcast. In addition, there is the Auto-Plus Report. This is issued three times a year. It shows who makes up the car-radio audience. It also shows the size of the audience in relation to the home audience. How do researchers find out what programs car owners listen to when they are driving? Very simple. Researchers examine cars in parking lots at different times of the day. They note the station at which the radio was turned off.

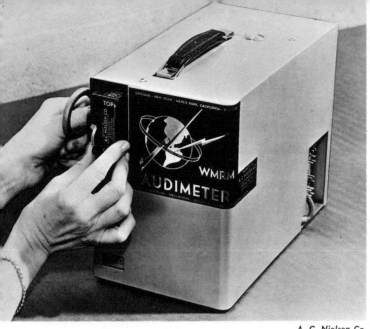

The A. C. Nielsen Company has placed about 1,200 audimeters in homes across the nation. These devices are attached to TV sets. They record what channels are turned on and how long they are on.

A. C. Nielsen Co.

The NTI is the most widely used guide of all the television reports. In this report, all sponsored network programs are arranged alphabetically in what is called the Program Ratings Summary. In a separate section, the programs are also arranged according to when they are on the air: (a) evening, (b) weekday, (c) weekend daytime. The time at which a program is shown is very important in determining its rating. For example, more people watch TV between eight and ten P.M. than at any other time. And more people watch TV on Saturday night than on any other night. Therefore the networks and local radio stations make sponsors pay much more to use these prime times. The sponsor must decide whether his program will sell enough of his product to make the high price he is paying for prime time worthwhile.

In spite of what the ratings tell us, strange things sometimes happen. For example, not long ago *Doctor Kildare* was running on prime air time on NBC. The show received an excellent rating. However, the sponsors wanted a still better rating. So they decided to change the show to another night. They kept the show on prime time but ran it at the same time as shows that had very low ratings on other networks. To the surprise of the sponsors, the rating fell. And the ratings of the competing shows went up. No one was able to explain this strange occurrence.

Another strange occurrence took place in 1958. A live dramatic daytime show called *Matinee Theater* was taken off the air because it had a very low rating. CBS promptly received millions of letters from viewers all over the country. They wanted the show to be continued. Many people even sent money to help put the show back on the air. The network was very impressed by this display of public indignation. It put the show back on.

In general, however, the rating system has been effective. It measures the overall popularity of a program. And a high rating usually means more sales for the sponsor's product. This is very important, since sponsors keep shows on the air.

For a number of years the most popular type of television show has been the "situation comedy," such as *I Love Lucy* and *The Beverly Hillbillies*. This type of show is a light, family comedy. Each episode presents a different plot or situation in the lives of the same central characters. In general the sales of products sponsored by this type of show match the high ratings given to it. So, in one respect at least, the rating services have proved to doubters that they are accurate and are here to stay.

Music
and Record Review

By HUBERT SAAL

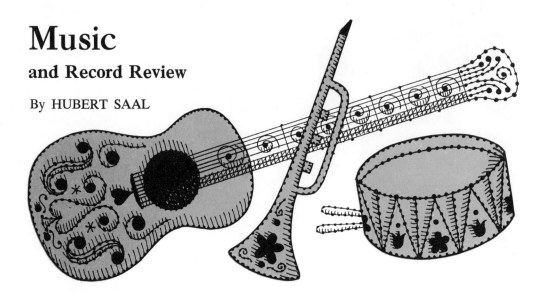

Classical and Opera

Richard Strauss, who composed both orchestral and operatic music during his long life, was born on June 11, 1864. Thus the centenary of his birth came in 1964. In Germany and Austria, municipalities competed with each other to see who could honor Strauss most. Munich won over cities like Berlin, Vienna and Dresden. Not only did they commemorate Strauss in Munich by issuing gold and silver coins, but they played every musical work he had ever written.

The United States paid somewhat less attention to the Strauss centennial. However, the Metropolitan Opera in its 1963-64 season presented his *Ariadne auf Naxos*. The Met also planned both *Der Rosenkavalier* and *Salome* for the 1964-65 season. The San Francisco Opera featured *Die Frau Ohne Schatten*. And Strauss' *Daphne* received its first American performance at the Santa Fe Opera.

The Metropolitan had two opera seasons. The first, 1963-64, was Rudolph Bing's fourteenth season as general manager. In this seventy-ninth Metropolitan season, Gian Carlo Menotti's eleventh opera, *The Last Savage,* was offered. It tells

the story of a Vassar girl who searches for the Abominable Snowman. The Met put on its biggest production in 1964 in honor of Shakespeare's four hundredth birthday. It was Verdi's *Falstaff,* which was sung by three different basses: Anzo Colzani, Fernando Corena and Geraint Evans. This production marked the Metropolitan debut of the permanent conductor of the New York Philharmonic, Leonard Bernstein. Also during the regular season, Renata Tebaldi returned to the Met as Mimi in *La Bohème.*

On February 15 at the matinee of *Otello,* the Met, for the first time since its doors opened in 1883, had no standees. Annoyed by some noisy enthusiasts, Mr. Bing outlawed standees. They took revenge by picketing the Met with signs reading, for example, "Exit Bing, Enter Callas." This was a reference to the quarrel between Mr. Bing and soprano Maria Callas that has kept her from singing at the Metropolitan for the last few years. Mr. Bing reversed his rule against standees after one performance. Before the year was over, he also announced that Miss Callas would return to the Met the following year.

Beginning April 27, the Metropolitan offered a special World's Fair season. It presented 16 highlights of the previous season. Among the outstanding singers who performed were Joan Sutherland, Birgit Nilsson, Leontyne Price, Miss Tebaldi, Richard Tucker, Cesare Siepi and Jerome Hines. The 1964 fall season opened on October 12, 1964, with Joan Sutherland in *Lucia di Lammermoor*. Another fall highlight was the Metropolitan debut of Elisabeth Schwartzkopf as the Marschallin in Strauss' *Der Rosenkavalier*.

San Francisco's spring season featured *Aïda* with Leontyne Price, and *The Italian Girl in Algeria* starring Marilyn Horne. Miss Horne's voice had already astounded New York twice during 1964. On February 18 she and Joan Sutherland participated in a concert version of Rossini's *Semiramide*. Her solo New York debut on April 22 was also warmly praised. San Francisco's 1964 fall season featured the American premiere of Dimitri Shostakovich's *Katerina Ismailova*.

Additional operatic news was made elsewhere. In Boston, Joan Sutherland sang Bellini's *I Puritani* with the Boston opera group. The great American composer Roger Sessions had his full-length opera *Montezuma* produced in Germany. *Montezuma* is based on the story of Cortez and the Spanish conquest of Mexico. In Central City, Colorado, Pulitzer-Prizewinning composer Robert Ward presented *The Lady from Colorado*. It has a libretto by Bernard Stambler, with whom Ward had previously written *The Crucible*. At Bristol Cathedral in England a short opera, *Martin's Lie* by Gian Carlo Menotti, was offered for the first time. At the Aldeburgh Festival in England, Benjamin Britten's new opera, *Curlew River,* received its world premiere. Later in the summer Mr. Britten received $30,000, the first Aspen (Colorado) Award in Humanities.

Other notable musical premieres in 1964 included the surprise unveiling of a tribute

Soprano Joan Sutherland in costume for the title role in Donizetti's "Lucia di Lammermoor," which opened the Metropolitan Opera's fall season.

Louis Mélançon, Metropolitan Opera Association

to John F. Kennedy by composer Igor Stravinsky and poet W. H. Auden. Their work was performed in Los Angeles on April 6. Stravinsky's short *Abraham and Isaac* cantata received its first performance in Tel Aviv on August 23. Leonard Bernstein's Symphony No. 3 (*Kaddish*) had its premiere in Boston on January 31. It was played by the Boston Symphony under the baton of Charles Munch. On April 9, composer Bernstein led the New York Philharmonic in the first New York performance of his new work. There was also Aaron Copland's *Music for a Great City* with the London Symphony Orchestra on May 26, the Sixth Symphony of Mexican composer Carlos Chavez on May 7, and Darius Milhaud's oratorio *Peace on Earth*. Milhaud set his music to the late Pope John's famous encyclical. It was performed in Paris in the cathedral of Notre Dame, which celebrated its 800th birthday in 1964.

Milestones in music included the deaths of conductor Pierre Monteux and composer Marc Blitzstein. After forty years, Howard Hanson retired as director of the Eastman School of Music. He was succeeded by Walter Hendl, formerly associate conductor of the Chicago Symphony. Herbert von Karajan resigned after eight years as artistic director of the Vienna State Opera. A Brazilian, Eleazar de Carvalho, became the new conductor of the St. Louis Symphony.

Jazz

In the world of jazz, many American musicians were traveling abroad. The cool jazz players, like Dave Brubeck, flutist Herbie Mann, the Modern Jazz Quartet and Charlie Mingus, were especially well received in Europe and in the Far East. George Wein, producer of the Newport Jazz Festival, planned a roaming jazz festival in Europe. Among those he lined up to go were the Miles Davis Quintet, the Dave Brubeck Quartet, Sonny Stitt, Coleman Hawkins, Bud Freeman and Pee Wee Russell. Trumpeter Chet Baker and pianist Bud Powell came back to the United States after long stays in Europe.

Avant-garde reed man Eric Dolphy died at the age of 36 in Paris. The year also saw the deaths of the great trombonist Jack Teagarden, of boogie-woogie pianist Meade Lux Lewis and pianist Teddy Napoleon.

Jazz festivals were held in many cities in the United States, in Europe and even in Tokyo. The biggest splash, of course, was Newport. There, everything from the hot jazz of Bud Freeman, Pee Wee Russell and Bobby Haggart to the cool jazz of Thelonius Monk, Dave Brubeck and Stan Getz was on hand. There too were Louis Armstrong and his All-Stars, stride pianist Willie "the Lion" Smith and trumpeter Max Kaminsky.

Among the big jazz dates of the year was July 20. On that day hot jazzmen like Billy Butterfield, Zutty Singleton, Bobby Hackett and Yank Lawson recalled the old days in a tribute to Eddie Condon, the Chicago-style guitarist. The tribute was played at Carnegie Hall. Earlier in the year the old Benny Goodman Quartet (Benny, Lionel Hampton on the vibraphones, drummer Gene Krupa and pianist Teddy Wilson) had gotten together and played at Carnegie Hall. On the West Coast, Disneyland had a big week for jazz in June. Count Basie, Duke Ellington and Benny Goodman—with their orchestras—all played there at the same time.

Several jazz musicians entertained at the White House. The first to be invited there was guitarist Charlie Byrd's trio. Then the Dave Brubeck Quartet played for President and Mrs. Johnson and their guest of honor, jazz fan King Hussein of Jordan. Later in the year, the Gerry Mulligan Quartet also played there.

Folk

In Mississippi during the summer a folk-music caravan toured in an attempt to increase voter registration. Such singers as Pete Seeger, Theodore Bikel, Judy Collins

Veteran trumpeter Louis Armstrong took the title song from Broadway's biggest hit, "Hello, Dolly!," gave it his unique vocal and musical interpretation and came up with a runaway best seller.

and Len Chandler were in the caravan. Pete Seeger also toured Russia. He won great success, paving the way for Leon Bibb, who sang there soon afterward. As usual, the Newport Folk Festival attracted the leaders in the folk-singing field. Nearly everyone, from Joan Baez and Bob Dylan to Young Phil Ochs and recently discovered bluesman Mississippi John Hurt, was there.

Popular

In popular music the news, of course, was all Beatles. They first invaded the United States on February 7, 1964. The country will probably never be the same again. Naturally their album *Meet the Beatles* was the most popular one of the year. A song from this album, "I Want to Hold Your Hand," was the most popular song of the year. "Hello, Dolly," played by Louis Armstrong, came in second to it.

This was the year that Harry James celebrated his twenty-fifth anniversary of leading big bands. Frank Sinatra continued to lead Elvis Presley as America's most popular vocalist. Connie Francis topped Brenda Lee, and Henry Mancini led all the bandleaders. Singing groups had strange names: The Animals, the Supremes, the Rolling Stones, the Beach Boys (who sang about cars in songs like "This Car of Mine"), and the Four Seasons with their hit, "Rag Doll." One of the prettiest songs of the year was "The Girl from Ipanema." In it Stan Getz and his saxophone wove neat designs around young Brazilian singer Astrud Gilberto.

RECORD REVIEW

Outstanding among the many records released during the 1963-64 season were:

Classical and Opera

Bach: *Well-Tempered Clavier*, Book I: Preludes and Fugues 9-16; Glenn Gould, piano. Columbia MS-6538.

Bartok: Music for Strings, Percussion, Celesta; New York Philharmonic, conducted by Leonard Bernstein. Columbia MS-6579.

Beethoven: Triple Concerto, in C (opus 56), with Rudolph Serkin, Jaime Laredo and Leslie Parnas, Columbia MS-6564.

Bellini: *I Puritani*, with Joan Sutherland; orchestra and chorus of Maggio Musicale Fiorentino, conducted by Richard Bonynge. London (OSA-1373).

Bernstein: Symphony No. 3 (*Kaddish*); New York Philharmonic, conducted by Leonard Bernstein. Columbia KS-6605.

Bizet: *Carmen*, with Leontyne Price, Franco Corelli; Vienna Philharmonic Orchestra, conducted by Herbert von Karajan. RCA Victor LDS-6164.

Brahms: Overtures: *Academic Festival Overture* (opus 80), Variations on a Theme by Haydn (opus 56a); Philadelphia Philharmonic Orchestra, conducted by Josef Krips. Angel S-36170.

Handel: *Israel in Egypt*; orchestra and chorus of Musica Aeterna, conducted by Frederic Waldman. Decca DXS-7178.

Haydn: Symphonies No. 95 in C minor and 101 in D (*Clock*); conducted by Fritz Reiner. RCA Victor LSC-2742.

Haydn: Quartet for Strings in C (opus 76), No. 3 (*Emperor*); Amadeus Quartet. Deutsche Grammophon SLPM-138886.

Milhaud: *A Frenchman in New York*; Boston Pops, conducted by Arthur Fiedler. RCA Victor LSC-2702.

Mozart: Sinfonia Concertante in E♭, K. 364, Duo in G, with Igor and David Oistrakh; Moscow Philharmonic, conducted by Kiril Kondrashin. London CS-6377.

Mozart: *The Marriage of Figaro*, K. 492, with Teresa Stitch-Randall, Rita Streich, Ronaldo Panarai; conducted by Hans Rosbaud. Vox Box OPBX-165.

Schubert: Fantasia in C, opus 15 (*Wanderer*); Sonata for Piano No. 13, in A (opus 120); Sviatoslav Richter. Angel S-36150.

Schubert: Quintet in C (opus 163, D. 956); Budapest Quartet, with Benar Heifetz, cello. Columbia MS-6536.

Schubert: *Winterreise*, D. 911; Dietrich Fischer-Dieskau. Angel S-3640.

Strauss, Richard: *Till Eulenspiegel* (opus 28); *Don Juan* (opus 20); *Salome: Dance of the Seven Veils*, Festival Prelude; Berlin Philharmonic, conducted by Karl Böhm. Deutsche Grammaphon SLPM-138866.

Tchaikovsky: *Swan Lake* (Ballet suite excerpts); Boston Pops, conducted by Arthur Fiedler. RCA Victor LSC-2688.

Verdi: *Falstaff*, with Geraint Evans; RCA Victor Chorus and Orchestra, conducted by Georg Solti. RCA Victor LSC-6163.

Jazz

Armstrong, Louis: *Hello, Dolly!* Kapp KS-3364.

Brubeck, Dave (Quartet): *Time Changes.* Columbia CS-8927.

Ellington, Duke: *Afro-Bossa.* Reprise R9-6069.

Fitzgerald, Ella: *These Are the Blues:* Verve V64062.

Gillespie, Dizzy: *New Wave!* Philips 600070.

Goodman, Benny: *Together Again!* RCA Victor LSP-2698.

Herman, Woody: *Woody Herman,* 1964. Philips PHS-600118.

Jazz Odyssey Vol. II: The Sound of Chicago 1923-1940, 48 selections. Columbia (mono) C3L32.

Reinhardt, Django (and the Quintet): *The Hot Club of France.* Capitol (mono) T2045.

Teagarden, Jack: *Tribute to Teagarden.* Capitol S-2076.

Folk

Baez, Joan: *Joan Baez in Concert,* Part 2. Vanguard 2123.

Bikel, Theodore: *A Folksinger's Choice.* Electra EKL 7250.

Hurt, Mississippi John: Folksongs and Blues. Piedmont (mono) 13157.

The Newport Festival-1963 (Vols. 1-2). Vanguard VSD 79148/9.

Seeger, Pete: *We Shall Overcome.* Columbia CS 8901.

The Serendipity Singers: *Twelve Songs.* Philips PHS 600134.

Popular

The Beatles: *Meet the Beatles.* Capitol ST-2047.

Getz, Stan: *Getz, Gilberto* (including "The Girl from Ipanema"). Verve S-8545.

The Dave Clark Five: *Glad All Over.* Epic 24093 (mono).

Funny Girl: original Broadway cast, starring Barbra Streisand. Capitol SVAS-2059.

Los Indios Tabajaras: *Ma ria Elena.* RCA Victor LSP-2822.

Mancini, Henry and his orchestra: *The Pink Panther.* RCA Victor LSP 2795.

Pavone, Rita: *The International Teenage Sensation.* RCA Victor LSP 2900.

Ray Charles Singers: *Something Special for Young Lovers.* Command 866SD.

Weill, Kurt: *Lady in the Dark* and *Down in the Valley.* RCA Victor LPV 503 (mono).

Wilson, Nancy: *Today, Tomorrow, Forever.* Capitol SI-2082.

MAKING A MOVIE

WHEN someone suggests going to the movies, he usually has in mind a trip to the neighborhood theater to see a feature film. With the feature he will often see other types of films. There may be a newsreel or a cartoon or a short subject, such as a travelogue or a documentary. Outside of theaters, movies are widely used to educate—in industry, science and schools. Television relies on filmed programs for educational as well as commercial viewing. Sports figures watch films of themselves and their competitors in order to improve their performance. However, movies still mean entertainment to most people. And in this section we are dealing with feature films that are made to entertain.

Feature films are often shot entirely in a studio. The typical movie studio is almost a self-contained community. It covers dozens of acres. Besides offices and laboratories and various specialized departments, there are huge sound stages, where both pictures and dialogue are recorded, and numerous elaborate sets. Today, however, more and more movies are being filmed outside the studio, on location. This practice makes it possible for films to make dramatic use of interesting or exotic places, or to make a movie seem more real.

The very minimum needed to make a movie is a man, a camera and some film. The first Hollywood movies were practically that simple. Through the years, however, the single man has turned into an army of specialists. Now representatives of almost three hundred professions or trades can be found in film studios. These include everyone from the star to sound dubbers, camera-crane operators and special-effects men such as the greensmen who create tropics, forests or fields as they are needed, or the powder men, who make smoke without fire. In this army of craftsmen, none are more important than the producer, the director, the actor and the cameraman. On the following pages, distinguished representatives of these four key professions discuss their craft.

Columbia Pictures Corp.

ACTING

By ELI WALLACH

In a scene from a recent movie, "The Victors," the author confronts French film star Jeanne Moreau.

GOOD acting—on stage or screen—means using your imagination. You must make believe that what you are doing is really happening, that you really are flying a plane or being shot.

Generally, screen acting, at least for the stage-trained actor, is not as satisfying as working on the stage. When he performs before a live audience, the stage actor lives through an experience or a role. The audience is his mirror. It provides him with an immediate response and reaction to his work. Because he gets the chance to go back and do it over, the actor can apply the insights that repeated playing before a live audience gives him. In this way he is able to correct and polish his role.

Screen acting is very different. Seeing yourself on the screen leaves you with a great sense of helplessness. "Is that me?" you ask. "Do I sound and look like that? If only I could go back and do it over!" But once the scene is shot, the actor rarely gets the chance to go back to correct, change or improve his performance. Filming is done in short scenes, often not in the sequence of the plot. The actor's performance is edited so that the final result is fitted together like a mosaic or a jigsaw puzzle. Also, on a movie screen the actor is brought up close to the viewer. The sharp and penetrating eye of the camera requires the utmost sense of truth in the actor's performance. Every nuance, inflection and even thought is captured by the camera.

Screen acting demands great concentration and patience. It sometimes takes hours to prepare scenes, light them, get horses or special effects ready. However, when "action" is finally called, regardless of how long you've been waiting you must be alert and prepared, so that you can come immediately to life before the camera. Each scene should appear fresh and spontaneous. No matter how many retakes there are, the actor must give the impression that it is all happening for the first time. In addition, he must be aware not only of what he has to say or do in the scene he is filming, but also of what happened just before the scene—where he came from and what his relationship is with the other people in the scene.

One delight that screen acting provides is traveling to strange and exotic locations. "Join the movies and see the world!" is now true. The screen actor may be sent wherever the story takes him—Cambodia, Spain, Greece, Yugoslavia. In this way he can absorb and use the customs, traditions and costumes of the locale.

DIRECTING

By OTTO PREMINGER

Vytas Valaitis

The author directs John Wayne in a scene from his new film "In Harm's Way."

THE popular image of the director is that of a man who tells actors when to enter and exit, to sit down and get up, to stand still or move, and—to some degree at least—how to read their lines. Working with actors is indeed a vital part of the director's function. The relationship between director and actor is very important to the final success of the whole project. It is an intimate relationship which depends on the personalities of both director and actor. Out of it grows the method of work, which is different in every individual case. Using his instinct and psychological experience, the director must find the right approach to the actor. He must get to him. The more intelligent the director and actor and the higher their mutual respect, the easier is the director's task. I do not believe that any director can make an untalented actor give a first-rate performance. But on the other hand, even the greatest actor cannot project his talent without direction. This is particularly true in films where, unlike on the stage, the actor has no direct contact with the audience. Thus the director becomes not only his guide but also his only sounding board.

However, the director's function starts long before the actors are even chosen. A finished stage play or film script may be submitted to him. Or he may start with an original idea, novel, or other material which is being adapted for the screen. In either case, the work he does with the writer is just as essential as his work with the actors. To give direction to the script, to influence and most often decide the final shape of it before he starts rehearsals, is the director's most vital contribution. The writer, like the actor, depends on the director to re-create his work on the screen.

But there are many other artistic elements which the director blends into the final form of the film. His responsibility is to guide the art director, the cameraman, the costume designer, the sound mixer and so on down to the last electrician. He must make them express their talents to the fullest. In some of these functions, like casting or final editing, the director might share authority with the producer. It has often been argued who is more important and should have more say. I believe this does not depend on the title but on the personalities. The stronger one will leave his mark on the completed work.

267

PRODUCING

By DAVID O. SELZNICK

The author, here with director King
Vidor, on the set of one of his films.

ANYBODY who has a camera and film
negative can produce a motion picture.
Films produced by college students for
limited exhibition sometimes show great
promise. However, producing films for
worldwide showing is quite another matter. It involves the selection and super-
vision of artists and craftsmen in various
fields, and enormous financial investments.

Film production in the United States is
primarily in the hands of large corporations. These corporations usually supply
film makers with physical facilities as well
as financing. They also lease (distribute)
films to thousands of theaters the world
over. In the past, sometimes the truly independent producer arranged the financing himself. He was in charge of a film
from its beginning through its showing to
the public. Now, with the ever rising costs
and the increasing gamble involved, the
independent producer has almost entirely
passed from the scene. (This is less true
abroad.) Most of the so-called independent producers of today are simply satellites of their financing companies. The
degree of their artistic control varies according to their prestige and previous
successes.

Originally, a producer had authority
over not only the financial and business
aspects of making a film, but all of the
creative aspects as well. He chose the
story and either wrote or collaborated in
the writing of the screenplay. He selected
and closely supervised the directors, actors, cameramen, art directors, costume
designers, film cutters, musicians and all
the other creators and department heads

necessary to the making of a commercial
motion picture. In those days there were
also associate producers who worked for
large studios under the final authority of
executive producers.

In recent years an increasing number
of directors have become producers and
vice versa. And lately the legend "produced by" has often been applied, con-
fusingly and mistakenly, to entrepreneurs
and promoters who are in no sense actually producers.

Because of the virtual collapse of the
big Hollywood (Southern California)
studio hierarchal system, there is now no
proper training or proving ground for new
producers. This is unfortunate for the
motion-picture industry and its audiences,
and for the development of cinema as an
art form. Those who wish to study the
producing craft would probably be best
advised to seek their training in television, which is more closely allied to theatrical film making than is the living stage.

CINEMA-TOGRAPHY

By JAMES WONG HOWE

The author accepts an Oscar as the year's best cameraman for his work on "Hud."

Wide World

A DIRECTOR of photography does not actually operate the camera. His job is to direct his camera operator and crew. However, this involves many members of the company and is a long, involved process.

First, I read the script, or screenplay. Then, I study each scene to determine my approach for photographically creating the mood of the story. With the director, I talk over my ideas for lighting-mood for each sequence. Camera movements and angles usually are decided upon later when the action is rehearsed with the players. There are many discussions. The art director goes over the design of the set, including whether or not ceilings are to be used. (Most sets are built without ceilings for easier lighting and saving time.) The costume designer shows the colors and types of material to be used, as well as the designs. Set dressers, the electrical department and makeup artists are also consulted. Makeup of the players is very important, especially for women. Men seldom wear makeup unless a special character is to be portrayed. All must be approved by the producer, director and production office.

Before actual camera work begins, many photographic tests are required for the players. These tests determine makeup, costumes, proper lighting and correct angles for shooting. Photogenically speaking, there are few, if any, perfect faces. So it is up to the director of photography to make all necessary corrections with his various lenses, diffusion disks and special lighting.

The photographer must give the whole film a visual as well as a dramatic impact with his creative use of composition, lenses, camera movement, lighting. Lighting is not only important for players and places, seasons, time of day or night, and individual interiors, but for creating the mood of the story in general. Sometimes, if nature does not cooperate at the exact time of shooting, say, for instance, with a sunset or moonlight, the photographer must "make" a sunset or moonlight.

The average time for photographing a feature film is six to eight weeks; the multimillion-dollar spectacles take six months to a year. Film exposed through the camera for the average picture is 150,000 to 200,000 feet and may reach 500,000 to 1,000,000 feet in the spectacles. There are 16 frames to one foot of 35mm. film. At normal speed, 24 frames, or $1\frac{1}{2}$ feet of film, pass through the camera each second. Length of the usual feature film is 8,000 to 10,000 feet.

There are no set rules beyond basic knowledge of motion-picture photography. Imagination makes the difference. The photographer must continually experiment with new techniques to improve his art. He is most successful when he and the director work in close communication to bring the story to the screen.

NEW SCHOOL

On the following pages are featured some school-related topics which in 1964 were either in the news or were given added emphasis in classrooms. For example, the 50th anniversary of World War I and the 25th anniversary of World War II were observed during the year. These anniversaries might have highlighted studies in modern history. In 1964, too, it was reported that certain French scholars had objected to the adoption of English words into the French language. In this section language authority Charles Berlitz discusses the possibility of English becoming a world language as more and more languages adopt English words. Also in this section are articles on one aspect of the new math—sets—and on geography and maps, which in 1964 gained new importance in school curricula.

Susan McCartney, Photo Researchers

moellons bruts à l'aide de la smille.

SMOKING n. m. (de l'angl. *smoking-jacket*, jaquette que l'on met après le dîner pour fumer). Costume habillé d'homme, à revers de soie.

SMORZANDO [*dzan'*] adv. Terme musical
Sn. symbole chimique de l'*étain* (stannum).

SNACK-BAR n. m. (mot angl.; de *snack*, portion et *bar*). Restaurant servant rapidement à toute heure.

SNOB adj. et n. (mot angl.). Qui fait preuve de snobisme.

SNOBISME n. m. Admiration pour tout ce qui est en vogue.

SNOW-BOOT [*snô-boût'*] n. m. (mot angl.). Chaussure caoutchoutée et fourrée, pour la neige.

SOBRE adj. (lat. *sobrius*). Tempérant dans le

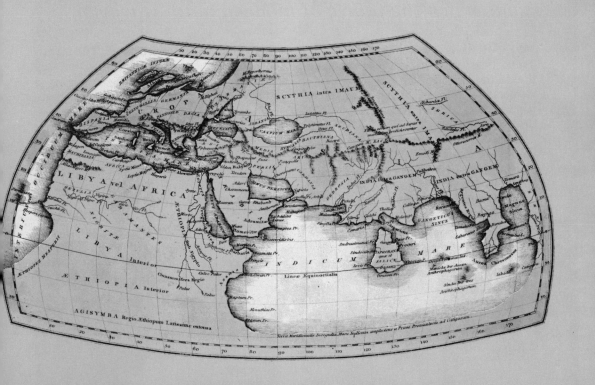

SETS

By BRYAN BUNCH

Photo Researchers

. . . a set is simply a collection of objects; still, set theory, operations and applications are the threads from which the fabric of modern math is woven.

TWELVE boys who are in Boy Scout Troop Four organized a paper drive with the Little League team, which has 15 members. Every boy showed up for the paper drive and there were 20 boys. How did this happen?

Probably you can guess that 7 boys were members of both Troop Four and the Little League team. Even though the numbers 12 and 15 add up to 27, when the two sets of boys got together there were not 27 boys. The mathematics of sets is different in some ways from the arithmetic children have been taught for many years. Today in many schools, children are learning the mathematics of sets along with the mathematics of numbers.

Children in these schools learn that a set is any collection of objects that is described

well enough. By "well enough," mathematicians mean that you must be able to tell whether or not a particular thing is a member of a given set. If it is a mathematical set, you can recognize its members. The boys in Troop Four form a set because it is clear that a boy is either a member of Troop Four or not.

This meaning for the word "set" should not be surprising. You have probably spoken of a set of dishes. A set of dishes includes dishes that are the same in design or color. If you have a cup and saucer that are white and a dinner plate that is white, probably you would feel that a brown or green dessert dish does not belong to the set.

It is also possible to have a set of objects that seem to be unrelated. But the objects must all be identified as belonging to the set. If the objects are unrelated, it is necessary to list them. For example, you might think of the set whose members are the torch on the Statue of Liberty, the River Nile, the letter Q, and Mount Rushmore.

To mathematicians, the most interesting sets are sets of numbers and sets of points. Mathematicians like to talk about the set of even numbers and its properties, or the fact that a circle is a set of points all at the same distance from a given point.

A set is often indicated by putting braces around the names of the objects in a set. For example, the set of counting numbers less than five can be indicated as

$$\{1, 2, 3, 4\}.$$

Another way to write this set is to use a short, vertical bar that means "such that" and a symbol such as Δ or **x**. These symbols can stand for any member of the set. Thus

$$\{\Delta/\Delta \text{ is a counting number less than 5}\}$$

is another way of showing the set

$$\{1, 2, 3, 4\}$$

The equal sign is used with sets that have the same members:

$\{1, 2, 3, 4\} = \{\Delta/\Delta$ is a counting number less than 5$\}$.

When two sets, such as the two sets of boys on the paper drive, are combined, the combination is called their union. The union of the two sets is the set that includes all the members of the two sets, but no other members. The set of boys on the paper drive was the union of these two sets:

$$\{\Delta/\Delta \text{ is in Troop Four}\}$$
and $\{\square/\square$ is in the Little League team$\}$.

The sign mathematicians use for union is like a capital U: $\cup$. Suppose we call the set of boys in Troop Four T, the set of boys on the Little League team L and the set of boys on the paper drive P. Then

$$T \cup L = P.$$

Consider the set $\{1, 2, 3, 4\}$ and the set $\{4, 5, 6\}$. What is their union? It is the set $\{1, 2, 3, 4, 5, 6\}$. Notice that the member 4 is included only once in the union, even though it is in both of the sets that form the union.

Say that the sets of points in the triangular regions below are named A and B as indicated on the diagram.

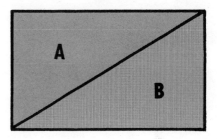

What is $A \cup B$? Is it the rectangular region?

Forming the union is not the only operation that can be performed on sets. Sometimes we want to know what members belong to both of two sets. The set of common members is called the intersection of the two sets. Do you remember that there were seven members in the intersection of the set of Scouts in Troop Four and the set of Little Leaguers?

The sign for set intersection is just the sign for set union turned upside down: $\cap$. We may write that

$$\{1, 2, 3, 4\} \cap \{4, 5, 6\} = 4.$$

The intersection of the set of points on line L and the set of points on circle O is just the two points labeled P and Q.

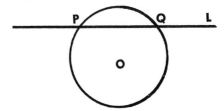

Can you find the intersection of the set of letters in your name and the set of vowels $\{a, e, i, o, u\}$?

273

The set shown below {white king, white queen} is a subset of the set shown in the photograph at the left, which is the set of all of the white chessmen in the game.

Suppose you say that the chessmen on the board in the left-hand picture form two sets: {black king, black pawn, black pawn} and {white rook, white king}. The set shown at right is the union of the two sets originally given. How is the union related to addition?

Harbrace Photos. Reproduced from "Mathematics—An Integrated Series, Book One," by H. Vernon Price, Philip Peak. Phillip S. Jones by permission of Harcourt, Brace & World, Inc.

What is the intersection of the set {1, 3, 5, 7, 9} and the set {2, 4, 6, 8}? These sets have no points in common. Their intersection is a set with no members. It is called the empty set and is very important in set mathematics. Consider the set of buildings taller than the Empire State Building. This set has no members, so it is one way of naming the empty set. Generally the empty set is represented by the sign ϕ. Do you think the following statement is true? The set of kings of the United States is ϕ.

We have seen one relation between sets. They may be equal. Suppose two sets are unequal. How can such sets be related? Consider the sets {1, 2, 3, 4} and {a, b, c, d}. Although they are not equal, these sets do seem to have something in common. Every member in the first set can be matched with exactly one member of the second set. And every member in the second set can be matched with exactly one member of the first:

$$\{1, \; 2, \; 3, \; 4\}$$
$$\updownarrow \; \updownarrow \; \updownarrow \; \updownarrow$$
$$\{a, \; b, \; c, \; d\}.$$

Such a matching is called a one-to-one correspondence. Two sets that can be so matched are said to be equivalent. Here are two sets that are not equivalent:

$$\bigcirc, \; \triangle, \; \square$$
$$\updownarrow \; \updownarrow \; \updownarrow$$
$$A, \; B, \; C, \; D.$$

All pairs of equal sets are equivalent. But equivalent sets need not be equal.

Consider the sets {1, 2, 3, 4} and {2, 3}. Are they equal? Are they equivalent? Although they are neither, there is a relation between the sets. Notice that every member of {2, 3} is also a member of {1, 2, 3, 4}. We say that {2, 3} is a subset of {1, 2, 3,

The set of pawns below can be separated into two sets: black and white. Are the two equivalent? Right: two equivalent sets have been taken from the board. Are the remaining sets equivalent?

Left: if you know there are 8 squares in each row, then the one-to-one correspondence between the set of pawns and the squares in a row proves the cardinal number of the set of pawns is 8. Right: are the two sets equal? No, because one has white elements, the other black. Are they equivalent?

4}. The sign for the subset relation is ⊆ :

$$\{2, 3\} \subseteq \{1, 2, 3, 4\}.$$

The subset relation has many uses in mathematics. For example, it is useful in geometry to view the set of squares as a subset of the set of rectangles.

The subset relation demands only that every member of set A be a member of set B for $A \subseteq B$ to be true. Therefore every set is a subset of itself:

$$\{a, b, c\} \subseteq \{a, b, c\}.$$

Also, although this is very hard to understand, mathematicians insist that ϕ is a subset of every set.

There is another possibility for a relation between two sets. Earlier we examined the sets {1, 3, 5, 7, 9} and {2, 4, 6, 8}. These two sets are not equal, and they are not equivalent. Neither one is a subset of the other. The fact that their intersection is empty is the main thing we know about these sets. When

$$A \cap B = \phi,$$

we say A and B are disjoint. The set of triangles and the set of circles are disjoint, since there are no triangles that are also circles.

Out of the operations of set union and intersection, and the relations of equality, equivalence, being a subset, and disjointedness, the theory of sets can be built. There are also other operations and relations.

The study of sets is less than one hundred years old. There are many questions about sets that no one can answer yet. Still, we are becoming more and more aware of the many uses of sets throughout mathematics, from kindergarten to research mathematics.

Geography and Maps

MAPS are pictures of places. But they are very special pictures. They can tell us what the weather is and where the stars and planets are. They can tell us how a continent is divided into different countries. They can also tell us the best way to get from one place to another. And they can tell us these things much better than words can.

All the different kinds of maps can be roughly divided into two groups: special maps and reference maps. Special maps illustrate a certain theme. They may show, for example, the distribution of population in a country. Or they may show how each part of a country voted in an election.

General reference maps tell us where continents, countries, states and cities are. They also show such features of the land as rivers and mountains. There are contour maps to tell us the shape of the land —where its hills and valleys are. Road maps and celestial maps are also reference maps.

A globe is the only true picture of the earth. But it has two important disadvantages. It is hard to carry around, and it is usually too small to have many details. A map is much easier to use.

Before you can use a map properly, you must know several things about it. The first thing to realize, of course, is that maps are drawn as if you were looking down on the area drawn. In other words, you have a bird's-eye view. Next you must realize that maps are drawn to scale. This means that everything on the map is drawn in the same proportion as it really is, but it is drawn much smaller. On the map, one inch may represent hundreds of real miles. A large-scale map is one that covers a small area in detail. A small-scale map may show the entire world, but it will not have many details. In an atlas, which is a whole book of maps, the scale of miles changes from map to map, even though the size of the pages stays the same. Thus, using different scales, a map of New York State can be drawn so that it is the same size as a map of the whole United States.

A great deal of information may be shown on a map by the use of color and symbols. Color can make clear at a glance the size and shape of countries or states. It can also give us all kinds of political information. For example, we could immediately tell which countries belong to NATO if the member countries were colored the same color on a map. Of course, the map legend would have to tell us what the color means.

Color can be used on physical maps too. On most such maps, certain standard colors show altitudes. Colors are used on most general maps in a similar way. For example, blue nearly always indicates rivers and bodies of water. Color is also used to describe the landscape. Various colors and shades of coloring can indicate types of soil and vegetation. The uses of color in maps are almost limitless.

Symbols are also important to the map reader. A map's symbols will usually be explained in the part of the map called the legend. A symbol can take almost any form. It may consist of dots, lines, geometric shapes such as triangles or circles, letters or, again, colors.

Symbols can show the natural or manmade features of an area. To make things easier for the map reader, the symbol often looks like what it is supposed to represent. For example, railroad tracks are often indicated by a long line with tiny lines crossing it. Forests may be seen as a tiny tree; dairy land by a drawing of a cow.

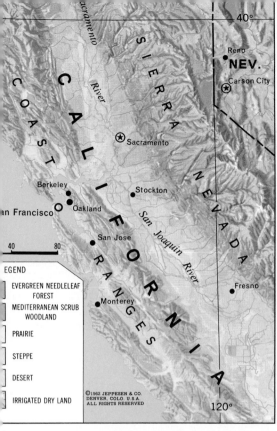

SIERRA NEVADA

CALIFORNIA

COAST RANGES

Reno
NEV.
Carson City ⊛

Sacramento ⊛

Berkeley
Stockton
San Francisco
Oakland
San Jose
San Joaquin River

Fresno
Monterey

40   80

120°

LEGEND

EVERGREEN NEEDLELEAF
FOREST

MEDITERRANEAN SCRUB
WOODLAND

PRAIRIE

STEPPE

DESERT

IRRIGATED DRY LAND

The map is the primary tool of the geographer and is used for plotting, studying, and interpreting the variety of distributions of phenomena with which he deals.

On this page are three maps of the same landscape, each designed to reveal a different aspect of the physical characteristics of the area or some aspect of man's use of it.

On the following three pages are additional maps, each of which describes some physical or cultural characteristic of the lands, or sets forth one of man's uses of the air and the seas.

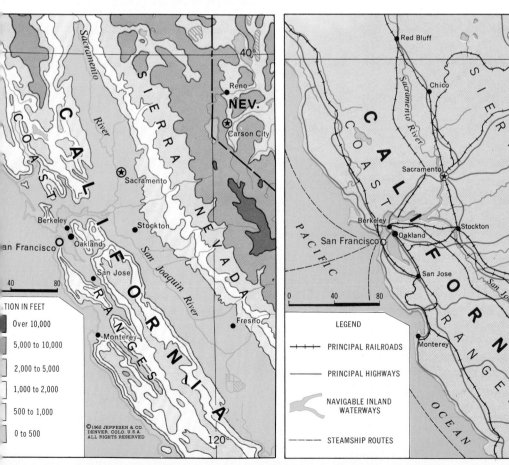

Sacramento River

SIERRA NEVADA

CALIFORNIA

COAST RANGES

Reno
NEV.
Carson City ⊛

Sacramento ⊛

Berkeley
Stockton
San Francisco
Oakland
San Jose
San Joaquin River

Fresno
Monterey

40   80

TION IN FEET

Over 10,000

5,000 to 10,000

2,000 to 5,000

1,000 to 2,000

500 to 1,000

0 to 500

120°

Red Bluff
Chico

Sacramento River

SIERRA NEVADA

CALIFORNIA

COAST

PACIFIC

Reno
NEV.
Carson City

Sacramento ⊛

Berkeley
Stockton
San Francisco
Oakland
San Jose
San Joaquin River

Fresno
Monterey
Hanford

OCEAN

0   40   80

LEGEND

+++ PRINCIPAL RAILROADS

PRINCIPAL HIGHWAYS

NAVIGABLE INLAND
WATERWAYS

--- STEAMSHIP ROUTES

40°

120°

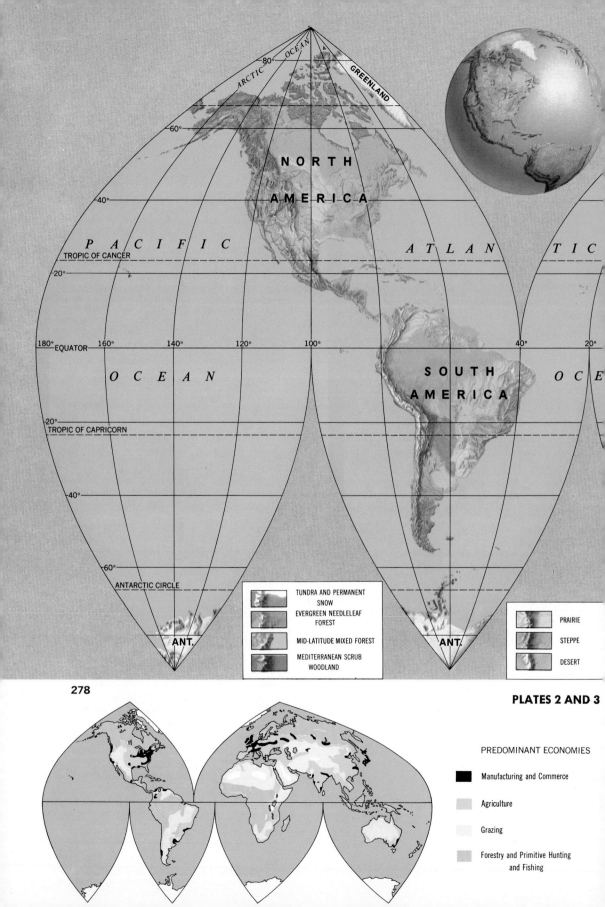

ARCTIC OCEAN

80°

GREENLAND

60°

NORTH

40°

AMERICA

P A C I F I C

A T L A N T I C

TROPIC OF CANCER

20°

180° EQUATOR 160° 140° 120° 100° 40° 20°

O C E A N

SOUTH

AMERICA

O C E

20°

TROPIC OF CAPRICORN

40°

60°

ANTARCTIC CIRCLE

	TUNDRA AND PERMANENT SNOW
	EVERGREEN NEEDLELEAF FOREST
	MID-LATITUDE MIXED FOREST
	MEDITERRANEAN SCRUB WOODLAND

ANT.   ANT.

	PRAIRIE
	STEPPE
	DESERT

PLATES 2 AND 3

PREDOMINANT ECONOMIES

	Manufacturing and Commerce
	Agriculture
	Grazing
	Forestry and Primitive Hunting and Fishing

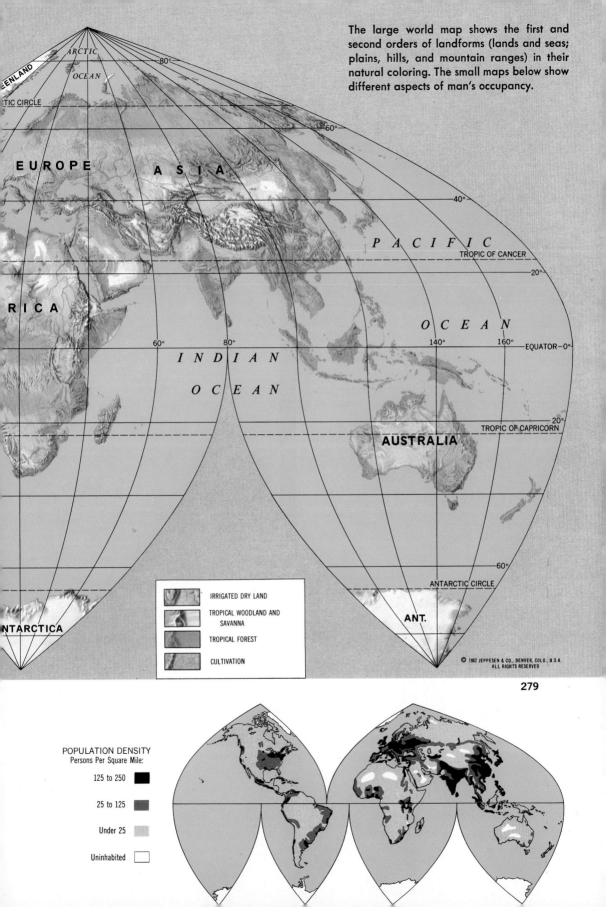

The large world map shows the first and second orders of landforms (lands and seas; plains, hills, and mountain ranges) in their natural coloring. The small maps below show different aspects of man's occupancy.

ARCTIC OCEAN

GREENLAND

ARCTIC CIRCLE

80°

60°

EUROPE

ASIA

AFRICA

40°

PACIFIC

TROPIC OF CANCER

20°

OCEAN

INDIAN

60°   80°   140°   160°   EQUATOR—0°

OCEAN

AUSTRALIA

20°
TROPIC OF CAPRICORN

60°

ANTARCTIC CIRCLE

ANTARCTICA

ANT.

	IRRIGATED DRY LAND
	TROPICAL WOODLAND AND SAVANNA
	TROPICAL FOREST
	CULTIVATION

POPULATION DENSITY
Persons Per Square Mile:

125 to 250	■
25 to 125	▨
Under 25	▤
Uninhabited	□

MAPS AS AN AID TO COMMERCE AND EXPLORATION

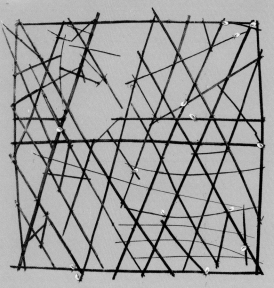

A primitive pilot chart prepared by islanders of the Pacific Ocean. The curved palm spines show prevailing wave fronts, the straight spines indicate sailing courses, and the shells locate islands.

A 16th-century portolan chart. Such charts were the earliest seafarers' maps that achieved wide distribution. The radial lines show compass directions from many different locations. These lines enabled mariners for the first time to set accurate sailing courses far out of sight of land, with fair expectation of reaching their destinations without losing time skirting the shores.

A portion of an accurate, modern air navigation chart.

Oktoba pancher FUTBOL hobby Far West FINISH beisbol BAW sorry hotodoqu

ENGLISH—A World Language ?

By CHARLES F. BERLITZ

. . . a noted language authority talks about the wide-spread use of English words in other languages

THE English language is more widely spoken than ever before in history. Even people who do not speak English understand and use at least a few English words. Certain English words and expressions are now part of languages in almost every part of the world. For example, *O.K., hello* and *stop* are used throughout the world. These may be the first words in a future "world" language.

There are many other English words that are used in almost every country. Golfers—even in Japan—herald their shots by shouting *fore!* And games such as poker, bridge and tennis usually keep their English names wherever they are played. English "travel" words have been popularized by English-speaking tourists. It is not odd for a European or a Latin American to use such words as *hotel, taxi, automobile, car, airport, club, sport, soda, sandwich, salad, steak, stewardess* and *hostess*. These words are often spelled differently in other languages. But when spoken they are easily understood by English-speaking people.

People whose native tongue is not English often do not like it when English words become part of their language. They tend to resist the adoption of English words, but for the most part they are not successful. There are many reasons why English words

keep invading other languages. In the first place, English is one of the most widely used languages. Some 275,000,000 people in different parts of the globe speak it as their first language. An equal number speak it as their second language.

English is spoken in the United States and the British Commonwealth countries. African and Asian nations have their own languages, but many of the leaders of these countries find English useful. Many of these leaders were trained by the British and went to schools in Great Britain. In some countries, such as India, many, many languages are spoken. Thus English is used as an official "compromise" language.

There are other reasons why English words are becoming more and more a part of other languages. Almost 100,000,000 of the world's telephones are in English-speaking countries. Thus most international calls are made in English. Most of the world's radio stations broadcast in English and 75 per cent of all international telegraph messages are sent in English. More than 50 per cent of the books, magazines and newspapers are printed in English. English is also the international language for air and sea communications. In addition, linguistic islands of English-speaking people are scattered throughout

281

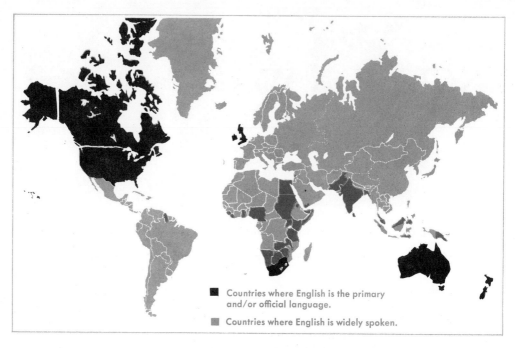

The fact that 275,000,000 people speak English as their first language, and another 275,000,000 use it as their second, makes English one of the world's most widely used languages.

the world. This has been especially true since World War II. These people have helped popularize English words among non-English-speaking peoples.

The United States has led the world in the military and space technology fields. Thus the names of most military and space items are in English. These names, too, have been adopted by foreign languages. Among them are *jet, rocket, radar, sonar, tank, mortar, jeep* and *bazooka*. The names of fabrics developed in the United States are also used in other languages: *rayon, Dacron* and *nylon*.

France is geographically close to Great Britain. Many of the English words that have come into use in the French language are commonly used in Britain: *weekend, business bar, five-o'clock tea, building, pullover, cardigan, smoking* (which means a tuxedo), *tennis, fair play, football* (not American football, but soccer), *camping* and *dancing* (which means a dance hall).

The French have also adopted many American-English words. American tourists, movies and television have been responsible for this. Among such words are *snack bar, parking, star, starlet, girl, outlaw, gangster, drugstore, derrick, Far West, gag, job, film* and *gang*. The following hybrid sentence would be perfectly understandable in modern French: "Hier soir, il y a eu un *holdup* dans le *snack bar* du coin, et les *gangsters* ont pris tout le *cash* mais ont laissé tous les *sandwichs!*" ("Last night there was a holdup at the snack bar on the corner and the gangsters took all the cash but left all the sandwiches.")

The German language, too, has adopted many English words. Among the most popular are *best seller, handicap, five-o'clock tea, manager, hobby, cottage, clown, clerk, transfer, detective, shorts, slogan* and *shock*. The following German sentence is one example of the invasion of English words into the German language:

ENGLISH WORDS IN THE HAWAIIAN LANGUAGE

ENGLISH	HAWAIIAN
bible	baibala
captain	kapena
coal	koala (to cook)
coffee	kope
cook	kuko
hammer	amara
hanky	hainaka
hymn	himeni
inch	iniha
ink	inika
man-of-war	manuwa
palm	puulima
pin	pini
plow	palau

"Der *Bartender* hat den *Cocktail O.K.* gemixt." Because of the basic similarity of English, German, Dutch and Scandinavian languages, it is fairly easy for the last three to adopt English words. English is essentially a German language.

Spanish, Italian and Portuguese adopt fewer English words than do French and German (apart from the usual sports terms). Also, these three languages tend to modify the English spelling. For example, in Spanish we have *coctel* (cocktail), *Yanqui* (Yankee), *nocaut* (knockout), *sueter* (sweater), and *sanwich* (sandwich). Baseball is a very popular sport in Spanish-speaking countries, especially in the Caribbean. So we have *jonron* (home run), *beisbol* (baseball) and *aut* (out). Also, in many Spanish-speaking countries, North American products are referred to by their trade names. In Spanish a sewing machine is called *el Singer*.

Japanese offers perhaps the most interesting example of wholesale adaptation of English vocabulary by a foreign language. Baseball was first brought to Japan in the late nineteenth century. Today it is that country's national game. In Japan baseball is called *beisboru*. The following baseball terms can be easily recognized in their Japanese pronunciation: *batto* (bat), *chansu* (chance), *pitchingu* (pitching), *kyatcha* (catcher), *ranna* (runner), *straiku* (strike), *seifu* (safe), *auto* (out).

Among the other English words used by Japanese are *rekodo* (record), *Te Bi* (TV), *Coka Kora* (Coca Cola), *hambagu* (hamburger), *hotodogu* (hot dog), *matchi* (matches), *modan* (modern), *taipu* (typewriter), *maskomu* (mass communications), *basuketo* (basketball), *shigaretto* (cigarette), *erebeta* (elevator), *dansu* (dance) and *kisu* (kiss).

Swahili is the most widely spoken African language. English words have invaded this language too. These words usually refer to something modern or mechanical: *motokaa* (motor car), *baiskeli* (bicycle), *breki* (brakes), *petroli* (petroleum), *mashingan* (machine gun), *banki* (bank), *posta* (post office), *blanketi* (blanket), *helikopta* (helicopter), *jipi* (jeep), *polisi* (police), *waya* (wire), *opereta* (operator). Even the months of the year have been adopted by Swahili-speaking Africans: *Oktoba* (October), *Novemba* (November) and *Disemba* (December).

Despite the iron curtain, some English words have even crept into the Russian language. These include *djentlmen* (gentlemen), *bifshteks* (beefsteak), *tennis, futbol,* (football), *bridge, poker, basketbol* (basketball), *finish* (race), *demping* (dumping).

And so it goes in country after country around the world. In Israel an automobile tire gets a *pancher* (puncture). In the United Arab Republic someone who bumps into you might say *Sorry!* In Indonesia you will hear the words *pencil* and *lego* (let go). And in China, children love to play *baw* (ball) games.

All the countries of the world have their own languages. But if the adoption of English words into these languages goes on at its present rate, it is not unlikely that within the next hundred years or so a simplified English may be in general use by the world's peoples as a means of international communication.

COLONIALISM

... it is coming to an end but there are still about 100 non-self-governing territories

By HELEN HYNSON MERRICK

AT one time or another, almost every major nation in the world has been accused of practicing colonialism. Colonialism is probably the most used—and misused—word in our political dictionary. Well, just what is colonialism? First, it must be understood that even experts on the subject define the word differently. For example, some experts have called colonialism "an overflow of nationality." Other experts have defined it as the domination of non-

Europeans by European nations. Still others have called it the acquisition of territories usually occupied by other races or peoples. And colonialism has been called a policy of creating a large state made up of many different national units that are ruled by a single, central government.

From these different but similar definitions we can form a single working definition for our purposes. We might say that in colonialism one area and the people who

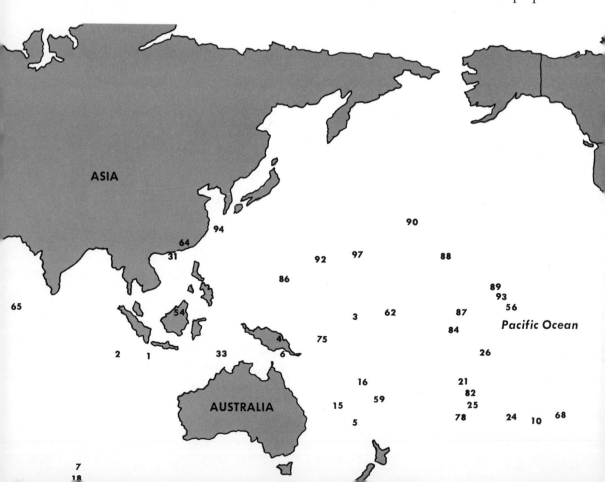

The Western world's remaining non-self-governing territories. They are listed under the nations that control them.

TERRITORY	LOCATION	AREA (sq. mi.)	POPULATION
AUSTRALIA			
1. Christmas I.	Indian Ocean	62	3,200
2. Cocos (Keeling) Is.	Indian Ocean	5	1,000
3. Nauru I.[1]	Central Pacific	6	4,849
4. Northeast New Guinea [1]	Southwest Pacific	93,000	1,500,000
5. Norfolk I.	Southwest Pacific	13	1,100
6. Papua	Southwest Pacific	90,540	540,000
FRANCE			
7. Amsterdam I.	Indian Ocean	16	0
8. Comoro Is.	Indian Ocean	838	190,600
9. Crozet Is.	Indian Ocean	193	0
10. French Polynesia	South-central Pacific	1,544	80,000
11. Guadeloupe I.	Caribbean	687	283,000
12. French Guiana	South America	31,135	35,000
13. Kerguelen Is.	Indian Ocean	2,703	100
14. Martinique I.	Caribbean	425	300,000
15. New Caledonia I.	Southwest Pacific	7,340	82,000
16. New Hebrides Arch.[2]	Southwest Pacific	5,700	68,000
17. Réunion I.	Indian Ocean	970	360,000
18. St. Paul I.	Indian Ocean	3	0
19. St. Pierre & Miquelon	North Atlantic	93	5,000
20. French Somaliland	Gulf of Aden	8,500	85,000
21. Wallis & Futuna Is.	Southwest Pacific	106	9,900

Continued on page 286

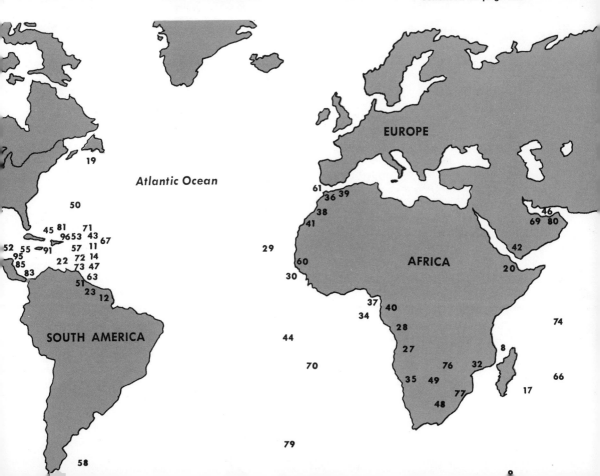

TERRITORY	LOCATION	AREA (sq. mi.)	POPULATION
NETHERLANDS			
22. Netherlands Antilles	Caribbean	394	200,000
23. Surinam (Dutch Guiana)	South America	55,144	340,000
NEW ZEALAND			
24. Cook Is.	South Pacific	93	20,000
25. Niue I.	South Pacific	100	5,000
26. Tokelau (Union) I.	South Pacific	4	2,000
PORTUGAL			
27. Angola	Africa	481,351	4,950,000
28. Cabinda	Africa	3,000	55,000
29. Cape Verde Is.	North Atlantic	1,557	220,000
30. Portuguese Guinea	Africa	13,948	565,000
31. Macao	South China Sea	6	180,000
32. Mozambique	Africa	302,250	6,800,000
33. Portuguese Timor	Indonesia	7,332	540,000
34. Sao Tomé & Principé Is.	Gulf of Guinea	372	65,000
SOUTH AFRICA			
35. South-West Africa [3]	Africa	318,100	575,000
SPAIN			
36. Ceuta	Africa	7	78,000
37. Fernando Po Is.	Gulf of Guinea	786	70,000
38. Ifni	Africa	579	55,000
39. Melilla	Africa	5	85,000
40. Rio Muni	Africa	10,045	212,000
41. Spanish Sahara	Africa	102,703	36,000
GREAT BRITAIN			
42. Federation of South Arabia	Arabian Peninsula	100,000	1,000,000
43. Antigua Is.	Caribbean	171	58,000
44. Ascension I.	South Atlantic	34	374
45. Bahama Is.	West Atlantic	4,000	120,000
46. Bahrain Is.	Persian Gulf	250	156,000
47. Barbados Is.	West Indies	166	240,000
48. Basutoland	Africa	11,716	708,000
49. Bechuanaland	Africa	222,000	360,000
50. Bermuda Is.	West Atlantic	21	46,000
51. British Guiana	South America	83,000	610,000
52. British Honduras	Central America	8,866	100,000
53. British Virgin Is.	Caribbean	59	8,200
54. Brunei	South China Sea	2,226	87,000
55. Cayman Is.	Caribbean	93	9,000
56. Christmas Is.	South Pacific	237	1,300
57. Dominica I.	Caribbean	290	65,000

live in that area are controlled by the government of another area.

Throughout history there have been many people who have said that colonialism is a good thing. They believed that the colonial nations helped the people in the areas they controlled. They said that they spread Christianity and Western ideas of law. That they built schools and roads and hospitals. That they brought modern technology to backward people. In many cases the colonial powers did do these things.

But on the other hand, the colonial powers did many bad things. They exploited the people and the resources of the land. Many natives in the colonies suffered a great deal. Some were forced into slavery. They had to work on plantations where living conditions were wretched. And the natives were made to feel that they were not as good as the people who ruled them. They were told that they were not capable of ruling themselves.

Why do nations acquire colonies? There are many reasons. First, there is the economic reason. A nation can make money selling goods to the people who live in its colonies. And it can do so without competition from other exporting nations. Also, many colonies are rich in minerals and

TERRITORY	LOCATION	AREA (sq. mi.)	POPULATION
58. Falkland Is.	South Atlantic	4,700	2,400
59. Fiji Is.	Central Pacific	7,055	440,000
60. Gambia*	Africa	4,003	320,000
61. Gibraltar	Mediterranean	2	26,000
62. Gilbert & Ellice Is.	Western Pacific	369	52,000
63. Grenada Is.	Caribbean	133	95,000
64. Hong Kong	Southeast China	398	3,530,000
65. Maldive Is.	Indian Ocean	115	95,000
66. Mauritius Is.	Indian Ocean	720	720,000
67. Montserrat I.	Caribbean	32	13,500
68. Pitcairn I.	South Pacific	2	148
69. Qatar	Persian Gulf	4,000	60,000
70. St. Helena I.	South Atlantic	47	5,000
71. St. Kitts-Nevis-Anguilla Is.	Caribbean	138	60,000
72. St. Lucia I.	Caribbean	238	95,000
73. St. Vincent I.	Caribbean	150	86,000
74. Seychelles Is.	Indian Ocean	156	45,000
75. Solomon Is.	Southwest Pacific	11,500	135,000
76. Southern Rhodesia	Africa	150,333	4,000,000
77. Swaziland	Africa	6,705	280,000
78. Tonga Is.	Southwest Pacific	270	70,000
79. Tristan da Cunha Is.	South Atlantic	38	250
80. Trucial States	Persian Gulf	30,000	115,000
81. Turks & Caicos Is.	West Pacific	166	6,200

UNITED STATES

TERRITORY	LOCATION	AREA (sq. mi.)	POPULATION
82. American Samoa	South Pacific	76	20,500
83. Panama Canal Zone	Central America	648	42,000
84. Canton & Enderbury Is.[4]	South Pacific	27	320
85. Corn Is.	Caribbean	3	3,200
86. Guam	West Pacific	209	67,000
87. Howland, Baker, Jarvis Is.	Mid-Pacific	3	0
88. Johnston & Sand Is.	Mid-Pacific	×	156
89. Kingman Reef	Mid-Pacific	×	0
90. Midway I.	Mid-Pacific	2	2,356
91. Navassa I.	Caribbean	1	0
92. Pacific Islands Trust Territory	West Pacific	700	81,000
93. Palmyra I.	Mid-Pacific	4	0
94. Ryukyu Is.	East China Sea	848	908,000
95. Swan Is.	Caribbean	1	28
96. U.S. Virgin Is.	Caribbean	133	37,000
97. Wake I.	Mid-Pacific	3	1,200

[1] UN trust territories. Nauru is administered by Australia on behalf of itself, New Zealand and Great Britain.
[2] Joint dominion of Great Britain and France.
[3] Formerly a League of Nations mandate.
[4] Joint dominion of Great Britain and the United States.
× Less than .5 sq. mi.
* Scheduled for independence on February 18, 1965.

other raw materials. These can be mined and used or sold by the nation that controls the colony. The native peoples of the colony usually do not benefit very much from the sale or use of these raw materials.

Many countries have obtained colonies to increase their prestige. And some colonialists thought it was their duty to spread their religion and civilization to other areas. Many people have also migrated to colonies because their own country was overpopulated, or they felt that they were discriminated against because of their religion or for other reasons.

Lastly, and perhaps most important in this century, nations have acquired colonies to improve their national defense. Some nations, such as Russia, have set up buffer states around their borders. In times of war these buffer states, which are in effect colonies, stand in the way of advancing hostile armies. Colonies also give troops in wartime. And colonies permit the placement of troops all over the world. This gives the colonial power easy access to troubled areas.

As you know from your study of history, the original American states and Canadian provinces were once colonies of Great Britain. But they were not the first colonies. Colonialism has been going on for thousands of years. The ancient Phoenicians set up colonies all around the Mediterranean Sea. They did this to increase their trade. Carthage was a colony of Phoenicia. But after Phoenicia became weak and was unable to control its colonies, Carthage broke away. Then Carthage became strong and set up its own colonies. They sprang up on Sardinia, Sicily and Malta.

Then came Rome. The Romans were the greatest colonizers of ancient times. At its height, Rome controlled the western part of Europe, North Africa, Syria and Greece.

The greatest period of colonization began at the end of the fifteenth century. This was when the great age of exploration began. Spain, Portugal, Great Britain, France and the Netherlands sent explorers all over the world. Then they sent people to colonize the newly discovered lands. By the middle of the eighteenth century, the nations of Europe had set up colonies on all the continents except Australia. Portugal and Spain planted colonies in Africa, South and Central America. Spain even set up a colony in Florida. Britain and France set up colonies in North America, Africa and Asia. The Dutch were most active in Africa, the Caribbean and the East Indies.

This great period of colonization ended around the middle of the eighteenth century. From then until around 1870, only a few new colonies were set up by European nations. British colonies were planted in Australia, New Zealand and South Africa. France took control of Algeria. But during this period, also, the first wars of independence were fought by colonies. Britain lost a large part of its American colonies. Spain and Portugal lost their holdings in South and Central America.

A new period of colonialism began around 1870. Britain and France set up more colonies in Africa and southeast Asia. Germany set up colonies in Togoland, Cameroun (Kamerun) and other places in Africa as well as in the Pacific.

From "The Four Corners of the World"
by Roger Duvoisin, © 1948 Alfred A. Knopf

Pizarro's conquistadores defeated the Incas in the 1530's and made Peru a Spanish colony.

Italy established the colonies of Eritrea, Italian Somaliland and Libya in Africa. Belgium took the Belgian Congo. Japan took control of many Pacific islands, including the Ryukyus and Formosa. By the beginning of World War I, almost all of Africa had been colonized.

The United States, too, has engaged in colonialism. But many of the areas controlled by the United States are very small. They are mostly islands in the Pacific where few people live. Thus they probably could never become independent. In contrast to most other colonial powers, the United States has usually acted in a very enlightened way. The native peoples were rarely mistreated or their lands exploited. Most important, the people who live under United States rule do not seem to want to change their status.

The areas that the United States acquired through the years were gotten in a variety of ways. The Virgin Islands were bought from Denmark. Alaska was bought from Russia. Guam and Puerto Rico were taken from Spain during the Spanish-American War of 1898. The Philippines were also taken from Spain in 1898. This many-island nation was given its independence in 1946.

The Panama Canal Zone and Hawaii are two areas acquired by the United States in rather devious ways. At the end of the nineteenth century, the United States wanted to build a canal across the Isthmus of Panama. At that time Panama was a province of Colombia. When Colombia delayed signing the treaty that would give the United States the right to build the canal, Americans helped start a revolt of the Panamanians against Colombia in 1903. The U. S. Navy actively supported the revolutionists. The revolt was a success; the Republic of Panama was set up. Then the new Panamanian Government gave the United States the right to build the canal.

Americans had started flocking to Hawaii in the early 1800's. These islands were then ruled by native kings and queens. During the following years, plans were made to annex the islands to the United States. By 1890, Hawaii was controlled by white planters. The native Hawaiians, who originally numbered over 200,000, had dwindled to 34,000. Queen Liliuokalani came to the throne in 1891. She did not want foreign rule, and opposed the white planters. Because of this, the Americans on the island revolted. The revolt was supported by the United States Government. The Queen had to give in. Hawaii was formally annexed by the United States in 1898. Today Hawaii is the fiftieth state of the United States.

The mid-twentieth century has seen practically an end to Western colonialism. After World War II, the subject peoples of the world demanded their freedom. They did not want to be ruled by other countries. In most cases these people did get their freedom.

There are now only two Western countries that refuse to give up the areas they control. These are Portugal and South Africa. Portugal's two biggest colonies are Angola and Mozambique in Africa. The people of Angola are now fighting for their independence.

South-West Africa is in a unique position. Before World War I it was a colony of Germany. After the war it became a League of Nations mandate. The League asked South Africa to administer South-West Africa and help the people there prepare for independence. But South Africa has not done this. It wants to keep control of South-West Africa.

With the exception of Portugal and South Africa, the Western colonial powers are making no great effort to hold on to their colonies. "On the contrary," says Woodruff Wallner, former U. S. deputy assistant secretary of state for international organization affairs, "sometimes the colonial powers are apt to get rid of them faster than the colonies would like. They are both a headache and an expense to run. Nobody makes money out of colonies these days." One colony that was surely given its freedom too soon was the Belgian Congo. Belgium pulled out in 1960. But it had not prepared the Congolese to take over the government and run the country. As a result the country has been in a state of turmoil and civil war for four years. The United Nations had to send in troops, but they were withdrawn in 1964.

Even with the great decline in the number of colonies, there are still about one hundred non-self-governing territories left. Of course, many of these are so small and have so few people that they are unlikely ever to become independent.

A Lesson

50 Years Ago: World War I

World War I began on July 28, 1914, when Austria-Hungary declared war on Serbia. The event that triggered the war was the assassination of Archduke Francis Ferdinand, heir to the Austro-Hungarian throne. Germany soon joined Austria-Hungary and became the dominant Central Power.

Brown Brothers

Wilhelm II, emperor of Germany, with his generals during World War I.

ALLIES

Belgium
Brazil
British Empire
China
Costa Rica
Cuba
France
Greece
Guatemala
Haiti
Honduras
Italy
Japan
Liberia
Montenegro
Nicaragua
Panama
Portugal
Rumania
Russia
San Marino
Serbia
Siam
United States

CENTRAL POWERS

Austria-Hungary
Bulgaria
Germany
Ottoman Empire (Turkey)

■ CENTRAL POWERS

25 *Years Ago: World War II*

ALLIES

Argentina
Australia
Belgium
Bolivia
Brazil
Canada
Chile
China
Colombia
Costa Rica
Cuba
Czechoslovakia
Denmark
Dominican Republic
Ecuador
Egypt
El Salvador
Ethiopia
France
Great Britain
Greece
Guatemala
Haiti
Honduras
India
Iran
Iraq
Lebanon
Liberia
Luxembourg
Mexico
Netherlands
New Zealand
Nicaragua
Norway
Panama
Paraguay
Peru
Poland
Russia
San Marino
Saudi Arabia
South Africa
Syria
Turkey
United States
Uruguay
Venezuela
Yugoslavia

AXIS

Bulgaria
Finland
Germany
Hungary
Italy
Japan
Rumania

World War II began on September 1, 1939, when nazi Germany, under the leadership of Adolf Hitler, attacked Poland. Nazi forces then went on to conquer most of Europe. By the end of World War II in 1945, most of the nations of the world had in some way been involved in this most destructive of all wars.

Underwood & Underwood

German Führer Adolf Hitler salutes nazi troops as they enter Warsaw.

■ AXIS POWERS

291

SCIENCE AN[D]

The most beautiful thing we can
experience is the mysterious. It is the
source of all true art and science.
Albert Einstein

NASA

TECHNOLOGY

The World's Largest Telescope

MOST radio telescopes have antennas, or reflectors, that can be rotated. But Cornell University's new telescope antenna near Arecibo, Puerto Rico, is so big that it could not be made to move. The cost would have been enormous. Thus the antenna was built into a natural bowl in the earth. It is made of steel mesh, and is known as a fixed antenna. This biggest-of-all antennas is 1,000 feet in diameter and 160 feet deep. It covers an area of 18½ acres.

Since the antenna cannot be moved and the energy aimed, movable feed lines are used. The feed, which is connected to a sensitive receiver, bounces radar beams off the mesh antenna, sending them into the earth's ionosphere and outer space. By moving the feed, scientists can point the telescope at any object within 20° of the zenith (the point directly overhead). The upper end of the feed is 435 feet above the reflector.

The most important function of the Arecibo Ionospheric Observatory is to study the earth's ionized upper atmosphere, the ionosphere. But the telescope can also be used in radar astronomy. As a radar telescope it can send a powerful signal to the moon, the sun and the nearby planets. This new telescope is thus enabling astronomers to make more accurate measurements of the solar system. By studying the returning signals, astronomers can also deduce the major surface features of the planets and the rotation rate of a planet on its axis.

295

Optical Spectra

HAVE you ever noticed that when a beam of white light is passed at an angle through a certain kind of glass, a rainbow results? White light is actually a mixture of colored light—violet, blue, green, yellow, orange and red. Usually light passes through a substance in a straight line. But if it passes through at an angle, the light rays bend. This bending is what causes the color in the white light to separate and make a rainbow. We can bend light with a wedge of glass called a prism.

Each color has its own wavelength. And, depending upon the wavelength, each color is bent by a different amount when it passes through the prism. The shorter the wavelength of light, the more it will bend. Violet light bends the most. Red waves, which are the longest, bend the least.

The pattern of colors that is formed when light passes through a prism is the spectrum of the substance giving off the light. By studying the spectrum we can learn a great deal about the source of light. Just as one set of fingerprints differs from every other, so every substance has its own spectrum. Examining its spectrum is a good way to identify the composition of a substance. This is called spectrum analysis. The instrument used is called a spectroscope. In its simplest form, a spectroscope is just a triangular glass prism. A small telescope is usually connected to the prism so the spectra can be studied in greater detail.

A more complicated instrument—the compound spectroscope—can show us the spectra of objects in the heavens such as stars and planets. The astronomer can tell a great deal from the spectra observed in this way. He can find out the chemical makeup of the sun and stars and the atmosphere of the planets. By measuring small shifts in the lines of the spectrum, he can also figure out the speed at which the object is moving toward or away from the earth. When the object is moving toward the earth, each of its light waves becomes a little shorter. Thus the lines shift toward the violet end of the object's spectrum. The amount of shift reveals the speed of the object. Temperature and pressure also affect spectra in certain ways. Thus spectra can tell the astronomer what the approximate temperature is of heavenly bodies. They can also help the astronomer measure the pressure of gases on such bodies.

Chemists and physicists use spectrum analysis to learn what the atomic and molecular structure of a material is. And industrial technicians use it to reveal any impurities that may exist in a product.

We have been discussing, on the whole, natural light. But there are many other kinds of light. Each of these has its own spectrum. Various filaments give off artificial light. Light is also given off by molten metals. Each of these produces a spectrum that shows all the colors. This pattern is called a continuous spectrum.

The spectra from incandescent gases are different. Only certain colors show up, in fine lines. Such patterns are called bright-line spectra.

The whole spectrum of rays is known as the electromagnetic spectrum. The visible spectrum—what we can see with our own eyes—is a very small part of this. Among the rays outside the visible spectrum are ultraviolet waves, infrared waves, X rays and gamma rays. Even though we cannot see them, these rays can be recorded on photographic film.

h wavelength of visible radiation produces light of
articular color. White light, such as that from the
or an incandescent lamp filament, results from the
bination of the many colors. A prism separates a
m of this light into its constituent colors by bending
waves in inverse proportion to their wavelength.
et waves, the shortest, are bent the most; red, the
gest, are bent the least. The color pattern so
ned is known as a spectrum. Since no two sub-
ces give rise to the same color pattern, spectra
e as a means of positive identification.

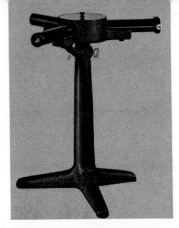

A spectroscope. One arm admits light
and focuses it through the prism. The
spectrum is viewed through the eye-
piece in the second arm, against a
scale projected from the third arm.

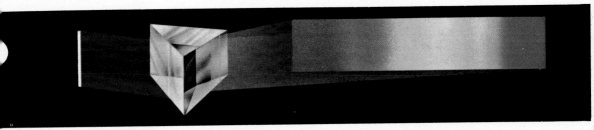

NTINUOUS SPECTRUM

emitted by glowing solids or liquids or by hot, dense gases
er great pressure is separated by a prism into a continuous
ation of color. Raindrops acting as prisms separate the sun's
into the most familiar continuous spectrum, the rainbow.

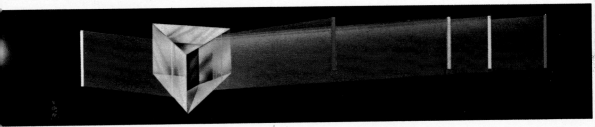

IISSION (BRIGHT-LINE) SPECTRUM

er less extreme conditions than exist on the sun and stars, hot
es emit light which separates into narrow lines of color charac-
stic of the substance. Spectral patterns differ not only in color,
also in the number and spacing of lines.

SORPTION (DARK-LINE) SPECTRUM

white light passes through a comparatively cool gas before
ering the prism, the gas absorbs the identical lines of color it
ld emit if hot. Absorption spectra are particularly useful in
lyzing substances that would decompose at high temperatures.

297

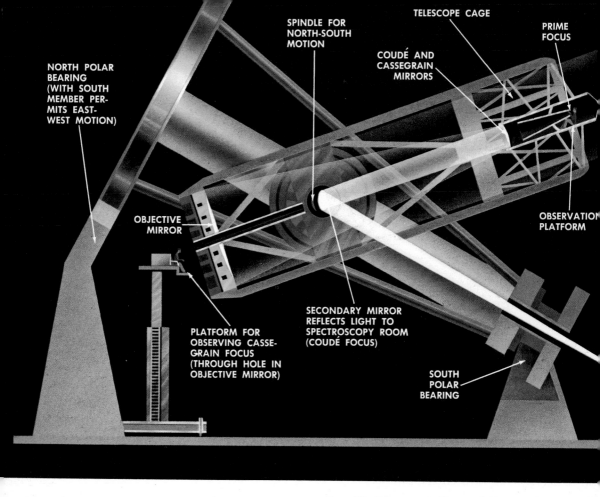

NORTH POLAR
BEARING
(WITH SOUTH
MEMBER PER-
MITS EAST-
WEST MOTION)

SPINDLE FOR
NORTH-SOUTH
MOTION

TELESCOPE CAGE

PRIME
FOCUS

COUDÉ AND
CASSEGRAIN
MIRRORS

OBSERVATION
PLATFORM

OBJECTIVE
MIRROR

SECONDARY MIRROR
REFLECTS LIGHT TO
SPECTROSCOPY ROOM
(COUDÉ FOCUS)

PLATFORM FOR
OBSERVING CASSE-
GRAIN FOCUS
(THROUGH HOLE IN
OBJECTIVE MIRROR)

SOUTH
POLAR
BEARING

Some identifying spectra. Photographs (spectrograms) of most of
the substances found on earth have been cataloged for reference

MERCURY LAMP

IRON ARC

BARIUM

CALCIUM

FRAUNHOFER LINES

TUNGSTEN LAMP

FLUORESCENT LAMP

The 200-in. Hale Telescope at Mount Palomar, Cal., collects and concentrates light from the brightest star, Sirius. Reflected into the spectroscopy room, the beam is separated into its spectrum and photographed. A small portion of the spectrogram is reproduced.

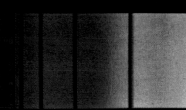

Illustrated by George Bakacs

The Fraunhofer lines are absorption lines in the solar spectrum. Like the black lines in Sirius' spectrum, they reveal the presence of specific substances. The tungsten and fluorescent lamps give continuous spectra; the others are bright-line spectra.

CULAR HYDROGEN

TOMIC HYDROGEN

SODIUM LAMP

HELIUM

NEON

LITHIUM

More than 400,000 stars have been classified in six principal spectral groups based on absorption lines and the region of maximum intensity (blue, white, yellow-white, yellow, orange, red) of the continuous background.

HERTZSPRUNG-RUSSELL DIAGRAM OF THE VARIOUS TYPES OF STARS

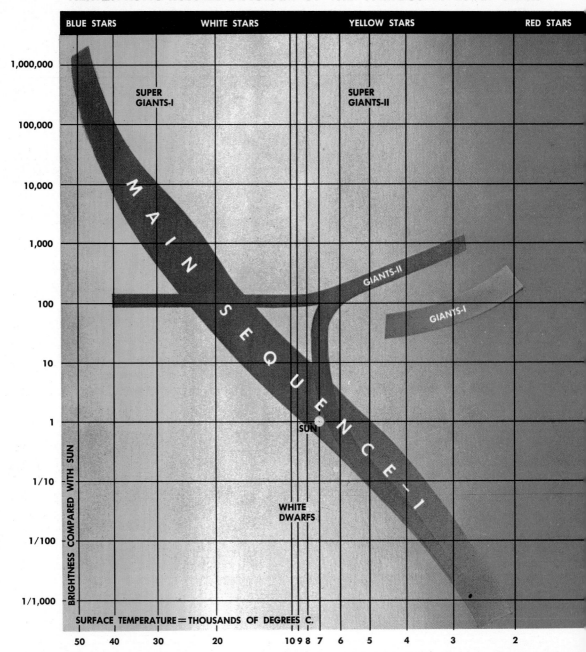

Color and brightness are determined by a star's surface temperature, which, in turn, is determined by its age and size. Population I stars are young, growing stars, located in the arms (stellar dusts) of galaxies. Dim red stars are small; bright blue stars are large.

The old, dying stars of Population II are usually found in clus[ters] at the center of galaxies. Many become giants, then white dwa[rfs] before burning out. Population I red giants and the super gi[ants] of both populations are abnormally large and bright.

International Years of the Quiet Sun

... scientists from more than 60 nations are studying the sun's effects on the earth

By EDWARD R. DYER, JR.

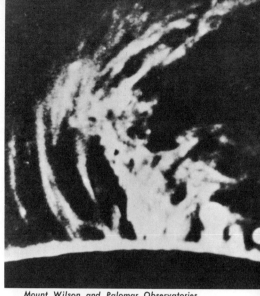

THE International Years of the Quiet Sun (IQSY) is the name of a two-year program of research. In this program, scientists from more than 60 nations are observing the sun and the earth's atmosphere and magnetic field. They are also examining the properties of space around the earth and sun. The two-year period of the IQSY began on January 1, 1964, and will last until December 31, 1965. This time was chosen for a very special reason. During this period the sun is relatively "quiet." This means that there is little or no activity, such as sunspots or flares.

The IQSY, then, is taking place during the quiet part of the present solar cycle. Each solar cycle lasts about 11 years. It consists of an active phase and a quiet phase. The times of these phases can be pretty well predicted. When the sun is active, as it was during the International Geophysical Year (IGY) 1957-58, it produces strong effects on earth. These effects include magnetic storms, changes in the flow of cosmic rays, radio disturbances and auroras. An active sun also heats up the upper atmosphere. And it changes the electrical properties of the upper atmosphere. These in turn affect the earth's weather in ways not clearly understood. Radio communications are also affected. It is thus very important to study these phenomena and the sun itself. To get as complete a picture as possible, we must

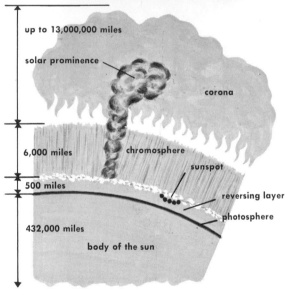

Top: A solar prominence at the sun's surface. The dot at the right represents the size of earth. Above: A diagram showing a cross section of the sun's gaseous layers. Also shown are solar disturbances—a prominence and sunspots.

study the sun during active as well as quiet or near-normal conditions. The results must then be compared. But this is a very big job. So scientists all over the world decided to combine their efforts and work together. They exchange ideas and results obtained from their observations.

301

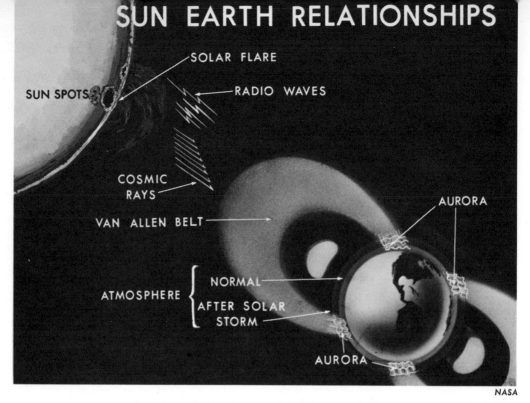

SUN EARTH RELATIONSHIPS

SOLAR FLARE

SUN SPOTS

RADIO WAVES

COSMIC RAYS

VAN ALLEN BELT

AURORA

ATMOSPHERE { NORMAL

AFTER SOLAR STORM

AURORA

Sunspots and solar flares and storms affect the earth's atmosphere and cause auroras. IQSY scientists are studying these and other earth-sun relationships.

Scientists first worked together on a truly world-wide scale during the International Geophysical Year. During this 18-month period, scientists from many nations studied the earth and its structure. They studied the oceans, the earth's ice cover and its atmosphere. And they studied the influence of the sun, which was then in an active period, on the other fields of study.

International expeditions were sent to such remote areas as the Antarctic and the Arctic. For the first time, rockets, space probes and artificial satellites were used a great deal. It was soon realized how important international cooperation is in scientific projects. Thus, after the IGY had ended, scientific cooperation continued. It became clear also that to get a complete picture, the sun and its relationship to the earth during the quiet portion of the solar cycle would have to be studied.

In 1961, President Kennedy approved United States participation in the IQSY. A U. S. Committee for IQSY was set up to be the clearing house for the activities of United States scientists. IQSY committees were also set up in many other nations. Today, some 60 nations have IQSY committees. An international IQSY Committee was also set up. This committee keeps the IQSY nations informed of each other's programs and progress. It also coordinates the efforts of scientists the world over.

The sun is about 93,000,000 miles from the earth. When we look at the sun it seems to have a sharply defined surface. That surface, called the photosphere, is really a layer of gas—mostly hydrogen. The photosphere is about 100 miles thick, and has a temperature of about 10,000° F. Beneath the photosphere is the sun's interior. The sun gets hotter and hotter toward the center, where it reaches a temperature of about 30,000,000° F.

Just above the photosphere is a very turbulent layer of gas 6,000 miles thick. This layer is called the chromosphere. The temperature of the chromosphere seems to vary quite a bit from place to place. It ranges up to about

100,000° F. in some of its "stormy" features. Outside the chromosphere is still another region. This one is called the corona. The corona is made up of very, very thin gas. It has a temperature of several million degrees. The corona stretches millions of miles into space. It fades off so gradually that no one knows exactly where it ends. The chromosphere and corona can be seen only during a total eclipse of the sun or with a special telescope (coronagraph or coronascope).

The photosphere is marked in places by what look like little dark regions. These are called sunspots. Sunspots are in reality neither little nor dark. Some of them in fact are several times as big as the earth. Since they are about only one tenth as bright as their surroundings, they seem dark in contrast. But they are still very bright. Sunspots are often accompanied by other, less visible activities on the sun. Since sunspots are easily recognized, a count of their number at any particular time is an easy way to measure the amount of solar activity. During the active part of the solar cycle, such as the IGY, many sunspots appeared. It is expected that during the IQSY only a few sunspots will be seen. These sunspots will not come quickly on the heels of those before. Their effects will not overlap and pile up. Thus it will be easier to study the effects of individual spots and the solar storms connected with them.

The sun's photosphere and chromosphere emit ultraviolet light. This is absorbed during the daytime by the thin air in the earth's atmosphere. As a result an electrified layer of air is created from about 40 miles above the earth on up. This layer is called the ionosphere. The ionosphere is made up of clouds of electrons and positively charged air molecules and atoms. This layer acts like a mirror. It reflects radio waves of a certain range of frequencies. Radio waves sent out from one given point on earth travel up in a straight line until they hit the ionsophere. The iono-sphere reflects them back to other points on earth. This makes possible long-distance radio and telephone communications. Powerful ultraviolet light and X rays from solar flares sometimes electrify the ionosphere more than usual. This causes the reflection of radio waves to stop. These temporary "radio blackouts" can disrupt long-distance communications. This phenomenon will be carefully studied during the IQSY.

There are many other disturbances on the sun that need to be studied. Some flares send out streams of highly charged particles. When these particles get near the earth, they cause changes in the earth's magnetic field. These are called magnetic storms. The particles also cause auroras— displays of northern and southern lights. The magnetic fields associated with solar activity prevent cosmic rays from reaching the earth in normal numbers. It is helpful to know in advance when such disturbances will happen. But in order to predict these disturbances scientists must understand the events on the sun that cause them.

Some special expeditions are planned for the IQSY period. One is going near the magnetic equator in India. This expedition is scheduled for the spring of 1965. United States scientists, in cooperation with Indian scientists, will send up balloons to great heights to measure wind patterns, cosmic-ray particles and other features of the upper atmosphere. Several expeditions will go to two islands in the South Pacific to observe the May 30, 1965, solar eclipse.

During the IQSY, scientists will explore the atmosphere and space with the newest equipment at their disposal. Improved balloons will float high above the earth for several days at a time. Rockets and satellites will carry instruments still higher into the atmosphere, up to the fringes of the atmosphere and beyond into space.

We cannot foresee what discoveries will be made during the IQSY. We do know that as some of the problems puzzling us now are solved, new and even more challenging questions will arise.

Space Review

By JOHN NEWBAUER

A model of the manned Gemini and unmanned Agena spacecraft rendezvousing and about to dock, a maneuver soon to be introduced into the U.S. space program.

ON October 12 the Russians launched the *Voskhod* (Sunrise), the world's first three-man spacecraft. It traveled on a 16-orbit, 24-hour, 17-minute flight. The *Voskhod* carried an astronaut-pilot, a flight physician and a scientist. (The physician studied the behavior of his companions.) The passengers wore no space suits, just light clothes. Their cabin was rather like a jet-airplane passenger cabin. The *Voskhod* used retro-rockets for landing, rather than a parachute. This was the first time this had been done.

The *Voskhod* weighed about 15,000 pounds. The rocket that put it into orbit probably had a thrust of nearly 1,000,000 pounds. The rocket itself may mean nothing new in the Russian space program. It does not match the power of the first United States Saturn rocket. But the three-man flight does mean that the Soviet Union has moved rapidly to take advantage of its earlier pioneering work. In two years the Russians should be ready to begin long flights out toward the moon and eventually around it, without landing. Also, it means that the Russians have moved much closer to knowing how to build a space station. The United States is still a full year away from orbiting a manned spacecraft that could begin to match the performance of the *Voskhod*.

Two unmanned launches shared honors as the year's most dramatic—Syncom III in August and Ranger 7 in July.

Syncom III is a synchronous satellite. This means that it can continuously relay telephone, teletype and television between one part of the world and another. It can do this because it is at an altitude of 22,300 miles over the Pacific Ocean, where the international date line and the equator meet. Because of its speed and location, Syncom III remains over this spot, even though the earth is rotating on its axis. For its dramatic debut, the satellite brought to the United States excellent pictures of the September Olympics in Tokyo, Japan.

In July the Ranger 7 spacecraft made a perfect flight to the moon. Its six TV cameras sent back more than 4,000 photographs of the moon's surface. These photos gave scientists their first close look at the moon. At their best, the pictures were 1,000 times better than any given by a telescope. Information gained from the photos is of great importance to future programs. It now seems, for example, that astronauts probably will not face a rugged terrain when they land on the moon.

More Rangers will be launched, paving the way for Surveyor spacecraft, which will land softly on the lunar surface and explore it with tools. The information that the Surveyor finds will determine what kind of landing gear the manned Lunar Excursion Module (LEM) of the Apollo spacecraft system will have. In 1964, scientists began to develop a Lunar Orbiter. Ranger 7 mapped the equator of the moon in one place. The Orbiter will map the moon's entire equator. This information will help scientists to choose the best place to land the LEM.

In the United States, preparations for manned flights included test launchings of Titan II rockets, Saturn I rockets and experimental Gemini and Apollo spacecraft. The Gemini project is an ambitious one. First an unmanned Agena spacecraft will be orbited. Then, hours later, a Titan II will launch a manned Gemini spacecraft into orbit near the Agena's orbit. In the Gemini will be two astronauts seated side by side. Both the Agena and the Gemini have rocket engines. The astronauts will use these to make the two spacecraft approach one another—rendezvous—and then dock. To dock, the nose of the Gemini

Adapted from "The New York Times"

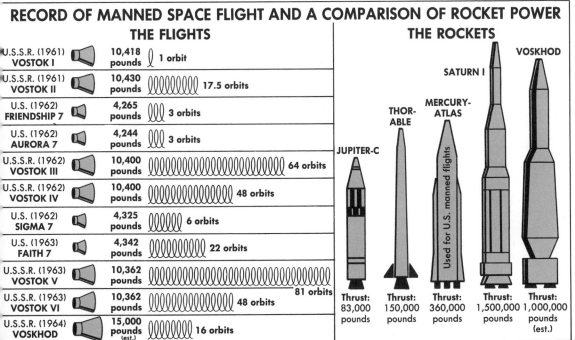

RECORD OF MANNED SPACE FLIGHT AND A COMPARISON OF ROCKET POWER

THE FLIGHTS

U.S.S.R. (1961) VOSTOK I	10,418 pounds	1 orbit
U.S.S.R. (1961) VOSTOK II	10,430 pounds	17.5 orbits
U.S. (1962) FRIENDSHIP 7	4,265 pounds	3 orbits
U.S. (1962) AURORA 7	4,244 pounds	3 orbits
U.S.S.R. (1962) VOSTOK III	10,400 pounds	64 orbits
U.S.S.R. (1962) VOSTOK IV	10,400 pounds	48 orbits
U.S. (1962) SIGMA 7	4,325 pounds	6 orbits
U.S. (1963) FAITH 7	4,342 pounds	22 orbits
U.S.S.R. (1963) VOSTOK V	10,362 pounds	81 orbits
U.S.S.R. (1963) VOSTOK VI	10,362 pounds	48 orbits
U.S.S.R. (1964) VOSKHOD	15,000 pounds (est.)	16 orbits

THE ROCKETS

JUPITER-C	THOR-ABLE	MERCURY-ATLAS	SATURN I	VOSKHOD
Thrust: 83,000 pounds	Thrust: 150,000 pounds	Thrust: 360,000 pounds	Thrust: 1,500,000 pounds	Thrust: 1,000,000 pounds (est.)

Used for U.S. manned flights

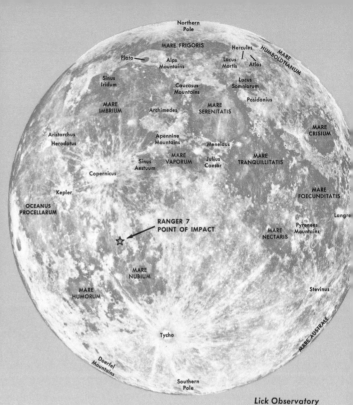

Northern
Pole

MARE FRIGORIS

Plato
Alps
Mountains

Hercules

Atlas

Lacus
Mortis

MARE
HUMBOLDTIANUM

Sinus
Iridum

Caucasus
Mountains

Lacus
Somniorum

MARE
IMBRIUM

Archimedes

MARE
SERENITATIS

Posidonius

MARE
CRISIUM

Aristarchus
Herodotus

Apennine
Mountains

Menelaus

Copernicus

Sinus
Aestuum

MARE
VAPORUM

Julius
Caesar

MARE
TRANQUILLITATIS

Kepler

MARE
FOECUNDITATIS

OCEANUS
PROCELLARUM

Langre

RANGER 7
POINT OF IMPACT

☆

Pyrenees
Mountains

MARE
NECTARIS

MARE
NUBIUM

MARE
HUMORUM

Stevinus

Tycho

MARE AUSTRALE

Doerfel
Mountains

Southern
Pole

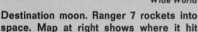

Destination moon. Ranger 7 rockets into space. Map at right shows where it hit the moon—after photographing it.

will be clipped into a ring on the Agena. Successful rendezvous and docking will mark a basic step forward in space technology. It will be especially important to the Apollo program. In the Apollo flight the LEM must dock twice with the mother spacecraft, once before and once after the lunar landing.

Gemini will tell scientists many other basic things about advanced space operations. For instance, the Gemini astronauts, wearing space suits, will expose themselves directly to the hard vacuum of space. Information gained from this will help prepare the way for operations requiring astronauts to leave their spacecraft while in space. Gemini astronauts will try to live in the spacecraft for up to two weeks. Scientists don't know yet if a man can stand weightlessness that long. The Gemini flights might answer this question. If the Gemini astronauts get sick, it may mean that spacecraft intended for long flights will have to rotate. Rotation would provide the astronauts with a force somewhat like the force of gravity here on earth.

In 1964 the Apollo program to put a man on the moon reached two landmarks. First the basic design was decided upon for the two man-carrying elements of the Apollo system—the command module and the LEM. Second, the Saturn I spacecraft completed seven perfect launches in a row. The Saturn is the most successful launch-vehicle on record. In 1965, Saturn I should launch an Apollo command module carrying three astronauts on an orbital test flight.

Millions of miles beyond the moon move the planets nearest earth—Mars and Venus. From the very beginning of the space program these planets have been prime targets for investigation by un-manned spacecraft. In 1962, Mariner 2 was launched into a path about the sun. At one point the Mariner came within 20,-000 miles of Venus. No spacecraft has yet reached Mars. The Soviet Union launched at least one spacecraft toward Mars in 1964. But it failed to function properly.

The United States Mariner 3 probe to Mars on November 5 also failed. But on

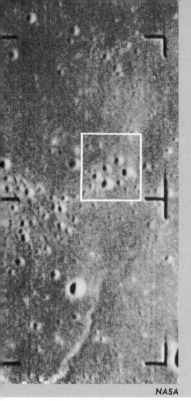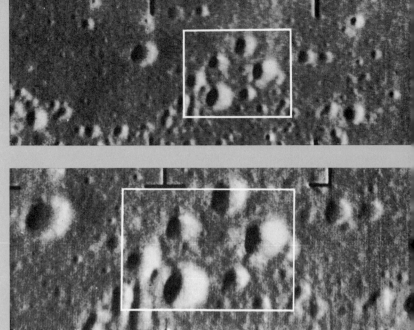

Photos of the same area of the moon, taken by Ranger 7 from an altitude of 85 miles (left), 37 miles (top) and 20 miles (above).

November 29 the United States launched Mariner 4 toward Mars. It is expected to reach the vicinity of that planet in July 1965. Like the successful Venus probe, it is called a Mariner. It will attempt to measure atmospheric and magnetic characteristics of the planet. It will also gather data in space on the way. The Mars Mariner carries TV equipment. If all goes well, we will see the first close view of a planet that has stirred the imagination of men for centuries.

There is a very special reason for wanting not only to see Mars but also, eventually, to land instruments and perhaps men on it. Mars is the only planet in our solar system besides earth that may harbor life. Most scientists hope at best to find there simple life-forms, such as small, tough plants. Spacecraft will have to land on the planet to identify living things, and such spacecraft cannot be launched, by the United States at least, until 1969 at the earliest.

What would some simple living thing found on Mars mean to us? Even if it were only a tiny dryish plant? It might mean that there is life on planets of other suns—millions of suns—in our galaxy, the Milky Way. This life could be at least as advanced as life on earth. Perhaps one day living beings will communicate by radio across the vast expanses of interstellar space. So far we cannot even imagine a spaceship that would have the power to leave our solar system and journey to another. But it will be fairly easy to build receivers that can pick up radio messages coming from 50 light-years away.

This is what scientists are thinking of as they open the exploration of Mars with the first, relatively simple Mariner. If entirely successful, this first Mariner, for instance, might show the best place to land a capsule on Mars and look for living things.

The year 1964 was the first half of the International Years of the Quiet Sun (IQSY). More than sixty nations cooperated to study earth-sun relationships. For a full report on this project, see the article "International Years of the Quiet Sun" on pages 301–03.

Aviation Highlights

By ERWIN J. BULBAN

THE rocket-powered X-15 is the world's fastest airplane. This plane is now being groomed to break all its own speed records. A new version, the X-15-A2, will be able to fly at about 5,450 miles per hour. This is 1,300 miles per hour faster than the old X-15. At this speed—eight times that of sound—the X-15-A2 will rocket through the air at better than 1½ miles per second.

The X-15-A2 will be a one-man flying laboratory. It will test new engines planned for future airplanes that will take off from the ground and zoom into space. The engines that the X-15-A2 will test are called ramjets. Ramjets are the simplest type of engine yet developed. A ramjet engine basically is a tube into which fuel is injected. The fuel mixes with the air that flows through the tube. Once the air-fuel mixture is ignited, it will burn and produce a thrust until the fuel is used up.

A ramjet has no moving parts. It is much less complicated than a turbojet engine. However, the ramjet will not work unless air flows through it at a high speed. This means that the airplane will also have to have turbojet or rocket engines. These develop the initial speed for the airplane. Once a high speed is reached, the ramjets can be started. The X-15-A2 will use its regular 57,000-pound-thrust rocket engines for this.

When an airplane flies at very high speeds, intense heat is generated. This heat is caused by the friction of the atmosphere on the plane's surface. To protect the X-15-A2 from this heat (perhaps 1,800° F.), the plane will have to be coated with a special material. This material will be very much like the material used to coat missile nose cones and spacecraft. If this coating were not used, the structure of the plane would soften.

In 1964 several important aviation records were set. Early in the year a 38-year-old mother of four sons, Mrs. Jerrie Mock, became the first woman to fly alone around the world. This Columbus, Ohio, housewife covered a total of 22,858.8 miles in 29 days in her single-engine airplane. For her feat Mrs. Mock was honored at a White House reception. President Johnson presented her with the Federal Aviation Agency's gold medal for outstanding aviation achievement.

On February 29, President Johnson announced that the United States had an airplane, the A-11, that could fly faster than 2,000 miles per hour. This plane, which is now called the YF-12A, can fly at an altitude of more than 70,000 feet. President Johnson said that this plane's performance "far exceeds that of any other aircraft in the world today."

Another record was set by a U. S. Army research helicopter. The Bell YUH-1B Iroquois set an unofficial speed record of 222 miles per hour. The previous record was 221 miles per hour. This was held

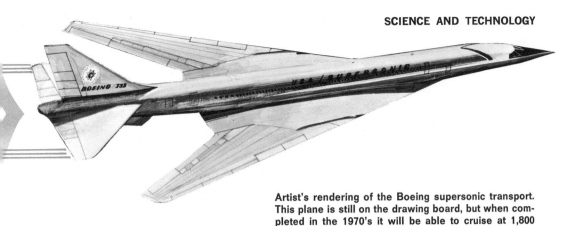

Artist's rendering of the Boeing supersonic transport. This plane is still on the drawing board, but when completed in the 1970's it will be able to cruise at 1,800 miles an hour at an altitude of 65,000 feet.

The Boeing Co.

by the Russians. The YUH-1B Iroquois has auxiliary jet engines on each side of its cabin. It also has small wings. These provide extra lifting power. It is hoped that this helicopter will fly at least 250 miles per hour in the near future.

In another test flight a special Lockheed NF-104A Starfighter supersonic jet fighter climbed to 118,860 feet. This is an unofficial world record for an airplane that has taken off from the ground under its own power. The NF-104A is designed to reach eventually an altitude of 130,000 feet. The absolute world altitude record is held by the X-15. This plane reached an altitude of 354,200 feet. But it was launched in midair from a B-52 jet bomber.

The NF-104A Starfighter has an auxiliary rocket engine in its tail. But a regular Starfighter was used by aviatrix Jacqueline Cochran to set yet another record. She flew this plane at an average speed of 1,429.297 miles per hour. This set a new women's straight-line speed record in the 15-25-kilometer distance class. The previous record was 1,273.109 miles per hour.

Commercial transport planes also set their share of records in 1964. An American Airlines 707 Astrojet flew from Dallas, Texas, to Los Angeles, California, in 1 hour, 56 minutes, 20 seconds. The previous record was 2 hours, 3 minutes, 3 seconds. Strong tail winds aided the 707 in this speedy, 1,200-mile flight.

In 1964 a jetliner made the longest flight on record by a commercial airline. A Swissair DC-8 flew from California to Beirut, Lebanon, without making a stop in between. The DC-8 covered the 7,903 miles at an average speed of 565 miles per hour. At one point during the flight the plane hit 690 miles per hour.

Development of new aircraft continued at a rapid pace in 1964.

Still in the planning stage is the supersonic transport. These planes will not be ready to carry passengers until the early 1970's. Two United States companies have been working on the supersonic transport —Boeing and Lockheed. Boeing has a design that makes use of a swiveling wing. The wing is set in the straight-out position for takeoff and landings. It is swept back to the tail for flights at speeds of almost three times that of sound. Lockheed will use a delta-wing shape that is very much like its YF-12A military plane.

Both of these planes will carry more than 200 passengers. Fully loaded they will weigh about 450,000 pounds. Boeing and Lockheed were expected to test scale models of their planes in wind tunnels late in 1964.

The British and French are working together to produce a supersonic transport. It is called the Concorde. The British-French plane is being designed to fly at twice the speed of sound. It will carry only half as many passengers as the United

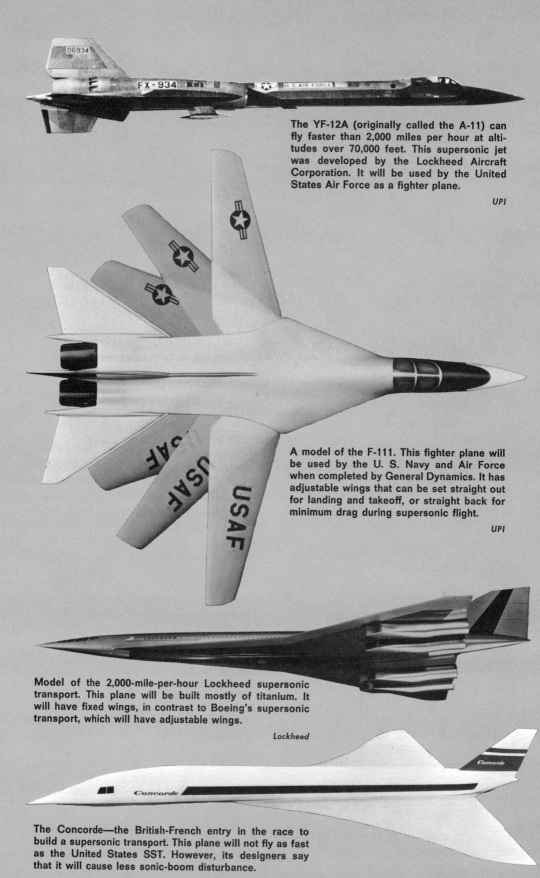

The YF-12A (originally called the A-11) can fly faster than 2,000 miles per hour at altitudes over 70,000 feet. This supersonic jet was developed by the Lockheed Aircraft Corporation. It will be used by the United States Air Force as a fighter plane.

UPI

A model of the F-111. This fighter plane will be used by the U. S. Navy and Air Force when completed by General Dynamics. It has adjustable wings that can be set straight out for landing and takeoff, or straight back for minimum drag during supersonic flight.

UPI

Model of the 2,000-mile-per-hour Lockheed supersonic transport. This plane will be built mostly of titanium. It will have fixed wings, in contrast to Boeing's supersonic transport, which will have adjustable wings.

Lockheed

The Concorde—the British-French entry in the race to build a supersonic transport. This plane will not fly as fast as the United States SST. However, its designers say that it will cause less sonic-boom disturbance.

Wide World

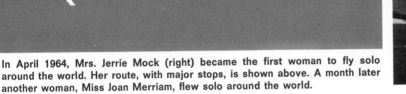

In April 1964, Mrs. Jerrie Mock (right) became the first woman to fly solo around the world. Her route, with major stops, is shown above. A month later another woman, Miss Joan Merriam, flew solo around the world.

States supersonic transport. The designers of this plane feel that since it will fly slower than the United States plane, it will not cause as much nuisance with the sonic boom.

The American designers feel that their plane will create even less sonic-boom nuisance than the British-French plane. The American plane will fly at altitudes much higher than the Concorde. At these high altitudes the air is very thin. Very thin air does not transmit shock waves so easily as denser air. The American plane designers also feel that they can design their planes so that they will not produce much of a shock wave to begin with.

Much will be learned about flying at three times the speed of sound when the giant new XB-70A bomber is tested. This delta-wing plane weighs about 500,000 pounds. It is 185 feet long and has a wing-span of 105 feet.

This plane will fly at 2,000 miles per hour. As a result a great deal of heat will be generated by the friction of the air on the plane. To keep the crew comfortable a special Freon refrigeration system will

be installed. Also, about 70 per cent of the plane is made of heat-resistant stainless steel.

Work also continued on the new F-111 two-man fighter plane. This aircraft has wings that can be swiveled back to the tail in flight. This will enable the plane to fly at speeds of about 2½ times the speed of sound. For takeoff and landings or for slow, cruising flight, the wings would be moved to a straight-out position.

Another unusual feature of this plane is the way in which the crew would escape in case of an emergency. They would not parachute from the plane. Instead they would trigger the entire nose section, in which the crew rides, to separate from the rest of the plane. This escape "capsule" would then be lowered to the ground by a large parachute. If it should land in water, the capsule would float and act as a life raft.

At least 2,000 of the F-111's will be built for the United States Air Force and Navy. Others have been ordered by Australia. The F-111 is expected to start flying early in 1965.

311

Ancestors of the Automobile

. . . the history and development of self-propelled land vehicles

By KEN PURDY

THE gasoline automobile as we know it today has been around only since the late 1800's. But before then, other types of self-propelled land vehicles were made. These vehicles are the ancestors of our automobile.

The very first self-propelled vehicles were really not self-propelled. They needed man power in one form or another. The driver had to work to make the vehicle move. One type, for example, ran on springs. The driver had to wind up these

springs. Leonardo da Vinci designed a spring-driven car almost five hundred years ago.

The first true self-propelled land vehicle was steam powered. It is believed that Ferdinand Verbiest, a Jesuit missionary in China, made the first steam car, in 1668. But it was only a model about two feet long. Its power source was a simple turbine engine. A jet of steam was directed against the blades of a paddle wheel. The paddle wheel was connected to the driving wheels by means of gears. So when the paddle wheel turned, the driving wheels turned. This model steam car could run for about one hour.

Today's automobiles use piston engines. Early work toward developing a piston engine was begun by Otto von Guericke (1602-86) of Germany, Christian Huygens (1629-95) of Holland and Denis Papin (1647-1712) of France. Guericke worked with vacuums. He invented the air pump and made metal pistons, connecting rods and cylinders. These are the basic parts of the reciprocating engine. Huygens logically extended the idea of the cannon. He exploded gunpowder in a cylinder. But instead of using a cannonball, he used a cylinder. Papin was the first to use steam to raise a piston.

Many people credit Nicholas Joseph Cugnot (1725-1804) with building the first true automobile. In 1769 this French Army engineer built a steam wagon. As have the inventors of all things from the shortbow to the missile, Cugnot thought of his invention as a useful war machine. He tried to interest French military officials in it. At first they liked his steam cart, which traveled at better than two miles an hour. The French Minister of War told Cugnot to build a larger vehicle. He wanted one that could transport artillery. Cugnot built the vehicle. It still exists. It is now in Paris in the Conservatoire des Arts et Métiers. The vehicle's chassis is made of heavy timbers. It has three wheels, the single one being in front. Its steam engine has two cylinders. Power for the engine is drawn from a big copper boiler that hangs out in front of the single wheel.

Cugnot made a great contribution to the development of the automobile. But his second steam cart never ran. The French Army decided to keep on using horses for transport.

The foremost name in steam-powered vehicles for road use is certainly Richard Trevithick (1771-1833). His father was a tin-mine manager. At an early age,

STEAM-DRIVEN VEHICLES

Cugnot's second steam vehicle, built in 1770. Cugnot's two vehicles are considered by many to be the first true automobiles.

Richard Trevithick's four-wheeled road vehicle was built and run in 1801. It could travel uphill "faster than a man could walk."

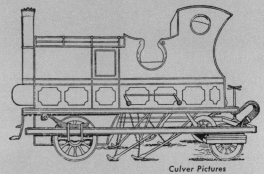

Culver Pictures

David Gordon's steam carriage of 1824. Gordon expected that the steam-driven legs —not the wheels—would propel the vehicle.

Trevithick became fascinated by the mine machinery. He used to watch the huge steam engines that were used to pump out the mine shafts. These engines ran at very low pressures and rates of speed. Trevithick later thought of using steam at high pressures. But this idea was not well received. James Watt, Matthew Boulton and other pioneers in the steam-engine field said that high pressures were very dangerous.

But Trevithick still built a toy-size model that ran on high-pressure steam. It worked very well. This machine is now in the Science Museum in Kensington in London. Trevithick's work was based on the idea that high-pressure steam could be used in an engine very much smaller than was usual at his time. He felt that a smaller machine could transport itself. This was something the two- and three-story-high mine-pumping machines could never do.

Trevithick also knew that iron-to-iron adhesion would give traction. Most of the inventors of his time did not know this. They thought that only drawing efforts, such as a man or horse uses, could move a vehicle. In fact, some early vehicles used a system of rods that pushed backward on the ground for propulsion.

Trevithick had two basic ideas. He wanted to use a small, self-propelled steam engine. And he wanted to mount this on metal wheels and run it on iron rails. This makes him the inventor of the steam locomotive and railroad.

This pioneer also ran a four-wheeled road vehicle, on Christmas Eve, 1801. A local newspaper account said the carriage managed a load of "several" persons. It traveled at a speed of four miles per hour uphill. This vehicle was later burned out when Trevithick left it unattended with the fire going.

Throughout his life Trevithick was plagued by poverty and bad luck. He had a brilliant mind and brilliant ideas. But he was never able to see his work completed. In 1812 he was commissioned to equip silver mines in Peru with steam-engine pumps. The equipment was built in Cornwall, England. It was then shipped around the Horn to the west coast of South America. From there it was brought by mule to the mine sites, 14,000 feet above sea level. The machinery was then installed. Shortly after that, revolutionists took over. They threw all the machinery down the mine shafts. Trevithick had to come back to England on borrowed money. He died a poor man in 1833.

The steam-driven vehicle continued to be improved upon during the first half of the nineteenth century. Much work was done in England. Sir Goldsworthy Gurney made and ran a car in 1825. He was one of those who thought that power applied through a wheel could not move a vehicle. He applied power through rear-facing iron legs that dug into the roadway. But in 1826 he made a second vehicle. This one used the pushing rods only for emergencies. With his third car the rods disappeared. Gurney made one trip of 84 miles on 48 bushels of coal. The trip took him 9½ hours. In 1829 he drove from London to Bath and back (200 miles) at an average speed of 15 miles per hour.

In 1833, Sir Charles Dance, another automobile pioneer, built and used a steam-powered "drag" (tractor or tow) to pull a 15-seat bus from London to Brighton.

Around the same time, Walter Hancock ran regular "bus" service from London to nearby communities. He built about ten steam coaches. Some of these were quite large. His *Era* carried 18 passengers, and his *Automaton,* 22. Hancock sometimes used the *Automaton* as a drag. One time it pulled four buses, carrying 50 passengers, through the streets of London. It traveled at about 10-14 miles per hour.

Many other steam-driven vehicles were built in England, Europe and the United States. But these vehicles had certain disadvantages. It was hard to steer them. They easily got out of hand if they went

Men cheered, women and children waved and dogs barked when the steam omnibus Enterprise began running in London in 1833.

too fast. They smoked furiously and threatened to blow their boilers. Generally speaking, once the novelty had worn off, the people were against them. And, of course, the people who ran the railroads and horse-drawn carriages were against them.

In the meantime the internal-combustion engine was being developed. The Italian scientist Alessandro Volta had exploded methane gas by setting a spark to it. John Barber of Great Britain burned a mixture of coal gas and air within a cylinder. A Swiss, Isaac de Rivas, patented an engine that used a system like Volta's. Samuel Brown of England built and ran an engine fueled by hydrogen gas. All of these men contributed to the development of the internal-combustion engine. In so doing they helped bring the modern automobile closer to reality.

Étienne Lenoir (1822-1900) invented an engine that was relatively similar to today's engine. It was a two-stroke engine that ran on coal gas which was ignited electrically. This engine was patented in 1860. It produced 1½ horsepower. In 1863 Lenoir made a vehicle and used this engine to power it. The car went only 6 miles per hour.

The Austrian inventor Siegfried Marcus (1831-99) ran a self-propelled vehicle in 1864 or 1865. It had a two-stroke internal-combustion engine. The chassis of the vehicle was very crude; it was made of wood. Marcus said he started it by having the janitor of his house, a strong man, lift the rear end so the driving wheels could be spun. Marcus ran this machine only once. In 1874-75 he made another vehicle. This one also had a very crude body. But its engine was very advanced in design. The car has been driven several times. It can go 4 miles an hour with four passengers aboard. Today it is on exhibit at the Vienna Technisches Museum.

Next in the line of auto pioneers were Karl Benz (1844-1929) and Gottlieb Daimler (1834-1900). Benz built and ran a three-wheeled internal-combustion vehicle in 1885. Daimler made a four-wheeled vehicle in the following year. Both of these were prototypes of today's auto.

Daimler and Benz never met. But the companies they founded were later joined as the giant Daimler-Benz organization. This is the oldest auto-manufacturing company in the world. It makes the famous Mercedes and Mercedes-Benz vehicles.

With the Daimler and Benz vehicles the modern auto came into existence. Only development and refinement were left to be done.

The Human Brain

... this 3-pound organ with its billions of nerve cells controls our every action

EACH year electronic engineers find something new for electronic brains, or computers, to do. These amazing machines can now play chess and compose music. They can take dictation and read mail. A large electronic brain can do more than eight thousand additions or subtractions in one second. It can also predict the weather and translate foreign languages into English. And it can design other computing machines. Some electronic brains can even find and then correct their own mistakes.

Electronic brains act faster than human brains. They are also more accurate than human brains. But electronic brains are limited: they cannot reason for themselves. If they are not "told" to do something in very clear terms, they cannot do it. Nor can they use past knowledge or experience when solving a problem. It is in this area that man's brain is unique.

The brain is the most important part of man's nervous system. This complex organ weighs only about three pounds. Yet it controls all our actions. Without a brain we would not be able to think, reason, learn or remember. We would not be able to see, taste, hear, smell or feel. Nor would we be able to walk, talk or even move effectively.

The amazing organ that allows us to do all these things is made up of three main sections. These are the forebrain, the midbrain and the hindbrain.

In the forebrain are the cerebrum and the hypothalamus. The cerebrum is the largest part of the brain. In fact it accounts for 90 per cent of the brain's bulk. This part of the brain is the seat of intelligence. It is the center of all our conscious mental processes, such as memory, reasoning and judgment. The cerebrum also controls our muscles, sight, hearing and speech.

The hypothalamus regulates the body's internal organs, such as the heart, lungs and liver.

Another very important part of the brain is the cerebellum. This organ is in the hindbrain. It controls our balance and coordinates our muscles.

The medulla oblongata is also in the hindbrain. This organ controls such things as circulation, digestion and respiration. It also controls our tongue muscles.

The four organs just described—the cerebrum, the hypothalamus, the cerebellum and the medulla oblongata—are the four most important parts of the brain.

The brain is connected to the spinal column by the brainstem. The brainstem runs from the spine right through the forebrain, the midbrain and the hindbrain. In fact the medulla oblongata (which is in the hindbrain), the entire midbrain and the hypothalamus (which is in the forebrain) are all parts of the brainstem.

Man's brain is very, very complex. There are still many things that we do not know about it. Scientists and medical men are still probing its mysteries. But—there is much that we do know. On the following pages are diagrams of various parts of the brain. These will help you to understand better how this organ and its various subsections work.

The human brain is the most complex structure known, consisting of billions of nerve cells richly interconnected in networks that still defy analysis. Here countless nerve impulses constantly play over what one physiologist called an "enchanted loom" of fiber pathways, recording the nature of the outside world, thinking, dreaming, feeling, and directing the muscles of the body. Basically the brain performs three types of activity: (a) it receives an input of sensory impulses from the eyes, ears, nose, and other sense structures; (b) it processes these impulses (thinking); and (c) it sends out impulses that direct muscular activity.

Shown in the diagram are the principal structures of the brain: (1) the cerebrum, which contains areas for higher thought, vision, hearing, speech, and muscle control; (2) the hypothalamus, which integrates emotion and body activity; (3) the cerebellum, which co-ordinates muscular activity; and (4) the medulla, which contains the respiratory center.

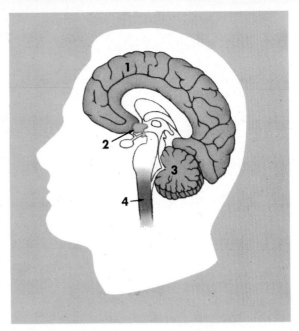

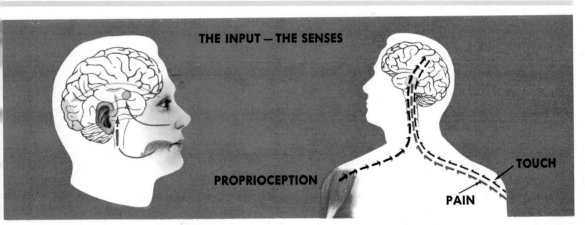

THE INPUT — THE SENSES

The sensations of sight, sound, taste, and smell reach the brain directly through the cranial nerves.

Muscle sensations (proprioception) and sensations of pain and touch from the trunk travel to the brain via the spinal cord. The proprioceptive impulses keep the brain informed of the state of muscular contraction.

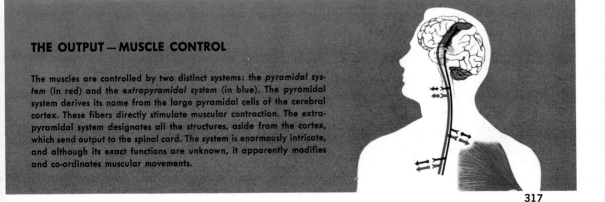

THE OUTPUT — MUSCLE CONTROL

The muscles are controlled by two distinct systems: the *pyramidal system* (in red) and the *extrapyramidal system* (in blue). The pyramidal system derives its name from the large pyramidal cells of the cerebral cortex. These fibers directly stimulate muscular contraction. The extrapyramidal system designates all the structures, aside from the cortex, which send output to the spinal cord. The system is enormously intricate, and although its exact functions are unknown, it apparently modifies and co-ordinates muscular movements.

317

Thinking, remembering, enjoying music and art, writing, and other similar activities most familiarly associated with the brain are primarily "associative," that is, they involve communication within the brain. An early concept of the brain as a mere switchboard co-ordinating incoming and outgoing impulses has be supplanted by the realization that the brain is the s of constant activity into which sensory impulses fe These impulses are interpreted, co-ordinated, thou about, and acted upon by the structures indicated he

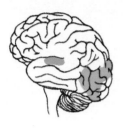

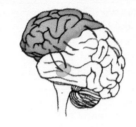

Sensory association areas surrounding the auditory and visual cortex function in the comprehension of sounds and images.

The frontal lobes were an early challenge to investigators because no specific function could be assigned to them. Even more puzzling was the discovery that these structures could be removed, often producing only slight effects on behavior. It is now believed that the lobes are important in abstract thinking. The arrows indicate the connections of the lobe with the thalamus of the lower brain and with other parts of the cerebrum.

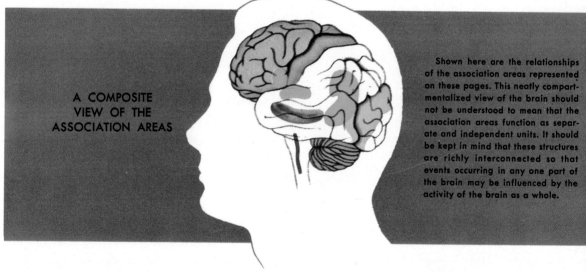

A COMPOSITE
VIEW OF THE
ASSOCIATION AREAS

Shown here are the relationships of the association areas represented on these pages. This neatly compartmentalized view of the brain should not be understood to mean that the association areas function as separate and independent units. It should be kept in mind that these structures are richly interconnected so that events occurring in any one part of the brain may be influenced by the activity of the brain as a whole.

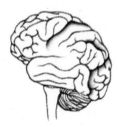

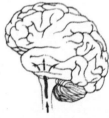

Suppressor areas inhibit the activity of adjacent brain tissues. Thus the motor suppressor area halts muscular movement.

The reticular system is an extensive network of fibers in the lower brain that is apparently involved in conciousness, attention, and feeling. The arrows indicate the radiation of impulses from the reticular system to the cerebral cortex and lower brain.

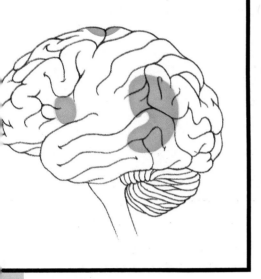

SPEECH

Three distinct speech areas are recognized and are unique in that all are located in one-half of the brain, usually the left hemisphere.

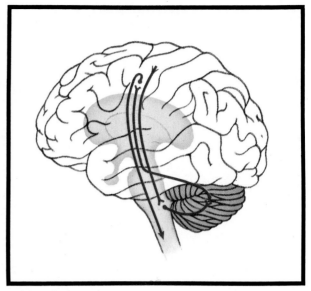

CEREBELLUM

This structure is important in movement. Impulses from the motor area of the cerebral cortex reach the cerebellum, which selects a pattern of action and relays it back to the cortex. The cortex then sends the selected impulse pattern to the muscles.

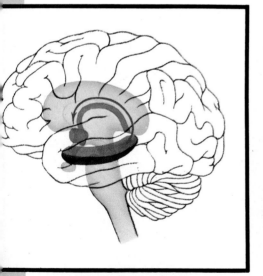

HIPPOCAMPAL SYSTEM

This consists of a group of structures which integrates impulses from other parts of the brain and is evidently involved in mood and emotional responses. The system expresses these actions on the body by way of its connections with the hypothalamus.

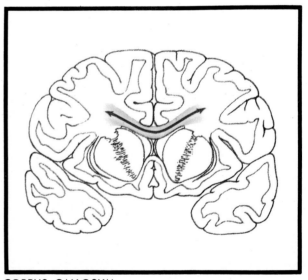

CORPUS CALLOSUM

The corpus callosum is an important integrating structure connecting the two halves of the brain. Experiments with monkeys have demonstrated that severing the corpus callosum permits each half of the brain to function independently. Such animals can learn two tasks in the time required for an ordinary animal to learn one.

319

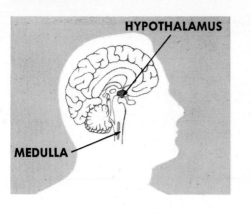

HYPOTHALAMUS

MEDULLA

THE BRAIN AND THE INTERNAL ORGANS

An important aspect of the brain-body relationship is the uncon
scious nervous control of the heartbeat rate, respiration, an
glandular activity. These actions enable the body to adjust t
external stresses. The prolonged action of the central nervou
system on the internal organs is believed to be the central facto
in psychosomatic illness. Some parts of the brain involved i
these control activities are shown in the diagram. The actio
may be accomplished by means of hormones traveling throug
the blood or by direct nerve pathways to the target organs.

BRAIN-HORMONE RELATIONSHIPS

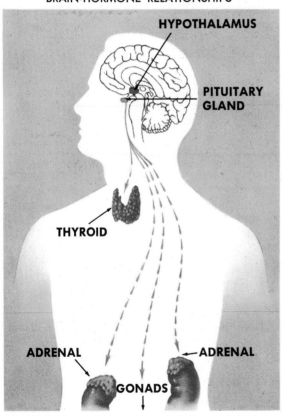

HYPOTHALAMUS

PITUITARY
GLAND

THYROID

ADRENAL

ADRENAL

GONADS

DIRECT NERVOUS CONTROL
OF INTERNAL ACTIVITY

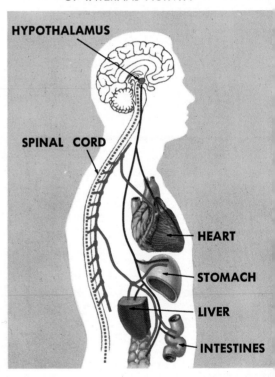

HYPOTHALAMUS

SPINAL CORD

HEART

STOMACH

LIVER

INTESTINES

Indicated here is the link between the nervous and endocrine gland
systems. Impulses from the hypothalamus act upon the pituitary,
the "master" endocrine gland. Pituitary hormones stimulate the
thyroid, adrenal, and sex glands. Brain-pituitary control may at
times have pronounced effects on body function. An excellent
example is the relation between stress, emotions, and the menstrual
period. Marked anxiety can delay the onset of menstruation
through pituitary control.

Direct nervous control of the heart, liver, blood vessels, and num
ous other internal structures is exercised by the brain through t
hypothalamus. The nerve pathways involved are those of t
autonomic, or visceral, nervous system. The sympathetic branch
red) of the system serves largely to mobilize the body for stress
diverting blood from the internal organs to the muscles by raisi
the blood pressure and by increasing the pulse rate. The pa
sympathetic branch (in blue) promotes digestion by stimulating t
secretions of the digestive organs.

Smoking and Health

By LUTHER L. TERRY

. . . the United States Surgeon General tells about the hazards of smoking

Fred Lyon

THERE has been a great deal of talk about the connection between smoking and health. Concern is shown by the many debates on the subject and in the amount of public interest that has been stirred. Studies of the subject began way back in 1900. They have increased in number and scope over the years as new and important facts came to light.

The United States Public Health Service is the main Federal agency concerned with the nation's health. Thus it has long been interested in the effect of smoking on human health. The Service has conducted, supported and summarized research on the subject. In the 1950's many independent studies were being carried on in several countries. On the basis of these studies, the Public Health Service issued a much-discussed statement in 1957. It said that "the weight of the evidence is increasingly pointing in one direction; that excessive smoking is one of the causative factors in lung cancer." In 1959 the Service repeated this belief. It said that cigarette smoking particularly is associated with an increased chance of developing lung cancer. Later research findings made scientists think that there is an even broader link between smoking and disease. Soon it became clear that further public-health action was needed.

In London the Royal College of Physicians issued a report early in 1962. Their conclusion was that "cigarette smoking is a cause of lung cancer and bronchitis, and probably contributes to the development of coronary heart disease and various other less common diseases." As a result of these findings, the British Government began waging a strong campaign against smoking. They also limited cigarette advertising on television, in the hope of discouraging would-be smokers.

In the United States various organizations urged that a presidential commission be formed to study the effects of smoking on health. These organizations were the American Cancer Society, the American Public Health Association, the American Heart Association and the National Tuberculosis Association. As a result, on June 7, 1962, the Public Health Service announced plans to establish a committee to review and evaluate all available knowledge on the subject. The ten noted scientists chosen to serve on the committee were selected from more than 150 top experts in several health fields. Those chosen had never before done research on the subject. Nor had any of them taken a definite position.

On January 11, 1964, these scientists— the Surgeon General's Advisory Committee on Smoking and Health—made their report. It was the most complete analysis ever made on the health effects of smoking.

The committee reached the conclusion that *cigarette smoking is a health hazard of sufficient importance in the United States to warrant appropriate remedial action.* The committee found that cigarette smoking contributes substantially to the overall death rate. It is linked to certain diseases, including several types of cancer and of ulcers, heart and artery diseases, chronic

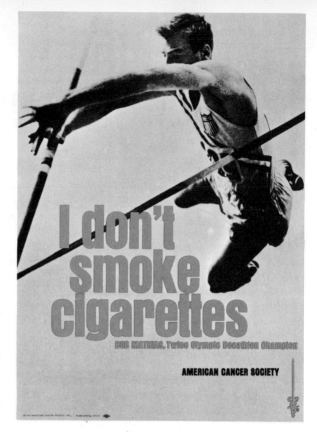

I don't smoke cigarettes

BOB MATHIAS, Twice Olympic Decathlon Champion

AMERICAN CANCER SOCIETY

At one time, famous athletes often endorsed their favorite brands of cigarettes. Now many well-known personalities—such as Bob Mathias, Bobby Richardson, Murray Rose and Pat Boone—are helping the American Cancer Society in its drive to discourage the American public from smoking.

bronchitis, and emphysema. Cigarette smoking also causes breathlessness and coughing. And it is related to accidental deaths from fires in the home.

The diseases mentioned are major causes of death in the United States. They claim more and more lives each year. For example, lung-cancer deaths totaled 41,000 in 1962. This is an increase of 34,500 from the total in 1942. The number of cigarette smokers who die from lung cancer is, in fact, 11 times greater than the number of nonsmokers who die from lung cancer. During these 20 years, deaths from heart disease increased by 183,100. And reported deaths from chronic bronchitis and emphysema rose from 1,960 to 15,000.

The number of cigarettes smoked in the United States has increased at a similarly rapid pace. At the turn of the century, each person (15 years and older) smoked, on the average, 50 cigarettes a year. By 1910 it had increased to 138. By 1961 it was at a peak of 3,986. The 1955 *Current Population Survey* showed that 68 per cent of the

men in the United States and 32.4 per cent of the women (18 years of age and over) were regular smokers of cigarettes. The percentages are even higher now.

As you might expect, smoking habits greatly affect the extent of the health hazard. For example, the more cigarettes smoked daily, the higher the death rate. Even for moderate smokers the death rate from all causes is about 40 per cent higher than for nonsmokers. A moderate smoker is one who smokes less than 10 cigarettes a day. For those who smoke from 10 to 19 cigarettes daily, the death rate is about 70 per cent higher than for nonsmokers; 20 to 39 cigarettes a day raise it to 90 per cent. And men who smoke two packs or more have a death rate that is 120 per cent higher than that of nonsmokers.

What about other forms of tobacco? Men who smoke less than 5 cigars daily seem to have about the same death rate as nonsmokers. More than 5 cigars a day raises the death rates slightly. There is some indication that these higher death rates

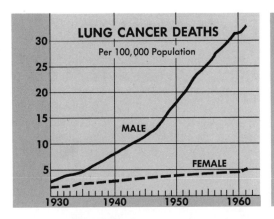

LUNG CANCER DEATHS	CIGARETTE CONSUMPTION
Per 100,000 Population	Per Person for Americans over 15

Both cigarette smoking and the number of deaths from lung cancer have risen steadily since 1930, as these graphs show. Because most lung can- cer victims turned out to be heavy cigarette smokers, a link was made between the two. Other studies tend to confirm this link.

occur mostly among men who have been smoking more than 30 years and who inhale the smoke. The death rates for pipe smokers are little if at all higher than for nonsmokers. This is true even of men who smoke 10 or more pipefuls a day, or of men who have smoked pipes more than 30 years. In fact the only risk for pipe smokers is that they are somewhat more likely to get cancer of the lip than nonsmokers.

Men who began smoking before they were 20 have a higher death rate than those who began after they were 25. In general the mortality risk of cigarette smokers increases the longer they have been smoking. Also, those who stop after age 55 are more susceptible than those who stop when they are younger.

The Public Health Service intends to take action against cigarette smoking through education and research. Educational efforts will be directed mostly toward young people. By making them aware of the dangers of smoking, the Service hopes to discourage them from taking up cigarettes. However, the Service realizes that many smokers will continue to smoke. So an effort must also be made to lessen ill effects on the health of those who keep smoking. For example, the Service urges that cigarette smokers cut down on the number of cigarettes they smoke. It is also helpful if they switch from cigarettes to pipes or cigars, or if they inhale less, since statistics indicate that inhaling seems to increase the mortality rate.

Research into the social and behavioral side of smoking is another important field. The evidence indicates that smoking is a habit that people form for psychological and social reasons. This conclusion does not, however, rule out the possibility that physiological factors make some people more likely to become smokers than others. At any rate, we need to know more about why people start smoking. We also need to know why they maintain this habit, and how they can stop once they have started. Still another research goal is to make smoking safer. Perhaps this may be done by developing better strains of tobacco and better methods of cultivating it.

Such education and research will be undertaken cooperatively by the Public Health Service and other Federal agencies. State and local agencies, nongovernmental organizations and the tobacco industry will help too. Their common goal will be to avoid or cut down on the human intake of harmful substances. Their success will be determined in large measure by the support the American people give them.

Dr. Harold E. Edgerton

. . . the man who stops bullets in flight

By RICHARD H. MILLER

All photos, Edgerton, Germeshausen & Grier

A bullet shot through an apple is caught by the camera.

HAVE you ever seen a bullet in flight? You never have and you never will, with your unaided eye. A regular bullet speeds toward its target at 1,800 miles an hour. Its speed is three times that of a modern jet airliner. If you stood at one end of a football field and fired at the opposite goal line, the bullet would cross the one hundred yards in one ninth of a second!

But just because something moves too fast to be seen, it doesn't mean that we cannot take its picture. Thanks to equipment developed by Dr. Harold E. Edgerton of the Massachusetts Institute of Technology, we now have photos of all sorts of things we never really saw before.

Until Dr. Edgerton developed a way of taking pictures at 1/1,000,000 of a second and less, no one had actually seen a golf ball leave the club head, at 198 feet a second. Nor had anyone clearly photo-

graphed a hummingbird with its tiny wings beating 3,600 times a minute. Truly, Dr. Edgerton can be called the Father of Modern Ultra-High-Speed Photography.

Like all famous inventors, Dr. Edgerton trained himself for his work. He didn't just wake up one morning, snap his fingers, and announce that he had discovered the correct way of photographing a bullet. It took him many years of hard work and study.

Dr. Edgerton was born in 1903 in Fremont, Nebraska. His father was a lawyer. But when he said he would rather study electricity than the law, his father let him go ahead. So, at the age of 16, he found himself a job as a janitor in an electric-light plant. He worked there before and after school. Sometimes his father had to shake him to get him out of bed on cold winter mornings.

"It was a wonderful job," Dr. Edgerton says, "and I learned how to climb light poles and how to run generators and motors.

"One time I was sent to a home to find out why the fuses kept blowing. My boss told me not to come back until I had discovered what the real trouble was. It didn't take me long—there was a little girl who kept sticking pins into the light cords. Don't you try it."

And he learned something that he keeps telling his students at MIT: "Once you start a job, finish it. Don't come back with excuses."

After graduating from high school, he went to the University of Nebraska. There he studied electrical engineering. Next he worked at the General Electric Company for a year. Then he went to the Massachusetts Institute of Technology for a Master's degree. He has been there ever since. Dr. Edgerton now holds the title of Professor of Electrical Measurements.

Thirty years ago Dr. Edgerton was studying electric motors in the laboratory. He wanted to see what they were doing when they were running at high speed. This was not easy, for the armature—the motor's main moving part—rotates several thousand times a minute.

He set up a stroboscope to help him. The word "stroboscope" comes from two ancient Greek words that, taken together, mean "whirling viewer." It is a very accurate term.

Let us see how a "strobe" works. Suppose you mark your initials on one blade of an ordinary electric fan. Turn it on and it will spin 18 times a second. All you will see is a blur. Now suppose you set up a light that flashes exactly 18 times a second. Each time your initials reach "12 o'clock," the light goes on for a tiny fraction of a second. If your timing is perfect —if flash and fan are synchronized—it will seem as if the fan were not moving at all. You will be able to read your initials clearly. But don't stick your finger

Ultra-high-speed photography has made possible these two amazing photos. The splash of milk was exposed at 100 millionths of a second.

into the fan no matter how still it looks!

The stroboscope is that simple, on paper at least. It was invented in 1832 by two men, Joseph A. F. Plateau of Belgium and a Viennese scientist named S. R. von Stampfer. But like many important inventions, it did not come into full use for a long while. In fact it was almost a century before Dr. Edgerton began to use the strobe for flash photography.

Dr. Edgerton took the basic ideas of Plateau, of Von Stampfer and of other scientists and used them to make modern equipment. For example, he discovered the way to get a very bright, very fast flash—a kind of man-made lightning bolt —inside a gas-filled tube. Then he worked out the controls so that his tube would flash 25,000 times a second, 5,000 times a second, 500 times a second, or only once.

At this point you may be puzzled. Some stroboscopes flash thousands of times a second. But when we take a high-speed picture, we use only one fast burst of light. Are we really talking about the same thing?

The answer is "yes" because the basic equipment is the same. The strobe light attached to a camera is designed to do a one-flash-per-picture job. It must weigh as little as possible. And it must work on lightweight batteries. A photographer does not want all the standard, heavy strobo-scope equipment.

Let us look at how Dr. Edgerton takes a picture of a bullet in flight. First, he sets up a pistol or rifle and fastens it in place so that when he pulls the trigger the bullet will hit the target automatically. He doesn't have the time to worry about whether his aim is good or not.

Then he sets up a strobe light—one of the many different ones he has helped to design. It will give a flash of less than 1/1,000,000 of a second. This is so much faster than any camera shutter that he simply leaves the shutter open and keeps the room dark so that stray light will not fog the film.

His next job is to work out a way of setting off the strobe light just as the bullet passes in front of the camera. A bullet is fast. But it still takes 1/1,000 of a second to travel a full yard from the pistol. So he sets a little microphone a foot away from the pistol. He knows that it will take about 1/1,000 of a second for the sound of the shot to arrive. (Sound travels at about 750 miles an hour.) The moment it does, it triggers the strobe lamp. Hope-fully the bullet is in the right spot at that moment. If it isn't, he tries again, after making some small adjustments.

Using a microphone is not the only way to set off a strobe lamp. A moving object could cut a wire or cross a light beam. If the photographer is taking pictures of a bird landing or of a boxer being felled by a sharp right to the jaw, the timing is not quite as important. The photographer can then trigger the flash himself by pressing a button.

Of course, not many people want to take pictures of bullets in flight or hum-mingbirds hovering. Thus the real impor-tance of Dr. Edgerton's work is that it has provided the basic high-speed flash equip-ment for all sorts of uses. Dr. Edgerton did not build the strobe light that you use with your camera. But some of his basic ideas went into it. This is his contribution to the amateur photographer.

He has also designed lights for use in underwater photography, and the lamps that are still flashing aboard the ANNA space satellite. The lamps aboard ANNA were designed to last at least a year. But they have lasted far longer than that.

The ANNA lamps were built by the electronics firm of Edgerton, Germeshaus-en and Grier, Inc., of which Dr. Edgerton is board chairman. These lights flash on at precisely timed intervals. Scientists on the earth photograph them against a back-ground of stars. They use these pictures to check on the exact size of the earth and the exact distances between places on the earth.

Dr. Edgerton is always up to something new. At present he is working with doctors who are trying to get series of photo-graphs of the fast-moving red blood cells in the white of a living person's eye. This must be done through a microscope be-cause two thousand red cells, side by side, cover only one inch.

"This is not easy," Dr. Edgerton says, "because we have to work with very small lamps, and there are many other prob-lems.

"But this is a whole new exciting field for flash photography."

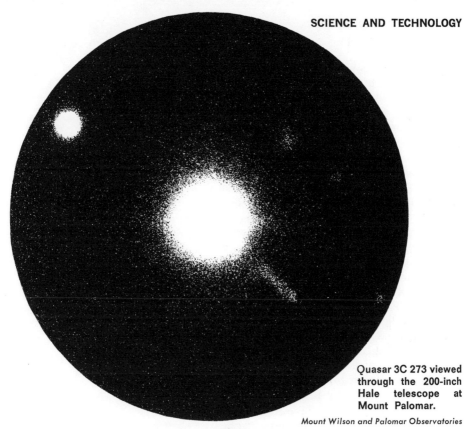

Quasar 3C 273 viewed through the 200-inch Hale telescope at Mount Palomar.

Mount Wilson and Palomar Observatories

Science Review

By BRYAN BUNCH

**Quasars: new mysteries
    in the heavens**

In 1964 there was a great deal of talk about the quasar. This is a kind of super-star. Earl Ubell, popular newspaper and radio science commentator, has called the discovery of quasars "the most exciting event in astronomy in a generation." The word "quasar" is short for quasi-stellar object. Quasars are bigger than stars but smaller than galaxies. They seem to be very far away. And they are getting farther away all the time. Tremendous amounts of energy pour out of the quasars—more than can be accounted for by present theories of how stars create energy. About 25 quasars have been located so far.

In addition to light, quasars send out radio waves. These were detected by radio astronomers. The radio astronomers then asked the optical astronomers to look around the area from which huge amounts of energy were being sent. The scientists found what appeared to be a dim star. But this object was not really dim. It only seemed dim because it was so far away—1,000,000,000 light-years away, to be exact. In absolute brightness the object was the brightest ever measured. Could it be a supernova? No, because supernovae are giant exploding stars that burn out in a few years. Photographs indicate that quasars have been around longer than that. Could the quasars be galaxies? No, because they are far too small. One quasar is about as wide as half the distance from the sun to the nearest star.

Some astronomers think a quasar is a galaxy that is falling in on itself. The energy released by falling could be great enough to account for the quasar's great brightness and tremendous output of radio energy. But this theory raises new problems. Through close study of old photographs, one quasar has been discovered to brighten and dim in a 13-year pattern. It does not seem possible for a collapsing galaxy to collapse fast for a while, then slow, then fast in a regular cycle. On the other hand, it does not seem possible for a quasar to pulsate at all. The quasar with the 13-year cycle seems to be a thousand light-years across. Suppose the change that caused the quasar to become less bright began in the center of the quasar. The signal could not reach the surface until at least five hundred years later. If there were any irregularity at all in the makeup of the quasar, one side would pulse at a different time from another.

Could a signal travel faster than the speed of light? If the answer is yes, then the entire structure of modern physics is rotten. If the answer is no, then how does one explain the quasar with the 13-year cycle?

Quasars can help solve some problems just by being there. Because they release such enormous amounts of energy, they can be seen farther than anything else in the universe. There is one quasar that seems to be the most distant object seen yet.

There are rival theories about the structure of the universe. These differ mainly in their explanations of what is happening at great distances. Examination of quasars may help prove whether the universe is curved or not. They may also give us information on whether the universe started with a bang or has always been the same. Finally it may help us find out whether the universe will continue to expand or will some day begin to contract.

C A N A D A

Ant cowboys and caterpillar cows

Gary Ross of Louisiana State University discovered unique herdsmen in the Tuxta Mountains of Mexico. The herdsmen are ants. Their herds are caterpillars.

Naturalists have known for many years that ants sometimes keep other insects. Ants need the nutritious fluids that these insects produce. But the care the Mexican ants give to their caterpillar cattle is something special. They shut the caterpillars up in a short burrow during the day. Before the ants let the caterpillars out, they carefully examine the plants that the caterpillars will eat from. They remove any spiders or harmful insects. Then the caterpillars are released. They are allowed to eat under the watchful eyes of their keepers. The ants then drink the caterpillar juice.

When the caterpillar turns into a chrysalis, the ants stay on guard. They protect the cocoon until the butterfly emerges.

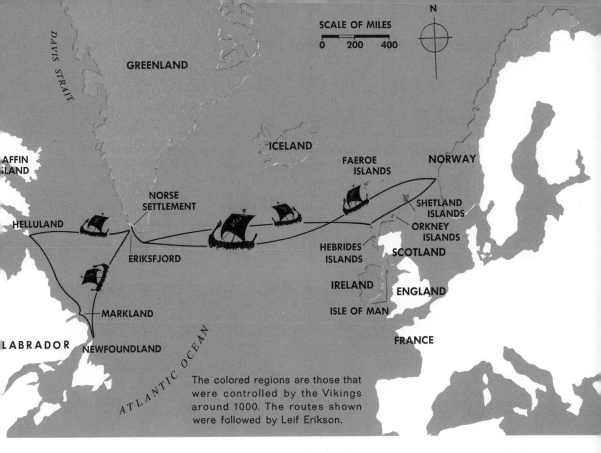

NSCALE OF MILES

0   200   400

DAVIS STRAIT

GREENLAND

ICELAND

BAFFIN
ISLAND

FAEROE
ISLANDS

NORWAY

NORSE
SETTLEMENT

SHETLAND
ISLANDS

HELLULAND

ORKNEY
ISLANDS

ERIKSFJORD

HEBRIDES
ISLANDS

SCOTLAND

IRELAND

ENGLAND

ISLE OF MAN

MARKLAND

LABRADOR   NEWFOUNDLAND

FRANCE

ATLANTIC OCEAN

The colored regions are those that
were controlled by the Vikings
around 1000. The routes shown
were followed by Leif Erikson.

Destroying cancer with a laser beam

The laser is a device that creates an intense, concentrated beam of light. Among other things, the laser has been used to destroy a type of skin cancer in hamsters. The cancer cells are destroyed where the laser hits. And, oddly enough, the destruction spreads throughout the patch of skin cancer. It stops only when non-cancerous skin is reached. This type of research is very important. It bears out the idea that there is some essential difference between cancerous cells and normal cells. If such a difference can be spotted chemically, a way might be opened to cure all sorts of cancer in humans.

Pre-Columbian Viking ruins discovered in Newfoundland

It often happens that scientists know (or suspect) that some particular thing exists (such as a predicted subatomic particle). But they often have trouble locating it. For example, scientists have long thought that the ancient Norse colony of Vinland was on the mainland of North America. Some thought Vinland might even be Rhode Island.

Norwegian archaeologist Helge Ingstad decided to try and find out exactly where Vinland was. He spent a long time studying old maps and legends. They suggested to him that Leif Ericson had founded Vinland on the northern shore of Newfoundland around A.D. 1000.

Ingstad and his wife then went to Newfoundland. They explored the northern shore and finally came across the first clearly proved ruins of European men in North America before Columbus. The ruins consist of the foundations of several houses, a ceremonial hall and a shed for cattle. There are also some artifacts.

It is quite clear that the ruins are Norse. Radiocarbon dating places the settlement at A.D. 1000, with a possible error of seventy years. Certainly the site matches

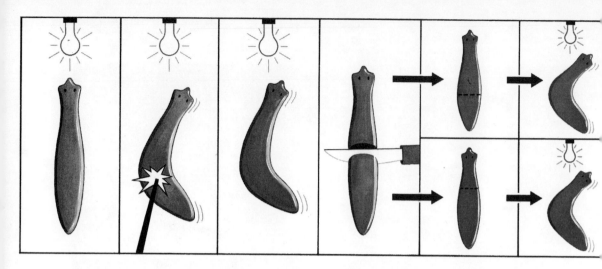

Now even flatworms can be educated. First they are shocked, which makes them contract, while a light is flashed. Thereafter whenever the light is flashed, they contract, though no shock is applied. They still respond to the light after being cut in two and growing a new half.

the descriptions of Vinland found in old Norse legends preserved in Iceland.

How to educate
a flatworm

About ten years ago James McConnell and Robert Thompson tried to see if they could teach anything to flatworms (planarias). These two phychologists believed that since planarias have primitive brains, they could be taught. A dog can learn to perform some simple tasks. Pigeons can be taught. Why not worms?

The two men put a worm in a trough. They then gave it an electric shock. This made the worm contract. At the same time that the shock was given, a 100-watt bulb was flashed at the worm. This was done a couple of hundred times. Then the shocks were stopped. Only the light bulb was flashed. But the worm still contracted. Apparently the worm had learned that light meant a shock.

If you cut a flatworm in half, both halves continue to live and grow. In time the head of the original flatworm grows a new tail. The original tail grows a new head. Some scientists believe that memories are stored throughout the body in the giant molecules of DNA. Others believe that memories are stored only in the brain.

McConnell and Thompson decided to find out who is correct.

They began by teaching the flatworms to react to light. Then they cut them in half and checked to see how much each half remembered after the halves had grown back into flatworms. If the tail (with a new head) reacted to the light, then memory must be stored throughout the body. And the tail did seem to remember!

Another test was then tried. If learning came from a chemical in the worm's body, might there be some way to put the chemical from educated worms into uneducated worms?

Planarias are cannibals. So the easiest way to do this would be to feed an uneducated worm on the bits and pieces of educated ones. The experiment was carried out. It seemed to work quite well. The well-fed cannibals seemed to learn faster than those on a normal diet.

At this point the scientific worm turned. Scientists in Utah and North Dakota disputed the results of the experiments. One said that the worms could not be taught in the first place. The controversy grew. Finally, in 1964, the United States Government gave a grant for an official three-year study of flatworm education.

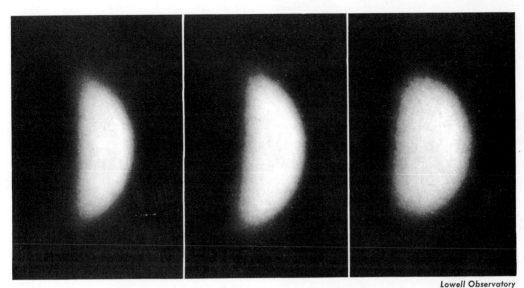

Lowell Observatory

SYMBOL FOR THE
PLANET MERCURY

Because Mercury travels in an orbit smaller than that of the earth, the part of the planet that is permanently sunlit is visible to observers on the earth in varying amounts. In other words, Mercury goes through phases similar to those of the earth's moon. The above photographs show Mercury as it appeared on (left to right) June 7, June 11 and June 12.

Radio astronomy determines
Mercury's temperature

Mercury's rate of revolution about its axis is the same as its rate of revolution around the sun. Thus one hemisphere always faces the sun; the other always faces away from it. The side that faces the sun is bathed in light, heat and radiation. The other side of the planet is always dark. And until 1964 it was assumed that Mercury's dark side was also very cold.

Radio telescopes can be used to determine the temperatures of bodies in space. In 1964, Australian astronomers used their 250-foot radio telescope at Parkes, New South Wales, to take the temperature of the dark side of Mercury. Instead of the expected reading of 400° F. below zero, the Australians obtained a balmy 60° F. above zero. How could this be? Something must transfer the heat from the sun side to the dark side. This is usually done by gases—that is, the planet's atmosphere. So if Mercury's dark side is warm, then the planet should have an atmosphere.

The fact that Mercury seems to have an atmosphere that transfers heat presents another problem. This is simply that Mercury seems too small to have an atmosphere. A molecule of gas on the hot side would travel at a speed well above the escape velocity for a small planet. (The escape velocity is the speed at which a body must be traveling to leave a planet and not return. For Earth it is about seven miles a second.)

Thus on the one hand, Mercury must have an atmosphere to transfer the heat from the hot side to the dark side. On the other hand, it would seem that any atmosphere would fly off into space. Perhaps this riddle will not be solved until observations can be made from space.

Australian News and Information Bureau

Astronomical thermometer: Australia's new radio telescope, which took Mercury's temperature and found it to be much warmer than expected.

Nuclear particles and the eightfold way

One of the areas in which scientists have had great success with predictions is particle physics. Many subatomic particles have been predicted, and most of the predictions have eventually worked out. At various times over the past few years, the last predicted particle would be found and everyone would breathe a sigh of relief. But then new particles would be predicted and the search would begin again.

A new theory, developed by physicists Murray Gell-Mann and Yuval Ne'eman, has now systematized the predictions. This theory, known as the eightfold way, is a classification scheme for particles, just as the periodic table is a classification scheme for the elements. Several new particles were detected in 1964. One was predicted by the eightfold way. The others seem to fit into the eightfold classification scheme.

The eightfold way is based upon a branch of mathematics known as group theory. A group is a closed system of a rather simple structure. An example of a group is the set of drill commands used in the army: attention, right face, left face and about-face. No matter how many times these commands are given in some sequence, the soldier will be in a position that could have been reached from attention with a single command. Suppose that the command "about-face" were deleted from the set. Would it still be a group? No, because the command "right face" given twice would put the soldier in a position that could not be reached by the commands "attention," "right face" or "left face" alone. As this particular group is defined, it must have four members.

Using eight criteria, the Gell-Mann-Ne'eman theory groups all subatomic particles into a small number of families. Each family has a predictable number of particles. Each particle is viewed as a different state, just as we might say that the soldier facing north is in a different state from the soldier facing east or south. Mathematicians have studied groups for over one hundred years and have classified various types. The type of group, or family, formed by the subatomic states can have 8 members, 10 members or 27 members. But it cannot have, say, 9 or 11 members. Thus when Gell-Mann recognized what appeared to be a group with 9 members, he was able to predict that a tenth would be found. He was also able to predict its mass. It is as if in the drill commands you noted that sometimes a soldier turned right and sometimes he turned left, and you had reason to believe that his turns should form a group. You could then predict that another command would exist (to make the required four). And you could even say that it would be the command to turn and face the opposite direction.

TRANSPORTATION OF THE FUTURE

Instead of ocean liners, trans-oceanic travelers may someday be taking passenger submarines similar to this one—the first ever—which was designed by Jacques Piccard. It now tours Lake Geneva, where it carries 42 passengers down 3,000 feet.

All photos, UPI

Science-fiction planes powered by invisible energy are no longer part of the unforeseeable future. In fact airborne travelers may soon be flying about in aircraft along the lines of the one shown here. It is driven by wireless microwave power beamed at it from the ground. Tethering lines keep the tiny helicopter centered over the transmitting antenna.

CONSERVATION AND NATURE

I went to the woods because I wished to live deliberately, to front only the essential facts of life, and see if I could not learn what it had to teach. . . .

Thoreau

Fritz Henle, Photo Researchers

DPI

Frederich Ayer, Photo Researchers

William E. Shapiro

DPI

George Holton, Photo Researchers

Fritz Henle, Photo Researchers

"Here's a Pretty Kettle of Fish!"

FISH were the first vertebrates (animals with backbones). They have existed for about 500,000,000 years. With their more than 25,000 species, they are also the most numerous of the vertebrates.

Fish come in many different forms, and they differ greatly in their habits. Because fish are so diverse, it is very difficult to find a definition that fits all of them. In fact the most that can be safely said about fish in general is that they are back-boned, cold-blooded animals with two-chambered hearts. The other characteristics associated with fish are not found in all species. For example, there are some fish that do not breathe through gills. Some fish have no fins, others have no scales. And a few partially breathe out of water and will even drown if held underwater too long.

Most fish seem to have at least five senses. These are sight, touch, hearing, taste and smell.

Some fish cannot see at all. Others, such as the trout, have excellent vision. The trout apparently can distinguish both the form and the color of a fisherman's bait. But no matter how well developed a fish's sight is, it is of no use in clouded water or at night. It is then that many fish must rely on their sense of smell. This sense is keenly developed in certain fish.

To some extent all fish are able to taste the water that surrounds them. The catfish has taste buds scattered over its skin. It uses taste as a way of finding food in muddy water.

Hearing and touch seem to be related to each other. The hearing organs of fish are internal. These organs also serve as a balancing mechanism. In most fish, pores penetrate each scale in a line along its sides. These are connected with a duct underneath the scales. In the water, sounds are translated into waves of pressure. These waves are received by the fish through the connected pores. Thus even a blind fish that lives in dark caves can avoid bumping into walls and rocks.

Water temperature is very important to fish. Therefore it is not very surprising that fish can tell when the temperature changes by as little as a degree or two. Some herring can even tell when the temperature changes by two tenths of a degree.

Noise too seems to play a part in the lives of many fish, particularly during the breeding season. Some fish grind their teeth. Others grunt. Still others make a drumming sound by vibrating parts of the swim bladder. Many marine fish can also communicate by means of light-producing organs which give them a phosphorescent glow.

Some fish have a sixth sense. This sense enables them to detect and be guided by tiny electric currents in the water. They do this by generating their own electricity by the action of one chemical on another. These fish are thus guided by the echoes of the series of electric discharges that they themselves send into the water. This sixth sense is very accurate in certain fish. They can swim through a hole with less than one-eighth-inch clearance on either side without touching the sides of the hole.

FAMILIAR AQUARIUM FISH

The **Double Swordtail Guppy** is one of many domestic varieties developed from the wild guppy, a fresh-water native of Trinidad.

The **Veiltail Goldfish** was developed from the wild goldfish, which is native to fresh waters in Asia.

The **Banded Distichodus**, a native of fresh water in central Africa, belongs to the characid family.

The **Neon Tetra**, a fresh-water native of South America, also belongs to the characid family.

The **Silver Hatchetfish**, of the Amazon basin in South America, can actually fly above the water by moving its pectoral fins.

The **Sailfin Mollie** occurs in brackish and fresh water in warmer parts of North America.

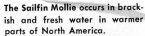

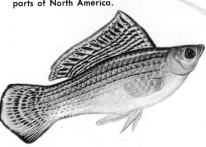

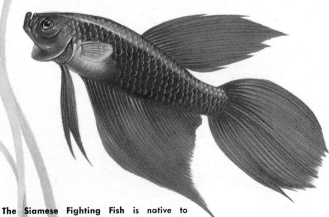

The **Siamese Fighting Fish** is native to fresh water in Thailand. The wild species is dull-colored and has small fins.

337

pages prepared with the co-operation
the American Museum of Natural History.
work by Leonard B. Cole.

MARINE GAME FISH

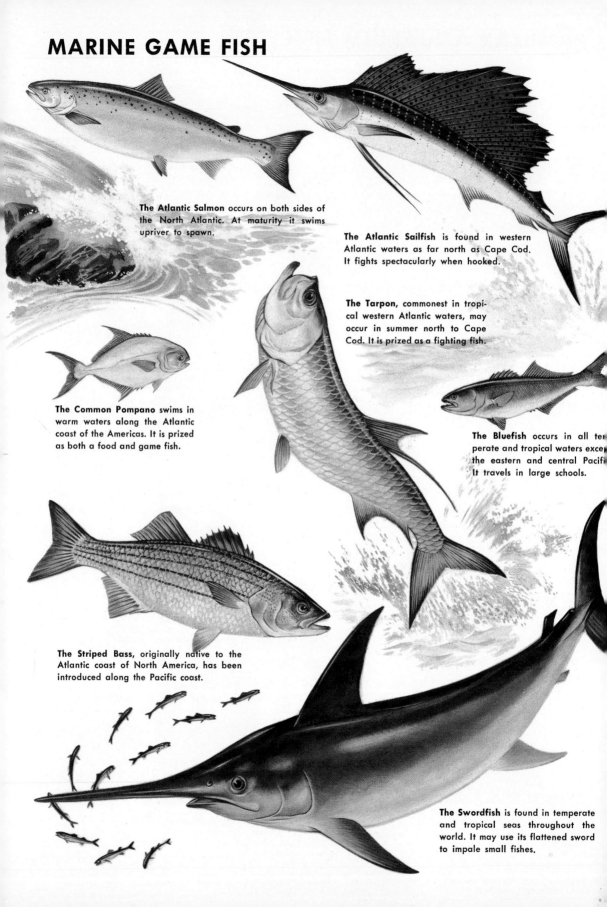

The **Atlantic Salmon** occurs on both sides of the North Atlantic. At maturity it swims upriver to spawn.

The **Atlantic Sailfish** is found in western Atlantic waters as far north as Cape Cod. It fights spectacularly when hooked.

The **Tarpon**, commonest in tropical western Atlantic waters, may occur in summer north to Cape Cod. It is prized as a fighting fish.

The **Common Pompano** swims in warm waters along the Atlantic coast of the Americas. It is prized as both a food and game fish.

The **Bluefish** occurs in all temperate and tropical waters except the eastern and central Pacific. It travels in large schools.

The **Striped Bass**, originally native to the Atlantic coast of North America, has been introduced along the Pacific coast.

The **Swordfish** is found in temperate and tropical seas throughout the world. It may use its flattened sword to impale small fishes.

FRESH-WATER GAME FISH

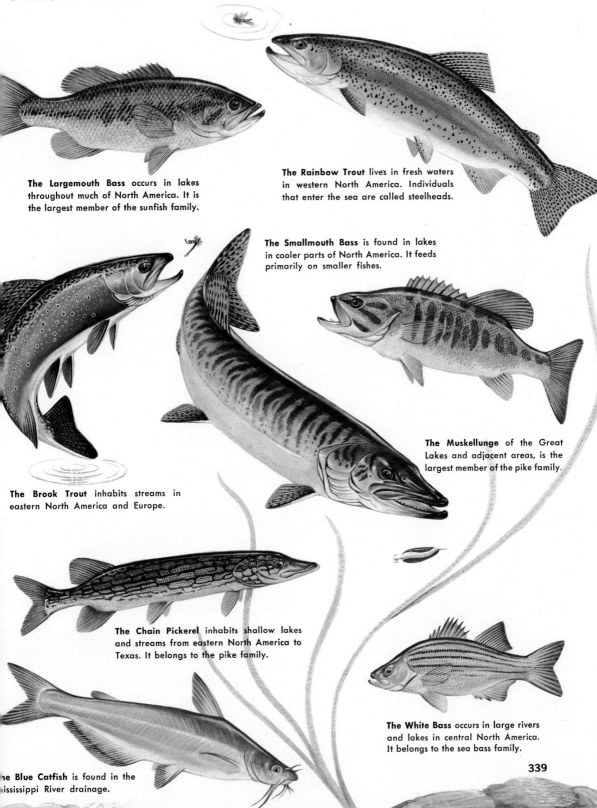

The Largemouth Bass occurs in lakes throughout much of North America. It is the largest member of the sunfish family.

The Rainbow Trout lives in fresh waters in western North America. Individuals that enter the sea are called steelheads.

The Smallmouth Bass is found in lakes in cooler parts of North America. It feeds primarily on smaller fishes.

The Brook Trout inhabits streams in eastern North America and Europe.

The Muskellunge of the Great Lakes and adjacent areas, is the largest member of the pike family.

The Chain Pickerel inhabits shallow lakes and streams from eastern North America to Texas. It belongs to the pike family.

The White Bass occurs in large rivers and lakes in central North America. It belongs to the sea bass family.

The **Blue Catfish** is found in the Mississippi River drainage.

CURIOSITIES OF THE FISH WORLD

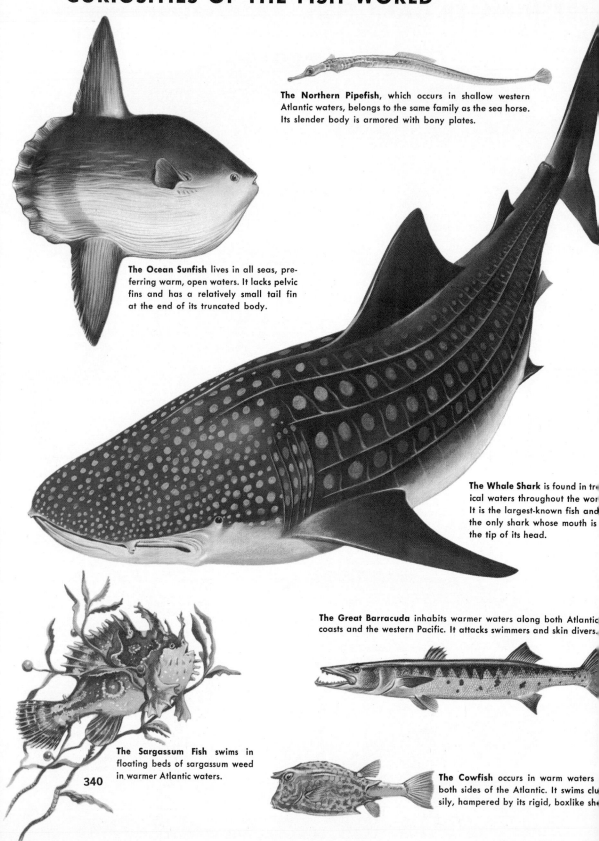

The Northern Pipefish, which occurs in shallow western Atlantic waters, belongs to the same family as the sea horse. Its slender body is armored with bony plates.

The Ocean Sunfish lives in all seas, preferring warm, open waters. It lacks pelvic fins and has a relatively small tail fin at the end of its truncated body.

The Whale Shark is found in tr[...] ical waters throughout the wor[...] It is the largest-known fish and[...] the only shark whose mouth is [...] the tip of its head.

The Great Barracuda inhabits warmer waters along both Atlantic coasts and the western Pacific. It attacks swimmers and skin divers.

The Sargassum Fish swims in floating beds of sargassum weed in warmer Atlantic waters.

The Cowfish occurs in warm waters [...] both sides of the Atlantic. It swims clu[...] sily, hampered by its rigid, boxlike sh[...]

Mudskipper, native to shallow waters the tropical Indo-Pacific, can hop about mud flats using its enlarged pectoral fins.

The Archerfish, found in fresh and salt water from India to Indonesia, shoots down insects by ejecting water through its mouth.

The Sawfish is found on both sides of the tropical and temperate Atlantic and in brackish and fresh waters. It uses its saw to club prey.

The Threespine Stickleback occurs in fresh and salt water throughout much of the Northern Hemisphere. After building a nest, the male lures the female into it.

Atlantic Sea Horse lives on the ntic coast from Nova Scotia to ntina. The male incubates the in a pouch on his underside.

The Porcupine Fish inhabits sub-tropical and tropical marine waters throughout the world. By swallowing water or air it can distend itself like a balloon.

MARINE FOOD FISH

The Albacore is found in offshore Atlantic and Pacific waters. Its flesh is the "whitemeat tuna" of commerce.

The Chinook Salmon occurs in cooler waters on both sides of the Pacific and swims far inland to spawn. It is the largest member of the salmon family.

The Scup lives along the North American Atlantic coast. It is popularly called the porgy.

The Atlantic Herring moves in large schools along both sides of the North Atlantic. Young herring are called "sardines" in the New England fishery.

The Spanish Mackerel occurs in warmer open and coastal Atlantic waters. It has the streamlined body typical of members of the tuna family.

The Atlantic Cod is found along both coasts of the North Atlantic. This is the "sacred cod" of Massachusetts.

The Atlantic Halibut is found on both sides of the North Atlantic. Its eyes are on the right side of its body and it swims on its left side.

The Southern Flounder occurs along the North American Atlantic coast. As it matures its eyes move to the left side of its body and it swims on its right side.

FRESH-WATER FOOD FISH

The Lake Trout inhabits deep lakes in Canada and northern United States. Its numbers in the Great Lakes have been reduced by the parasitic sea lamprey.

The Channel Catfish occurs in clear, moving rivers through central North America. Its spotted markings usually disappear at maturity.

The Lake Whitefish lives in larger lakes in Canada and northern United States. The sea lamprey has reduced its numbers.

The Northern Pike is found in cool streams and lakes in North America and Eurasia. It is also a popular game fish.

The Walleye lives in lakes and streams in eastern North America. Is a member of the perch family.

The Cisco occurs in the same region as the lake whitefish, to which it is closely related. Ciscos swim in large schools, usually near the water's surface.

The Carp, native to the region between the Black and Caspian seas, has been introduced into fresh water throughout the world.

The Lake Sturgeon inhabits large lakes in temperate North America. It swims on the bottom, sucking in small invertebrates with its tubular mouth.

TROPICAL REEF FISH

The Queen Angelfish inhabits coastal reefs from the Gulf of Mexico to Brazil. Young fish have blue stripes on their sides.

The Ocean Triggerfish is found among from Florida to the West Indies. It is to lock its first two dorsal spines in position, preventing predators from re ing it from a coral reef crevice.

The Green Moray lives among coral reefs along the warmer western Atlantic coast. It attacks viciously if disturbed.

The Longspine Squirrelfish occurs in western Atlantic reefs from the Carolinas to Colombia. It was named for its squirrellike eyes.

The Rainbow Parrotfish, found in tropic and subtropical reefs on both sides of t Atlantic, was named for its parrotlike "beak

Animals of the Arctic

...today the Eskimo still depends on many animals for his survival

By CHARLES PAUL MAY

THE animals of the Arctic have been for many years essential to the survival of the Eskimo. In fact before the white man came to the Arctic, the Eskimo depended entirely on what he caught hunting and fishing. The very word "Eskimo" means "eater of raw meat." And the traditional Eskimo culture is a triumph of man's adaptation to an extremely difficult environment. But now, with the advent of firearms, the animals are becoming scarce. To help offset this problem, the United States and Canadian governments have been importing animals such as the reindeer.

March 1965 marks the thirtieth anniversary of the end of the greatest reindeer drive in history. This trek was undertaken to benefit the Eskimos of Canada's Mackenzie River delta. But some Government officials still wonder if the drive was worth the effort.

All across northern Europe and Asia, Lapps, Chukchi, Samoyeds and Kamchadals depend heavily on their domesticated reindeer. The animals provide them with food, leather and transportation. These peoples rarely know the periods of starvation that Eskimos sometimes face when wild game is scarce.

It was for this reason that Dr. Wilfred Grenfell brought reindeer to Labrador more than half a century ago. He dreamed of making herders of the Eskimos there. Lapps even came to Labrador to show the Eskimos how to care for reindeer. But Eskimos, being hunters instead of herders, slaughtered the deer at every opportunity. The European herders found themselves acting as guards for the animals.

In spite of this, Canadian officials decided to bring reindeer to the Mackenzie River delta. In Alaska a small reindeer industry had gradually been built up since the deer were introduced there in the 1890's. With three thousand Alaskan reindeer, a handful of Lapps and Eskimos started the 1,500-mile reindeer drive at Christmastime in 1929. It was thought they would reach the Mackenzie River in less than two years.

Arctic winters were severe during the early 1930's. Blizzards regularly slowed the drive, making the deer difficult to handle, since it is their nature to remain in one place during stormy weather. Hidden by curtains of wind-whipped snow, wolves stalked the reindeer unseen. Only when the predators rushed into the herd were the herders aware of their presence. By the time men reached the scene of an attack, a few deer would be dying while others were stampeding. The drive would halt for hours, perhaps days until the runaway reindeer were rounded up.

The "two-year" drive took five years and three months. Only about 400 of the original 3,000 deer completed the journey. But calves born along the way helped make up for losses. The Eskimos were delighted to see so much meat trotting about. They would have shot the deer immediately had they been allowed to.

It was assumed, and rightly, that older people would not adapt well to new ways. Officials therefore picked young men and teen-agers to train as herders under the guidance of Lapps. Even then, early signs indicated that the project might fail. Why

The polar bear is hunted by the Eskimo; its thick fur makes warm clothing.

The Alaskan malamute. This sled dog provides dependable transportation in the frozen north.

This gray-seal pup, resting comfortably here, will grow up only to be hunted by the Eskimo, who depend on the seal for food and oil.

should a boy spend dull hours looking after deer he wasn't allowed to slaughter when he could be out following a trapline?

However, in the 1950's, fur prices began to drop. Even if a trapper were successful, his reward might be so small that he could purchase little food. Though it is a comparatively quiet life, reindeer herding is more appealing than slow starvation. So

today Eskimos are showing more interest in the deer.

Closely related to the reindeer, but larger and more sturdy, is the wild caribou. For years this animal has been extremely important in the life of the Eskimo. Some Eskimos in central Canada, for example, depend on the caribou for their food, clothing, weapons, tools and even their *kayaks,* the small skin boats which hold a single man. Now heavy hunting has reduced the caribou's numbers. Where once there were thousands of caribou now there are hundreds.

Firearms, plus the northward advance of civilization, have changed the pattern of caribou life. At one time enormous herds of these animals followed certain migration routes every spring and every fall. It was simple for hunters to wait along the routes. Roads and settlements have caused the big deer to turn aside. Consequently Eskimos

A herd of migrating caribou in Alaska. For the Eskimo, this animal is
a source of food, clothing, weapons and tools.

may wait beside an old trail for days without seeing a caribou. When the hunters realize that the deer will not come, it may be too late to seek them elsewhere, for the animals travel far. Having great endurance, they cover mile after mile without pausing.

Scientists say the caribou could be domesticated. Some efforts to tame the big deer have been made, but setbacks have discouraged experimenters. It seems easier to bring in reindeer from Europe and Asia.

Whatever success the Eskimo has in domesticating the reindeer, it is unlikely that he will ever turn to the reindeer as a major means of transportation. He is too attached to his sturdy sled dog. Most sled dogs are called huskies, though accurately there are four breeds—Eskimo dogs, Siberian Huskies, Malamutes and Samoyeds. They generally stand about two feet high at the shoulders and have broad chests, powerful leg muscles. And, for warmth, they have a

The Pacific walrus lives along the Siberian and north Alaskan coasts. This aquatic mammal is related to the seal; it is a source of food to the Eskimo.

long outer fur coat over a short inner one.

Sled dogs are noted for their loyalty to their masters. There have been cases where they have actually starved or died of exhaustion in harness. The Eskimo driver, in turn, may share his last strip of dried seal with his dogs.

Some huskies resemble wolves, for Eskimos capture wolf cubs, raise them, and

347

breed them with their sled dogs. The mixed breeds inherit endurance from their wild ancestors but may lack the loyal dispositions of their domesticated forebears.

The gray wolves of the Arctic are not among the animals on which Eskimos rely regularly for food or furs. On the contrary, wolves and men are competitors. They look on each other with mutual fear. Eskimos worry that starvation will turn the predators into man-killers.

Also competing with man, especially for seals, is the polar bear. This yellowish white giant rears up to a height of ten or more feet. It always lives along the coasts, for its food supply comes from the Arctic Ocean or Hudson Bay.

On the ocean floor, a polar bear searches for shellfish. Between the seabed and the surface, this bear catches fish, while on the surface it feasts on seals. It can swim slowly with only its nose and eyes showing above water. Looking almost like a drifting fragment of ice, it silently approaches a seal napping on an ice floe. Before a ripple or swish of water alerts the seal to danger, the bear is close enough to lunge forward and strike.

Polar-bear fur provides Eskimos with warm clothes and blankets. Some Eskimos even eat bear meat, enjoying its strong, slightly spoiled flavor.

The wolverine is another predator of the far north. Although it is a little smaller than a husky, it is such a fierce animal that even polar bears, unless starving, will leave a carcass rather than fight with the wolverine. Eskimos despise the animal, for it kills furbearing animals needlessly, breaks into cabins, and fouls the air with the skunk-like musk characteristic of all members of the weasel family.

Eskimos use wolverine fur to line their parkas. This fur is unusually oily and does not frost over quickly. Although a man's breath will cause frost to form on it in time, this can be knocked off more easily than from most furs.

Not all creatures of the far north vie with man for food. Seals and walrus provide food during much of the year. Seals are extremely wary, closing their eyes for brief naps of only seconds at a time. To slip up on one an Eskimo must be clever. Worming across the ice on his belly, he stops the instant the intended victim raises its head. Then he inches ahead again as the seal closes its eyes. Good hunters can get close enough to hurl a harpoon.

Today most Eskimos hunt with guns. This eliminates some of the adventure and much of the danger from daily life. Hunting walrus was particularly risky when Eskimos had only harpoons.

A bull walrus may weigh a ton and a half. Two great teeth, or tusks, grow out of the walrus' mouth. These sharp weapons sometimes measure two feet in length. To dredge the ocean floor for shellfish, the walrus sinks its tusks into the mud and swims backward, plowing a double furrow. If once a walrus sinks these teeth into an Eskimo, the man will usually decide to seek other game from then on.

Seals and walrus are kept warm by thick layers of fat under their hides. This fat, or blubber, represents food to Eskimos. They eat it raw, boil it, and mix it with roots to make stew.

A milder meat comes from the Arctic hare. The ptarmigan, too, like other members of the grouse family, is good to eat. The Eskimo turns to these creatures during severe winters, but may pass them by when he has good luck hunting other animals. He will even use the fur of the hare for clothing, but prefers the hides of bear, seal and caribou. When he traps the fox, lynx, mink and marten, he is getting pelts to sell rather than for his own personal use.

Although it might sound as though there are plenty of animals in the far north, some of them are scarce. In stormy weather all of them are difficult to hunt. Thus the idea of maintaining a herd of domesticated animals, such as the reindeer, could prove to be a very good one. The Eskimo would have a year-round supply of food.

Uncontrolled slaughter, typified by the nineteenth-century buffalo shoot shown above, can mean extinction for our wildlife.

Within the image:

Railway Excursion
and
Buffalo Hunt

An excursion train will leave Leavenworth at 8
A. M. and Lawrence at 10 A. M. on Tuesday, October
27, 1868, and return on Friday.
This train will stop at the principal stations both going and returning. Ample time will be had for a grand
BUFFALO HUNT ON THE PLAINS.
Buffaloes are so numerous along the road that they
are shot from the cars nearly every day. On our last
excursion twenty buffaloes were killed in a hunt of
six hours.
All passengers can have refreshments on the cars at
reasonable prices.
Tickets for round trip from Leavenworth, $10.

Protecting Our Wildlife

... man is now trying to save animal species that are close to extinction

By JOHN HAYDEN

FOR generations Arab hunters have scouted the vast Arabian deserts for herds of Arabian, or white, oryx. They have killed these light-colored antelopes for their long, slender horns. Yet the oryx was in no danger of disappearing so long as the hunt was conducted on camelback. The swift oryx can outrun even a horse. But when Arab princes began to use modern weapons and motorized transportation—even airplanes—during a hunt, the number of oryx soon dwindled. The species was on the brink of extinction.

The Fauna Preservation Society of London saw what was happening, and in 1962 they launched Operation Oryx. Their aim was to capture some oryx and send them to other countries where they could breed. But the oryx had become so scarce that a two-month expedition netted only one female and two males. However, a London zoo contributed another female. All four

349

One of the several Arabian oryx which the Phoenix Zoo hopes will thrive and build up into a herd.

were then sent to the Phoenix Maytag Zoo, where the climate is similar to that of Arabia. Since then, two calves have been born in captivity, and four more oryx have been sent from Saudi Arabia.

Other species of animals have survived and their numbers increased in captivity. One of the most interesting of these is the Père David's deer of China. This strange deer, which has cowlike hooves and a donkeylike tail, was already extinct in the wild when it was discovered by a French naturalist in the gardens of the summer palace at Peking in 1865. Before the beginning of the twentieth century, some of these animals were shipped to Europe. If not for this, the Père David's deer would now be extinct. During the Boxer uprising in 1900 the herd in China was entirely destroyed. It was not until 1957 that four of the deer from the European herd were sent back to China. It was only by luck that the Père David's deer survived. Other species were not so fortunate.

Since the early 1800's, 44 species of mammals and an even greater number of bird species have disappeared. In many cases, man has been directly responsible for these losses. The dodo bird, for example, became extinct because of man's ignorance.

When the Dutch settled the island of Mauritius in 1598, they brought with them pigs and dogs. Up to that time, the dodo, which could not fly, had no enemies on Mauritius. Thus it had no defense against these imported animals, which ate the young birds and destroyed the eggs. By 1681 the dodo was extinct.

A more recent story can be told of Hawaii's state bird, the Hawaiian goose, or nene. But this story has a happy ending. When settlers first went to Hawaii, they brought with them the mongoose, dogs and pigs. As with the dodo, these animals attacked and ate the nene. By 1955 only 22 nene were counted in the wild. A few had been taken to Great Britain, and in 1963 thirty were shipped back to Hawaii. With careful tending, these birds will help increase the flock. The nene live on the slopes of Mauna Kea, a dormant volcano on the island of Hawaii.

The dodo became extinct, and the nene near-extinct, because out of ignorance man upset the balance of nature. There are also many examples of animals becoming extinct or near-extinct because of man's ruthless exploitation of his fellow creatures.

At one time there were enormous numbers of passenger pigeons in North America. John James Audubon, the famous naturalist, told of one flock that flew overhead for nearly four hours. Audubon estimated its number at 1,000,000,000 birds.

When European settlers came to North America, they found the passenger pigeon to be a tasty food. And they thought the supply would never end. They began to kill these birds by the thousands. Yet there were so many passenger pigeons that the species might have survived even this. But after the Civil War, the newly built railroads gave professional pigeon hunters a cheap, easy way of transporting tens of millions of pigeons to city markets each year. By the 1880's some people saw what was happening. But in spite of their warnings, the slaughter continued. In 1914, incredible as it seems, the last passenger

THE GREAT SWAMP

A mere thirty miles from the hustle and bustle of New York City lies New Jersey's Great Swamp, which officially became a Wildlife Refuge during 1964. Seven miles long and three miles wide, the swamp is a great natural marshland populated only by wild animals and birds. Here nature lovers will soon be able to study at a brand-new nature center, stroll through marked trails and examine labeled plants and shrubs. Among the animals they may glimpse on such strolls are the whitetail doe, left, and the American otter, below. They may also see many kinds of migratory birds resting in the Great Swamp.

Both photos, Annan Photos

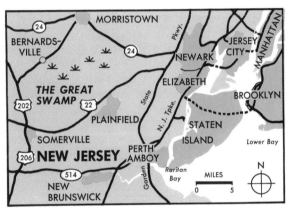

pigeon died at the Cincinnati Zoological Gardens. This bird is now on exhibit at the Smithsonian Institution in Washington, D. C. It serves as a reminder of what man can do when exploitation of our wildlife is not controlled, especially when a bird or animal has commercial value.

Man has brought other animals close to extinction through thoughtless exploitation. The North American bison, often called the buffalo, at one time roamed the plains in vast herds. There were perhaps sixty million bison in North America when the first European settlers arrived. These animals were killed mainly for their skins and for their tongues, which were considered a delicacy. In the late 1800's the slaughter of bison reached enormous proportions. By

1900 only a few hundred were left. Fortunately some had been sent to zoos in the United States and Europe. Over the years, the remaining bison increased in number. Today some eight thousand roam safely in various herds within the National Park System.

A North American bird that came close to extinction is the whooping crane. So many of these birds were killed for their plumage that in 1938 only 14 were counted. There are now 40 whooping cranes. Eight of these are in captivity. Two of the whoopers—Josephine and Crip—live in the Audubon Park Zoo at New Orleans. They have successfully raised 4 offspring. But the whooping cranes that live in the wild must journey from their wintering grounds

351

in Aransas National Wildlife Refuge, in Texas, 2,500 miles north to Canada every spring. In the fall they travel back to Texas. These long, hazardous migrations make it doubtful that the whooping crane will survive and increase its numbers in the wild.

As the population of the world grows, man competes more and more with wildlife for space to live in. New housing developments in the suburbs displace wild creatures. Farms also deprive animals of food supplies. In the nineteenth century, as Americans moved westward across the continent, settlers cleared many of the hardwood forests for farming sites. As a result the ivory-billed woodpecker probably became extinct. This bird depended on wood borers for its food supply. These insects lived in dead or dying trees. When the trees were destroyed the woodpecker lost its food supply. Today this bird is believed to be extinct in North America.

Other species have decreased in number because their environment has been altered. Even such a seemingly harmless thing as replacing hedgerows with wire fencing is enough to reduce the numbers of such birds as quail. These birds depend upon the hedgerows for nesting sites.

The population will continue to expand, and people will continue to build new homes and factories in previously wild areas. One way to preserve our wildlife is to set aside sanctuaries in wilderness areas, such as the one for the California condor in the Los Angeles National Forest. There are now several wildlife sanctuaries in state and national parks. Private societies, such as the National Audubon Society, also maintain sanctuaries.

Sometimes, private citizens form groups to protect the wildlife in their area. In 1960 the Port of New York Authority wanted to build a jet airport on the site of the Great Swamp of Morris County, New Jersey. The people of Morris County raised enough money to buy about 2,500 acres as a wildlife refuge. They eventually hope to increase this to 6,000 acres. This refuge is only 25 miles from New York City. Yet it boasts 165 species of waterfowl and is a haven for whitetail deer, fox, mink, otter, raccoon and muskrat. This swamp and other wetlands along the eastern seaboard also provide resting places for migratory birds.

The problem of protecting wildlife is not peculiar to the United States. Efforts are being made to encourage African nations to maintain their vast wildlife preserves. But even with preserves, poachers in Africa are a constant threat to wildlife. They hunt many kinds of antelope for biltong (dried meat). And they kill giraffes not for meat but because their tails make such good flyswatters. Yet this is no more senseless than killing leopards, whose numbers are rapidly diminishing, for fashionable fur coats.

In countries all over the world, efforts are being made to protect rare species of animals. In India nearly one third of the remaining great Indian rhinoceros are safe in Kaziranga Wildlife Sanctuary, a 166-square-mile preserve. They live there along with lions, elephants, tigers and other animals whose numbers are diminishing.

Conservation programs are aimed primarily at preserving species in the wild. But when a species seems unable to survive in the wild, another course of action becomes necessary. One such course of action has been taken by the New York Zoological Society. It has set up a wildlife survival center in the Bronx Zoo. There one hundred acres of land have been set aside for the breeding of birds, mammals and reptiles that are being threatened with extinction in the wild or that exist only in captivity. The Zoological Society hopes to have such rarities as the Mongolian Przhevalski's horse, the Cambodian wild ox and, among the rare birds, the Nubian ibis. No doubt other zoological parks will follow this course. This is one way to assure that herds of rare animals and flocks of near-extinct birds will be maintained in several places to avoid extermination of the species.

OYSTERS

By DAVID LYLE

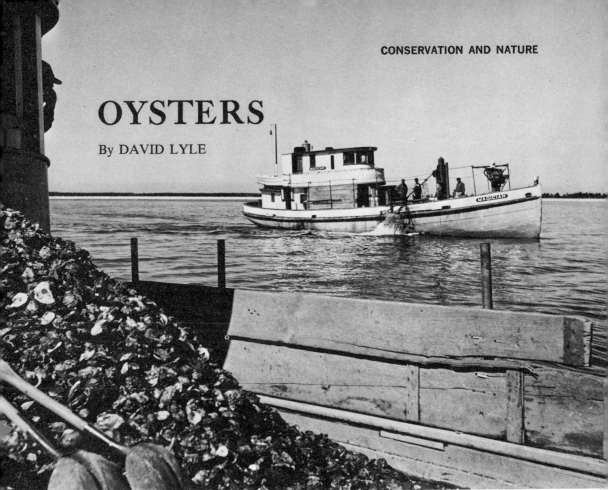

Van Ark, Bluepoints Co.

A catch of Bluepoint oysters is hauled aboard a dredger.

. . . for the edible oyster, the world is definitely no oyster

THE oyster is a small, rather drab and very lazy animal. Yet it has created a great deal of commotion in the world. Poets and painters have been inspired by it. Scientists have devoted their lives to it. The longest "war" in American history has been fought over it. And fortunes have been made and lost because of this delightfully tasty relative of the octopus.

For thousands of years man has sought the oyster with enthusiasm and eaten it with great pleasure. It may be true, of course, as John Gay, the English poet and dramatist, wrote, that:

The man had sure a palate covered o'er
With brass or steel, that on the rocky
*   shore*
First broke the oozy oyster's pearly coat,
And risked the living morsel down his
*   throat.*

But having risked the morsel, that man, whoever he was, evidently liked the effect and told his friends. The oyster's fame has been growing ever since. Some of the world's best-known artists—Jan Steen, Manet, Braque—have put the oyster on canvas. In literature, the oyster appears in the

A veteran Canadian oysterman shoulders the long-handled tongs he uses to gather oysters.

works of Chaucer, Horace, Juvenal, Shakespeare and Shaw.

Who hasn't heard this line from Shakespeare's *Merry Wives of Windsor*?:

Falstaff: *I will not lend thee a penny.*
Pistol: *Why, then the world's mine oyster,*
          Which I with sword will open.

Shaw, a vegetarian, wrote this tribute to the oyster in *Caesar and Cleopatra:*

Caesar: *I have been in Britain, that western land of romance. . . . I went there in search for its famous pearls. The British pearl was a fable; but in searching for it I found the British oyster.*

Apollodorus: *All posterity will bless you for it.*

Men have been eating oysters for a long, long time. Oysters became so popular that in many places the natural oyster beds were picked clean. But people found it both possible and profitable to refill the natural beds and to make artificial beds in which they cultivated the oyster.

The Romans especially treasured the oyster. And they cultivated it as a crop. They ground up the shells to make medicine and cement. And at banquets they ate oysters by the thousands. Gibbon, the historian, reports that "beastly Vitellius ate one thousand at a single sitting." In Britain, as Shaw indicates, the Romans discovered the English oyster. They liked it so much that they found a way to transport it back to Rome (possibly in snow-filled sacks). "Poor Britons," wrote Sallust in 50 B.C., "there is some good in them after all—they produce an oyster."

The oyster, then, was cultivated two thousand years ago. Now there are oyster farmers all over the world. Thousands of people are employed in bringing in and marketing a world crop of between one and two billion oysters each year. This crop is worth millions of dollars. And while the average oysterman is not a wealthy man, fortunes have been made and lost in the trade over and over again. This helps explain why there is an oyster ground in the United States today which, even under ten feet of water, sells for $500 or more an acre. It also helps explain why the oyster war began.

The oyster war involving Maryland and Virginia began well over one hundred years ago. It is not a make-believe war. Men have

been killed and wounded in it during the last decade. The dispute centers on the Potomac River oyster grounds. These are among the finest in the world. They lie in the river that forms the boundary between Maryland and Virginia. This has caused the trouble. The shooting began over who had the right to fish where. When that question was more or less settled, the shooting continued over how the oysters were to be taken.

In 1931 Maryland began restricting oystering on the Potomac to tonging. This is a very long and difficult operation. The oysterman can pluck only a few shells at a time from the riverbed with long-handled tongs. This method of gathering oysters tends to conserve the oyster beds. Dredging is a quicker method of gathering oysters. But this tends to tear up the beds. The Marylanders accused the Virginians of dredging the Potomac beds at night. Maryland then put armed patrol boats on the river to stop

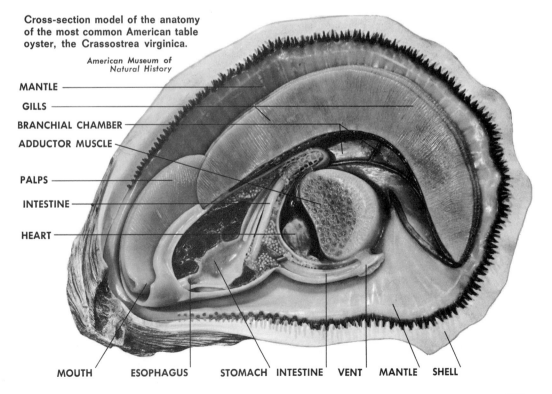

Cross-section model of the anatomy of the most common American table oyster, the Crassostrea virginica.

American Museum of Natural History

MANTLE

GILLS

BRANCHIAL CHAMBER

ADDUCTOR MUSCLE

PALPS

INTESTINE

HEART

MOUTH   ESOPHAGUS   STOMACH INTESTINE VENT   MANTLE   SHELL this. But the dredging continued. This led to shootings between the dredgers and the patrol boats. Recently things have been fairly quiet along the Potomac. But in a war as old as this one it is still too early to say that a permanent peace has settled over the oyster beds.

Oysters are mollusks. So are clams, whelks, mussels and, oddly enough, the octopus and the squid. Oysters live in the shallow bays and sounds of all the continents. But they avoid the polar regions. The common table oyster belongs to the genus *Crassostrea,* which includes more than one hundred species. The common American oyster is *Crassostrea virginica.* This oyster usually appears on the menu as Bluepoint, Cotuit, Chincoteague or some other equally appetizing name.

The average *Crassostrea virginica* is, when harvested, four or five inches long. But specimens up to 18 inches have been found. The oyster has no brain. In fact it has no head. It has no eyes worth talking about, no sense of smell, no way of attacking its enemies and no way of fleeing them. What can an oyster do when it is in a tight spot? Just clamp its shell shut tight with its powerful adductor muscle and wait for the trouble to go away.

When the shell isn't closed tight, the oyster is probably eating. It does this by waving the hairlike cilia on its gills so that a steady current of water passes through the shell. The water brings an oxygen supply as well as the microscopic, floating plant and animal life on which the oyster feeds. The oyster's pumping system works very well. It may pump one hundred gallons of water through the shell in a single day.

One of the most mysterious things about the oyster is its habit of changing sex. During its first season, *Crassostrea virginica* is, as a rule, male. Later this young male may become a female, and later still a male again, and so on for the rest of his (or her) life. Oysters have been known to change sex four times within 13 months.

Oysters spawn in the summer and early fall. A female may release as many as 100,000,000 eggs in a season. At least some of these will unite with male sperm, which have also been released into the water. When egg and sperm unite an embryo results. With luck, this embryo will develop into a full-grown oyster.

For the first two or three weeks of life, the young oyster is a free-swimming animal. It is microscopic in size. And it looks a bit like a watermelon seed with a fringe of hair. These young oysters are called spat. Many of them drift far from their birthplace on the tide. They are often a prey to fish, barnacles, jellyfish and other marine animals. By the end of the free-swimming period, the oysters have begun to grow shells. They then settle to the bottom. This is called spatfall. It is a crucial period in the life of any oyster. If the baby oyster falls on a muddy bottom, that's the end of him. He will die there. But if he settles on something suitable, such as a submerged branch or an old shell, he will cement himself to it. And there he will stay for the rest of his life.

No article about oysters would be complete without a word on pearls. Pearls are masses of mineral matter formed by mollusks out of the same material from which they produce their shells. Even table oysters can produce pearls. But as a rule these are dull-looking. They are rarely of any value. The true marine pearl oyster belongs to the genus *Pinctada.* It has a larger and more lustrous shell than the eating oyster.

True pearls are the only products produced by animals that are considered gems. As such they have been valued highly since prehistoric times. The world's main pearl-fisheries are in the Persian Gulf, the Indian Ocean, the South Pacific and the Gulf of California. Today, as they have for thousands of years, men risk their lives diving for pearls. Sometimes they are attacked by sharks. Usually the oysters they bring up will contain nothing but the mother-of-pearl shell. But one shell in a thousand will contain a pearl. For the pearl fisherman, that is reason enough to keep on diving.

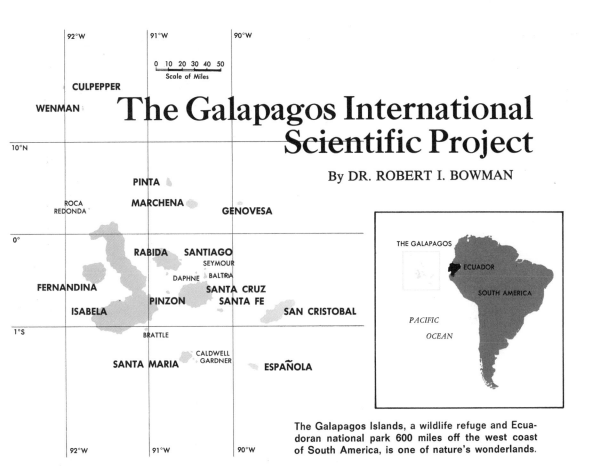

The Galapagos International Scientific Project

By DR. ROBERT I. BOWMAN

The Galapagos Islands, a wildlife refuge and Ecuadoran national park 600 miles off the west coast of South America, is one of nature's wonderlands.

ABOUT 600 miles west of Ecuador, in the Pacific Ocean, is a group of islands once called the Enchanted Isles but now known as the Galapagos. There are 15 major islands in this group. The total land area is about 3,123 square miles. Isabela, the largest island, is about 75 miles long. It accounts for more than half the group's land area.

Although the island group's name has changed, these islands still seem enchanted, for on them are some of the strangest species of wildlife known to man. You can find there a small fish with four eyes. Its eyes are arranged so that it can see both above and below the water's surface at the same time. Three-foot-long marine iguanas that enter the ocean to feed on

seaweed also live on the islands. Another resident of the Galapagos is a cormorant whose wings are so small that the bird cannot fly.

Most penguins live in or near the frigid Antarctic. But the Galapagos Islands, which sit astride the equator, boast one species of penguins. And there are many species of songbirds called Darwin's finches. Some of these birds use tools to help catch their dinner. Holding one end of a twig in its beak, the finch pokes the other end into a crack in a tree to force out an insect. But perhaps the most famous trademark of the islands is the giant tortoise. In fact it was from these tortoises that the island group got its name. Galapagos is a Spanish word for tortoises. Some of these tortoises are over 100 years old. They weigh as much as 500 pounds and are some of the oldest living animals in existence.

The Galapagos were discovered in 1535 by the Bishop of Panama, Tomas de Berlanga. During the seventeenth century, the islands became a haven for many pirates and buccaneers. Whalers, too, would stop at the Galapagos to take on supplies of food and fuel. The islands belonged to Spain from the time they were discovered until 1832. In that year, Ecuador claimed them. It has ruled the islands ever since.

Charles Darwin, the noted British scientist, visited the Galapagos Islands in 1835. At the time, he was serving as naturalist aboard the HMS *Beagle*. So impressed was he with the curious animals on the islands that he began to turn over in his mind the possible ways in which these creatures first came into being. He wondered how they had developed from types that existed before them. His observations of the creatures on the Galapagos reinforced his theories about evolution. These theories were published 24 years later in *The Origin of Species*. This book is one of the great modern classics of scientific literature.

Darwin's visit may be considered the first scientific expedition to the Galapagos. There have been others since. The most recent was early in 1964. From January 7 to March 8, 1964, the Galapagos were discussed, studied and visited by 66 scientists from eight countries. Their work was part of the Galapagos International Scientific Project. This expedition was sponsored by the National Science Foundation and the University of California.

The members of the project gathered in Berkeley, California, in early January. There they took part in two days of lectures on the scientific history of the Galapagos. They also discussed the research they would conduct there. Sir Julian Huxley of Great Britain, the first director general of UNESCO and outspoken supporter of

A. M. Bailey, National Audubon Society

A giant tortoise on Santa Cruz Island. Some of these tortoises weigh as much as 500 pounds.

nature conservation in the Galapagos, was there. So was the late Professor Victor Van Straelen of Belgium, who was the first president of the Charles Darwin Foundation for the Galapagos Islands.

After the lectures in Berkeley, the group sailed from Vallejo, California, aboard the *Golden Bear,* a training ship for merchant-marine officers. For the next nine days they met on board ship and discussed the Galapagos and related subjects. Also, each scientist told about the work he planned to do in the islands.

The *Golden Bear* arrived at Academy Bay, Santa Cruz Island, on January 19. Headquarters for the project were set up there. By January 21, over one hundred delegates had come together there for the dedication of the newly finished Charles Darwin Research Station.

Two days later the scientists began their field research. Getting from one place to another is almost as difficult in the Galapagos as it is in the Antarctic. But the transportation problems were solved by the Ecuadoran Air Force and Navy, local fishermen and the United States Air Force and Navy. Helicopters were especially helpful. They quickly carried field parties to out-of-the-way spots.

One exploring party consisted of 11 scientists—specialists on birds, lizards, insects, plants and rocks. Loaded with food and equipment, they were carried by helicopters to the top of Culpepper Island. It was the first time in history that anyone had reached the summit of this most northerly island of the Galapagos. Culpepper Island is less than a mile square and is surrounded by sheer cliffs several hundred feet high. It teems with thousands of nesting birds, such as sooty terns and red-footed boobies. These birds are not afraid of man. This island also has 12-inch-long centipedes that are eaten by tiny mockingbirds. There are no land mammals or snakes on Culpepper Island. The marine iguana is the only lizard there. On this field trip many new plants and insects were collected. Some of Darwin's finches were taken alive for further study in San Francisco.

The field studies of the scientists were many and varied. Members of the project observed the reaction of boobies and marine iguanas to the intense heat of the sun at different times of the day. The egg-laying and sleeping habits of the tortoises were followed closely. The songs of Darwin's finches were tape-recorded. Scientists will try to figure out how the birds communicate with their neighbors. The penguin and the cormorant are two distantly related birds. Neither of them can fly. Their presence on the Galapagos makes it possible to study how changes in the wings and other parts of the body affect locomotion on land and water.

Several scientists studied ways in which plants and animals interact with each other. For example, one project was concerned with the growth-shape of the prickly-pear cactus. The tortoises feed on the spiny pads of these cacti. The scientists wanted to see whether the presence or absence of tortoises on islands where the cacti grow make any difference in the shape of the cacti. In another study, the changes in the body temperature deep within the stomach and intestines of cold-blooded reptiles were measured. To do this, very small thermometers were connected to tiny radio transmitters. These were put into the animal's food. Without knowing it the animals swallowed them when they ate. By standing near an animal that had swallowed the instrument, the scientists could monitor the coded radio signals on a transistorized receiver.

On February 27, after nearly six weeks on the islands, the scientists left for Guayaquil, the main port city of Ecuador. There they held a series of meetings for four days. On March 6, the scientists left Ecuador aboard the *Golden Bear*. They went to Cocos Island, 300 miles southwest of Costa Rica. They stopped there for two days to study the island's natural history, which is quite similar to that of the Galapagos. Then, on March 18, the ship arrived in San Diego, California, bringing to an end the Galapagos International Scientific Project.

The results of the project will become known gradually in the months and years ahead. The scientists must first sort and analyze their information. A volume of collected material about the trip and a popular scientific book on the Galapagos will be published in 1965.

The project also had good results in the field of conservation. The Galapagos have been an Ecuadoran national park and wildlife refuge since 1959. But while the group was there, the Government of Ecuador issued two executive decrees providing for a practical plan of wildlife protection. The Government and the Charles Darwin Foundation have already taken steps to guard the remaining tortoises. They will be protected in special preserves patrolled by a conservation officer.

Animal Camouflage and Disguise

By K. L. BOYNTON

. . . the ways in which nature protects animals are many, but none are as ingenious as camouflage and mimicry

THE Arctic fox pushed on over the snow to the crest of the hill. Hungry, he eyed the snowy plain about him, eager for a sign of a rabbit. The fox held his short nose high. He sniffed the wind and cocked a rounded ear, straining for the slightest sound. But there was only the unbroken whiteness of the snow, empty and still, all around him.

Suddenly a patch of snow seemed to move. The fox tensed for a chase. Staring at the spot, he saw a big white form get up from the snow. It shook itself and started padding slowly uphill toward him.

The fox slunk back down over the brow of the hill. He moved swiftly, belly low. Intent on escaping the advancing polar bear, he did not see the snowshoe rabbit that crouched motionless almost in his very path, its fur blending with the snow.

Reaching flatter ground, the fox streaked away, tail streaming out behind. Finally, satisfied that he had gone far enough, he curled up to rest. The fox was now warm and safe in his thick white coat with his bushy tail covering his nose and eyes. He too became a small white mound in the vastness of the Arctic snow.

This little episode in the life of the Arctic fox shows how an animal is protected because it blends with its background. If the animal remains still, it actually disappears into its surroundings. The eye will pass over it. This is camouflage. The dust-colored coats worn by desert animals work the same way. These animals blend into the faded background of their desert home. Animals living on the open plains —prairie dogs, coyotes, jackrabbits, African lions—all wear neutral-colored coats.

In the Tularosa Basin in New Mexico there are two regions. One section has pale desert soils. Just a few miles away basaltic lava makes the soil black. The same kinds of animals live in both of these regions. But where the soil is pale the pack rats and pocket mice are pale gray. Where the soil is black the rats and mice are black. This is one more example of animal camouflage.

Insects too use camouflage. The rhododipsa moth is red and yellow. This moth likes to sleep in a gaillardia flower. When it does, it settles down with the yellow part of its body fitting exactly on the yellow ray of the flower. Its red wings rest on the red part of the flower. Rocked by the breeze, it is safely hidden in its flower bed.

In tangled grasses or in places where there is a play of light and shade, stripes and speckles are the best camouflage for animals. These stripes and speckles fool the eye. They break up the animal's outline until it is lost in the background confusion. No wonder deer fawns with spotted

(*text continued on page 365*)

PROTECTIVE COLORATION AND MIMICRY

Every animal, in whatever habitat it may live, is adapted in some way to protect itself from enemies. Some animals have structural defenses (the turtle's shell) or functional ones (the bee's stinger). More subtle, and in some ways more effective, protective features are the various types of animal camouflage. Through its protective coloration an animal is rendered less visible to its enemies. Through its resemblance (mimicry) to another animal that has few enemies or to an inanimate object, the more vulnerable animal gains protection. The accompanying photographs illustrate some of the ways in which protective coloration and mimicry camouflage animals in different surroundings.

The **Ruffed Grouse** is almost hidden among the leaves by its coloring and because the intricate pattern of its plumage breaks up its outline, making the bird seem to merge with its background.

361

Eastman Kodak

The Cottontail Rabbit, like the ruffed grouse, is colored like background and marked in such a way that its outline is obscure

The White-Tailed Deer has camouflaging spots when young, a enhances the value of its camouflage by remaining immobile.

Herbert Lanks—Shostal

Leonard Lee Rue III—National Audubon Soc

Kenneth Chambers—The American Museum of Natural History

C. J. Ott—National Audubon Soc

The Short-Tailed Weasel, or ermine, is protectively colored throughout the year. In summer *(left)* it blends in with leaves and grasses; in winter *(right)*, with snow.

Ozzie Sweet—Shostal

The Tarpon, like many fishes, exhibits countershaded colorat Viewed from above, its dark back matches the apparent colo water. Viewed from beneath, its light underside blends with the

The Sargassum Fish, because of its coloration and body forr almost invisible amid the beds of sargassum weed where it li

George Lower—National Audubon Soc

The **Toad's** protective coloration is made even more effective by its warty skin, which is similar in texture to its background.

Walter Dawn

The **Copperhead Snake** has complex patterning, serving to dissolve its body outline, and is also colored like the leaves on which it lies.

Leonard Lee Rue III—National Audubon Society

William G. Froelich, Jr.

The **Lizard** has coloration and skin texture similar to the ground and remains immobile to avoid detection by predators.

Walter Dawn

The **Mole Cricket** illustrates how near-perfect camouflage is achieved through coloration, body form, and skin texture.

The **Metallic Wood Borer's** hard body covering has color and texture similar to the moss-covered rock on which it moves.

Karl Maslowski—Photo Researchers

Walter Dawn

The **Waved Sphinx Moth** is camouflaged by color and pattern when at rest. Its hind wings and abdomen, exposed in flight, are colorfully marked for recognition by others of its species.

MIMICRY

Resemblance to another animal or to an object is perhaps the most effective type of camouflage. Commonly called mimicry, camouflage through resemblance is dependent on body form, coloration, and, to a great extent, on the animal's posture and gait. Mimicry is an especially helpful adaptation in animals which lack a means of effective defense or are unable to move rapidly to escape from predators.

S.E.F.—Photo Researchers

The Dead Leaf Mantid is an effective mimic largely because of its posture, aided, of course, by its coloration.

Russ Kinne—Photo Researcher

The Walking Leaf Insect illustrates the value of mimicry in relation to mobility. The female *(shown here)* is unable to fly. The male, which can fly, does not resemble a leaf.

Roman Vishniac

The American Museum of Natural Histor

The Viceroy Butterfly *(left)* mimics the **Monarch Butterfly**, presumably because the latter is considered unpalatable by predators

The Geometrid Moth Caterpillar eludes predators by remaining absolutely still and holding its body at a twiglike angle.

coats are safely hidden if they lie still in the dappled sunlight of their forest home. Young ground-nesting birds are protected by the patterns of their feathers. Stripes hide the tiger in tall grass. The bittern has a feather pattern of stripes. This marsh bird is practically invisible in reeds. It even acts like reeds, swaying its body if a breeze stirs the reeds about. A zebra's stripes cross its body outline. From a distance the horselike form cannot be seen.

Some wildlife camouflage experts disguise themselves with material from their background. For example, spider crabs attach pieces of seaweed or sponge to their bodies. Thus they hide themselves in a mass of material that is exactly like what is growing around them. Crabs know what they are doing. If they are taken from a seaweedy place to where only sponges grow, they will throw away their seaweed camouflage and put on pieces of sponge. The caddis-fly larva, during its underwater life, builds a case around itself of bits of wood, pebbles, shells or pieces of plants. This camouflage saves it from being eaten by fish.

One kind of geometrid-moth caterpillar has triangular-shaped plates on its body. Each plate is topped with a spur. This caterpillar attaches matched pieces of blossoms to its tail and front spines on each side. It attaches pieces of leaves to the spurs. Later it transfers this pretty camouflage to the outside of its cocoon.

Animals whose bodies actually look like parts of plants have the best camouflage. The leafy sea dragon, for example, looks just like a piece of seaweed. So to hide from its enemies it attaches itself to seaweed by its tail.

When *Kallima,* the dead-leaf butterfly, flies it shows the beautiful purple and orange of the upper part of its wings. But should a bird come after it, this butterfly will suddenly drop into a bush. There it will look just like a dry leaf. The underside of its wings, folded at rest, is dead-leaf brown. The wings also have decay-like spots, and dark lines that look like leaf veins. A tip at the end of its hind wing looks just like a leaf stem.

Some animals can change color to match their background. Their body covering has special cells that contain color, or dark pigments. These pigments can be shifted around. The color changes in these animals are controlled by the nervous system, by hormones or by a combination of both, depending upon the animal. Usually a message from the eyes will start the color change. But temperature changes, being touched or light striking the pigment cells directly will make some animals change color.

Crab spiders live in flowers. They are protected from their enemies because they can change color to match some of the different colored flowers that bloom through the season.

Palaemonetes, a shrimp, has a very fancy color system. Its pigment cells carry red, blue and yellow. This shrimp can match any color seaweed or even a black background.

The ability to change color very fast will give an animal a good deal of protection. Twenty-eight species of reef fish can change color instantly. Flounders, which are bottom-dwelling flatfish, can match solid black or white backgrounds. They can also make large and small skin patterns. A flounder placed on a lit-up checkerboard matches it so exactly in a very short time that a game could be played on it!

In the wilds it seems that almost everybody has hungry neighbors. So if timid and unarmed animals can somehow manage to vanish into their surroundings or look like something that is not good to eat, they stand a much better chance of staying alive.

The most important thing in animal camouflage is holding still. In the drama of the Arctic fox, movement gave away the polar bear. Sitting tight, not moving a whisker, saved the snowshoe rabbit.

CAREERS

Blessed is he who has found his work;
let him ask no other blessedness.
Thomas Carlyle

The Foreign Service

By JOHN CABOT

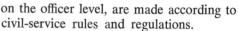

. . . the U. S. Ambassador to Poland talks about a career in foreign lands

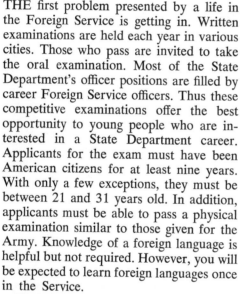

THE first problem presented by a life in the Foreign Service is getting in. Written examinations are held each year in various cities. Those who pass are invited to take the oral examination. Most of the State Department's officer positions are filled by career Foreign Service officers. Thus these competitive examinations offer the best opportunity to young people who are interested in a State Department career. Applicants for the exam must have been American citizens for at least nine years. With only a few exceptions, they must be between 21 and 31 years old. In addition, applicants must be able to pass a physical examination similar to those given for the Army. Knowledge of a foreign language is helpful but not required. However, you will be expected to learn foreign languages once in the Service.

To help its officers and to carry out its everyday work, the Foreign Service has a number of staff members. The staff is made up of stenographers, clerks and technical personnel in the lower and middle grades. Usually the greatest need is for secretaries, stenographers, communications clerks and general clerical personnel. But now and then a need arises for diplomatic couriers, nurses and telecommunications technicians. As you might expect, the basic requirements for being a nontechnical staff member are less difficult to meet than those for officers. All appointments, including those on the officer level, are made according to civil-service rules and regulations.

Do not think that once you are in the Foreign Service life is going to be a bed of roses. There are of course the glamorous posts where life should be delightful. Still, it frequently isn't. Even in Western Europe —Paris, London, Rome—the work may be dull. Tourists may buzz around like mosquitoes in June, and the routine may be never ending.

A lot of posts are not at all glamorous. On the contrary, many are hot, cold, isolated or primitive. In many places, you have to guard against diseases rarely found in the United States. These include plague, cholera and smallpox. Food and drink may not be safe. And you may not relish the local varieties even when they are safe. Living conditions are often poor. Housing may be below any American standard or totally unobtainable. You often have to learn an obscure and difficult language in order to accomplish anything or even to get the necessities for living from day to day. The resulting strain on your family may be serious.

You must become accustomed to strange customs and procedures. Yet at the same time it is essential not to lose your fundamental Americanism. You may have to deal with hostile or devious governments and officials. And one of the most trying things in the Foreign Service is to deal with governments that expect us to do for them what we feel they should do for themselves.

There are also dangerous aspects of a Foreign Service career. Not all travel is done by luxurious ocean liner or scheduled flight in times of peace and universal sunshine. Often it is necessary to travel by those means available—however crude or haphazard they may be—at times you would rather not venture forth at all. There is also the possibility of violence.

There are frustrations as well as dangers in the Foreign Service. You must always keep your temper and your wits when seeing people, even if they are unscrupulous, or if they anger you. A Foreign Service officer must try to avoid making hasty decisions, even as he must be prepared to make them when necessary. In the Service there are times when the work is never done. But even for the most justifiable of reasons, you must not give in to fatigue.

A Foreign Service officer must always be discreet. He obviously cannot criticize governments or officials—not only of his own country but also of most others. He cannot betray confidences or reveal secret information.

If, then, life in the Foreign Service can be tough, exacting, frustrating and difficult, it also can have great rewards. Every Foreign Service officer should feel something of a sense of history in his work. For him a corner of the curtain that separates the public from the stage is lifted. He can observe how the performance is prepared. From his vantage point he can watch the course of relations between the United States and the country where he is stationed. He can also see a good deal of the international panorama. Right from the first, he is likely to meet some of the great men of the time. In some cases, he may come to know them well enough so that he can form his own opinion of their abilities and defects.

A Foreign Service officer will probably serve in several foreign countries in the course of his career. These countries will usually be quite varied. If life in some is not comfortable or convenient, it may still be fascinating and exotic. It is in the out-of-the-way corners of the world that an officer's reputation is often made. Life in many posts is rather rugged. But things have improved over the years. Today there are commissaries, government housing and furnishings, medical facilities and swift transport in places where not so many years ago these things were unknown. Yet one of the great fascinations of the Foreign Service is to participate fully in the life of the community where you are stationed. The facilities we have now may in some ways be a handicap.

Few officers think they get ahead in the Foreign Service as fast as they should. Everyone is disappointed at some time. An officer may spurt ahead or lag behind at different times. Yet over the years he is likely to get just about where he deserves to be. If one chief is bad, another may be particularly inspiring and helpful. If a Foreign Service officer gets in the doghouse with the powers that be, the powers will change and the new ones may be more friendly.

And so, some officers reach the top. When they do they often look back on the good old days when all they had to do was their job, and freewheeling was still possible. A chief of mission's life is an endless round of callers, visitors, dinners, ceremonies and other inescapable duties. In fact, you must be careful not to let yourself just drift in the diplomatic whirl. You must be sure to direct your life toward accomplishing your mission.

But if being chief of mission is almost invariably a grind, if insolvable problems present themselves at regular intervals, it is still a rewarding job. You participate in history. You may make history. You may even shape history. For those who seek to serve their country and mankind, this is a great reward.

UNITED STATES AMBASSADORS AND MINISTERS[†]

AFGHANISTAN John M. Steeves

ALGERIA William J. Porter

ARGENTINA Edwin M. Martin

AUSTRALIA Jack W. Lydman*

AUSTRIA James W. Riddleberger

BELGIUM Douglas MacArthur 2d

BOLIVIA Douglas Henderson

BRAZIL Lincoln Gordon

BULGARIA Mrs. Eugenie Anderson

BURMA Henry A. Byroade

BURUNDI Donald A. Dumont

CAMBODIA Randolph A. Kidder

CAMEROUN Leland Barrows

CANADA W. Walton Butterworth

CENTRAL AFRICAN REPUBLIC Claude G. Ross

CEYLON Cecil B. Lyon

CHAD Brewster H. Morris

CHILE Ralph A. Dungan

CHINA (Taiwan) Admiral Jerauld Wright

COLOMBIA Covey T. Oliver

CONGO (Brazzaville) Henry L. T. Koren

CONGO (Leopoldville) G. McMurtrie Godley

COSTA RICA Raymond Telles

CYPRUS Taylor G. Belcher

CZECHOSLOVAKIA Outerbridge Horsey

DAHOMEY Clinton E. Knox

DENMARK Mrs. Katharine Elkus White

DOMINICAN REPUBLIC W. Tapley Bennett, Jr.

ECUADOR Maurice M. Bernbaum

EL SALVADOR Raul H. Castro

ETHIOPIA Edward M. Korry

FINLAND Tyler Thompson

FRANCE Charles E. Bohlen

GABON Charles F. Darlington

GERMANY (West) George C. McGhee

GHANA William P. Mahoney, Jr.

GREAT BRITAIN David K. E. Bruce

GREECE Henry R. Labouisse

GUATEMALA John O. Bell

GUINEA James I. Loeb

HAITI Benson E. L. Timmons III

HONDURAS Charles R. Burrows

HUNGARY Elim O'Shaughnessy*

ICELAND James K. Penfield

INDIA Chester Bowles

INDONESIA Howard P. Jones

IRAN Julius C. Holmes

IRAQ Robert C. Strong

IRELAND Robert P. Chalker*

ISRAEL Walworth Barbour

ITALY G. Frederick Reinhardt

IVORY COAST James Wine

JAMAICA Lewis M. Purnell*

JAPAN Edwin O. Reischauer

JORDAN Robert G. Barnes

KENYA William Attwood

KOREA (South) Winthrop Gilman Brown

KUWAIT Howard Rex Cottam

LAOS William Sullivan

LEBANON Armin H. Meyer

LIBERIA Ben Hill Brown, Jr.

LIBYA E. Allan Lightner, Jr.

LUXEMBOURG William R. Rivkin

MALAGASY REPUBLIC C. Vaughan Ferguson, Jr.

MALAWI Sam P. Gilstrap

MALAYSIA James D. Bell

MALI Bayard King*

MALTA Harrison Lewis*

MAURITANIA Richard S. Dawson*

MEXICO Fulton Freeman

MOROCCO L. Dean Brown*

NEPAL Henry E. Stebbins

NETHERLANDS Fisher Howe

NEW ZEALAND General Herbert B. Powell

NICARAGUA Aaron S. Brown

NIGER Robert J. Ryan

NIGERIA Elbert G. Mathews

NORWAY Miss Margaret Joy Tibbetts

PAKISTAN Walter P. McConaughy

PANAMA Jack Hood Vaughn

PARAGUAY William P. Snow

PERU J. Wesley Jones

PHILIPPINES William McCormick Blair, Jr.

POLAND John M. Cabot

PORTUGAL Admiral George W. Anderson, Jr.

RUMANIA William A. Crawford

RWANDA Charles D. Withers

SAUDI ARABIA Parker T. Hart

SENEGAL Mercer Cook

SIERRA LEONE Andrew V. Corry

SOMALI REPUBLIC Horace G. Torbert, Jr.

SOUTH AFRICA Joseph C. Satterthwaite

SPAIN Robert F. Woodward

SUDAN William M. Rountree

SWEDEN J. Graham Parsons

SWITZERLAND W. True Davis, Jr.

SYRIA Ridgway B. Knight

TANZANIA William Leonhart

THAILAND Graham A. Martin

TOGO William Witman II

TRINIDAD AND TOBAGO Robert G. Miner

TUNISIA Francis H. Russell

TURKEY Raymond A. Hare

UGANDA Olcott H. Deming

U.S.S.R. Foy D. Kohler

UNITED ARAB REPUBLIC Lucius D. Battle

UPPER VOLTA Thomas S. Estes

URUGUAY Wymberley DeR. Coerr

VENEZUELA C. Allan Stewart

VIETNAM (South) General Maxwell D. Taylor

YEMEN Harlan B. Clark*

YUGOSLAVIA C. Burke Elbrick

ZAMBIA no one appointed as of Dec. 1

AMBASSADOR AT LARGE Llewellyn E. Thompson

SPECIAL MISSIONS

NORTH ATLANTIC TREATY ORGANIZATION Thomas K. Finletter

U. S. MISSION TO THE EUROPEAN COMMUNITIES John W. Tuthill

UNITED NATIONS Adlai E. Stevenson

INTERNATIONAL ATOMIC ENERGY COMMISSION Henry DeWolf Smyth

EUROPEAN OFFICE OF THE UN AND OTHER INTERNATIONAL ORGANIZATIONS Roger W. Tubby

† as of December 1, 1964

* chargé d'affaires

Fashion Designing

By OLEG CASSINI

. . . the United States' best-known designer tells how you too can become a couturiere

Students at work at the Fashion Institute of Technology in New York City.

Fashion Institute of Technology

DO you draw well? Can you sew? Are you good at following patterns? Do you make your own clothes? Well, if you want to become a fashion designer these things don't really matter at all. It is more important to have good taste, an observant eye and a distinctive personality. And you must be willing to work, keep learning, and work some more.

Fashion designing, basically, is not a very technical skill. I do not mean to downgrade technique. It is very important. But compare two designers who can draw equally well, and who have equal knowledge of anatomy, fabrics and color coordination. The one who will stand out is the one with the personal—as opposed to the "safe"—point of view. He will be the one who has something original to say. And he will know how to say it with just the proper degree of daring.

I would ask a youngster who says he or she would like to become a fashion designer: "Do you sincerely feel that you have a genuine aptitude for such a way of life?" I mean "way of life," not "line of work." The worlds of fashion and design must be with you during your every waking (and quite often sleeping) hour. The profession demands it. To succeed you must have a devotion that won't let your mind and eye rest. You'll always be searching for new ideas, new variations.

Moreover, you must always be aware of contemporary events. You must observe and criticize society and its culture. And you must be able to bring together current design and color trends.

Fashion is a business, like it or not. This means that you must learn to please your customers. You have to honor their tastes and preferences and provide for

371

their needs. At the same time, you must fix your individual stamp on the fashions you create for them. Is this, then, the kind of life you want to live?

What people may admiringly refer to as inborn talent is mostly plain hard work—or, as I like to call it, "a long patience." Therefore, my next question to the would-be designer is "Can you accept and learn from honest, informed criticism—however severe—and still keep your self-confidence? And are you willing to work hard to learn the techniques you need to have to put your ideas into practice?"

Just what are these techniques? First of all, there's sketching—putting your ideas on paper. The beginner should concentrate on this. However, he does not need to become a drawing master. Fashion design, however creative it may be, is quite different from fine art. In fact the most successful designers do very little finished sketching. They have assistants to do it for them. When a fashion designer sketches, it is not with the aim of winning first prize at an art show. Much as with the architect, his sketches are blueprints of his ideas. They must be accurate, informative and legible. Then they can be followed and translated into fabric.

The designer should have a good knowledge of human anatomy. His job is to drape the human form. He must therefore be very familiar with its structure. And he must know how the parts are related. Most important, he must know how the body changes in movement. People walk, sit, bend, stride, stretch, twist, kneel and perform countless other movements. The fashion designer must take into account all these possible movements. A garment must never bind the wearer. It must above all be wearable.

Next on the list is a knowledge of the "anatomy," or grain, of fabrics. You must know how these fabrics are affected by movement. Each fabric reacts differently, cuts differently, "lies" differently. Each has different properties of weight, texture,

strength, porosity, workability, wearability, creasability, cleanability and so on. These qualities must be considered in selecting the proper fabric or fabrics for an outfit designed for a particular purpose.

The fashion designer must also be thoroughly familiar with colors and how they combine. He must know how they look when used with one another. And he must be aware of the various degrees of hue, value and chroma. Otherwise he will not know which colors will be best for the design he has created.

A budding fashion designer must also do a lot of research. To know what can be done, he must know what has been done. In addition, he must know what has been tried but couldn't be done. He must be familiar with the designs of the "old masters" of fashion and with clothes from distant countries and past years. This is a continuing study. The leading fashion publications should be his everyday bibles.

These, then, are the basics. A designer must know these subjects so well that they become second nature to him. Only then can he with confidence go on to develop his own style. Similarly a musician's fingers must be so well trained that he needn't think about technical problems. Instead he can proceed to matters of interpretation and expression.

There are two ways of learning these techniques and breaking into the field of fashion design. One is by apprenticeship. As an apprentice, you would start young, without much formal training. You would then work your way up through the ranks. The other way to learn is by attending a specialized school. Both methods—and especially the first—require quite a bit of independent, self-inspired study.

The apprentice, or journeyman, route involves joining the staff of an established designer or fashion house. At the outset you will be doing a lot of small, petty, boring things. If you can take it, however, the experience gained has much to recommend it. You really get to know the work-

A new Cassini creation—from sketch to finish. The rough sketch at left gives written details on colors and accessories. Center, the finished sketch. Right, the manufactured garment.

ings of the world of fashion. Rising through the ranks is not too common today. Emphasis is placed on newcomers who are well-trained in the basic techniques. They come to learn, to be sure. But primarily they are hired to produce. To do this, they must be well-schooled semiprofessionals who can immediately make solid contributions.

If you decide, then, to choose the second route, I cannot emphasize too strongly that you seek out the very finest school you can afford. Make a financial sacrifice if need be. In this area, at least, you get what you pay for. I know several now-successful designers who worked their way through school. They would attend classes by day and add to their incomes by night by doing the most lowly tasks. They wouldn't settle for second best. They wanted the best schooling money could buy.

I am not an authority on fashion-design schools. But I would say that the best I've come across—in this country at least—are located in New York City. This is the hub of the American fashion industry. I have no doubt that there are some fine schools in other fashion centers—such as California—but I'm not familiar with them.

After you've mastered the basic techniques, what's your next step? My advice is to go to one of the world's great fashion centers. This means New York or Paris. Perhaps by the time you're ready, it may also be Rome or London or Madrid. Once there, present your credentials to a reputable house, show your work and keep your fingers crossed. Hopefully, you will be taken on as an assistant to a designer. Then your job will mainly be to prepare sketches from the designer's roughs or from ideas he has described to you. You will offer suggestions for details. And you will shop the markets for fabrics and novelties (trimmings). All of this is valuable experience.

If you're good, if you have original, creative ideas, and if you're willing to work long and hard, you will in time be a full-fledged fashion designer.

At his drawing board, the author outlines an idea for a design.

A Career in Architecture

... this challenging profession is as ancient as man himself

By EDWARD DURELL STONE

ARCHITECTURE is, in a manner of speaking, as old as man's need to shelter himself and his family against heat, cold, wind, rain and snow. When men decided to live on the surface of the earth rather than beneath it, they were presented with many new problems. For as well as needing protection from the weather, they had to

erect safeguards against wild animals and against hostile tribes. They also had to try as best they could to defend themselves against natural hazards such as forest fires and floods.

At first, of course, men built no more than simple lean-tos. They raised makeshift roofs onto poles, placed platforms in trees and stretched hides for walls. But as the need for making different kinds of buildings for different purposes became clear, the builder's craft grew more complicated. There were separate structures for living and sleeping, for storing food and supplies, for holding community meetings, for defense and so on. All such building projects had to be planned. Thus, when some early builder picked up a stick and drew a picture of what he wanted to construct, he had made a plan. Just then, having drawn a plan, Man the Builder became Man the Architect.

Thus architecture is just about as old as civilization. And it has gone far beyond its primary function of protecting man from the weather. Architecture has, over the centuries, developed into a great art. Indeed, in its highest forms, architecture stands for man's best hopes and fulfills his most precious dreams. For any given moment in history, the quality of man's creative skills can be measured by how well or how badly he designed and built his buildings. As one of man's major activities, architecture lies in the mainstream of human thought. When it is good, it constitutes a noble record of how man lived on earth.

For such reasons, architecture is a very attractive profession. To choose it as a career, however, means that you must be willing to devote your whole life to it. It is an exacting, demanding art, full of details. Furthermore, very early in the game you must realize that few architects get to the top. For every architect who gains some kind of recognition, there are thousands who, even though they may possess great talent, remain obscure. Sometimes, becoming famous is a matter of luck. Most of the time though, success in architecture is simply the result of complete devotion and very hard work. There are no shortcuts, no easy ways to "succeed in business without really trying." As a result, the foremost architects of our time "arrive" late in life. Most of them are mature, experienced men.

They are equal to the large responsibilities they are asked to assume.

In spite of these rather severe drawbacks, architecture—like medicine, law, science, literature and many other professions—has genuine rewards. Few things in life, for example, can match the architect's thrill as he watches his own thoughts and ideas taking shape as a building. Then too, he feels a great creative satisfaction in knowing that for a long time to come, people will enjoy looking at and using the rooms and spaces he has planned for them.

What does it take to be an architect? Well, it takes a combination of many things. But first and foremost, one should be willing to take the time to learn to draw. Drawings are the basic language of the profession, so before anything else, an architect must be an artist. He must be able to set down on paper what he sees, what he imagines and what he wants others to see and understand. He must know how to create the illusion of perspective on paper. He must know how to express complicated forms with light and shadow. And he must know how to suggest tone, color and atmosphere. The ability to draw, therefore, is the first skill an architect needs. The better he draws, the easier it will be to convey his ideas to others.

Like a sculptor, an architect must be able to visualize in three dimensions—"in the round" as the saying goes. Actually, going a step beyond sculpture, he should be able to think in four dimensions. All buildings are, of course, three-dimensional: that is, they are so long, so wide and so high. But the space inside the building may be thought of as a fourth dimension. The main reason for building buildings is to create different sizes and kinds of enclosed spaces in which people can live or work happily, comfortably and efficiently. Surely the way buildings look on the outside is very important. But how buildings work on the inside is even more important. This relationship of inside to outside and outside

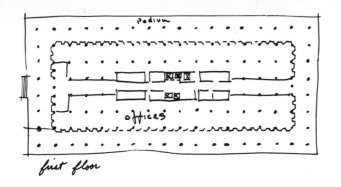

first floor

Plans for a building begin at the architect's drawing board, where he makes rough sketches showing how the rooms on each floor will be arranged when it is finished.

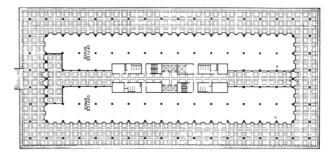

Rough sketches are done with increasing detail (right) until finally blueprints, with exact specifications filled in, are prepared for the building contractor to use.

to inside is what we mean by being able to think in a fourth dimension.

Another essential part of an architect's career is knowing how to handle words. He should be able to write and talk clearly about his work when he presents his plans. Since architecture is mainly the business of drawing pictures of buildings, this may sound unimportant. But oddly enough, pictures by themselves can seldom fully explain an idea. Pictures alone or words alone do not describe a concept so fully as a combination of both. The old Chinese saying that a picture is worth ten thousand words is only half the story. The whole story is that pictures can be better understood if they are accompanied by words.

An architect should also have a solid understanding of engineering techniques and standard mathematics. Arithmetic is essential. But a working knowledge of algebra and geometry is also helpful. This is not so much because they help simplify planning procedures, but because they lend order and practicality when you are sorting out several solutions to a design problem.

Next, an understanding of structure, or more specifically structural engineering, is a valuable thing to have. In almost any

kind of building these days, architects work very closely with engineers. However, unless an architect has a solid feeling for structure himself (that is, a feeling for what is or is not practical to build), he can waste a lot of time drawing meaningless plans. After all, an architect simply must be able to design buildings that will stand firmly for years, maybe centuries, to come. In fact all cities and states now have very rigid rules and regulations about how buildings are constructed. So, if somehow an architect did design an unsafe building, he would soon be in trouble with the law.

To the essential requirements for a career in architecture, I might also add a familiarity with business administration and office procedures. Many a good architect has floundered because he forgot about or just didn't bother to learn certain basic business techniques. An architect should know how to plan budgets as well as buildings. And he should know how to read a profit-and-loss statement, especially his own. We must not forget that architects are responsible for spending large amounts of other people's money. A good architect who is also a dependable businessman evokes trust in people.

The plans at left were among those that resulted in Edward Durell Stone's New Town Federal Building of reinforced concrete in Hyattsville, Maryland.

Just an average fulfillment of all the above requirements adds up to years of training and study. And even after you become a graduate architect, there must follow more years of internship, of realistic, actual experience. Unless you are very lucky or gifted beyond the wildest dreams, you simply cannot walk out of architectural school and open an architectural office on your own. This part of an architectural career should be spent working with other architects—perhaps as a junior member of a large firm or perhaps as an associate in a small group. In either case this particular period is crucial. For it is during this time that you will find out about the real business of architecture and develop maturity, judgment and taste. Here theory is turned into practice. Here you are better able to judge your own ideas against the ideas of others.

Finally, and this is very important, an architect must travel. The more he sees of the great buildings, squares and gardens of the world, the better he will design his own. Looking at pictures or reading about the world's architectural masterpieces is no substitute for actually walking around and through them. The exact nature of the beauty that has pleased and inspired men for so long in these structures is hidden in countless secrets of their construction and in that vital balance between space, form and scale known as "proportion." Unless you actually stand in the vast nave of the great cathedral at Chartres, for example, or unless you actually stroll across the magnificent Piazza San Marco in Venice, these secrets will never be fully revealed to you. Nor will great architecture be fully appreciated for what it is: an art with a powerful influence for good on man's way of life. Thus an architect must somehow find a way to go and study the things men have built in honor of their better natures or in celebration of their own achievements.

In the coming years the need for thoughtful, well-trained architects will be enormous. As populations grow and cities expand, the people will turn to the planners and the designers to help save them from chaos. Even now, conscientious federal and city officials all over the world look upon the present with alarm and the future with hopelessness. Only the planners will be able to restore the tranquility we all yearn for. Most of this burden is bound to fall on the architects.

Photography

By MARGARET BOURKE-WHITE

The author's favorite portrait, taken when she was a war correspondent with the United States 8th Air Force in Europe in 1943.

. . . photography's First Lady discusses her career and the qualities needed by a photographer

PHOTOGRAPHY is an open door to the world. It is a career in which you are your own captain. You can choose the branch of photography you want to specialize in. You can choose the subjects you want to photograph. If some subject interests you very much, it probably will interest others.

What qualities does the photographer need? He should have a good sense of design and an eye for composition. He should have a sense of the dramatic. He should also have enough technique to be able to carry through the type of photographs he wants to make. New techniques are being developed constantly, but the photographer should not feel that technique is an end in itself. It should be a means to an end.

What qualities does the photojournalist need? He must have or develop the ability to see things straight. He should not be too influenced by other people. He must have honesty and integrity. He must have a sense of responsibility because there will be occasions when he will be photographing history. It is important for him to look at all sides of a question and not accept an easy answer. To do this, he must understand people and situations.

What goes on in front of the camera is not so important as what goes on in back of it. If a photographer has an interesting mind, his pictures will interest others. If he has a dull mind, they will be dull pictures. Everything can be of use to the photojournalist. He should listen to what people say. He should hoard knowledge about every subject.

Nowadays, there are many schools and universities where photography is taught. But when I was a student, photography was not considered a serious academic subject.

I became a photographer almost by accident. My father had died and I had to work my way through school. I tried to get a job as a waitress on the campus. How grateful I am now that that job was not available, because instead I turned to an old camera. It had a crack right through its lens. Still, I began taking pictures of campus buildings and other college scenes at Cornell University. After much trial and error, these met with more enthusiasm than I had dared to hope for. When I graduated, I decided to give up biology for photography.

My little Cleveland apartment served as my studio. I did my developing in the bathtub and my printing in the kitchenette. The living room was my reception room.

I kept myself going with various small jobs. I wanted to get into industrial photography. The nearest subject to my heart, the one I really wanted to photograph, was a steel mill. I was not aware that I had chosen the most difficult subject for lighting. Even with today's equipment the deep blacks of the steel mill and the sudden brilliant bursts of light from the molten steel are very hard to photograph. In those days the mills had never been photographed from a dramatic or artistic point of view. There were few tools with which to do this.

The steel-mill owners thought I was going to come down once or twice to make a few snapshots. Instead I went to the steel mill every night for a whole winter. I filled many wastebaskets with gummy, poorly exposed film. Finally I succeeded in producing 12 shots that captured something of the magic of the mills.

That winter of work in the steel mills shaped my whole career. The pictures were widely used. They attracted the attention of Henry R. Luce of Time, Inc., who was then just getting ready to publish *Fortune* magazine. It was a wonderful outlet for my industrial photographs. I began as *Fortune's* first and only photographer in 1929, about eight months before the magazine was published. I moved from there to *Life* when that maga-

Toward the end of World War II, Margaret Bourke-White captured on film the horror and inhumanity of German concentration camps.

zine was started in 1936. I have been with the organization ever since.

Up to that time, photographs had been used to illustrate stories. But it was not until *Life* was started that pictures were used to actually tell the story. This was the beginning of photojournalism.

Photojournalism is very hard work. No one should go into it unless he has a great deal of energy. You work long hours. You are often in difficult places and may have to crouch in uncomfortable positions. There are tensions and worries, especially when you are working away from home base. Even when you are working as far away as India or Korea, your films are usually flown to your magazine or newspaper for developing. Because of this, I felt as though I were working in a vacuum until I got the first report from the office. Only then, when I learned that the pictures were satisfactory, did I hit my stride.

Some assignments can prove to be very demanding. For example, I needed every resource that I had when I covered the Union of South Africa for *Life* in 1950. Racial tensions were at a peak there. It was very hard to move around and get information freely. One of the sequences I wanted to do was to trace the daily life of a gold miner. When I asked the officials of the mine if I might photograph a certain pair of miners, they consented. But when they found that the miners I had chosen were working in the deepest part of the mines—two miles straight down—they tried to discourage me. They said, "We will move the men to a more comfortable place for you to work where the mines aren't so deep, and the heat is not so great. Then you can take your pictures." I refused. I was determined to photograph the miners as they really were. Finally the officials consented. The picture of the two miners with perspiration rolling down their chests turned out to be the lead picture of my photo-essay on South Africa.

Of course, photography isn't all photojournalism of this type. It has a thousand uses—from advertising to baby pictures. The photographer thus can choose the fields in which he wants to work and for which he has talent.

People often ask me if photography is a good field for women. I believe that it is. A woman, if she is sensitive, may notice things a man would miss. And if she has charm she can break down barriers. I feel very strongly that a woman should stay as feminine as possible. I feel equally strongly that she must do her work twice as well as it has to be done. Although she may gain advantages because of her sex, this in no way lightens her responsibility to do the best work she can.

As a war correspondent in World War II, I was bombed in Moscow and torpedoed in the Mediterranean at the beginning of the North African invasion. I slogged with the GI's through the mud of Italy. I flew on a combat mission in the lead ship of a B-17 formation and in a tiny unarmed artillery spotting plane which was jumped by four German fighters. I accompanied General Patton's army through the Rhine crossings and into Buchenwald and other nazi concentration camps. In the Korean war, I covered fierce guerrilla warfare in the wild mountains of Korea. For war-correspondence work, it was sometimes a disadvantage to be a woman. The generals and high officials tended to discourage and overprotect female photographers and journalists. But the closer I got to the actual front, the more enthusiastically I, as a woman, was welcomed by the GI's.

It has been exciting and fascinating to be able to photograph such notables as Gandhi, Nehru, Stalin, Pope Pius XII and Churchill. But it is the average human being who holds my interest most. In the endless march of history, it is the common man who really counts.

I am sure that other photojournalists believe, as I do, that in small events as well as large, they are writing history with the camera.

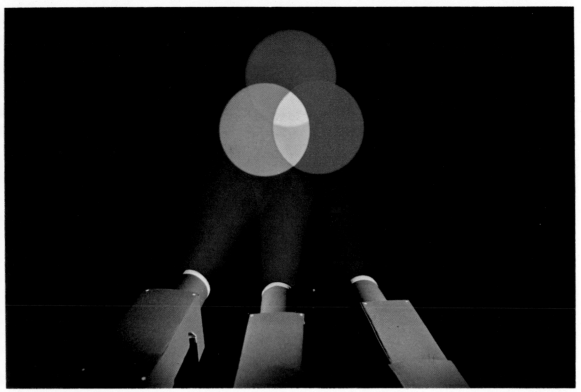

Overlapping two or more colored beams of light to create the appearance of another color is known as additive mixing. An overlap of red and blue produces magenta; of blue and green, cyan; of green and red, yellow; and of red, blue, and green, white.

COLOR PHOTOGRAPHY

THE STRUCTURE OF COLOR FILM

LIGHT

FILM BASE

Color film is composed of layers of light-sensitive emulsion attached to a plastic film base. The top diagram illustrates the penetration of the emulsion layers by light rays of different color. The upper part of the bottom diagram shows the colors that the layers record, and the lower part the actual additive colors that, in combination, produce the colors in the finished film.

Additive mixing of light is of primary importance in color photography. The film has three emulsion layers, one for each of the primary light colors: the top layer is sensitive to blue light, the middle layer to green light, and the bottom layer to red light. The first two are combined with filters which prevent passage of blue and green light beyond the respective layer. Each layer records different shades of color just as black-and-white film records shades of gray. Exposed and developed, the film filters and mixes light in colors corresponding to those in the original scene. The emulsion layers are extremely thin, and variations in terms of millionths of an inch in the thickness of any one of them renders the film unusable.

381

COLOR ESSENTIALS

The reaction time of color film is slower than that of black-and-white film, hence color pictures require brighter light or longer exposure time. There is less margin for error in exposure time with color film, and adjustments for overexposure or underexposure cannot be made in the darkroom. Since psychological factors affect the reliability of the eye in judging lighting conditions, the use of an exposure meter is recommended. Instructions for using various combinations of shutter speeds and lens openings usually accompany each roll of film. The shadows in a color photograph always appear darker than in the original scene, and reflectors and flash bulbs should be used as fill-in light to eliminate them, indoors and out. Consideration should also be given to the contrasting and complementary colors of the subject matter, keeping in mind that the sensitive film will record reflections that ordinarily go unnoticed. Heat and humidity cause rapid deterioration of the color-producing chemicals in the film.

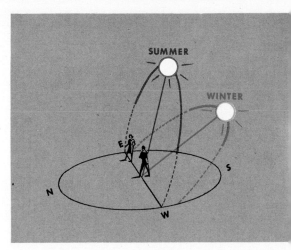

The solid portions of the two arcs represent the hours during which pictures with normal color balance can be obtained in northern latitudes. When the sun is less than 20° above either horizon, the rays travel a longer distance through the denser portions of the earth's atmosphere and much of the blue and green light is filtered out.

HOW TIME OF DAY AFFECTS COLOR

In the early morning hours the long red rays of the rising sun combine with the normal scattering of blue sky light.

In the late afternoon the atmosphere blocks off the short blue and green rays and the red and yellow rays predominate.

During recommended hours all wave lengths of the sun's spectrum penetrate the atmosphere and colors appear normal

FILM CHARACTERISTICS

Different light sources have different color characteristics, and various types of film are manufactured accordingly. Daylight film compensates for the blue-white light of the sun and indoor film for the yellow and red of artificial light. Under some circumstances the types can be interchanged, but this is not recommended.

Indoor film, balanced to make up for the blue lacking in artificial light, overemphasizes the blue of natural light.

Daylight film, balanced to reduce blue light, gives an equally unsatisfactory reproduction of an indoor scene.

CONTRAST

Massie — Fundamental Photographs

When there is a considerable difference in brightness between areas, the exposure is based on the most important element.

With a more normal brightness contrast, exposure can be based on the skin tones, or any medium-toned area.

In a low contrast subject an error in exposure is least noticeable.

POLAROID COLOR PHOTOGRAPHY

Although only 0.002 in. thick, Polaroid color film has 13 layers. The top four — positive base, acid polymer, spacer, and image layer — are the film's positive and the lower nine — blue sensitive, developer-yellow dye, spacer, green sensitive, developer-magenta dye, spacer, red sensitive, developer-cyan dye, and negative base—the film's negative. The developer-dye combinations are new chemicals created expressly for the film. Between the positive and negative sets is a pod which, when crushed by rollers in the camera, frees the chemicals needed to touch off the developing.

These five Polaroid photographs were removed from the camera at different time intervals to show the stages of development within the 50-60 second period required for complete processing. A chemical reaction between the acid polymer and its spacer seals in the finished picture. Once a frame is exposed and pulled through the rollers, another exposure can be made.

HOME MOVIES IN COLOR

Unless a large area of scenery is being filmed, the subject should move, not the camera. The pictures are made one at a time, and if the camera is not properly focused or is not held steady, the movies will be blurred or jumpy. The average "take" lasts about six seconds. Minimum duration is two; maximum should be about twelve.

OUTDOORS

The daylight types of film should be used, and exposure instructions followed carefully. Excessive contrasts in color and lighting should be avoided. Cloudy-day and night sequences add variety.

INDOORS ·

The indoor types of film should be used, with lighting as recommended. Since doubling the distance decreases the illumination by one-fourth, the distance between the light source and the subject is important for proper exposures.

Bright days and colorful subjects can make lively pictures.

Camera-mounted floodlamps insure proper illumination.

Films should be edited and sequences rearranged by splicing so that they show to best advantage. Projector-film co-ordination is essential, but the type of screen surface is a matter of choice. A rectangular screen is more effective for showing movies, but if slides are to be viewed also, a square screen is recommended.

SCREEN SIZES (in inches)	PROJECTOR-TO-SCREEN DISTANCE (in fee	
	8mm — ¾-inch lens	8mm — 1-inch lens o 16mm — 2-inch lens
30 x 40	13	18
37 x 50	17	22
45 x 60	20	27

Union Pacific Railroad

NATURE

ADVERTISING

U. S. Steel

INDUSTRIAL

Wide World

PHOTOJOURNALISM

1964 Scholastic Photography Awards

ART, or CREATIVE

Warner Brothers

PORTRAIT

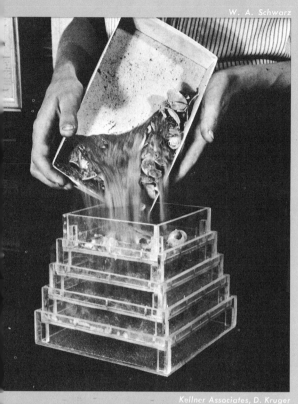

W. A. Schwarz

Kellner Associates, D. Kruger

When a man's busy, why, leisure
Strikes him as wonderful pleasure;
'Faith, and at leisure once is he?
Straightway he wants to be busy.
                    Robert Browning

Hatami, R-G

FADS

By DORA JANE HAMBLIN

Both photos, "Life" magazine © 1960 Time Inc.

Zoot Suit   **Phone-Booth Stuffing**

Robert J. Smith, Black Star

Hula Hoop

... from zoot suits to Beatlemania

FADS are temporary crazes that now and then flash across the United States and the world. A fad usually consists of a very odd activity or a peculiarity of dress. When a new fad appears, it comes without warning to occupy people's time, attention and conversation. It then vanishes as rapidly as it appeared.

One of the noisiest of 1964 fads centered around the Beatles, four mop-haired young men from Liverpool, England. John Lennon, Paul McCartney, George Harrison and Ringo Starr delighted millions of Americans with their singing and guitar playing. In return, these admirers pelted the Beatles with jelly beans, their favorite

Marathon Dancing

Yo-Yo

England's Beatles

candy. They broke down police barriers to touch the Beatles. And they screamed "yeah, yeah, yeah" after each Beatle song. Beatlemania brought chaos to New York's John F. Kennedy International Airport, the Ed Sullivan TV Show and Carnegie Hall. Then the Beatles left for home. The flight of the Beatles, like the flights of locusts in Biblical times, left behind it a startled silence and a gradual dazed re-awakening of normal life.

The Beatle fad, like most fads, was concentrated among young people. But some, like 1958's Hula Hoop craze, are taken up even by adults. In the United States, the Hula Hoop fad started in California. Manufacturers of the brightly colored plastic circles introduced them in schoolyards. Western youngsters took them up with enthusiasm. But at first Easterners sniffed with scorn. They thought that the hoops were made to be rolled down streets.

To the East's way of thinking, too many things were already rolling down Eastern streets. But when Easterners discovered that the Hula Hoop was worn, not rolled, the rush was on. Before it ended, almost forty million hoops were sold. Half the people in the United States were risking backstrain trying to wriggle with the proper rhythm to keep the hoops flying about their bulging torsos. And to the great embarrassment of most adults, they were unable to do it half so well as kindergartners. After less than a year the Hula Hoop fad vanished into oblivion. There it joined other strenuous has-beens such as a dance called the Big Apple (circa 1937) and the even wilder jitterbug.

Implicit in dance fads, the Hula Hoop and even the Yo-Yo is the quite natural urge of people to move to rhythm. Rhythmic activity is good for the muscles and reflexes. And it can result in the mastery of a minor skill as satisfactory to its performer as bowling a strike or serving an ace on the tennis court. The expression of rhythm through dance fads, song fads, game fads goes on and on. Only the form changes, often every few months. Remember the bongo drums and the nonsense songs?

Some rhythm games, such as the jumping rope and the bouncing ball, stay with us forever. One longtime favorite is the Yo-Yo, which came to the United States about 1929. It was introduced by a man who had seen Filipinos perform wonders of skill and accuracy making a wooden disk run up and down a string. It became such a fad that for a few years it turned up everywhere from parties to Boy Scout jamborees. There is some evidence that the Yo-Yo was known, in one form or another, to the ancient Greeks. But the story most Americans like best is that it was invented by Filipino hunters who climbed trees and thunked passing animals on the head to kill them for food. According to this account, one fellow finally got tired of climbing up and down to get his weapon. So he attached it to a string and was thus able to whiz it down, clunk

his prey, and then coax it back up the string again. Whatever it may have been originally, the Yo-Yo comes back every few years to delight another generation.

No practical uses or rhythmic pleasure are connected with the maddest fads of all—the ones that usually spring up on college campuses. The craziest in modern times was goldfish swallowing. That one began at Harvard in 1939 with Lothrop Withington, Jr. He was a freshman who wanted publicity to aid his campaign for a student office. He summoned the press to watch him gulp down a live goldfish with a mashed-potato chaser. Withington didn't win the election, but he started a wave of campus goldfish gulping that got so bad that the Animal Rescue League protested. The unofficial world record was set by an M. I. T. student, who downed 42 wriggling fish at one sitting.

Some adults felt that goldfish eating was a sign of the troubled times just before World War II. But there have been fads that are just as wacky since then. The 1960's have been full of them. Bed pushing is one example. This practice began among British students in African universities. It moved to the United States by way of Canada. College students armed with any kind of bed on rollers vied with each other to see how far they could walk—or run—pushing their beds. All the pushers were put to shame by two British students. These champions tied a brass Victorian bedstead to oil drums, hooked up an outboard motor and put-putted clear across the English Channel.

After bed pushing came telephone-booth stuffing. The idea here was to see how many students could get into a phone booth. The record was 34. Hollow-tree stuffing intrigued even the girls. But it was a team of boys at the University of Maine who set the record in 1961 by getting 16 into one trunk. Other students invented ice-cube tossing (how many times can you toss an ice cube back and forth before it melts?). Some Texans claimed to have made 531 tosses. In Wisconsin, where cooler weather was perhaps an unfair advantage, students said they had completed 1,000 tosses.

In 1963, students at Iowa State University, at Abilene, Texas, and at Montana State University competed to see who could stay longest inside a rotating clothes dryer. It is not clear who won because, as they emerged dizzily, they claimed two different standards of measurement. One had counted revolutions; two had counted time inside.

Also in 1963 came piano wrecking. Teams of students broke pianos into pieces small enough to be thrust through holes eight or nine inches in diameter. Detroit's Wayne State University claimed the record by totally wrecking a piano in 4 minutes, 51 seconds.

Psychologists and counselors consider most campus fads as relatively harmless ways of working off too much energy. But oddly enough most fads also have in them clues to two warring sides of human nature. There is the desire to be different, to break away from conventional social customs. And on the other hand there is the desire to conform, to do "what the gang does." Clothing fads among high-school and college students particularly express this. Somebody gets an idea for a crazy outfit that makes everybody laugh—or makes adults shudder—and then everybody joins in. Such a fad in the late 1930's was the zoot suit. This originated in New York's Harlem and spread to teen-agers across the country. It included ballooning trousers pulled tight at the ankles and reaching up almost to the armpits, and a jacket that came almost to the knees. An outsized bow tie and a long, looping key chain over which the unwary were likely to trip completed the costume. The zoot suit vanished with World War II. Men exchanged it for khaki uniforms, and wartime material shortages cut down such waste. And girls cut down on waste by lifting the hemlines of their skirts above their knees. But when the war ended, the girls brought back the exaggerated effect in the long skirts of the New Look.

Clothing fads have since gone from bobby socks to the Davy Crockett coonskin cap to mismatched shoes and hand-decorated white sneakers to sweat shirts decorated with silly slogans or portraits of Beethoven and Brahms. A pair of coeds at the University of Illinois, doodling with their knitting needles in 1961, invented the "snoot boot," designed to protect the nose in cold weather. It became the rage of the season.

Almost none of today's fads have the unpleasant undertones of those two fads of the 1930's—marathon dancing and flagpole sitting. In the former, groups of people met in public places to see how long they could keep dancing until they dropped from fatigue. In the latter, individuals perched themselves on tiny platforms atop flagpoles to see how long they could stand the height, the isolation and the exposure to the weather. The United States was then in its worst economic depression. Many of the people who sat on flagpoles or danced until they dropped did so to earn a little money. And, sadly, other people were willing to pay money to watch them. These fads became a social commentary. Their recollection brings a slight shudder of disbelief today.

Most recollections of fads, however, bring nothing more than a whiff of nostalgia. Long before the Beatles or even Elvis Presley, there was Frankie Boy, the young Sinatra of the 1940's with his droopy tie and droopy hair. Before him, teen-agers swooned and screamed for the Crooner, Bing Crosby of the dreamy eyes and *buh-buh-buh-boo.* And should any adult truly object to bed pushing and piano wrecking, he might remember that Grandpa too had his fads. One of Grandpa's biggest fads was to take apart a horse-drawn wagon, haul it up to the top of the courthouse, and there reassemble it around the spire on Halloween.

Amer. Mus. of Nat. Hist.

The Amateu

By JOHN W. SHRUM

A striking insect fossil—an ant that has been preserved in amber. Amber is a hardened, translucent fossil resin.

DO you like to hike in the country? Do you like to visit new places? Do you like to study plants and animals and collect unusual things? Then join the ranks of the amateur fossil collectors. Few hobbies offer as much fun and satisfaction for such a small investment of time and money. As a fossil hunter, you can work with your hobby all year long. In good weather you can visit places where fossils may be found. In cold or rainy weather you can work at home with the fossils you have already collected.

What is a fossil? For one thing, the remains of plants and animals that lived in past ages are called fossils. These remains have been preserved in the earth's crust by natural processes. They are found in rocks or in finely divided rock particles, such as dust, mud, sand and soil. Sometimes plants and animals have been preserved as fossils by being frozen, or dried out, or "pickled" in a brine solution. Some fossils have been found embedded in amber or trapped in tar pits. Among the commonest fossils are shells, bones and impressions of leaves or other parts of plants and animals. In some cases, the entire organism is preserved. Fossils also include footprints, tracks and trails.

Where fossils
are to be found

Most fossils (about 99 per cent of them) occur in sedimentary rocks. These are made up of particles eroded from other rocks. Or the rocks have been formed from

such things as corals and plants. Some sedimentary rocks come from deposit of minerals that were dissolved in water. These particles have become compacted or cemented together. They have been changed into such sedimentary formations as shale, sandstone and limestone. It is important for the fossil collector to be able to tell sedimentary rocks from either igneous rocks or metamorphic rocks.

The chances are very good that you live in or near a region where the bedrock is sedimentary. Geologic maps of various areas show where sedimentary rocks lie. You can obtain such maps from your state Geological Survey or from the United States Geological Survey, Washington, D. C. You will also learn a good deal about fossil-collecting locations in the United States in the *Illustrated Guide to Fossil Collecting* by R. Casanova, Naturegraph Company, San Mateo, California, 1957.

Are you in or near a region of sedimentary rocks? Do you plan to visit other parts of the country where there are sedimentary rocks? If your answer is "Yes" to either question, you can begin to plan trips into the field to look for fossils.

Once sedimentary deposits are found, is it likely that they will contain fossils? It is possible for any sedimentary rock to contain fossils. But some sedimentary rocks contain many specimens; others have almost none. Rocks formed from sediments deposited in a body of water, especially a shallow sea, are the source of many good fossils. Thus, if the rock is a

ossil Hunter

. . . hunting for and collecting plant and animal fossils is a rewarding and educational hobby for young and old alike

marine sandstone, shale or limestone, the chances that you will find fossils are quite good. Lake and swamp sediments are good sources of fossils also. Sediments deposited by streams on land such as floodplains and sandbars often contain fossils of land animals and freshwater animals. In general, however, there are fewer fossils in stream deposits than in marine and lake deposits. Also, fossils found in lake deposits are not well preserved.

In most places, sedimentary rocks are covered by the regolith. The regolith is the loose materials, such as sand and gravel, that overlie bedrock. Fossils may be found in the regolith but not so frequently as in bedrock.

The bedrock is well exposed when a stream has cut down to it through the regolith. Along the valley wall of such a stream, one or more strata may be studied to determine if fossils are present or not. Chunks of rock that have broken off from the bedrock layers may be found downslope from the formation. They can also be found in the stream itself.

Bedrock is also exposed in stone quarries. If you wish to collect in quarries, bear in mind that most of them are privately owned. You will have to get the permission of the owner or caretaker before doing any exploring or collecting. A site similar to a quarry is an excavation for a new building. But these are usually available only for a short time. You will need permission to collect fossils there also.

W. A. Schwarz

A carbonized ray found in Wyoming. This interesting fossil is now in the Academy of Natural Sciences of Philadelphia.

The construction of a highway has exposed sedimentary bedrock in many localities. These road cuts may be excellent sites for fossil collecting. Be sure, however, that you take safety measures if you are working close to a busy highway. If work is still being done on the road, you should get permission from the construction company before collecting fossils. Even with permission, you should be very careful. And avoid getting in the way of the men and machinery. You may have to collect at a time when the construction crew is not working.

All the sites we have just mentioned may be good for fossil collecting. Certainly there are other good locations that you will notice as you begin to explore areas near your home.

393

ACTIVITIES

Young fossil collectors in the field. (A) A member of the Delaware Valley Amateur Paleontological Society has just uncovered a fossil snail which had been embedded in Pleistocene clay along the Potomac River. This specimen is now in the Academy of Natural Sciences of Philadelphia. (B) Collecting in a sandstone quarry near Lyons, Colorado. (C) A promising fossil site: an eroded hillside near Boulder, Colorado.

H. G. Richards

John W. Shrum

John W. Shrum

How to collect fossils

To collect fossils you need some equipment. You should also know how to use field techniques.

Equipment. This will vary slightly. It depends upon the kind of specimens and the nature of the rock with which you are working. For collecting fossils of animals without backbones (invertebrates), small vertebrates and plants, you need a hammer for breaking and trimming rocks. You also need a collecting bag, one or more chisels, a notebook and pencil, and paper for wrapping and labeling specimens. A regular mason's or bricklayer's hammer is excellent for fossil collecting. You will find that a canvas hunting bag, knapsack or book bag with a shoulder strap is quite satisfactory for carrying equipment, specimens and lunches. A notebook with hard covers about five by seven inches in size is convenient and useful for recording where each specimen was found and for keeping a record of all your observations. The chisels can be regular stonecutter's chisels or good-quality metalworking chisels. Both a small and a large chisel are useful in chipping specimens out of the rock. You can wrap the specimens in newspaper or put them in paper bags. Delicate specimens should be wrapped in tissue paper. Small sheets of plain paper with an identifying number can be wrapped with each specimen.

Other items of equipment are also helpful. A five- to ten-power hand lens is useful for getting a better look at specimens in the field. String, rubber bands and small boxes are useful in working with small or broken specimens out of the rock. You can wrap of strata and formations with a six- or ten-inch tape. A small shovel, such as the folding foxhole type available in army surplus stores, can be used to remove clay, sand and soil.

You will find various types of maps useful in your work. We have already mentioned the value of geologic maps.

A fossil hunter's equipment. At the top left are field notes, a road map and a topographic map. At the bottom of the topographic map are magni- fying lenses, a cold chisel and a mason's hammer. At the right, from top to bottom, are tissue paper, newspaper, masking tape and knapsack.

Topographic maps are also very helpful. They show the location of roads, railroads, houses and other buildings, and features of the land surface, such as streams, lakes, hills and valleys. You can get these maps from your state Geological Survey or from the United States Geological Survey, Washington, D. C. Road maps are useful for pinpointing promising localities and for recording where collections have been made.

The same equipment that is used in the field will be useful in working with the specimens at home. Additional tools will improve the quality of your work in your home laboratory. We discuss these tools later in the article.

Field techniques. The object of any technique is to get the best specimen possible and as much information about it as you can. Sometimes this amounts to just picking up specimens that have weathered out of the bedrock, wrapping them up and identifying where they were found. No matter how the specimens were obtained, wrapping and identifying techniques are similar. Each fossil should be wrapped by itself in a newspaper or a small sack. Then all specimens from the same location should be wrapped in a larger bundle. Place a slip of paper with a record of your finds in the larger bundle. You may want to make a separate record for each specimen.

The record may be written out in detail or it can consist only of a code word or number referring to the record made in your notebook. The complete record should include the geographic location, where the fossil was found in the rock formation and the name of the rock formation, if this can be determined. It might be well to add other observations. These could include the characteristics of the rocks exposed, the relative abundance of fossils and the variety of fossils in the formation.

Good specimens are frequently those that have weathered out of the bedrock. These may be found in thin layers of soil overlying the bedrock, in the accumulation of rocks that have weathered and fallen or slid from a cliff or steep valley wall, and in beds of clay between rock layers. Where fossils occur this way, you may have to sift through the soil or rock fragments or wash the fossils out of the material in a nearby stream.

Where fossils occur in solid rock, the task of removing them is more difficult. This is when you need a hammer or chisel or both. *Caution: when working with hammer or chisel, always wear safety goggles to protect your eyes from flying chips of stone.*

The chunks of rock containing the fossil can be pried loose and broken with the hammer in some cases. Sometimes you will have to remove the part of the rock you want by chiseling around the fossil. Experience will show you how best to do this for various fossils and rocks. Generally you should chisel a groove around the fossil, being careful to keep the groove far enough away so that the fossil will not be damaged. Chisel deep enough to split the rock underneath the fossil. Never try to trim a specimen closely in the field. Wait until you get home. Then you can use more precise tools.

The preparation
of specimens at home

Fossils brought in from the field need to be prepared for further study, identification and storage or display. Remove excess rock with a hammer, using a chisel if necessary. If you have several sizes of chisels and hammers, you will be able to select the best one for working with each specimen. *Remember to use safety goggles when working with either hammer or chisel.* A hacksaw can be used to saw through the rock in some specimens. Remove only small pieces of rock at any one time. This way you will avoid breaking the fossil. When most of the rock has been removed, you can work away on the remaining material with small chisels, ice picks, wire brushes, pliers and knife blades. Hatpins or other strong, sharp-pointed instruments can be used to remove bits of rock from the fossil. Small paintbrushes and a wire brush can be used to clean up the fossil.

Soaking in water will sometimes soften the rock enough so that it can readily be removed from the specimen with the use of the tools mentioned above. Dilute hydrochloric acid is useful in dissolving limestone from some fossils. But be very careful when using acid. Do not get any on your skin. Wash your hands frequently while working with it. Remember, too, that in dissolving limestone the acid will also dissolve the fossil if it consists of calcium carbonate (calcite). Put a drop of dilute acid on an inconspicuous spot on the fossil. If the acid starts to dissolve the fossil, you will see gas bubbles in the acid. Immerse the fossil in a bucket of clean water to stop the action of the acid.

The object of preparing the fossil is to remove as much of the rock material as possible. Then the fossil can be studied in detail. Remember that many fossils are millions of years old. Hence we are interested in getting all the information we can about them. Careful preparation of the fossils will reveal details that would not be seen otherwise.

Identifying
fossil specimens

If you can identify the fossils that you find, your collection will have added value and interest. You should begin by acquiring a good understanding of the classification system used in the study of plants and animals. The system in use today is based on one proposed by the Swedish biologist Carl von Linne, better known by the Latinized form of his name —Carolus Linnaeus. His system has been modified as paleontologists and biologists have learned more about the relationships among plants and animals.

To identify your fossils, compare your specimens with those described in reference books. An excellent one to start with is *The Fossil Book* by C. L. Fenton and M. A. Fenton, Doubleday and Company, Inc., New York, 1958. This book is well illustrated. And it contains excellent descriptions of the plants and animals that are found as fossils. It will probably be in

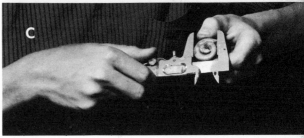

W. A. Schwarz

Basic equipment for preparing fossil specimens. Shown here are calipers, ball-peen hammer, geologist's hammer, chisel, high-powered magnifying glass, curved tweezers, metal tongs, straight tweezers, small paintbrush, short stiff-bristle brush, toothbrush, dental probes, and awls. Photos at right show a collector preparing a fossil specimen. He picks out or loosens clay or earth from the fossil (A). The loosened particles are then removed with a stiff-bristle brush (B). Finally the fossil is carefully measured with calipers (C).

your school library or public library. Another good reference book is *Index Fossils of North America* by H. W. Shimer and R. R. Shrock.

In addition to these reference books, many books and pamphlets contain information that will help you identify fossils found in various localities in the United States. Write to your state Geological Survey, in the state capital, for a list of the fossil publications available for your area.

The important task
of labeling your finds

A fossil collector should have a good labeling system for his fossils. This will help him to locate specimens when needed, to maintain a permanent record and to keep the identification of each fossil clearly in mind.

One or more specimens of the same fossil can be stored in a small box along with an identifying label. The label should be made from good-quality paper or lightweight cardboard. The information on the label should include the identification of the specimen, the name of the rock formation and of the geographic location in which it was found and its geologic age. You can also add the date the fossil was found, page references to your notebook, the sources used in identification and various other notations of special interest.

Often it is desirable to have an identifying mark on each fossil. The best way to do this is to place on the fossil a spot of light-colored paint about one quarter of an inch in diameter. Put the spot where it will not obscure any of the features that you may want to study. Quick-drying enamel, fingernail polish or airplane-model enamel can be used. When the paint spot is dry, write an identifying number on the paint with India ink. A coat of clear nail polish or colorless airplane dope will protect the numbered spot.

Whatever system you use in marking your fossils, you should keep a permanent record giving detailed information for each specimen.

Experiments in Astronomy

By NORMAN D. ANDERSON

THE professional astronomer uses both optical and radio telescopes, plus many other pieces of equipment, in his work. Even without such devices, you can make a number of interesting astronomical observations. You can also carry out various projects and experiments that will illustrate basic ideas in astronomy. In the following pages, we shall give some idea of what can be done even by a beginner without elaborate equipment. The rotation of the earth would be a good starting point.

The rotation
of the earth

You can easily observe the daily motions of the sun, moon, planets and stars across the sky from east to west. Until the time of astronomer Nicolaus Copernicus (1473-1543), most men interpreted these observations as evidence that the celestial objects revolved around a stationary earth. We now explain these same observations with a theory, or model, of a solar system with the sun at the center. In our present model, the earth spins on its axis, completing one rotation each 24 hours.

The flattening of the earth at the poles. The earth is not a perfect sphere. It is

slightly flattened at the poles, and it bulges a little at the equator. This has resulted from its rotation. According to a widely held theory, while the earth was still in a molten state, its spin caused particles to be forced outward from its axis. The particles were piled up least of all at the poles and most of all at the equator. By the time a solid crust had formed at the surface of the sphere, it had become slightly distorted. We know that this distortion exists because the earth's diameter is 7,927 miles at the equator and only 7,900 miles from pole to pole (Figure 1).

You can show how flattening of a sphere results from rotation by setting up a piece of equipment in your home workshop or in a school laboratory. You will need a long and short stick and a spool (Tinker Toys will work very well), plus a strip of heavy paper, ¾ inches wide and approximately 12 inches long. Assemble these pieces as shown in Figure 2. The lower ends of the paper strip should be secured to the spool. A hole should be made in the top of the paper loop so that it is free to slide up and down on the stick.

Place the device in a hand drill as shown, and set it to rotating rapidly. The circular

Figure 1. By measuring the earth's equatorial and polar diameters, we can tell that the earth is flattened at the poles.

Figure 2. Rotation causes a circular loop of paper to become an ellipse.

All photos, Kellner Associates—D. Krueger

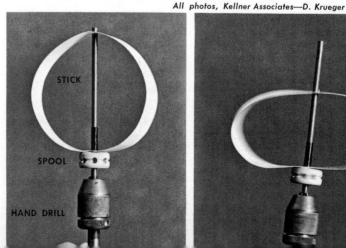

loop will then be flattened into the shape of an ellipse. The flattening will be much more pronounced than that of the earth, but it will be based on the same general principle.

The revolution of the earth around the sun

The earth completes an elliptical orbit around the sun in one year—approximately 365¼ days. The earth makes this yearly revolution with its axis tipped at an angle of 23½°, relative to the plane of its path around the sun.

The following project will help you visualize sun-earth relationships as they appear from outside of our solar system. All that is needed is a globe (mounted on a base), a dark room and a source of light—a slide projector, flashlight or small electric lamp with the shade removed. Probably the best source of light is an electric light bulb of low wattage—perhaps 15 W. Place this in the socket of an extension cord. The globe should be about six inches in diameter and should clearly show the earth's geographical features. Attach the globe to a spool and set the spool on a stick. Then insert the stick in a hole drilled at an angle of 23½° in a block of wood ¾ inches by 6 inches by 8 inches (Figure 3). The diameter of the hole is to be just large enough so that the stick will fit tightly.

Set the source of light, which represents our sun, in the central part of a darkened room. It can be placed on a table or on the floor. It is to be at the center of a circle 6 feet in diameter (indicated by the dotted lines in Figure 4). This circle represents the earth's orbit. Set the globe in the position for December, as indicated in Figure 4. The center of the light source is to be level with the center of the globe. The axis of the globe is to point away from the source of light, as shown. This represents the relative positions of the earth and sun in the month of December, at the beginning of winter. To show the relative positions in March, set the globe in the position labeled

Figure 3. How to prepare the toy globe that will represent the earth, as described in the text. The stick is inserted in a hole in the base at a 23½° angle. Spool and globe are then slid onto the stick.

March in Figure 4. Two other months—June and September—are indicated in the figure. Note that the axis is to continue to point in the same direction throughout. You should be able to position the globe correctly for any month of the year. For example, for January the globe should be set on its supposed orbit one third of the way to its March position.

Set the globe in the appropriate position for the month in which you are working on this project. Slowly rotate the globe while observing it directly from above. Can you follow your hometown or state as it moves through the zones of light and darkness? (Note that 15° of rotation—that is, 15° of longitude—corresponds to one hour of time.) Can you predict the number of hours of daylight for your hometown during the different months of the year? How many hours of darkness would there be for a person whose home is on the equator?

How to use our knowledge of the earth's movements

Once you have developed an understanding of the earth's movements within the solar system, it is possible to apply this knowledge to the solution of certain problems. Finding the latitude and longitude of your hometown would be two such problems.

How to determine latitude. In order to find out at what latitude you are, without consulting a map, you will have to measure the altitude (angle) of the sun. There are

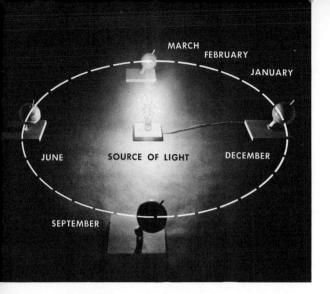

Figure 4. How the globe, mounted at an angle (the earth's axis is always tipped in the same direction), is used to illustrate the effects of the earth's orbit around the sun.

various ways of doing this. If you measure the length of the shadow cast by a vertical stick of known height, you can calculate the angle, using the mathematics of trigonometry.

If you do not know trigonometry, you can make an approximate direct measurement of the sun's altitude with the device shown in Figure 5. It consists of a 180° protractor attached to a soda straw by means of Scotch tape. A string with a paper clip fastened to the end is attached to the middle of the protractor, also with Scotch tape.

Hold a piece of white paper or cardboard a few inches from the lower end of the straw and point the straw at the sun. Caution: *Do not look directly at the sun without the protection of a special filter or goggles.* Make the necessary vertical and horizontal adjustments until the shadow cast by the straw on the paper or cardboard will be in the form of a ring enclosing a light area. Record the protractor reading (starting from the 0 mark nearer the sun) at the point through which the string passes. Subtract 90° from this reading and you will have the sun's altitude.

You are now ready to find your latitude. Your task will be simple if you set about it

on the first day of spring (about March 21) or the first day of autumn (about September 23). On these days, the sun appears to be directly overhead (that is, at an altitude of 90°) at noon to an observer at the earth's equator. Measure the altitude of the sun above the southern horizon at noon. Then subtract the number of degrees in this measurement from 90°, and you will have the latitude of the place where you are taking the observation. If you were at the equator, the altitude of the sun would be 90°; the latitude would be 90° − 90° = 0. If you were at Chicago, Illinois, the altitude of the sun would be 48°; the latitude would be 90° − 48° = 42°. You can check your own latitude figure by consulting a map.

If you wish to determine your latitude on some day other than the first day of spring or autumn, you must take into account the sun's declination. This represents the number of degrees the sun appears to be north or south of the equator. During the northern fall and winter, the sun appears to be a certain number of degrees (varying according to the date) south of the equator. This number must be added to the measured altitude of the sun. During the northern spring and summer, the sun appears to be a certain number of degrees north of the equator. In this case the number must be subtracted from the sun's altitude. The amount to be added or subtracted for a given date can be obtained from Table 1.

Here is how to use the table. First take a reading of the sun's altitude. Either add to or subtract from this figure the one given in Table 1 for the date on which you are taking the observation. Then subtract the result from 90° and you will have the latitude. For dates not listed in the table, use the figure given for the nearest date listed.

Let us consider an example. A person in New York City measures the altitude of the sun at noon on February 17 and finds it to be 37°. Consulting Table 1, he notes that since his observation was made on February 17, he must add 12° to this figure,

$37° + 12° = 49°$. Subtracting $49°$ from $90°$, he gets $41°$ as the latitude of New York City.

Apparent solar time and mean solar time. In order to determine one's longitude, it is necessary to find out the difference between apparent solar time and mean solar time for a given date. Let us see what is meant by these two kinds of time.

As everybody knows, the day is made up of 24 hours. This is based on the rotation of the earth, or the apparent daily movement of the sun around the earth. When the sun is at its highest point in the heavens, it is 12:00 o'clock noon as indicated on a sundial. An astronomer would say that the sun is at the meridian. The meridian of a given place is the great circle passing through the poles and the zenith of that place. Will the 12:00 o'clock reading of the sundial correspond to the hour as given on your watch or clock?

If you construct the sundial shown in Figure 6, you will be able to find the answer to your question. The gnomon, or triangular piece that casts the shadow, should be made so that the angle that its upper edge forms with the base will be equal to your latitude. The base should be level; this can be done with a carpenter's level. The gnomon should point due north. To line it up properly, sight along its upper edge to the North Star. Once the sundial has been correctly positioned do not move it.

When the sun is at the meridian, the shadow cast by the gnomon will point due north. This is the time when the reading of your dial will be 12:00 o'clock. It is called apparent solar time, because it is based on the apparent movement of the sun around the earth. What time will it be on your watch? (Be sure that your watch is running correctly.) The chances are that the time as given on your watch will be either before or after 12:00 noon as recorded on the sundial. As a matter of fact, if you take a series of readings over a long period of time, you will note that your watch will record a wide

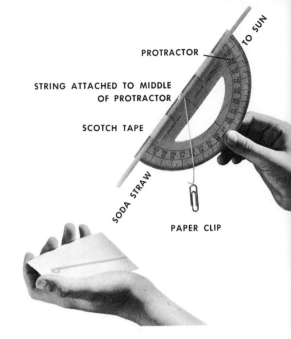

Figure 5. Measuring the altitude of the sun with the device described on page 400.

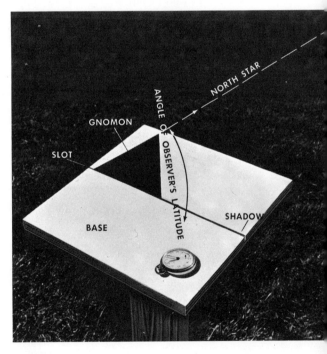

Figure 6. The angle that the upper edge of the gnomon forms with the base is 41° (the latitude of New York City, where the sundial was put up). Photo was taken October 1. The sun was at the meridian; this represents 12:00 noon apparent solar time. The watch shows mean solar time—12:10.

range of deviations from apparent solar time.

These deviations are due to the fact that the sun runs, or seems to run, at irregular speeds. In its orbit around the sun, the earth is now nearer to it, now farther away from it. The nearer the earth is to the sun, the faster it travels; the farther away it is from the sun, the slower it travels. As the earth goes faster, it causes the sun to seem to travel faster; as the earth goes slower, it causes the sun to seem to travel slower.

Imagine the difficulties we would get into if we measured the length of one day as the time between two successive appearances of the sun at the meridian (12:00 noon apparent solar time). We would have days of varying length ranging from 23 hours, 45 minutes, to 24 hours, 15 minutes. With days of varying length, we would have to reset all of our watches and clocks every 24 hours!

In order to have days of uniform length, we base our time system on the average length of time between one appearance of the sun at the meridian and the next appearance. This is called mean solar time because it is based on a mean (that is, average) sun.

Astronomers use the term "equation of time" to represent the difference between the time of apparent solar noon (sundial time) and the time of mean solar noon (watch time). Some values for the equation of time are given in Table 2. These values are to be added to your watch time or subtracted from your watch time in order to give apparent solar time.

How to determine longitude. You are now ready to find the longitude of the place where you live. You will have to note what progress the sun is making in its apparent journey around the earth. You will also have to apply the equation of time.

The sun covers 360° in 24 hours every time it makes a circuit of the earth. Therefore it covers 15 degrees (360° ÷ 24°) every hour. On the basis of the sun's apparent journey, the world is divided into 24 time zones, each having a width of 15 degrees of longitude. The time as indicated by a watch or clock is the same for any place within a given time zone. If it is 3:45 P.M. in town A in a given zone, it is 3:45 P.M. in town B in the same zone. As a person moves eastward from one time zone to the other, he must move his watch ahead an hour. If he made no such change, it would ultimately be late in the afternoon while his watch still recorded 12:00.

Table 1   To find an observer's latitude, add to or subtract from the sun's altitude the appropriate number of degrees given below; then subtract from 90°

TO BE ADDED TO SUN'S ALTITUDE				TO BE SUBTRACTED FROM SUN'S ALTITUDE			
Date	Degrees	Date	Degrees	Date	Degrees	Date	Degrees
Sept. 24	0	Jan. 1	23	March 21	0	July 2	23
Oct. 3	4	" 5	23	" 31	4	" 6	23
" 10	6	" 11	22	Apr. 6	6	" 13	22
" 13	7	" 18	21	" 10	8	" 21	21
" 24	11	" 20	20	" 20	11	" 23	20
" 29	13	" 30	18	" 23	12	Aug. 2	18
Nov. 3	15	Feb. 2	17	May 1	15	" 5	17
" 10	17	" 9	15	" 8	17	" 13	15
" 13	18	" 17	12	" 11	18	" 21	12
" 23	20	" 19	12	" 22	20	" 24	11
" 25	21	March 1	8	" 23	20	Sept. 3	8
Dec. 3	22	" 5	6	June 1	22	" 7	6
" 8	23	" 11	4	" 7	23	" 13	4
" 12	23	" 21	0	" 11	23	" 24	0
" 22	23½			" 22	23½		

There are four time zones in the United States. There is the Eastern Time Zone, extending theoretically 7½° on either side of 75° west longitude, which is the center of the zone; the Central Time Zone, centered about 90° west longitude; the Mountain Time Zone, centered about 105° west longitude; and the Pacific Time Zone, centered about 120° west longitude. 75°, 90°, 105° and 120° are called standard meridian; so are 135° west longitude, 150° west longitude and the rest.

At all locations at 75° west longitude, when the mean time is 12:00, apparent solar time may range from about 15 minutes after 12:00 to 15 minutes before 12:00, depending upon the day of the year, as indicated in Table 2. For example, on September 19, when mean solar time is 12:00, apparent solar time comes 6 minutes later: that is, at 12:06.

The farther west we go, the later the apparent solar time will come with respect to the standard time (mean solar time) for a given time zone. This is because the sun is traveling farther westward all the time. Each degree of longitude that the sun travels corresponds to 4 minutes of time (one hour, or 60 minutes, divided by 15). Hence at one degree west of 75° west longitude—that is, at 76° west longitude— apparent solar time would come 4 minutes later than at 75° west longitude. On September 19, therefore, apparent solar time would come at 12:10 P.M.

Now suppose an observer at Columbus, Ohio, which is the Eastern Time Zone, finds the shadow on his sundial pointing directly north at 12:38 EST (Eastern Standard Time) on September 19. The apparent solar time (when the sundial shadow points due north) at 75° west longitude for September 19, as we have seen, corresponds to 12:06 watch time (mean solar time). The difference between our Columbus observer's apparent time and that at 75° west longitude is 32 minutes (12:38 minus 12:06). Since 4 minutes of time correspond to one degree of longitude, 32 minutes of time would correspond to 32 ÷ 4 degrees, or 8 degrees, of longitude. Hence Columbus, Ohio, is at 75° + 8°, or 83°, west longitude.

Table 2   **EQUATION OF TIME**

Mean solar noon (12:00 noon on your watch) plus or minus the values given below gives the time of apparent solar noon (noon on the sundial).

Date	Equ. (in minutes)	Date	Equ. (in minutes)
Jan. 1	−3	July 19	−6
" 3	−4	" 27	−6⅓
" 5	−5	Aug. 5	−6
" 7	−6	" 13	−5
" 9	−7	" 18	−4
" 12	−8	" 22	−3
" 15	−9	" 26	−2
" 18	−10	" 29	−1
" 21	−11	Sept. 2	0
" 24	−12	" 5	+1
" 29	−13	" 8	+2
Feb. 4	−14	" 11	+3
" 12	−14⅓	" 14	+4
" 20	−14	" 17	+5
" 24	−13½	" 19	+6
" 27	−13	" 22	+7
Mar. 4	−12	" 25	+8
" 8	−11	" 28	+9
" 12	−10	Oct. 1	+10
" 16	−9	" 4	+11
" 20	−8	" 7	+12
" 23	−7	" 11	+13
" 26	−6	" 15	+14
" 29	−5	" 20	+15
Apr. 2	−4	" 27	+16
" 5	−3	Nov. 4	+16⅓
" 8	−2	" 11	+16
" 12	−1	" 18	+15
" 16	0	" 22	+14
" 20	+1	" 26	+13
" 25	+2	" 29	+12
May 2	+3	Dec. 1	+11
" 7	+3½	" 4	+10
" 15	+3¾	" 7	+9
" 23	+3½	" 9	+8
" 28	+3	" 11	+7
June 4	+2	" 13	+6
" 10	+1	" 16	+5
" 15	0	" 18	+4
" 19	−1	" 20	+3
" 24	−2	" 22	+2
" 29	−3	" 24	+1
July 4	−4	" 30	−2
" 10	−5	" 26	0
" 14	−5½	" 28	−1

Ecology Projects and Experiments

...examining the environments of living things

By ROBERT W. HOWE

ALL living things, plants and animals alike, are deeply influenced by their environment. The environment includes such factors as water, heat, light, soil and other plants and animals. The environment determines where a given plant or animal can live and how effectively it will be able to maintain life.

You can observe the effects of environment upon living things when you walk through the woods. For example, while hiking one day, I observed a small pond surrounded by a grassy field that bordered a forest. A frog was at one end of the pond

Figure 1. Experiments for finding out the water-holding capacity of different soils. Left, the two types of cans used for the experiment. Water will be poured into the can at left; note the six small holes through which the water will pass. The can at the right will hold the soil; a small-mesh wire screen is attached to the bottom of this can. Below, the setup for the experiment.

All photos, Kellner Associates—D. Kruger

CANS CONTAINING WATER

CANS CONTAINING SOIL

BRICK OR WOOD BLOCKS

ALUMINUM FOIL

feeding on insects. Three ducks glided along the water and appeared to be searching for food.

Continuing across the field and into the woods, I observed two squirrels scampering between the trees. Several trees had been blown down by a strong windstorm a few years before. Signs of bark beetles were evident on many of the fallen firs.

While observing the beauty of the woodland, I thought of several possible questions for study. How had the life in the wooded area been changed by the wind? What changes would I observe during the winter? What would be the effects on plant and animal life of the area if the pond should become filled with soil or drained?

Problems such as these are investigated by specialists in ecology. This is the science that studies the relationships between living things and their environments. The scientists who engage in this study are known as ecologists.

You do not have to be an ecologist to observe and investigate the secrets of plant and animal life in the country and even in built-up areas, such as towns and cities. You will acquire a new understanding that will add to your enjoyment of your plant and animal neighbors. You will also become aware of how we human beings influence the lives of other living things.

The following projects and experiments will introduce you to this fascinating field of study. In working on them, you will be applying some of the techniques, or research methods, used by ecologists.

**How does soil affect the
lives of animals and plants?**

The soil of an area may show great variation: it may range from sandy or clayey soil to rich loam. Plant and animal life is often related to a particular type of soil: it is affected by various soil characteristics.

One important characteristic is the capacity for holding moisture. Here is an interesting experiment that will enable you to tell whether one soil can hold more water than another.

Collect three types of soil (sandy, clay and loam) from root regions of plants or other sources. Spread the soil in pans and dry overnight in an oven at 220° F. Obtain three size #2½ cans. (They are 4½ inches high and have a diameter of 4 inches.) Cut off the top (if this is still in place) and the bottom of each can. Attach a small-mesh wire screen to the bottom of each; the screen can be held in place by friction tape. Fill each can with a different soil to within ½ inch of the top. Set the cans on bricks or wooden blocks, as shown in Figure 1, with aluminum foil underneath.

Prepare three other size #2½ cans for dripping water on the soil. Cut the top off each can and puncture six small holes in the bottom with a sharp nail. Be certain that the holes are very small. Suspend the cans from a broomstick or wooden pole, as shown in Figure 1, and fill each can with a measured amount of water. Drip water on the soils until each is thoroughly wet, and water drips from the bottom cans.

Determine the amount of water that each soil sample held. Compare the soils for water-holding capacity. The amount of moisture within a given soil may affect plant growth in different ways. For example, if there is not enough water, the plant will wither away. If there is too much, the soil will become waterlogged. Water will fill up the air spaces in the soil and will deprive the plant of the oxygen it needs for respiration and for root growth. If this condition continues, the plant will die.

Another important characteristic of soils is the rate at which they dry. Soils that dry relatively quickly tend to become warmer in the spring than those that stay damp. This is a vital difference, since soils that warm early in the spring aid in the germination of seeds and in the rapid growth of life in the soil.

Let us examine the drying rates of sand, clay and loam. Place the three cans of wet soil inside your house, where they can dry

Figure 2. How to study changing enviroment in a limited area. Markers are set in the corners of a grassy area of a given size. The types of animals and plants in the area are recorded. Then a section of the grass is covered with a board. After a few days the life observed under the board and in the surrounding area is recorded. The observations are repeated at specified intervals.

at room temperature—from 68° F. to 70° F. Insert a thermometer into each soil sample to a depth of two inches. Leave the thermometer in the soil until the temperature reading is constant. Then record this temperature. Continue taking temperature readings daily until all the soils have become dry. Which soil—sand, clay or loam—would aid the early growth of plant and animal life?

The nature of the soil surface affects plant life. For effective plant growth a soil should be crumbly. If it forms a hard, caked surface, moisture will not be able to penetrate it, and the supply of air to the soil will be reduced. (As we have seen, the oxygen contained in the air is necessary for the plant.) Investigate the surface characteristics of your three types of soil. Which of them forms a hard surface after drying?

How do changes in the environment affect living things?

Ecologists have made many studies of the effects of changing environments on plant and animal life. Here is a project that will illustrate these effects dramatically.

Select a square grassy area 2 feet on a side (Figure 2) and set markers on the corners. Carefully record the types of animals and plants that you can observe in the selected area. Next cover a section of the grass with a board about 1 foot by 1 foot, as in Figure 2. After 4 days observe the life around the board and under the board. Record your observations every 4 days for 24 days, recording the life that you observe under the board and in the surrounding grassy area. What changes have taken place?

I carried out an observation of this type during the spring and summer. Before setting the board in place, I identified various kinds of grasses, weeds, beetles, ants, spiders and mites in the selected area. After the board was set down, the grass and weeds under it turned yellow and began to decay. Pill bugs, millipedes, earthworms and the larvae of beetles and other insects were found. Various fungus growths also developed. Compare your observations with mine.

How does a change in temperature affect animals?

In many areas of the United States the temperature may rise above 90° F. in the summer, and fall below 0° F. in the winter. Temperatures may even vary as much as 40° F. between night and day during the summer. How do these changes influence living things?

An experiment with a goldfish will give you some idea of the effects of temperature on animals. Place a small goldfish in a pint jar filled with water to within about an inch of the top. Record the temperature of the water. Count the number of times the gill cover moves per minute. Next place the jar in a shallow pan or bowl. Fill the pan with ice water. Record the temperature and then count the number of movements of the gill cover per minute. Empty the pan and keep filling it with water at different temperatures ranging up to moderately warm—say about 100° F. Count the gill-cover movements per minute at each different temperature after recording the thermometer reading.

Figure 3. An experimental garden plot. Does the depth at which you plant the seeds have any effect on the development of the plants?

Figure 4. A windowsill laboratory. The box may be kept inside or outside so long as it gets enough sunlight and water.

More reliable results can be obtained by taking three readings at each temperature and averaging the results.

How did the movement of the gills vary with temperature? Not all animals of the same species have equal respiration rates. Does a large goldfish have a different rate from a small goldfish at equal temperatures?

You can also investigate the respiration rate of a human. Ask a friend to help you with your experiment: you will determine his respiration rate and he will determine yours. Conduct the experiment at a time when the temperature outside is from 10° F. to 15° F. above or below the house temperature. Go outside with your friend and remain there for at least 20 minutes to allow your body to adjust. Record the outside temperature. Then count the number of breaths per minute that your friend takes while seated. Have him determine your respiration rate in the same way. It is best to use a watch with a sweep-second hand for timing. Your friend and you are now to come into the house, where the temperature will probably be from 68° F.

to 70° F. Remain in the house for 20 minutes. Check the temperature. Each of you is then to note the respiration rate of the other as before.

Do your respiration rates vary with temperature? Do your friend and you have equal respiration rates? How do these rates compare to that of the goldfish at equal temperatures?

A laboratory in a garden, a window box or a flowerpot

If you live in a house with a yard, you can set aside a garden area for conducting ecology studies (Figure 3). If you do not have a yard where you could start an experimental garden, you can prepare a box that can be set on a windowsill (Figure 4). The box should be constructed of a weather-resistant material, such as cedar or redwood. The size will depend to some extent on the space you have available. A box 3 feet by 10 inches by 9 inches has been found satisfactory for growing a number of plants at one time. A 2-inch layer of gravel is set at the bottom of the box. Then comes an inch of peat moss; this in turn is topped by potting soil. Flowerpots can also be used for your experiments (Figure 5).

There are any number of problems you can investigate with your garden-area or windowsill or flowerpot laboratory. Here are a few possibilities:

A. Effect of depth on seed germination.
    1. Obtain 30 of each of the following seeds: corn, bean, carrot.
    2. Plant seeds in the garden, window box or flowerpots.
    3. Plant 10 of each kind of seed three inches deep. Set up a marker with the appropriate label.
    4. Plant 10 of each kind of seed one inch deep. Set up a marker.
    5. Place 10 of each type of seed on top of the soil. Set up a marker.
    6. Water with equal amounts of water.
    7. After 14 days observe your results.

Did the depth have an effect on the development of the plants? Were all the seeds affected in the same way? From your experiment can you determine some of the reasons why all seeds do not develop into mature plants? Would you get different results if you used more water? Less water? Would a different soil produce different results?

B. Effect of heat on germination of seeds.
    1. Obtain 30 seeds of each of the following: corn, tomato.
    2. Fill three flowerpots with soil.
    3. Plant 10 corn seeds at a depth of one inch in each container.
    4. Place one pot out of doors. Obtain an empty box and set it, bottom side up, over the pot so that it covers the latter completely. Check the temperature.
    5. Place a second pot in a room and cover it with a box as previously described. Check the temperature.
    6. Place the third pot in a refrigerator. Check the temperature.
    7. Keep the soil moist, but not too wet, by applying an equal amount of water to the pots as needed.
    8. Observe daily.
    9. Repeat the experiment with the tomato seeds.

How does heat influence the development of corn seeds? Were the results you obtained with the tomato seeds similar to those obtained with the corn seeds?

C. Your influence on plant and animal life.
    1. Put soil in three flowerpots or select three equal areas a foot wide in your garden and prepare the soil for planting.
    2. Do not plant any seeds in one pot or in one garden area. Allow all plants to grow.
    3. In a second pot or garden area plant 20 beet seeds. Allow all plants to grow.
    4. In a third pot or garden area plant 20 beet seeds. Allow the beet seeds to grow but remove any other plants that may appear.
    5. Water each area with an equal amount of water.
    6. Observe daily and make a record of the different forms of plant and animal life that appear. Note the differences between the three areas, including the soil conditions.

How did you influence the environment? What happened when you made no effort to influence the environment? What effect does the presence of plants have on the soil?

INDEX

a

C

f

g

Gabon, 142-43
Galapagos International Scientific Project, with illus. and map, 357-59
Game fish, illus., 338-39
Games, *see* Sports and names of sports
Gandhi, Mohandas K., 119, 120, 149
Garment center, New York City, illus., 33
GATT, *see* General Agreement on Tariffs and Trade
Gay, John, 353
Gbenye, Christophe, 141
Geesink, Anton, illus., 202
Gell-Mann, Murray, 332
Gemini spacecraft, 305-06, illus., 304
Gems, in jewelry, 224, illus., 226-28
General Agreement on Tariffs and Trade, 168-69
General Motors exhibit at N. Y. World's Fair, illus., 40
Geography, maps, use of, 276-79
Geology, fossil collecting, with illus., 392-97
Georgian architecture, in New York, 26
German reunification, 115
Germany, illus., 290-91
    colonialism, 288, 289
    concentration camp, 380, illus., 379
    East Germany, 165
    English words in German language, 282-83
    Erhard, Ludwig, with illus., 112-15
    foreign policy, 168
    Leipzig Fairs, 46
Germination of seeds, studies, with illus., 407-08
Ghana, 142
Gheorghui-Dej, Gheorghe, 164
Giacometti, Alberto, with illus., 116-18
Giannattasio, Luis, 157
Gibson, Virginia, illus., 255
Gilligan, Thomas R., 64, 69
Giraffes, illus., 334-35
Globe Theater, London, scale model, illus., 234
Goitschel, Christine and Marielle, 208-09
Golden Gate International Exposition, 49
Goldfish-swallowing fad, 390
Goldwater, Barry M., 63, 64, 78, 82, 86, 88, illus., 65
Golf, 218
Gonzales, Joseph, illus., 203
Gordon, David, illus., 313
Gothic architecture
    New York City, with illus., 27
Goulart, João, 58, 155
Government
    colonialism, 284, 286
    heads of government, 196-97
    Japanese women in government, 194
    Quebec separatism, with illus., 189-91
Governors, election of, 88
Governor's Palace, Williamsburg, illus., 91
Graves, Robert, with illus., 235-37
Great Britain, 53
    aviation, 309, 311
    colonialism, 288, list, 286-87
    Cyprus, 56
    East Africa, aid to, 144, illus., 140
    elections, 70, 166
    fairs, 45, 48
    Yemen, relations with, 160
Great Exhibition, London, 48
Great Swamp, N. J., 352, illus. and map, 351
Greece
    Cyprus, 56, 66, 161, 168, map, 159
    jewelry, ancient, 224, illus., 225
Greek Revival architecture, New York City, 26-27
Greenberg, Jack, illus., 108
Grenfell, Wilfred, 345
Group theory of mathematics, 332
Grouse, illus., 361
Guantanamo water supply, 81, 156, 172, with illus., 54-55

Guatemala, illus., 180
Guericke, Otto von, 313
Guevara, Ernesto, with illus., 75
Guggenheim Museum, 28, illus., 27
Guinness, Alec, illus., 251
Gulf of Tonkin, 66, 80, 147-48
Gurney, Goldsworthy, 314

h

Haiti, 59, 157
Hale Telescope, Mt. Palomar, illus., 298-99
Hamlet, play, 253, illus., 250
Hancock, Walter, 314
Hard Day's Night, A, film, 249
Harding, Warren G., 100
Hardwicke, Cedric, 67
Hare, Arctic, 348
Hartack, Bill, with illus., 219
Hawaii, map, 94
    English words in Hawaiian language, 283
    United States acquired, 289
Hawaiian goose or nene, 350
Hayes, Bob, with illus., 200
Hecht, Ben, 59
Helicopters, 308-09
Hello, Dolly! musical play, 252, illus., 251
Helou, Charles, 161
Hemingway, Ernest, with illus., 231
Herding reindeer, 345-46
Herlie, Eileen, illus., 250
Hertzsprung-Russell diagram of stars, 300
Heuga, Jimmy, 209
High-speed photography, with illus., 324-26
Hindbrain, 316
History of nursery rhymes, 246
Hitler, Adolf, illus., 291
Hobbies, fossil collecting, with illus., 392-97
Hochhuth, Rolf, 253
Hockey, 217
Hodgkin, Dorothy C., 71
Hogarth, William, illus., 44
Hollywood Palace, TV show, 256
Holy Land, Pope's trip, 133, illus., 131
Holy Trinity Church, Stratford, illus., 233
Hoover, Herbert Clark, with illus., 71
Hope Diamond, illus., 228
Hormone-brain relationships, illus., 320
Horne, Marilyn, 261
Horse racing, with illus., 218-20
House of Representatives, *see* Congress
Houses and housing
    Betsy Ross House, illus., 96
    New York City, illus., 20
    oldest in U. S., illus., 89
Howe, James Wong, with illus., 269
Hud, film, illus., 248
Hula-Hoop fad, 389-90, illus., 388
Humphrey, Hubert Horatio, Jr., 66, 72, 82, 86, with illus., 122-25, illus., 78
Humphrey, Muriel, 122, 123, 125, illus., 123
Hungary, 164, 165
Hunting, in Arctic, 346-48
Huntley, Chet, 256, illus., 254
Huong, Tran Van, 146
Huskies, dogs, 347, illus., 346
Hussein, king of Jordan, 160, illus., 196
Huxley, Julian, 358
Huygens, Christian, 313
Hydroelectricity, Aswan High Dam, 160
Hypothalamus, 316, illus., 317, 319

i

Ice skating
    Olympic Games, 204, 208, 209, illus., 208

Lebanon, 159, 161
Legislation, U. S., 83-85
    Civil Rights Act of 1964, 62, 82
    Humphrey, as legislator, 124-25
    Johnson, Lyndon Baines, 128
Leipzig Fairs, 46
Lenoir, Etienne, 315
Leoni, Raul, 155
Lewis, John, illus., 108
Liberal Party, Canada, 153
Life magazine, 379-80
Light, optical spectra, with illus., 296-300
Lilies of the Field, film, illus., 247
Lincoln Center Repertory Theater, 250, 253
Linnaeus, Carolus, 296
Liston, Sonny, 215
Literature
    Graves, Robert, with illus., 235-37
    Latin American poetry, with illus., 238-43
    nursery rhymes, with illus., 244-46
    See also Books
Little Congress, 127
Livestock, shows, 46-47
Living conditions
    foreign service, 368-69
    Japan, 194-95
    poverty, in U.S., with illus., 101-04
Living things and environment, with illus., 404-08
Lizard, illus., 334, 363
Lockheed Aircraft Corporation
    supersonic planes, 308, 309, 311, illus., 310
Lodge, Henry Cabot, 63, 80, 86
London, early engraving, illus., 232-33
    fairs and exhibitions, 48
Longitude, determining, 401-03
Lübke, Heinrich, 65, illus., 169
Lullabies, 244-45
Lumber, Canada, illus., 182-83
Lunar probe, 305-07, illus., 306-07
Luther, play, 250
Luxembourg, 169
Lynen, Feodor, 71

m

McAdoo, William G., 100
MacArthur, Douglas, with illus., 58-59
McCarver, Tim, illus., 215
McConnell, James, 330
McDermott, Terry, 208
McNamara, Robert, 73, 80, illus., 67
Macy's, department store, illus., 34
Maddox, USS, attack on, 80, 147-48
Magnetic field of earth, with illus., 303
Magnetic storms, study of, 303
Major-league baseball, 210, 212-13
    standings and leaders, 211
Makarios, Archbishop, 56, 66, illus., 196
Malamute, 347, illus., 345
Malawi, 65, 144
Malaysia, 148-49, illus., 145
Malta, 69
Manhattan Island, purchasing of, 32
Maps
    Canada, 184-85
    Caribbean area and Central America, 178-79
    election, 1964, 87
    English language, where spoken, 281
    fossil collecting, use in, 392, 394-95
    Galapagos Islands, 357
    Middle East, 175
    non-self-governing territories, 284-85
    nuclear testing areas, 147
    Panama Canal, 53, 75
    poverty in U.S., 103
    Tanzania (United Republic of Tanganyika and Zanzibar), 143

Maps (*cont.*)
    United States, 92-95
    use of, with illus., 276-80
    Vikings, regions controlled by, 329
    wildlife refuge, New Jersey, 351
    world flight, Jerrie Mock, 311
Marathon dancing, 391, illus., 389
Marcus, Siegfried, 315
Marine fish, illus., 338, 342
Mariner spacecrafts, 306, 307
Marriage and divorce, Japan, 193-94
Mars probe, 307
Martin, Joseph, 100
Marx, Harpo, 69
Mary Poppins, film, 249
Maryland
    New Town Federal Building, illus., 377
Maryland-Virginia oyster war, 355-56
Massachusetts
    Massasoit, statue, illus., 90
    Minuteman, statue, illus., 91
Massasoit, statue, illus., 90
Masses, Vallejo, 242, 243
Mathematics, essential to architect, 376
    group theory, 332
    sets, with illus., 272-75
Matinee Theater, TV show, 259
Mauritius, dodo bird, 350
May, Charles Paul, illus., 230
M'Ba, Leon, 143
Mean solar time, with illus., 401-03, table, 403
Medicare, 84
Medulla oblongata, 316, illus., 317, 320
Memorial Building, Charlottetown, 153
Memory, theories about, 330
Menotti, Gian Carlo, 260, 261
Mercury, planet, with illus., 331
Meridian, 401
Mesa Verde National Park, Colo., illus., 89
Metropolitan Opera, 260-61
Mexico, 156, illus., 138
    pavilion at N. Y. World's Fair, illus., 38
Michelangelo's Pieta, illus., 38
Middle Ages, 14-15, 45, 224, illus., 226
Middle East, 172, with illus. and map, 158-61, 175, illus., 173-76
Mikoyan, Anastas, 65
Milan, Italy, Pope Paul VI, 132
Military aid, Vietnam, 81
Military aircraft, 311, illus., 310
Military bases, closing of, 73
Miller, Arthur, 253
Miller, Frank R., 153
Miller, William E., 78, 86, with illus., 64
Mimicry, animals, illus., 361-64
Mindszenty, Cardinal, 165
Mines and mining
    Bolivia, 157
    Timmins, Ontario, 152
    unemployed miner, illus., 101, 102
Minimum subsistence, 101-02
Ministers, United States, 370
Minnesota, Hubert Humphrey, 123-25
Minority groups, in New York City, with illus., 22-23
Minuteman, statue, illus., 91
Mission of San Luis Rey de Francis, Calif., illus., 96
Mississippi, murder of civil rights workers, 63, 67, 74, 83, illus., 62
Mitarai, Takeshi, 195
Mock, Jerrie, 308, illus. and map, 311
Modern architecture, New York City, 28, illus., 25, 28
Mollusks, oysters, with illus., 353-56
Moment of Wonder, The, edited by Richard Lewis, 230, illus., 229
Monkeys, illus., 334
Montego Bay, Jamaica, illus., 177
Monteux, Pierre, 65

n

o

p

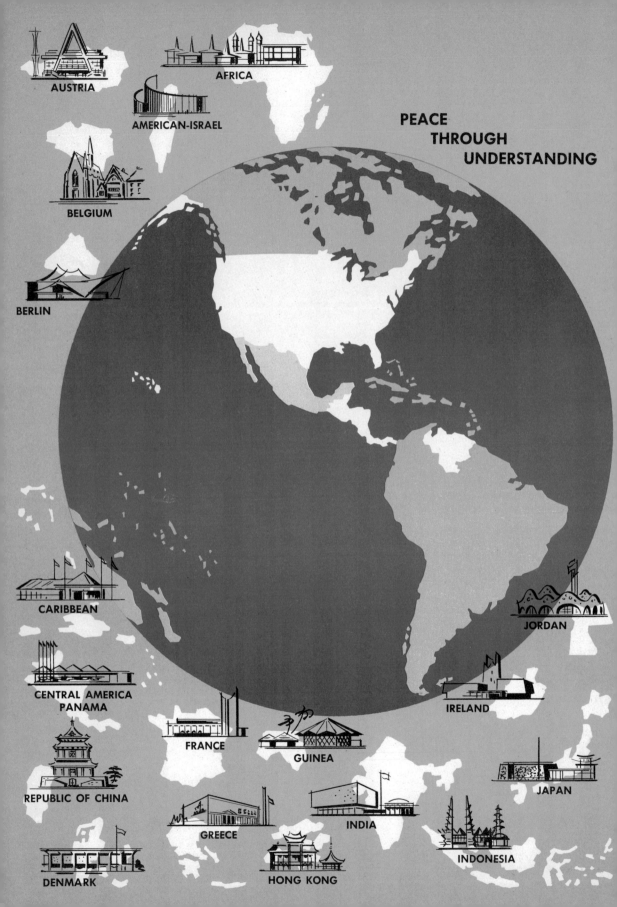

AUSTRIA

AFRICA

AMERICAN-ISRAEL

PEACE
THROUGH
UNDERSTANDING

BELGIUM

BERLIN

CARIBBEAN

JORDAN

CENTRAL AMERICA
PANAMA

IRELAND

FRANCE

GUINEA

REPUBLIC OF CHINA

JAPAN

GREECE

INDIA

DENMARK

HONG KONG

INDONESIA